Studies in Jewish and Christian Literature

Messiah and the Throne, Timo Eskola
Defilement and Purgation in the Book of Hebrews, William G. Johnsson
Father, Son, and Spirit in Romans 8, Ron C. Fay
Within the Veil, Félix H. Cortez
Jude's Apocalyptic Eschatology as Theological Exclusivism, William Wilson
Intertextuality and Prophetic Exegesis in the War Scroll of Qumran, César Melgar
The Past is Yet to Come: Exodus Typology in Revelation, Barbara A. Isbell

I0389796

INTERTEXTUALITY AND PROPHETIC EXEGESIS
IN THE WAR SCROLL OF QUMRAN

Intertextuality and Prophetic Exegesis in the War Scroll of Qumran

César Melgar

Fontes

Intertextuality and Prophetic Exegesis in the War Scroll of Qumran

Copyright © 2022 by César Melgar

ISBN-13: 978-1-948048-70-5 (hardback)

ISBN-13: 978-1-948048-65-1 (paperback)

All rights reserved. No part of this publication may be reproduced, stored in a retrieval system, or transmitted in any form or by any means—electronic, mechanical, photocopy, recording, or any other—except for brief quotations in printed reviews, without the prior permission of the publisher. Translations are the author's own, although influenced by the Legacy Standard Bible.

Fontes Press
Dallas, TX
www.fontespress.com

CONTENTS

ABBREVIATIONS ix

INTRODUCTION 1
- a. Scriptural Traditions in 1QM 3
- b. Thesis Statement 13
- c. Content and Purpose of 1QM 10–12 15
- d. Organization of the Present Study 17

1. METHODOLOGY 21
   - a. Intertextuality 22
     - i. Post-Structuralist Intertextuality 22
     - ii. Feminist Intertextuality 26
     - iii. Sectarian Intertextuality 30
   - b. Intertextual Features 34
     - i. Allusions 34
     - ii. Citations 46
   - c. Summary 53

2. PROPHETIC EXEGESIS 55
   - a. Prophetic Exegesis in Post-Exilic Times 56
     - i. Interpretation of Scripture Traditions 56
     - ii. Beginnings of Prophetic Exegesis 61
   - b. Prophetic Exegesis in the Dead Sea Scrolls 66
     - i. Thematic Pesharim 66
     - ii. Rule Books 83
   - c. Summary 96

3. PROPHETIC EXEGESIS IN 1QM 10 99
   - a. 1QM 10.1–8a: God Fighting for the Sectarian Army 101
     - i. Text and Translation 101
     - ii. Content 102
     - iii. Sectarian Intertextuality 105
     - iv. Scriptural Intertextuality 110
     - v. Prophetic Exegesis 123
   - b. 1QM 10.8b–18: God the Sovereign Teacher 125
     - i. Text and Translation 125
     - ii. Content 126
     - iii. Sectarian Intertextuality 127
     - iv. Scriptural Intertextuality 135
       - *God the Warrior* 135
       - *God the Deliverer of the Weak* 139
       - *God the Wise Teacher* 141
     - v. Prophetic Exegesis 143
   - c. Summary 146

4. Prophetic Exegesis in 1QM 11...149
   a. 1QM 11.1–7a: God's War (לכה המלחמה).........................152
      i. Text and Translation...152
      ii. Content 153
      iii. Sectarian Intertextuality..155
          Prophetic David 155
          Messianic David..159
          Prophecy of Balaam 166
      iv. Scriptural Intertextuality 170
          לכה המלחמה *in Chronicles*...........................171
          לכה המלחמה *in Maccabees*...........................176
      v. Prophetic Exegesis 178
   b. 1QM 11.7b–17: God's Future Exaltation 182
      i. Text and Translation...182
      ii. Content 183
      iii. Sectarian Intertextuality..184
          The Agency of the אביונים...............................185
      iv. Scriptural Intertextuality 188
          Pharaoh's Defeat in the ים סוף...........................189
          Assyria's Defeat by the חרב לוא איש 191
          Gog's Defeat from the השמים 192
      v. Prophetic Exegesis 194
   c. Summary...196
5. Prophetic Exegesis in 1QM 12 199
   a. 1QM 12.1–5: Israel as the Chosen People 202
      i. Text and Translation...202
      ii. Content 203
      iii. Sectarian Intertextuality..203
      iv. Scriptural Intertextuality 207
      v. Prophetic Exegesis 210
   b. 1QM 12.7–18: Final Restoration of Zion 211
      i. Text and Translation...211
      ii. Content 212
      iii. Sectarian Intertextuality..214
      iv. Scriptural Intertextuality 222
      v. Prophetic Exegesis 226
   c. Summary...231

Conclusion...235
   a. Intertextuality in 1QM...235
   b. Prophetic Exegesis..237
   c. 1QM 10–12 and their Role in the War Scroll 238
   d. Next Steps in the Study of 1QM 240

Bibliography 243

Index 257

Abbreviations

Bib	*Biblica*
BibInt	*Biblical Interpretation*
CutTM	*Currents in Theology and Mission*
DSD	*Dead Sea Discoveries*
DJD	*Discoveries in the Judean Desert*
EDSS	*Encyclopedia of the Dead Sea Scrolls*. Edited by Lawrence H. Schiffman and James C. VanderKam. 2 vols. New York: Oxford University Press, 2000
FAT	*Forschungen zum Alten Testament*
FRLANT	*Forschungen zur Religion und Literatur des Alten und Neuen Testaments*
HS	*Hebrew Studies*
HUCA	*Hebrew Union College Annual*
HvTSt	*Hervormde teologiese Studies*
JSOT	*Journal for Study of the Old Testament*
JSJ	*Journal for the Study of Judaism*
JSP	*Journal for the Study of the Pseudepigrapha*
JANER	*Journal of Ancient Near Eastern Religions*
JJS	*Journal of Jewish Studies*
JNES	*Journal of Near Eastern Studies*
Numen	*Numen*

PMLA	*Proceedings of the Modern Language Association*
Poetics	*Poetics*
RB	*Revue Biblique*
RHR	*Revue de l'histoire des religions*
ScEs	*Science et Esprit*
SBLSP	*Society of Biblical Literature Seminar Papers*
STDJ	*Studies on the Texts of the Desert of Judah*
SEÅ	*Svensk exegetisk årsbok*
TSAJ	*Texte und Studien zum antiken Judentum*
BA	*Biblical Archaeologist*
TZ	*Theologische Zeitschrift*
VT	*Vetus Testamentum*
ZAW	*Zeitschrift für die alttestamentliche Wissenschaft*

Introduction

I N 1947 SEVEN MANUSCRIPTS of what we know today as the Dead Sea Scrolls (DSS) were discovered in a cave near Khirbet Qumran. One of these manuscripts describes in great detail a battle that will take place between the "Sons of Light" (בני אור) against Belial and the "the Sons of Darkness" (בני חושך). In both his early reports and a later edition published posthumously in 1954, Professor Eleazar Sukenik entitled this manuscript the *War Scroll* (1QMilhamah, long for 1QM).[1] 1QM along with other manuscripts from Cave 4 (4Q285; 4Q471; 4Q91–4Q95) and Cave 11 (11Q14) reveal a holy war ideology among the people that preserved these works. This ideology fueled by an interpretation of the traditions of Scripture[2] combines law, prophecy, and liturgy to further the belief that the army was the recipient of God's favor. Because of this combination of tradition and ideology scholars have come up with different opinions to describe the genre of this text.

Some consider 1QM either as a "military manual" (Yigael Yadin) or a "tactical treatise" comparable to Greco-Roman treatises (Jean Duhaime). Others prefer to see it as an "apocalyptic text" (Henri Michaud) or even as a "liturgical drama" (Robert North).[3] Although the purpose of this study is not to

---

1 Eleazar L. Sukenik, *The Dead Sea Scrolls of the Hebrew University* (Jerusalem: Magness Press, 1955 [Hebrew 1954]).

2 Throughout this work we will refer to the Scriptures and avoid terms like "bible" or "Hebrew Bible" which might suggest that at this point in history there was a fixed set of writings. Instead when we use Scriptures, we mean not only some of the traditional writings (i.e. Torah, Prophets, and Psalms), but also other texts like Enoch and Jubilees that are not only referred to in 1QM but were also used among the DSS. For a discussion about Scripture in the Dead Sea Scrolls, see: James VanderKam, *The Dead Sea Scrolls and the Bible* (Grand Rapids: Eerdmans, 2012), 49–70.

3 For a survey of the different interpretations that scholars have presented regarding the genre of 1QM, see: Jean Duhaime, *The War Texts: 1QM and Related Manuscripts* (London: T & T Clark, 2004), 45–61. Yigael Yadin, *The Scroll of the War of the Sons of Light Against the Sons of*

ascertain the genre of 1QM, we believe that a careful look at how 1QM interprets the sacred traditions of Scripture will help to clarify this question. Before we state our thesis statement, it is necessary to broadly explore the parts that make up 1QM.

The *War Scroll* consists of nineteen well preserved columns that can be divided into two overarching stages.[4] Columns 2–9, commonly labeled as the War of Divisions, describe a thirty-five-year war against foreign powers (1QM 2.9b–16). These columns also relay the details of the composition of the army, the battle formations, and the cultic duties that the army needs to follow. Columns 2 and 7 provide the recruiting and cultic aspects that guide the army. Columns 3–5, 9 contain the standards for the trumpets, the banners, and the formation of the fighting battalions established by three rules: the Rule of the Banners of the Congregation (3.13; 4.9), the Rule of the Formation of the Fighting Battalions (5.3), and the Rule for Changing the Order of the Battle Divisions (9.10). Columns 6 and 8 deal with the deployment of the army during the skirmish and other tactical details. One of the distinctive qualities of these accounts is the continuous reference to passages in Scripture via allusions, to establish not just the stipulations of who can be part of the army but also the details of the paraphernalia that will be used in the war.

1QM 15–19 on the other hand describe the War Against the Kittim. This stage of the war is anchored by three prayers from the High Priest in 1QM 15.4–16.1, 16.13–17.9, and 18.5–14. Between these prayers there are instructions that the army shall follow with the priests leading the army through the sounding of the trumpets. Column 19 wraps up with a triumphal procession to Zion, which is also attested in 1QM 12 and 4Q492. Different from the War of Divisions, columns 15–19 assume that the army is already formed and ready for battle. For that matter the High Priest exhortations work to remind the combatants of God's promises to Israel and how God and the angels will act on their behalf in this battle. 1QM 16.1 states that "the God of Israel has called a sword against all the nations and with the holy ones of his people he will do mightily."[5] The War Against the Kittim, like the War of Divisions, depends on the promises in Scripture especially on the prophetic testimony from Daniel 11–12 where God and the angels intervene to deliver Israel.[6]

Darkness, trans. Batya Rabin and Chaim Rabim (London: Oxford University Press, 1962). Henri Michaud, "Une apocalypse nouvelle: La guerre des fils de lumière contre les fils des ténèbres," *Positions Luthériennes* 3: 64-76, (1955). Robert North, "'Kittim' War or 'Sectaries' Liturgy?" *Bib* 39: 84-93, (1958).

4 1QM has fragments of a 20th column but these fragments are too incomplete to be analyzed. For a discussion on the content of 1QM, see: Duhaime, *The War Texts*, 12–19.

5 Translations of the Hebrew texts are mine unless otherwise noted.

6 The influence of Daniel on 1QM appears not only in columns 15–19, but also on 1QM 1

Introduction 3

Right in the middle of the War of Divisions (1QM 2–9) and the War
Against the Kittim (1QM 15–19), columns 10–14 consist of a set of prayers
whose one consistent attribute is their explicit use of the traditions of Scripture. In his seminal work Yigael Yadin believes that 1QM 10–14 were part of a
liturgical book that he identified with the "Book of the Rule of Its Time" (ספר
סרך עתו) mentioned in 1QM 15.5.[7] For his part, Philip Davies concurs with
Yadin that these prayers point to an outside source, and added that these liturgies were included in 1QM at a later redactional stage.[8] Brian Schultz, like
Davies, is also interested in the redactional history of this manuscript, but
different from Davies he retrieves the intersection points that connect these
columns to each of the major parts of the scroll in order to read the manuscript as a cohesive whole. Our study will proceed, like Schultz above, in reading 1QM as a single work. However, rather than addressing questions that deal
with the redactional layers of this manuscript, we will attempt to deal with
the fact that the Scriptures play a primordial role and address what this use
reveals about the religious ideology of the people who preserved 1QM. More
specifically we will focus on 1QM 10–12 because these passages have the only
explicit citations to Scripture in the entire scroll (Deut 7:21–22, 20:2–5; Num
10:9 in 1QM 10; Num 24:17–19 and Isa 31:8 in 1QM 11) as well as numerous allusions to important moments in Israel's history.

The ensuing analysis of these columns will provide a clue to the interpretative method within 1QM, and how these traditions were used prophetically to
anticipate the future of Israel. Before we develop this thesis we must review
some of the most important works that deal with the use of Scripture in 1QM.

a.   Scriptural Traditions in 1QM

The early works on 1QM were done by scholars whose contribution included the reconstruction, translation, and commentaries on this scroll.[9] Jean
Carmignac was one of the first scholars to publish on the topic of Scriptural traditions in 1QM. Carmignac begins his exploration by describing what

---

where the introduction lays out the chronology of the battle following the prophecies of Daniel 11–12.

7 Yadin, 198–228. Yadin labels columns 10–14 as Ritual *Serekh* Series where prayers and
thanksgiving songs take place.

8 Philip R. Davies, *1QM, the War Scroll from Qumran: Its Structure and History* (Rome: Biblical Institute Press, 1977), 91–111.

9 Jean Carmignac, *La Règle de la Guerre Des Fils de Lumière Contre les Fils de Ténèbres* (Paris: Letouzey et Ané, 1958). Johannes van der Ploeg, "La Règle de la Guerre: Traduction et Notes,"
VT 5 (1955): 373–420. Johannes van der Ploeg, *Le Rouleau de la Guerre: Traduit et Annoté avec
une Introduction* (Leiden: Brill, 1959).

other scholars have commented about the literary character of this scroll.[10] He notes that some have described it as a "good specimen" of the anthological style, and that its discourse is constructed as a "mosaic of biblical texts" or a "tissue of biblical texts." These opinions led Carmignac to engage in a systematic study of 1QM with the hope that it would contribute to decipher both the sources that influenced the author's thought and the modifications that the author imposed on these traditions.

Carmignac recognizes the difficulty in providing a comprehensive list of the many sources that comprise 1QM and is careful to label his work as a "provisionary inventory." He divides this inventory into a list of passages that are explicitly cited in 1QM 10–12 and a bigger catalog of implicit traditions recorded throughout the scroll. In terms of the former, Carmignac states that the author used these texts to awake the courage of the warriors prior to the skirmish against the Sons of Darkness and to emphasize the promises that God had given to the Jewish people. In terms of the implicit passages, Carmignac clarifies that his aim is not to provide a complete list of every text that falls into this category, but to focus on the most salient examples in order to assess what these uses demonstrate about the authoritative role of the Scriptures and the author's "psychology."[11] He concludes that the different traditions in 1QM sprang from the writer's memory and sense of devotion, and that they also compensated for the apparent lack of imagination.[12]

Carmignac's work broke ground in the research of the scroll. His list of references and the analysis of the different interpretive moves are valuable resources that give us a starting point to analyze the ideology within 1QM. His point about the authoritative status of the Scriptures is self-evident, although we cannot necessarily assume that every reference in this scroll represents an authoritative tradition. His point about the author's lack of creativity is questionable, however, because it takes a significant amount of sophistication to integrate prior traditions into a completely new work. Plus, we know that the Second Temple Period was a time rich in the production of new texts, as evinced in subsequent readings of the sacred traditions (e.g. the book of Jubilees) and the ingenious exegesis that read prophecy in light of current historical events (e.g. Pesharim).

In the same year of Carmignac's article, Yadin published the most

---

10 Jean Carmignac, "Les Citation de l'Ancien Testament dans la 'Guerre des Fils de Lumière Contre des Fils de Ténèbres'," *RB* 63 (1956): 234–260. Raymond Tournay, "Les anciens manuscrits hébreux récemment découverts," *RB* 56 (1949): 218. André Dupont-Sommer, *Aperçus préliminaires sur les manuscrits de la Mer Morte* (Paris: Librairie Maisonneuve, 1950), 102.

11 Ibid.

12 Ibid., 239.

Introduction   5

comprehensive study of 1QM. Yadin's work is a foundational piece, because it explores in great detail every aspect of this text along with a complete translation and commentary.[13] Yadin believes that 1QM has all the characteristics of a sectarian writing whose purpose was to supply its readers with a detailed set of regulations and plans by which they were to act on the day of battle. He adds that the author of 1QM sought to answer some of the issues affecting the community, such as: when will the final war happen and against whom? What are the laws and the commandments of war? What are the tactics of warfare practices by the nations and how they connect with the Torah? And how will the war be conducted?[14] Yadin holds that the structure of 1QM is organized where it relies on textual sources that would speak to each of these questions.

For instance, the time and plan of the war are based on the apocalyptic and eschatological parts of Scriptures. The descriptions in Isaiah, the apocalypse and angelology of Daniel, and the references to Belial as the head of the enemy armies (e.g. 1 Enoch) are the main sources for the introduction of the war (1QM 1) and the Kittim Series (1QM 15–19). The *Serekh* series comprised of 1QM 2–14 relies on the legal and cultic precepts found in Torah (such as Numbers and Deuteronomy). The descriptions of the weaponry and the organization of the army rely on military sources and the books of Maccabees. Yadin closes his introductory remarks by stating that along with the Scriptures other sectarian sources, like the "Book of the Rule of Its Time" in 1QM 15.5, were foundational for the composition of the ritual series in 1QM 10–14.[15]

We can gather from the initial observations by both Carmignac and Yadin that 1QM contextualizes the traditions of the past that directly apply to the future skirmish. Other interpreters recognize this rhetorical approach in conversation with other Jewish sources. In 1971 Daniel Patte published his monograph *Early Jewish Hermeneutic in Palestine*. In this comprehensive work Patte integrates the hermeneutics of 1QM and other DSS into the wider discussion about interpretive traditions in the Second Temple Period. He notices that 1QM fulfills a similar role like the *Manual of Discipline* (1QS) in that it presents all the foundational disciplines that each of the members of the community needs to follow to maintain her/his place within the sect, and it relays the stipulations that the warriors must keep to partake in the eschatological war. Patte, following Yadin, divides 1QM in three parts: the introduction of the

---

13 Yadin, *The Scroll of the War of the Sons of Light Against the Sons of Darkness*, 1962.
14 Ibid., 4-6.
15 Yadin acknowledged that there was no tangible record of the ספר סרך עתו. He nonetheless was open to the possibility that such a source would be discovered among the manuscripts that were still uncovered at that time.

eschatological war (1QM 1–2), the rule of the war (1QM 3–14), and the final phase of the war (1QM 15–19).[16] He recognizes that the introduction adopts an anthological style that uses the language of passages in Psalms and most notably Daniel. He adds that this "matter-of-fact" introduction describes the future events as self-evident and adopts a "quasi liturgical" style, that enables the community to express its identity in light of the eschatological revelation.[17]

As for the second part of the scroll, Patte observes both a weak and a strong anthological style. In the regulations of the war (1QM 3–9), where the author echoes the holy wars of Yahweh the anthological style is weak. In contrast, the rituals before the war (1QM 10–14), with its five explicit citations from Scriptures and the retelling of Israel's historical moments display a dense anthological style. Patte believes that the hortatory character of this section interprets history as a sacred continuum, where each passage constitutes a "proof-text" that instills confidence in God for the upcoming conflict. In the final phase of the war (1QM 15–19), Patte observes a mix of both the weak and dense anthological styles.

Patte concludes that 1QM's use of Scripture is comparable to that of the *Hodayot* (1QH), the *Manual of Discipline* (1QS) and the *Damascus Document* (CD), in that Scripture is not used as a mere speculation, but as the "prolongation of the lines of the sacred history even beyond the community [and] into the future."[18] He adds that the people associated with 1QM believed that they were part of this sacred history and the main beneficiaries of God's future deeds. Patte's view about 1QM and sacred history is an important concept to consider, especially as the use of the principles and passages of Scripture not only show an interaction with the sacred texts but they bring up questions about how the users of this manuscript view themselves in light of the past traditions and other interpreters of these same passages. Patte does not necessarily address these questions when dealing with 1QM, but we will find out that the sectarians of the scrolls not only believed they were part of the sacred history, but that they were the direct recipients for whom the promises were stored. History points to them as the remnant that God preserved and as the fulfillment of the prophecies.

Another foundational text like Yadin's work comes from Davies whose monograph sets out to do a literary-critical analysis of 1QM.[19] Davies holds

---

16 Daniel Patte, *Early Jewish Hermeneutics in Palestine* (Missoula: Scholars Press, 1971), 281–282.

17 Ibid., 284.

18 Ibid., 287.

19 Davies, *1QM, The War Scroll from Qumran*, 11–23. Although he labels his method as form-critical, a careful reading shows that Davies devotes more attention to issues of redaction

Introduction 7

that 1QM can be divided into three major distinctive parts: columns 2–9, columns 15–19, and columns 10–14 with column 1 representing the latest text that provides an overall introduction to the scroll. He goes on to observe that different from columns 2–9 and 15–19, columns 10–14 do not have structural markers that identify it as a unit; there are no introduction or conclusion, plus they lack unity of style, subject matter, and historical background. Instead, they are prayers and hymns that revolve around the topic of war. In particular, Davies singles out columns 10–12 as a discrete unit that he connects with the priestly prayer in 1QM 15.4–6 that mentions a liturgical book.[20] Davies believes that these seemingly random passages form part of a collection of liturgies contained in this book. He supports this thesis by observing that 1QM 19 and 1QM 12 recite the same hymn whose inclusion in 1QM can be explained by assuming that they both come from the same source; that is, the "Book of the Rule of Its Time."

After positing this thesis Davies analyzes each of the constituent parts of 1QM 10–12 looking for clues that point to their redactional history. Davies' connection of the prayers in columns 10–12 with the "Book of the Rule of Its Time" brings up important aspects to consider no just from the standpoint of the source of these liturgies, but the rhetorical purpose of adding them to the scroll. Davies does not devote time to this last issue because that was not his original goal, as he looked for the clues that point to redactional moves from the part of the author(s) of 1QM. Nevertheless, if we consider this proposal as well as his observation that column 1 is a later redactional layer that provides an introduction to the entire scroll, then we can see that by integrating these texts the author(s) not only wants to provide the timing of these events but also to establish the prophetic foundation that envision the restoration of Israel. This last point will become more apparent once we analyze 1QM 12 and its allusion to the prophecies of Daniel 11–12, which are also referenced in 1QM 1.

The next publication that deals with Scripture in 1QM comes in the 1990s. Dean O. Wenthe picks up the discussion that begun with Carmignac's work. His aim is to provide a survey that would explore the extent to which the Scriptures appear in 1QM, and to compare each reference with its original source looking for redactional moves and hermeneutical assumptions.[21] Once he deals with the critical issues of composition date, form, and structure, Wenthe proceeds with his survey. He begins by delineating some of the

---

and how the parts of 1QM were incorporated into this scroll.

20 Ibid., 92.

21 Dean O. Wenthe, "The Use of the Hebrew Scriptures in 1QM," *DSD* 5 (1998): 290–319.

challenges he faces in this study by posing different questions: should the analysis move from more explicit to less explicit citations and/or allusions? Or, should the study proceed from start to end in linear direction? And what aspects of these usages should be highlighted? In the end Wenthe adopts a linear approach that goes from the start of 1QM to its ending. He considers that this direction would allow him to cover each part of 1QM and to demonstrate that even an allusive use of Scripture reveals an attitude toward these traditions. With this last point Wenthe agrees with Fitzmyer in that the DSS much like the NT adopts an anthological style, where the language of sacred history forms the very fabric of the texts.[22]

At the end of his survey Wenthe points out the complexity of this scroll because it alludes to the books of Daniel, the Torah, prophetic texts, the Apocrypha, and the Pseudepigrapha. He concludes that aside from the five explicit citations in 1QM 10–11, the use of other textual traditions underscores that the author did not discriminate between the modern categories of "canonical" versus "non-canonical," and concedes that there is a certain level of artificiality when using labels like "hermeneutics" or "implied exegesis" to try to interpret 1QM. Nevertheless he argues that the implicit exegesis seen throughout this scroll displays many aspects that are comparable to Rabbinic Midrash, the Apocrypha, and Pseudepigrapha. In the end Wenthe asserts that the author of 1QM used both "typological" and "pesher" hermeneutics that defined the present and future based on Scriptural traditions.[23] Wenthe's work is a good continuation of Carmignac's article; whereas Carmignac used the evidence in 1QM to compare it with the Scriptural passages it references, Wenthe went a step further as he asked questions about exegesis and interpretation that result from the pervasive presence of Scripture in this scroll. Wenthe's approach is informative to our work as we will consider not just the presence of particular passages in columns 10–12, but like him we want to ask about the implications that the use of the Scriptures reveals about the ideology of the sectarians and what hopes/aspirations can we discern by the selective process of tapping certain passages.

In *Conquering the World: The War Scroll (1QM) Reconsidered,* Schultz provides a comprehensive study of 1QM.[24] His goal, much like it was for Davies, is to provide an analysis of the redactional history of 1QM. Where he differs from his predecessor is that he wants to start from the vantage point of

---

22 Joseph Fitzmyer, "The Use of Explicit OT Quotations in the Qumran Literature and in the NT," in *Essays on the Semitic Background of the NT* (London: Geoffrey Chapman, 1971), 3–58.

23 Wenthe, "The Use of the Hebrew Scriptures in 1QM," 319.

24 Brian Schultz, *Conquering the World: The War Scroll (1QM) Reconsidered* (Leiden: Brill, 2009), 1–9.

Introduction 9

analyzing 1QM in its final form, and from this analysis to provide an explanation of its compositional history. Whereas Davies sees the different parts of
this scroll as proofs of its redactional history, Schultz takes 1QM as a finished
text and he transitions into the analysis of its compositional layers. Another aspect that Schultz concedes is that different from other works his work
benefits from the publication of other war texts from Caves 4 and 11. Thus,
he includes an analysis of the manuscripts from these caves. His aim in using
these manuscripts is not to provide a comparative inventory of the evidence
between the Cave 4 and 11 manuscripts and 1QM. Rather, he wants to tap into
these witnesses to discern if there are any indications that contribute to the
overarching conclusions regarding the development of the war material in
Qumran. Schultz also acknowledges that the fragmentary nature of the Cave
4 and 11 war texts precludes us from understanding these texts in the same
light as 1QM, and that studies of these texts will be forced to examine the evidence in light of the more complete framework in 1QM. Schultz's direction
in the study of 1QM as a finished text in conversation with the Cave 4 and 11
manuscripts is significant, because it not only recognizes that the war ideology existed within the *War Scroll* but that it was present in other works as well.
This inherently brings up additional questions about the sectarian identity
vis-à-vis other groups and why they relied in the war material to illustrate the
future and how they, as a close group, would inherent the promises. In addition, by acknowledging that the parts of the scroll represent different compositional layers that work jointly to form a composition Schultz goes beyond
pointing the obvious, but he triggers additional discussions about the purpose of joining these parts into this one manuscript.

Lastly, in his essay "The Literary Unit of 1QM and its Three-Stage War,"
Todd Scacewater has proposed that 1QM can be read as a literary unit broken
down into three stages.[25] In his estimation this approach gives more justice
to the author's (redactor's) competency in using the language of Scripture, to
illustrate the various stages of the war. Plus, it seeks to smooth out possible
contradictions that come up when trying to understand how the stages of the
war fit together.[26] Scacewater observes that 1QM begins in column 1 with a
war within Israel launched against the Kittim and Belial. This first attack continues with a second stage, in the War of Divisions columns 2–9, where the
army subdues the surrounding nations per 1QM 2.10–14. The third and final

---

25 Todd A. Scacewater, "The Literary Unity of 1QM and Its Three-Stage War," *RevQ* 27
(2015): 225–248.

26 Ibid., 237–238. In asserting the unity of 1QM, Scacewater sides with scholars like Yadin,
Carmignac, and Schultz who believe in the unity of 1QM. In particular, Schultz's theory of a
two stage war proves influential on the stages that Scacewater later proposes.

stage is therefore an attack on the remnants of the nations and the Kittim in columns 15–19.[27] Scacewater wraps up his study by addressing the prayers in 1QM 10–14.

He observes that it is unclear where these prayers fit within the two major stages of the war, since there are elements in 1QM 10.1–8 that correlate to the War of Divisions and other references in 1QM 11.13–12.5 that point to the War Against the Kittim. He concedes that the mixed nature of these prayers can be explained by the fact that the same army that fought the battle in columns 2–9 proceeds to fight against nations in columns 15–19. The prayers are therefore indicators of the consolidation of this army and their adherence to the precepts of law, where a priest recites a prayer before the battle.[28] Scacewater's observation about the mixed nature of these prayers is an important one, because it underscores that these accounts do not belong to either of the main stages of the war (i.e. columns 2–9 and 15–19). In addition, it is in line with the proposal originally presented by Yadin that these columns are part of the "Book of the Rule of Its Time." Furthermore, as we will suggest below, they are the prophetic testimony (both as foretelling and forthtelling) from the mouth of a priest for the success in the final war against the Kittim.

Aside from these overarching works, others have tried to address the links between 1QM and specific traditions. Perhaps one of the most intriguing connections in 1QM is the use of the book of Daniel. In 1976, John J. Collins published an article entitled "The Mythology of Holy War in Daniel and the Qumran War Scroll: A Point of Transition in Jewish Apocalyptic" where he describes the holy war imagery that is present in both of these writings and expounds on the different sources that influenced each of them. [29] He notices that whereas the holy war in Daniel is patterned according to Canaanite myth with its descriptions of cosmic chaos and restoration brought by God (e.g. Daniel 7), the War Scroll adopts Persian dualism evinced in its distinction of the Sons of Darkness and the Sons of Light as well as in the development of ethical concerns. He adds that the Zoroastrian myth in Plutarch's *De Iside et Osiride* 45–47 can inform some of the dualistic ideology seen in 1QM.[30]

Collins believes that the three-thousand-year conflict between Horomazes (born of light) and Areimanios (born of darkness) and their trading victories until the time when Hades passes away has striking similarities with

---

27 Ibid., 239–242.

28 Ibid., 243–246.

29 John J. Collins, "The Mythology of Holy War in Daniel and the Qumran War Scroll: A Point of Transition in Jewish Apocalyptic," *VT* 25 (1975): 596–612.

30 Ibid., 603–605.

Introduction

1QM. The schematization of the war into six discreet periods, the deadlock between the rivals, the differentiation between light and darkness, and the leaders of the two factions are the main intersecting points. These similarities lead Collins to suggest that 1QM is a novelty in Israelite religion with its distinctive Persian language, which changed the nationalistic language in the book of Daniel into a dualistic perspective that pitted the forces of light and darkness against each other. He reiterates that the dualism of the Persian myth was basic for the Qumran people and its portrayal of the universe, and that the conception of light and darkness became an oversimplification of the human condition, which is typical of overzealous sectarian and nationalistic movements.[31]

Eight years later Gregory Beale produced a thorough study of the use of Daniel in Jewish literature. Within this work Beale devotes a section on the relationship of Daniel and 1QM 1. He sets the stage for his analysis by constructing the criteria that would determine whether a particular passage is an allusion or an echo. Once he establishes these principles, Beale proceeds to analyze 1QM 1 and the different connections that appear in this passage. He proposes that the author of 1QM wrote with the context of Daniel 11–12 in his mind and that these two chapters provided the thematic as well as the unifying structure for the first column. Although Beale accepts that there are some contextual differences between Daniel 11–12 and 1QM 1, he explains these by suggesting that the author of 1QM used the descriptions in Daniel 12 as the starting point to interpret the historical events in chapter 11. In the end Beale holds that 1QM 1 reveals a typological interpretation of Scripture, which makes it an eschatological midrash of Daniel.[32]

Similar to Beale, Hanna Vanonen addresses the links between Daniel and 1QM 1 from the standpoint of intertextuality.[33] Using the works on Scriptural citations in the DSS from Moshe Bernstein and of literary allusions in the *Hodayot* (1QH) from Julie Hughes,[34] Vanonen establishes the approach that will steer her study. She recognizes that the relationship of Daniel and 1QM 1 is not without its problems as there is a marked discrepancy between these

---

31 Ibid., 612.

32 Gregory K. Beale, *The Use of Daniel in Jewish Apocalyptic Literature and in the Revelation of St. John* (Lanham: University Press of America, 1984), 42–66.

33 Hanna Vanonen, "The Textual Connections Between 1QM 1 and the Book of Daniel," in *Changes in Scripture,* ed. Hanne von Weissenberg, Juha Pakkala, and Marko Marttila (Berlin: De Gruyter, 2011), 223–246.

34 Moshe Bernstein, "Scriptures: Quotation and Use," in *Encyclopedia of the Dead Sea Scrolls,* ed. Lawrence H. Schiffman and James C. VanderKam (Oxford: Oxford University Press, 2000), 839–842. Julie Hughes, *Scriptural Allusions and Exegesis in the Hodayot* (Leiden: Brill, 2006).

two texts on how the events leading up to the end will transpire. The different redactional moves within 1QM 1 preclude certainty that the "biblical" version of Daniel is at the core of this chapter, and she proposes two possible solutions to this issue: a) either the author of 1QM used Daniel and adjusted its content in order to go deeper into the interpretation of these passages, or b) the author used a different text linked to another Danielic tradition. Vanonen favors the former solution and describes the use of Daniel in 1QM 1 as "allusive." This means that the writer of 1QM evokes the texts of Daniel trusting in the competence of the audience to recognize these passages and their different applications.

The previous survey demonstrates the different methods that scholars have adopted to explain the presence of the traditions of Scripture in 1QM. We can see from the early works of Carmignac and Yadin an effort to ascertain the traditions that 1QM alludes to and to what extent these traditions are kept and/or modified within the scroll. These early efforts gave way to additional questions, by scholars like Davies and Schultz, about the redaction of the scroll and how we can discern from the presence of particular traditions the various layers of composition that took place at different times in history. Because of these important contributions and the subsequent discovery of additional war texts from Cave 4, we are now in a position to ask additional questions that not only focus on the sources and redaction of the scroll but can begin to assess its war ideology and how the traditions of Scripture spurred this type of thinking among the sectarians. The focus of this study is not necessarily to provide the answers to these important questions. Instead, the aim is more circumscribed in that it seeks to explore how war ideology is influenced by Scripture and creates its own interpretation. We argue that this phenomenon can be seen in 1QM 10–12, where the prayers depend on the words of traditions to encourage the armies but they also illustrate in a prophetic fashion a new vision for the army as a fulfillment of prophecy.[35] We propose that the authors (redactors) of these columns, and for that matter the other war scrolls, do not just gather sources to explain the future, but they dialog with these texts using their own agency to illustrate how the events will unfold on behalf of the sectarians.

---

35 Although 1QM 10–12 form part of the liturgical section of the scroll that spans to columns 13–14, the present study focuses on these columns because of its explicit use of the Scriptural traditions. 1QM 10–11 has the only citations in the entire scroll and it makes references to prophetic teachings from Scripture. Moreover, columns 13 and 14 introduce new prayers that apply to a different stage of the war: 1QM 13.1 begins with a prayer where the priests and Levites bless God and curse Belial while 1QM 14 relays a prayer that happens when the combatants return to the camp. Although all of these prayers depend on traditions 1QM 13–14 take place in a different context than columns 10–12.

Introduction   13

b. Thesis Statement

The author(s) of 1QM 10–12 use their own agency to interpret that the prophecies of the past meet their ultimate fulfillment in the life of the sectarians as
the true Israel. To ascertain this interpretation 1QM 10–12 includes different
passages of Scripture using an interpretive approach that we label as "prophetic exegesis." By prophetic exegesis we mean that these prayers use the
words of Scripture both in predicting the future, based on past deliverance,
and also in calling the army to live by the principles of faith; they are both
foretelling and forthtelling. Further, these utterances act like markers that
trigger the combatants' memories and stamp in their minds the promises
that God has given to Israel. They are intersection points, where the present
and future are seen in light of the past. As a result of this interpretive direction, the Scriptural words (from law, prophecy, poetry, wisdom and liturgy)
become signs that need to be decoded, they are the keys that open the doors
to discern God's plan from ages past. Scripture is therefore this well of wisdom and instruction that steers the sectarians in both their tactics and faith
in God in the midst of the battle.[36]

    We can see this prophetic exegesis in full display as the explicit citations
and allusions advance the belief that the sectarians are the instruments that
God will use to bring to fruition the plan for Israel. The words of Moses recorded in both Numbers and Deuteronomy become the exhortation that the
priest gives to the warriors in 1QM 10.1–8a. The use of verbs of proclamation
(נגד) and instruction (למד) within these lines demonstrates not only that the
teachings of Moses are seen as prophecy but also as insight that the army can
use when they come across their oppressor. This is also evident when 1QM
11.1–7a ascribes the encounter to God by continuously repeating the refrain
"the battle is yours" (לכה המלחמה). This refrain along with the allusions to
historical moments like David's defeat of Goliath and Israel's kings submis-
sion of the Philistines, recall how God defeated their enemies. This hymn is
capped by an oracle, where the star and the scepter (as signs of Israel's power)
overcome the enemies. Further, the motif of overcoming the foes continues
in the latter part of column 11, where the "sword of no man" (חרב לא אדם)
from Isa 31:8 brings the powerful armies of Assyria (associated with the Kittim) to the feet of the meek. The culmination of this reversal of fortunes happens in 1QM 12 with the heavenly gathering of the chosen ones (i.e. chosen
of the holy people) who along with the angels celebrate God's victory on the

---

36 Our use of prophetic exegesis is informed by the work of Alex Jassen who deals with
prophecy and revelation in the DSS. See: Alex P. Jassen, *Mediating the Divine: Prophecy and Revelation in the Dead Sea Scrolls and Second Temple Judaism* (Leiden: Brill, 2007), 197–213.

earth. The procession to Zion and the restoration of Jerusalem, as a microcosm of the earth, aligns with the prophetic anticipations seen in accounts like Amos 9 and Ezekiel 38–48. Finally, the clearest example of prophetic exegesis comes in 1QM 11.7b–8. In this subtle but powerful statement the scroll describes that God has "declared" (נגד) via the "anointed ones and seers of decrees" (משיחיכה חוזי תעודות) the times and the purpose of the war: "to cover yourself with glory" (להׂ{לחם}כבד). This statement is of great significance, as it underscores that the process of deciphering the prophetic word for the current times was foundational to the sectarian beliefs. It also highlights that in the sectarian religious worldview the glorification of God could not come except via an extermination of the elements that they associated with wickedness. Thus, 1QM 11.7b–8 reveal the method for interpreting Scripture and the religious basis for this approach.

The contribution that this work makes to the study of 1QM and of the DSS, is that it highlights that prophetic interpretation of Scripture is foundational to this scroll as it is to other manuscripts like the *Damascus Document*, the *Rule of the Yahad*, the *Hodayot* among others.[37] We will see in our research that during the times following the return from the exile in Babylon, the study and interpretation of Scripture became the "prophetic voice" that steered the people of Israel. Scripture was the locus of authority and hope for the people who aspired for a new Israel, one that would be reconstituted in

---

37 One of the major topics of discussion in the study of the DSS is the identification of the people behind these manuscripts. The most popular option is that the community of the scrolls are the Essenes. The writings of Philo in *Quod Omnis Probus Liber Sit* 1.75–91 and in *De Vita Contemplative* 1.1 describe this group as individuals devoted to matters of purity and the service of God, which resemble in many ways the piety of the group(s) associated with the scrolls. Likewise, Josephus in *Antiquities* 13, 15, 17–18 describes the Essenes as a group that strives for the rewards of righteousness and to live in a community that serves one another. These depictions correlate to the image that comes from texts like the Rule Books in the DSS, where each community is trained to live in purity and to share everything among themselves under the leadership of teachers and/or priests who guide them in the observance of the words of Scripture. The fact is that the Rule Books, the Pesharim and other manuscripts in the DSS library do not attest to a single community. This reality has moved some scholars, like John Collins (see John J. Collins, *Beyond the Qumran Community* [Grand Rapids: Eerdmans, 2010]) to speak of "complementary communities" that were part of a larger movement that aspired to a higher degree of holiness. Although the purpose of our study is not to ascertain who the people behind the scrolls are, we will proceed instead with a more generic description of this people as "sectarians." The use of the term sectarians is not laden with a negative connotation, but it is rather used as a sociological term that better explains the organization and ethos of this people as well as their level of tension with the surrounding religious environment in early Judaism. For studies that deal with the Qumran sectarians from a sociological and comparative approaches, see: Jutta Jokiranta, "'Sectarianism' of the Qumran 'Sect:' Sociological Notes," *RevQ* 20 (2001): 223–239. Eyal Regev, "Comparing Sectarian Practice and Organization: The Qumran Sects in Light of the Regulations of the Shakers, Hutterites, Mennonites and Amish," *Numen* 51 (2004): 146–181.

Introduction 15

its proper worship of God via the cult and ethics. 1QM bears this characteristic, as it displays a method of analyzing the minute details of Scripture to
indicate that every passage points in a futuristic fashion to its realization and
consummation in the life of the sectarians. For that matter, throughout our
study we will argue that the explicit/implicit references to Scripture and their
subsequent interpretation underscore the sectarian identity and their aspirations as the true Israel.

c.   Content and Purpose of 1QM 10–12

1QM 10–12 comprise prayers, hymns, and visions where the prophecies of
Scripture take center stage. Our study will analyze each of these columns
separately for the sake of drawing the intertextual connections that each of
these passages has with other texts. Although the division of these columns
and the place where each prayer begins and ends is open to interpretation,
we will proceed with the following breakdown: 1QM 10.1–8a, 1QM 10.8b–18,
1QM 11.1–7a, 1QM 11.7b–18, 1QM 12.1–5, and 1QM 12.7–18.

The first part in 1QM 10.1–8a is the culmination of the War of Divisions,
more specifically of the Rule of Changing of the Order of the Combat Battalions (סרך לשנות סדר דגלי המלחמה), where the priest and the officers address the army prior to the battle. These leaders also appear in 1QM 7.12–18,
where they exhort the army to believe in God before the battle. In addition to
the priestly presence, the use of trumpets to guide the warriors in the midst
of battle corroborate the connections between 1QM 10.1–8a and 1QM 7. Although 1QM 10.1–8a fits as a capstone to the content and purpose of the War
of Divisions, we will include it among the passages to be analyzed for this
study. The three explicit citations to the Scriptures as well as the reference to
the prophetic testimony from Moses support our choice. The reference to the
explicit passages from Deuteronomy and Numbers demonstrate that these
lines were most likely added to the tail end of the War of Divisions.[38]

1QM 10.8b–18 transitions from the end of the War of Divisions to the beginning of a new stage with a song to God and Israel. In this piece the questions "who is like you, O God of Israel" (מיא כמוכה אל ישראל) and "who is
like your people Israel" (מיא כעמכה ישראל) provide the religious foundation that God will favor Israel and deliver them, because the sectarians are
the people of the covenant who are endowed with the mysteries of creation
and of the appointed times.

---

38 This is something that Davies originally proposed in his assessment of columns 10–14.
See, Davies, *1QM, The War Scroll from Qumran*, 11–23.

Subsequently, 1QM 11.1–7a continues with the theme of God favoring Israel with a hymn that ascribes the war to God. This piece is capped by the oracle in Num 24:17–19, where the star and scepter of Israel overcome the enemies; thus, prophecy and history meet to establish the hope for the future. In 1QM 11.7b–18 the testimony of the "anointed seers of decrees" depicts the turn of events where Belial and the Seven Nations of Futility will be defeated like Pharaoh, Assyria, and Gog of Magog. In these lines we begin to see markers that connect to the War Against the Kittim, as Belial and the Kittim are the targets of God's wrath. Also, the allusion to the prophecies of Ezekiel, Isaiah, and Daniel in column 12, connect with the images in the War Against the Kittim in columns 15–19. Column 12, therefore, concludes this section with two passages: a vision in heaven where the "chosen of the holy people" (בחירי עם קודש) celebrate with the holy angels in the presence of God. This vision alludes to the prophecy in Daniel 12, where the משכלים rise to everlasting life. In the same fashion the sectarians identify themselves as the chosen ones who will share in the heavenly abode with God. The final section in 1QM 12.7–18 is a triumphant march to Zion that appears also in 1QM 19 and in 4Q492. In this procession Psalm 24 figures as the key text that envisions, in eschatological fashion, God as the King of Glory and the War Hero that takes back the city. Column 12, like 1QM 10–11, has markers that point to both stages of the war. In the partnership of the warriors and the horsemen with God's angel we have a link to the War of Divisions, and in its universalistic tone via the procession to Zion we see the first connections with the War Against the Kittim. The presence of themes from both stages of the war brings up the fundamental question about the purpose of these liturgies.

1QM 10-12 provide the transition point from the end of the War of Divisions and into the War Against the Kittim.[39] The evidence of themes from both stages of the war corroborates that these columns do not belong to either part of the scroll, but they were strategically added to offer the religious foundation for Israel's success. From a structural standpoint the address in 1QM 10.1–8a precedes the prayers in 1QM 15–19, where the High Priest consistently comes before the army to encourage them as they head to battle. Thus, 1QM 10.1–8a finishes the War of Divisions and shifts the narrative as priestly addresses (i.e. High Priest prayer) take center stage (see 1QM 15.4–6, 1QM 16.13–17, and 1QM 18.5b–14). This transition in column 10 also points to a shift in teaching approach, where the instructional and cultic regulations in columns 2–9 proceed into a hortatory recollection of the promises and teachings

---

39 This proposal does not deny the possibility that these prayers are part of the ספר סרך עתו in 1QM 15.5 as proposed above by Yadin.

Introduction   17

of Scripture. Therefore, once the army is formed in the War of Divisions with
a proper observance of the purity teachings (1QM 7), the priests continue to
instruct the army in taking the victory that God has already guaranteed.

d. Organization of the Present Study

The structure of our investigation proceeds from establishing first the methodological foundations that will assist in the reading of 1QM. Once these
principles have been explained, we will proceed into an in-depth reading
of the passages in 1QM 10–12. The conclusion will summarize the findings
and suggest new avenues of inquiry for 1QM 10–12 and for the *War Scroll* as a
whole. Initially, we will establish the methodology that we will use to assess
the literary features in 1QM 10–12.

We have chosen intertextuality because we want to trace the dialogical exchanges that these columns create with other texts, and the rhetorical effect that these connections produce. We will proceed with a critical
analysis of intertextuality as a literary concept born from the work of French
post-structuralism. This discussion will lead into a closer look into the feminist version of intertextuality, where the female author counters the idea of
the "death of the author" originally proposed in post-structuralism. The feminist version of intertextuality will prove to be a fruitful tool to use for the analysis of 1QM, since it emphasizes the agency of the author to create her own
text. In the same manner, the sectarians assert their agency and ideological
beliefs in the *War Scroll*, as every detail from the texts they allude to indicate
that they are the main actors and beneficiaries of God's promises. The sectarians in their own agency to choose and make their own text make it explicitly
clear that they are the true Israel for whom the mysteries have been revealed.

Following this discussion, we will turn our attention to the literary features of allusions and citations. We will pay special attention to the works of
literary critics and draw out from these pieces the principles that will be used
to interpret these literary features in 1QM. Lastly, we will establish two axes for
studying the passages in 1QM. One of these axes includes the sectarian axis
where we will look at particular words, that carry religious and ideological
connotations particular to the scrolls, as well as Scriptural traditions attested
within the sectarian texts and other scrolls found in Qumran. The Scriptural
axis, on the other hand, looks at a particular tradition that is referenced, either
via a citation or allusion, and traces its development in texts outside of Qumran. The combination of these readings, however, is not mutually exclusive but
rather integrated as there is a continuous exchange that happens between the

sectarian texts and Scripture. Nevertheless, these axes will be helpful in focusing our attention on particular texts and providing a more complete picture of how the sacred traditions were used prophetically within this scroll.[40]

To create this picture, we will adopt the concept of "prophetic exegesis." Initially we will analyze with specific examples the background that set the stage for the flourishing of this type of exegetical method. The goal of this part is to gather enough evidence from the primary sources, to demonstrate that the DSS came in a time when there was a flourishing of exegetical tradition(s) that became a prophetic mode of teaching. We believe that Israel's historical vicissitudes led to the use of the sacred traditions and to the surge of a charismatic and sapiential class of interpreters, whose keen ability to discern the mysteries of Scripture became a form of divine teaching. After we have gone over some of the factors that gave rise to this phenomenon we will do a close reading of some of the most salient examples of prophetic exegesis within the DSS that have ideological and/or thematic affinities with 1QM like the Thematic Pesharim (i.e. *4QFlorelegium* and *11QMelchizedek*) and the Rule Books (i.e. *1QS* and *CD*). The goal of this initial exploration is to demonstrate that prophetic exegesis is not a phenomenon seen only in 1QM, but it was widespread among the communities associated with the scrolls.

Once the literary and historical foundations of our method have been presented, we will proceed in analyzing 1QM 10. Here we will divide column 10 into two distinct pieces: lines 1–8a consist of a priestly speech to encourage the warriors prior to the war, and lines 8b–18 consist of a song that celebrates God and Israel as the chosen people. In addition, lines 1–8a represent the end of the War of Divisions and the transition into the new stage of the war, where prayers, hymns and visions take center stage until column 14. The song in lines 8b–18 alludes to Scriptural songs like Exod 15, where God is exalted, and Israel is the chosen people. With this allusion 1QM demonstrates that the sectarians are the direct beneficiaries of God's favor and thus the new Israel. The combination of themes of wisdom, cultic celebrations, and calendar matters demonstrate that the sectarians are the ones endowed with the knowledge of the mysteries of God, and as we will see in column 11, they are the ones for whom the eschatological battle will be won.

1QM 11.1–7a ascribes the battle to God with a continuous refrain "the battle is yours". Not only does the hymn ascribe the battle to God, but in doing

---

40 One example where these axes merge happens in the study of David in 1QM 11. This column alludes to the encounter between David and Goliath in 1 Sam 17. In alluding to this passage, the allusion not only recalls this passage, but in doing so it brings ups questions about David's portrayal among the scrolls, which other texts like CD 5, 4Q174, and 11Q5 37–38 provide ample information.

Introduction   19

so it alludes to history as proof that God has indeed fought Israel's battle. The
thrust of this piece is to inspire the combatants in the face of a powerful enemy by recalling history and ascribing the conflict to God. In lines 7b–18 the
scroll transitions into a piece where the teaching of the "seers of decrees" provides the prophetic testimony that establishes the faith of the combatants. As
in the previous piece, here too the scroll recalls God's defeat of more powerful
forces like: Pharaoh and his army dying in the Sea of Reeds, Assyria falling by
"the sword of no man", and Gog and his hordes succumbing to God from the
heavens. The consistent thread across this column is that those who are weak
are suddenly emboldened to defeat their enemies by God's power. There are
the instances of David's encounter versus Goliath as well as Israel versus Pharaoh, Assyria, and Gog. Plus, the "poor" (אביונים) and those whose "face is
to the dust" (כורעי עפר) carry out God's judgment against the mighty. This
combination of historical references and prophetic hope emboldens the sectarians to face the battle by looking back in their collective memory of how
God favored them.

Lastly, in 1QM 12 we have a heavenly gathering that wraps up with a
triumphant celebration to Zion. 1QM 12.1–5 consists of a vision where God
chooses a holy people and establishes their names for eternity. The second
piece in 1QM 12.7–18 is a celebratory march that ends, as the Scriptural counterparts, with a procession to Zion. We will observe that this column presents
the consecration of a chosen people and it describes how this remnant will
partner with the angels and God in taking back Zion. As such, column 12 is
heavily influenced by the prophecies in Daniel 11–12 and Psalm 24. In addition, we will notice that lines 7–18 are the same piece that appears in 1QM
19 and in 4Q492. The comparison of this passage in column 12 with the other
versions will demonstrate that in column 12 the scroll introduces themes that
coincide with the depictions in the War of Divisions. This evidence will underscore what we have observed before, that these columns are a transition
between the major stages of the war. Also, the discussion in column 12 will
demonstrate that these accounts envision a turn of events, a victory similar
to what we find in Amos 9 and Ezekiel 38–48, where God empowers Israel to
defeat its enemies and reconstitute the city where God lives.

Following this exegetical analysis, we will summarize the evidence that
our study has gathered from the discussion of intertextuality and prophetic
exegesis, and we will provide a final interpretation of columns 10–12 and how
these columns fit in the overarching trajectory from the War of Divisions to
the War Against the Kittim. In the end we will provide some possible next
steps in the study of 1QM.

CHAPTER 1

METHODOLOGY

THE PRESENT CHAPTER WILL ESTABLISH the methodology that we will use to assess the literary features in 1QM 10–12. We have chosen intertextuality as our method because it will help in both tracing the dialogical exchanges that these columns engage with other texts and the rhetorical effect that these textual connections produce. 1QM is a rich text that alludes to and cites passages from the Scriptures, Jewish writings of the Second Temple period, and other sectarian texts from Qumran. Because of its allusive quality we posit that 1QM is a textual tapestry that paints an eschatological vision for the sectarian army, where they will enjoy closeness to God following the overthrow of their enemies. Intertextuality will, therefore, allow us to ask different questions and to go deeper into the references that the scroll makes and what it is trying to convey to its readers. Before we begin our use of intertextuality it will be worthwhile to clarify what we mean by it.

Literary critics and biblical scholars have used intertextuality to analyze the allusive character of texts.[1] Although intertextuality became a popular concept since Julia Kristeva first coined the term in the 1960s, recently it has become a catchall term that lacks specificity and methodological clarity. A careful delineation of what we mean by intertextuality will be a positive step to draw out the connections that we observe in 1QM. In addition, a clear definition of allusions and citations will be needed as we seek to discern the rhetorical effect that these features produce. Our argument is that the allusions and citations to Scripture in columns 10–12, and for that matter in 1QM as a whole, point not just to sources of influence per se, but they are windows

---

1 Graham Allen, *Intertextuality* (New York: Routledge, 2011), 1–2. Allen describes in his work that intertextuality has been variously defined using different categories. He adds that intertextuality is in danger of losing specificity and that it could become nothing more than what any particular critic wishes it to mean.

from which we can peek into the complex intertextual relationships as texts effect meaning into one another, and they reveal the religious aspirations of the author(s). When 1QM alludes to or directly cites Scripture, it follows an agenda that aims to persuade the sectarians to consider what God has already revealed in the past and to apply this revelation as something that is being directly fulfilled in their time. This collection of references culled together in 1QM, therefore, produces a new interpretation that becomes a firm belief that God will grant victory in the looming eschatological battle.

Before we are in a position to assess how 1QM accomplishes these rhetorical goals, it is necessary to establish the theoretical foundation of our work. First, we will proceed with a critical analysis of intertextuality as a literary concept born from the work of French post-structuralism. Afterwards we will contrast the post-structuralist project with a feminist version of intertextuality that counters the "death of the author" with the assertion of the woman's agency to create her own text. This discussion will lead into a delineation of the type of intertextuality that will inform our study. The sectarians of 1QM like the feminist writer establish their agency through the selective interpretation of Scripture and the continuous attempt to encourage the audience to believe in the promises of God. To see this authorial agency in full display we will operate on two levels: one where we assess how the sectarians interpret Scriptural traditions and the other where we compare 1QM with fellow sectarian writings. This dual focus will reveal the creative ways that 1QM uses the sacred traditions in line with the sectarian hopes and aspirations.

After establishing this type of intertextuality, our attention will turn to the literary features of allusions and citations. We will pay special attention to the works of literary critics and draw out from these pieces the principles that will be used to interpret these literary features in 1QM. The end will summarize the previous discussion and reiterate the reading strategy that will be used in the exegesis of 1QM.

a.   Intertextuality

i.   Post-Structuralist Intertextuality

The epicenter of intertextuality is located in the work of French post-structuralism associated with the *Tel Quel* group. Figures such as Jacques Derrida, Michel Foucault, Roland Barthes, and Julia Kristeva are key representatives of this movement who in the 1960s began to go against the boundaries established by traditional models of philosophy and literature. One of Kristeva's

Methodology 23

greatest contributions to this group and for that matter to the fields of literary and critical theory, is that she brought to light the work of the Russian theorist Mikhail Bakhtin. A philosopher and literary theorist who had for the most part remained unknown to French culture, Bakhtin had a profound effect on Kristeva's work and her development of intertextuality. A couple of essays will demonstrate the impact that Bakhtin had on Kristeva.

In "Word, Dialogue, and Novel," Kristeva credits Bakhtin with challenging the structural models of literary analysis within Russian Formalism.[2] She notes that for Bakhtin literature does not just exist, but it is generated through the close interaction of various sources. Literature is dynamic rather than stable, and the "literary word" represents the minimal structural unit where all these interactions take place. The word as a linguistic and historical object is the intersection where author, reader, and contemporary/earlier context engage in a dialogue. For Kristeva, Bakhtin's dynamic dimension of the word places literature within the continuum of history and society, in which the author inserts herself through the process of reading and writing. History and society, therefore, become "texts" that the author reads and transcends by re-writing them.

From Bakhtin's dialogical approach Kristeva formulates her own three-dimensional conceptualization of the text. These coordinates of dialogue as she labels them include: the writing subject, the addressee, and the exterior texts. In presenting these coordinates, Kristeva combines Bakhtin's ideas with Saussurean structural and linguistic analysis.[3] She transforms the literary word and Bakhtin's dialogical dimensions of language into structural points within a synchronic and diachronic plane. The synchronic dimension, she explains, happens when a particular text relates to other texts and/or to the surrounding environment, while the diachronic dimension takes place when a text mediates the exchange between writer and addressee. This tri-dimensional model of the text catapults Kristeva's notion of intertextuality as a "mosaic of quotations" that both absorb and transform other texts.[4]

For Kristeva this absorption and transformation of other texts brings forth "ambivalence." To explain what she means by ambivalence, Kristeva goes back to Bakhtin. She states that Bakhtin believed there were three categories of words within a narrative.[5] One is the "direct word," which the writer

---

2 Julia Kristeva, "Word, Dialogue, and Novel," in *Desire in Language: A Semiotic Approach to Literature and Art,* ed. Leon S. Roudiez (New York: Columbia University Press, 1980), 64–65.

3 For a good discussion about Saussurean linguistics and its influence on theories of the text, see: Allen, *Intertextuality,* 8–13.

4 Kristeva, "Word, Dialogue, and Novel," 66.

5 Ibid., 72–73.

uses to infiltrate history and society. Second is the "object-oriented" word that happens in the discourse between characters in a narrative. The last one is the "ambivalent word" where an author uses material from another writer. Kristeva indicates that there is a negotiation that takes place at the moment a writer adopts another's speech; either the author preserves the precursor's speech or changes it. This continuous negotiation brings forth ambivalence, which is something that Kristeva sees taking place in full force in the modern novel. For a deeper look into Kristeva's negotiation with Bakhtinian ideas we turn to her essay entitled "The Bounded Text."[6]

In this piece Kristeva further develops her ideas about the "text." She starts off by describing the text as "productivity," which she explains as the transformation of trans-linguistic operations into synchronic utterances that meet in the text. The text is, therefore, a permutation of other texts and the space where the utterances from other texts and/or the social environment meet and neutralize one another. Kristeva adds that the materialization of this productivity forms the "ideologeme," which is the intersection of the text's structure with the utterances that it assimilates from other texts. The ideologeme as intertextuality is what gives a text both its social and historical coordinates.[7] The concepts of the text as productivity and the ideologeme serve Kristeva to set the foundation of her analysis of the modern novel and the author's role in this enterprise. We will not go in-depth into what Kristeva thinks of both. Suffice to say that Kristeva believes that literature prior to the modern novel is characterized by a representation of transcendent "symbols" as universal values.[8] These symbols depicted in genres such as epics, folk tales, and/or songs of heroic deeds all illustrate a well-defined concept of the world heavily informed by religious perspectives.[9] In contrast, the modern novel is a semiotic "sign" where the author concatenates discourse to that of other sources whether these are texts and/or speech acts.[10] She concludes that the novel has a double semiotic status; on the one hand, it is a linguistic phenomenon illustrated throughout the narrative, and it is also a discursive circuit wrapped up in literature. The process of completing a novel

---

6 Julia Kristeva, "The Bounded Text," in *Desire in Language: A Semiotic Approach to Literature and Art,* ed. Leon S. Rowdies (New York: Columbia University Press, 1980), 36–65.

7 Ibid., 36–37.

8 Here we can see Bakhtin's influence on Kristeva. For Bakhtin, the dialogical dimensions of language in terms of contestation became apparent first in the modern novel. Bakhtin was clear that ancient writings, such as the epic and Scripture, presented a monologue rather than a dialogue. See Mikhail Bakhtin, *The Dialogic Imagination: Four Essays,* ed. Michael Holquist, trans. Caryl Emerson and Michael Holquist (Austin: University of Texas Press, 1981), 3–40.

9 Ibid., 38–41.

10 Ibid., 45.

Methodology 25

constitutes a social practice of the cultural text, as it confronts speech with its own death, that is, with writing.[11]

The connection of death with writing becomes a theme that Roland Barthes picks up and makes it a core of his ideas about intertextuality. In his piece "The Death of the Author," Barthes starts off by using an ambiguous sentence from *Sarrasine*, where Balzac describes a castrato disguised as a woman. In this example Barthes suggests that when we read a text, we do not fully know who is speaking. Is it the main character who is speaking? Or is it the author who is speaking through this character? Barthes argues that these questions cannot be answered, because ambiguity is the essential quality of writing. Writing for Barthes is the destruction of every voice and point of origin; it is the neutral space where all identity, beginning with the author's, is lost.[12] The example from *Sarrasine* serves Barthes to push for a reconceptualization of the author's role in the text.

Barthes describes that the author has dominated the discussion in literary circles since the Middle Ages. He adds that the interpretation of literary works has been characterized by this tyrannical approach that focuses on the author as the locus of meaning. Contrary to this position, Barthes holds that a text does not represent a single voice that the author confides to the reader. Instead he depicts the author as a "scriptor" who gathers portions of different texts that live in the environment and connects them into his/her own text.[13] He adds that since the text is a tissue of quotations that meet and neutralize one another, the writer can only imitate something that already exists. The writer as scriptor has only one power, which is to gather these external sources and organize them in such a way as to counter previous works. The scriptor is no longer this "Author-God" figure that releases a single "theological" meaning, but she/he is a subject that possesses an immense dictionary that transforms writing into a source of infinitely inferred signs.[14]

Once he presents his ideas about the scriptor, Barthes goes on to describe what he believes is the new center for literary analysis. The reader instead of the author should be the source from where the interpretation of literary texts shall emerge, and the final destination where all the quotations that make up a text are united and ultimately deciphered. The reader is not any particular person, but it is that "someone" who is without history, biography, and psychology. Barthes concludes this piece with the aggressive assertion

---

11 Ibid., 57.

12 Roland Barthes, "The Death of the Author," in *Image, Music, Text,* trans. Stephen Heath (London: Fontana, 1977), 142.

13 Ibid., 143.

14 Ibid., 146–147.

26   INTERTEXTUALITY AND PROPHETIC EXEGESIS IN THE WAR SCROLL OF QUMRAN

that if writing has a future, the myth of author-centered interpretation that has pervaded literature needs to be abolished. Thus, the birth of the reader must come at the cost of the death of the author.[15]

After Barthes kills the author and introduces the reader as the locus of meaning, he presents his propositions of the text in his essay entitled "From Work to Text."[16] Of all these propositions two in particular jump out as relevant to our work. First, Barthes believes that the text is irreducible. By this he means that a text does not necessarily have a multiplicity of meanings, but that it accomplishes the very essence of plurality, that is, an explosion of meanings that cannot be contained. To illustrate the plurality of the text, Barthes compares it to an individual strolling in the forest and experiencing all the sensations of light, sound, and smell that a forest provides.

The text in the same fashion engages the senses and brings forth a set of stimuli that precludes a simple interpretation.[17] The irreducibility of the text leads into Barthes' last proposition where he represents the text as a network that increases through combinations of other texts. A text does not demand respect, but it can be broken and read without the author's signature. In this statement we can see how Barthes continues with some of the ideas he presented in the "Death of the Author." Whereas in that essay he killed the author, here he concedes that the author can come back to the text not as a ruler but as a "guest." The author is no longer necessary to explain the text, but she/he is part of the text's development as the "I" that lives within the text.[18]

ii.   Feminist Intertextuality

The adoption of intertextuality in North American critical circles came with a fair share of methodological adjustments. A particular issue that scholars have had with their French counterparts is their commitment to remove the language of "influence" from the discussion about writing. Also, the "death of the author" has proved problematic, since it threatens to erase the agency that writers, such as feminist critics, have fought to assert.[19]

In "Weavings: Intertextuality and the (Re)Birth of the Author," Susan

---

15 Ibid., 147–148.

16 Roland Barthes, "From Work to Text," in *Image, Music, Text,* trans. Stephen Heath (London: Fontana, 1977), 155–156.

17 Ibid., 159–160.

18 Ibid., 161–162.

19 Jonathan Culler, *The Pursuit of Signs: Semiotics, Literature, Deconstruction* (Ithaca: Cornell University Press, 1981), 103–114. In this essay Culler offers a critique of the intertextuality that emerges from French post-structuralism. He crafts his critique by contrasting intertextuality with Harold Bloom's model of influence. Culler argues that somewhere in between these

Methodology   27

Stanford-Friedman starts from the position that both influence and intertextuality cannot be separated from one another.[20] To establish this thesis she shrewdly begins by exploring the history of how intertextuality came to be, and points out that Kristeva developed intertextuality as a by-product of the influence that Bakhtin exerted on her work. In bringing up this historical fact, Stanford-Friedman highlights the paradoxical nature of the conversation regarding writing, where post-structuralists want to remove influence and authorial intent while failing to recognize that even their work came about because of a pre-cursor's influence. She clarifies that her aim in illustrating this is to show that the ideas of influence and intertextuality do not need to be mutually exclusive, but rather interconnected.[21]

Stanford-Friedman continues her critique of post-structuralism by describing the reluctance among American critics to remove the "self" from the discussion about writing.[22] She notes that the "self" as individualistic, independent, and self-reliant is deeply rooted in American history and culture. For groups whose agency has been denied because of race, economic class, gender, religion, ethnicity, and sexual orientation, the appropriation of the "self" has been fundamental in their search for cultural and political relevance. For Stanford-Friedman, feminist critics like Nancy K. Miller have been at the vanguard of change and the embrace of intertextuality while maintaining the centrality of the female writer.[23]

In "Changing the Subject: Authorship, Writing, and the Reader," Nancy K. Miller addresses the question of authorship in reaction to Barthes' "Death of the Author."[24] Miller's issue with Barthes is that his perspectives about writing have substituted this generic concept of language for the individuals who actually participate in the process of writing and reading. She adds that the "transcendental anonymity" that Barthes borrows from Foucault is not helpful because it denotes that the identity of the writer is irrelevant. Plus, it limits the differentiation of readers and their subjective identity, which goes back to Barthes' claims that a reader is "without history, biography, and psychology."

---

two extremes, intertextuality can function as a concept that recognizes that every text is part of a prior discourse where the author plays a key role in fashioning the text.

20 Susan Stanford-Friedman, "Weavings: Intertextuality and the (Re) Birth of the Author," in *Influence and Intertextuality in Literary History,* ed. Jay Clayton and Eric Rothstein (Madison: University of Wisconsin Press, 1991), 146.

21 Ibid., 154–155.

22 Ibid., 157.

23 Ibid., 157–161.

24 Nancy K. Miller, "Changing the Subject: Authorship, Writing, and the Reader," in *Feminist Studies - Critical Studies,* ed. Teresa de Lauretis (Bloomington: Indiana University Press, 1986), 102–105.

Miller argues that French Post-Structuralism does not work for women writers because the belief that the author and her agency are dead forecloses the question of identity for women and women's writing.[25] Also, since women have been "decentered" and "deinstitutionalized," issues of integrity, textuality, desire, and authority are structurally different for them than they are for men. Miller, instead, advocates for the feminist critic to bring forward the question of her subjectivity and to oppose masculine structures of "regulative psychobiography" because universal discourse has often excluded female identity and testimony.[26] This does not mean that Miller seeks a complete rejection of "male" models. In fact, she states rather astutely that if women's studies are going to effect the much-needed institutional change, then feminist critics need to adopt the signifiers of "masculinity" while maintaining their agency as women.[27] In this piece Miller mainly addresses the issue of female agency, which feeds into her overarching question about writing and reading as a woman.

In "Arachnologies: The Woman, The Text and the Critic" Miller provides a fuller perspective of the kind of intertextuality that she envisions, by using the representation of the text as a spider's web and the "spider" as the writer.[28] In revisiting the Greek myth of Arachne, Miller demonstrates that the spider was a woman weaver of texts. Her story is a classic representation of women's relation to the dominant culture of text production and a parable of feminist poetics.[29] Likewise, it is a model of how women's writing has been understood and read throughout history. To counter this trajectory Miller introduces the practice of "overreading," which traces the instances where the figure of the female artist is produced within the text. The aim of overreading is to shake the classical models of interpretation that assume to know what women's writing is. More specifically, it is a paradigm shift in reading, whereby it approaches women's writing not as something already known but as something that has not been encountered before.[30]

Miller concludes that even though Athena cuts off Arachne's artistry, she does not erase her posterity.[31] The task of feminist criticism, therefore, is to read for Arachne and her female signature. It is to be aware of her place in the production of texts, and to recover those texts from the vacuum of aesthetic

---

25 Ibid., 106.
26 Ibid., 107.
27 Ibid., 115–116.
28 Nancy K. Miller, "Arachnologies: The Woman, the Text, and the Critic," in *The Poetics of Gender*, ed. Nancy K. Miller (New York: Columbia University Press, 1986), 270–296.
29 Ibid., 270–272.
30 Ibid., 274–275.
31 Ibid., 286–288.

Methodology   29

indifference postulated by post-structuralism. It also recognizes that those "gendered bodies that may have lived in history."[32] The connection of women's writings and history in Miller's work is something that other feminist critics will pick up in their quest to recover women's agency. For Elaine Showalter women's writing can be metaphorically and historically connected to the art of quilting.

In "Piecing and Writing", Showalter describes the history of quilting and its implications for the discussion at hand.[33] Showalter recounts that in American history quilting was an art form that crossed racial, regional, and class boundaries. It was a place, like the "quilting bees," where women would gather to learn new skills, share techniques, and in some cases even discuss about politics. The history of quilting is, therefore, intimately connected to the American female experience that refuses to be seen as anonymous sources.[34]

Showalter uses the functions of stitching fragments from different patches into a quilt as a helpful model to interpret the nuances of American women's writing. She sees that the creativity and ingenious design that takes place in quilting is reminiscent to the thoughtful process by which female writers craft their own writings. Showalter, however, is careful to clarify that she does not see quilting, and for that matter women's writing, exclusively as a group activity that removes the individuality of each of the women who participate in it. She notes that even though art historians and museum curators have often ignored the identity of the quilters, these pieces were not anonymous. In fact, there are accounts where women quilters often signed and dated their quilts and included them in their wills with specific instructions on who shall inherit them and how they should be cared for. Showalter concludes that in the same way the history of quilting has to be redeemed from anonymity, women's writing needs to be seen as an imaginative piecing of different texts through the hands of female writers that can achieve true artistic stature and genius.[35]

The preceding discussion deals with some of the concepts that will inform our analysis of 1QM. Post-structuralist intertextuality establishes that texts are social objects that stem from the exchange of ideas that happen in society. Indeed, texts are social objects and they come about not in a vacuum, but in the author's dialogue with the context around her/him. This social aspect of the text points, therefore, to the most significant shortcoming of the

---

32 Ibid., 288.
33 Elaine Showalter, "Piecing and Writing," in *The Poetics of Gender*, ed. Nancy K. Miller (New York: Columbia University Press, 1986), 223.
34 Ibid., 224–225.
35 Ibid., 229.

post-structuralist agenda in its attempt to erase the identity of the writer as creator of the work in favor of an anonymous version that is free from the voice of the writer. The difficulty with the anonymity pushed by post-structuralism was intuitively detected by feminist theorists who adopted intertextuality while at the same time highlighting the ability of the female writer to assert her agency. The resistance on the part of feminist writers to have their voice reduced to nothing recalls the great lengths that those in the periphery have to go, in order to preserve their artistic selves and not subjugate their ideas to those who are in power. Something similar can be seen in the writings of the Qumran sectarian communities who lived outside of the confines of the Judaism of their day and held to their own particular interpretation of the Scriptures and the religious traditions observed in Israel.[36] In the Qumran writings we see an interaction between the influence of the traditions of Scripture and the agency of the sectarians who interpret these texts in their manner and for their own ideology. Our reading of 1QM, therefore, will try to display this balance as it proceeds from the post-structuralist perception of texts as mosaics made from dialogical traces of other works while it retains the perspective that these same texts display the voice and persona of the author(s) who shaped these lines into a new vision. To accomplish this type of reading we will adopt a two-pronged approach that will on the one hand analyze the texts alluded to in 1QM 10–12 with their Scriptural references and on the other hand it will place these traditions in conversation with other sectarian texts. This dual scope will subsequently provide a fuller picture of how these sacred texts were interpreted and became useful to develop the ideology that the sectarian writer(s) wanted to promote.

iii. Sectarian Intertextuality

1QM evinces a balance between the influence of tradition and the authorial interpretation of these texts. This balance can be observed through two dimensions or axes that we will label Scriptural and Sectarian. The following chart illustrates the intersectionality of these interpretive directions.

The A-B axis is where we encounter the interpretation of traditions by the group associated with the scrolls. This axis does not necessarily represent a specific point in time, but it rather focuses on the immediate context surrounding 1QM. We observe that 1QM is part of a bigger set of writings that we have labeled "Sectarian Texts," because they use sectarian language

---

36 John J. Collins, *Beyond the Qumran Community: The Sectarian Movement of the Dead Sea Scrolls* (Grand Rapids: Eerdmans, 2010), 6–11.

Methodology   31

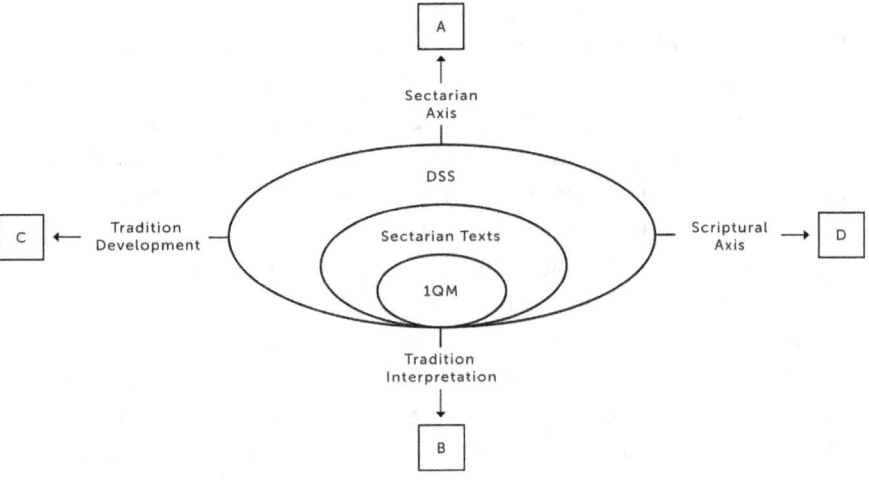

that points to one or more groups that separated from main stream Judaism.[37]
Some of these Sectarian Texts include 1QS, 1QSa, 1QHa, CD as well as some of
the Pesharim. Because of their ideological and religious proximity, these writings provide the first point of reference that we must carefully consult as we
try to analyze 1QM's interpretation and use of the Scriptures. Beyond the sectarian texts there is the broader collection of writings in the DSS library that
has several manuscripts from the Scriptures (including Jubilees and Enoch)
as well as other non-sectarian texts. At this junction we want to explore how
the ideas in 1QM compare and contrast with these other witnesses. The fact
that the manuscripts in the DSS were incorporated and preserved by the
sectarians, underscores that these texts were part of the ideological milieu
where 1QM flourished. As we analyze 1QM our first point of dialogue will be
within the immediate context that surrounded 1QM. The second dimension
that we will consider is represented by the C-D axis.

In this axis we encounter how particular traditions evolved through time.
The significance of this axis is that it allows us to be able to trace, as best
as we can with the available evidence, the different points where a tradition
appears and how it changed through time. Also, this axis helps us discern
the various interpretive moves that a particular witness made on a tradition
based on the historical and religious expediencies that affected the writer
and the people to whom she/he addresses (e.g. Jeremiah's 70-year prophecy in Ezra and Daniel). Thus, the Scriptural axis represents our second point

---

37 Devorah Dimant, "Sectarian and Non-Sectarian Texts from Qumran: The Pertinence
and Usage of a Taxonomy," *RevQ* 24 (2009): 7–18. Francesco Zanella, "Sectarian and Non-Sectarian Texts: A Possible Semantic Approach," *RevQ* 24 (2009): 19–34.

32   INTERTEXTUALITY AND PROPHETIC EXEGESIS IN THE WAR SCROLL OF QUMRAN

of dialogue, where we take the evidence from 1QM and we begin to inquire about the evolution of the tradition that it references, and we ask what the sectarian author is potentially doing with this tradition. This latter point will become key as we grapple with the use of Scriptural allusions and citations and how those references not just continue the evolution of the tradition but also take on new directions. An example of how axes interact with one another will help illustrate our method more clearly.

1QM 1 introduces the battle that will take place between the Sons of Light against the Sons of Darkness and the Kittim of Asshur. The mention of the Kittim is not the only appearance of these enemies within the scrolls.[38] In the Pesharim, such as 1QpHab and 1QpPs, the Kittim are also perceived as the enemies of the sectarians. The question as to who these historical characters are has remained open to debate. Some scholars side with the option that the Kittim refers to the Romans while others interpret them as the Greeks.[39] Although the precise identification of the Kittim with a particular historical group is contested, what remains undisputed is that they are one of the main adversaries that threatened the very existence of the sectarians as a group. However, if we compare this evidence with Scriptural traditions, we begin to see a different picture which leads us to investigate the wider context.

In Scripture the Kittim are mentioned as the descendants of Javan who themselves are descendants of Japheth, son of Noah (Gen 10:4; 1 Chr 1:7). They also appear in the part of Balaam's oracle where he predicts that the ships from Kittim shall appear and oppress Asshur (Num 24:24). Daniel 11:30 also mentions them as the people whose ships will come to battle against the King of the South, and finally 1 Macc 1:1 mentions Alexander son of Philip who came from the land of the Kittim and defeated Darius. We can gather from these references that the Kittim are foreign peoples mostly known for their maritime expertise who do not necessarily present an eminent threat to the people of Israel. Perhaps the closest parallel to what we encounter in Qumran

---

38 Overall, there are 56 references to the Kittim in the DSS. There are two particular spellings of the Kittim that appear in the scrolls:

הכתיאים in 1QpHab 2.12–16, 3.4–15, 4.5–10, 6.1–10, 9.7; 1QpPs 9–10.1–4; 4QpIsa-a 8–10.7–12; 4Q332 3.2; 4Q491 10ii.8–12, 11ii.1–8, 19–20, 13.3–5.

כתיי 1QM 1.2.

כתיים 1.4–12, 11.11, 15.2, 16.3–9, 17.12–15, 18.2–4, 19.10–13; 4QpNah 3–4i.3; 4Q247 6; 4Q285 3.4, 4.5, 7.6; 4Q492 1.9–12; 4Q496 3.6.

39 For the Romans, see: Yigael Yadin, *The Scroll of the War of the Sons of Light Against the Sons of Darkness* (Oxford: Oxford University Press, 1962), 244–246. For the Greeks, see: John Collins, *Apocalypticism in the Dead Sea Scrolls* (London: Routledge, 1997), 107. Timothy Lim, "Kittim," in *EncDSS1* (2000): 469–471. For a good summary of the scholarly arguments regarding the identity of the Kittim, see: Jean Duhaime, *The War Texts: 1QM and Related Manuscripts* (New York: T&T Clark, 2004), 77–81.

Methodology   33

comes from 1 Maccabees where the Kittim are invading forces, but even in this case it cannot be used as direct influence for the sectarian perception of the Kittim.

The previous comparison discloses that the traditional view of the Kittim as foreign sea peoples has been developed within the sectarians, where it no longer refers to a specific group. Instead, it suggests that the Kittim could potentially mean any foreign power that exerts its influence and threatens the people of Israel. Hanan Eshel has recently proposed that the Kittim was a term that may have originally applied to the Greeks, but that later it was used to refer to the Romans.[40] He observes that the Kittim in 1QM refers to the Greeks, as the reference to Asshur in 1.2 correlates with the Seleucids. He also changes the sense of line 1.4 where it refers to the Kittim "in" Egypt rather than the Kittim "of" Egypt.[41] On the other hand, Eshel also accounts for the connection of the Kittim with the Romans in some of the Pesharim as a change in the use of the tradition of the Kittim. He suggests also that the Pesharim ceased to be copied after 63 BCE alluding to a shift in the historical concept and arguing that it was easier to change the oral tradition rather than the written one.[42] Although the evidence for a Greek or Roman interpretation of the Kittim continues to be debated, a better approach perhaps is to take this question on a text by text basis. In this way we can mediate both sides of the debate and at the same time acknowledge that regardless of the historical reference, the Kittim have undergone a change in meaning and application from the traditions of Scripture. In any case, this example is illustrative of the types of questions that we will encounter and how we must align a methodology in an attempt to address them. For that matter we will use a set of steps as we read 1QM 10–12. The steps include:

1. Set the passage in question in a dialogue with other Sectarian Texts, by looking for particular terms that 1QM uses that may also appear in these other texts. This will help in retrieving a possible sectarian ideology represented in 1QM.
2. The next phase will be to take the preceding comparison and observe if such terms appear elsewhere in the DSS, in order to draw a fuller picture of the evidence from the sectarian and non-sectarian scrolls.

---

40 Hanan Eshel "The Kittim in the War Scroll and in the Pesharim," in *Historical Perspectives: From the Hasmoneans to Bar Kochba in Light of the Dead Sea Scrolls,* ed. D. Goodblatt, A. Pinnick, and D. R. Schwartz (Leiden: Brill, 2001), 29–44.

41 Ibid., 32–37.

42 Ibid., 43–44.

3. After exhausting the analysis of the sectarian context in steps 1 and 2, we will transition to the Scriptural dimension where we will trace the different points of either continuation or departure that the passage in question has made with the Scriptures.

4. Lastly, we will assess how this passage in 1QM evinces prophetic exegesis by taking together the evidence from steps 1–3.

Essentially, the two axes approach would allow us to be sensitive to the sectarian interpretation of Scripture and other texts as well as to be able to discern how particular traditions evolved through time. Also, this methodology seeks to spur more discussion about 1QM and how it creates its own vision for the future by incorporating the promises from the past. The next issue that must be addressed deals with how 1QM interacts with other sources through allusions and citations. Before these poetic interactions can be fully assessed, the theoretical foundation for each of them must be established.

b. Intertextual Features

i. Allusions

In her essay "The Poetics of Literary Allusion," Ziva Ben-Porat sets out to define literary allusions.[43] She intuitively recognizes that the term "literary allusion" can create confusion, since it may connote that it is separate from allusion as a feature of language. In fact, she adds, literary allusions evolved from the realm of linguistics, which defines allusions as references, hints, or known nuggets of information that a sender and receiver share. A literary allusion, for that matter, is the activation of two texts that results from the manipulation of a sign or what she labels as a "marker." Therefore, a literary allusion happens at the moment an informed reader recognizes the marker and begins to trace the intertextual relationships that this marker establishes with other text(s).[44]

Further, Ben-Porat describes these intertextual relationships as either "metaphoric" or "metonymic."[45] She clarifies that metaphoric connections happen when an alluding text brings similarities and correspondences with

---

43 Ziva Ben-Porat, "The Poetics of Literary Allusion," *A Journal for Descriptive Poetics and Theory of Literature* 1 (1976): 105–128.

44 Ibid., 107–110.

45 Ibid., 117. Here she borrows from Roman Jakobson who states: "one topic may lead to another either through their similarity or their contiguity. The metaphoric way would be the most appropriate term for the first case, and the metonymic way for the second, since they find their most condensed expression in metaphor and metonymy respectively." See: Roman

Methodology   35

the sources that it evokes. One example of metaphoric relationship happens in 1QM 1 and its similarities with Daniel 11–12. For instance, we see how the sectarian author describes God's intervention for the sake of the Sons of Light in the same fashion as God intervened on behalf of the משכלים in Daniel. Also, the descriptions in Daniel of kings and their armies going through different regions engaging in war happen as well in 1QM 1, where a mysterious character will battle against the kings of the north (1QM 1.5). An informed reader would, therefore, recognize some of these features and be able to see that 1QM 1 and Daniel 11–12 are similar types of texts; they are eschatological passages where the language of holy war is adopted to illustrate a common theme, which is that God will eventually turn history in favor of a holy remnant.

On the other hand, metonymic allusions also connect two texts but instead of showing their similarity they leave the impression that we are dealing with two different types of works. An example of this type of allusions happens in 1QM 2–9. These columns describe the formation of the army and its preparation prior to the skirmish. The descriptions in these columns echo passages in Leviticus and Numbers, where armies are formed and where halakhic standards are set for the people of Israel to follow.[46] However, the literary connections that we can establish between 1QM 2–9 and the Pentateuch do not necessarily leave us with the impression that we are dealing with texts that mirror each other or have a stronger connection beyond these similarities. Instead, we can see that 1QM 2–9 is a text that is looking at the past traditions to create a new future as cultic and historical sources are used as guiding principles for the formation and mobilization of the eschatological army.

Despite the differences between "metaphoric" and "metonymic" intertextual relationships, Ben-Porat reiterates that allusions create a fuller text.[47] Although Ben-Porat does not elaborate on what she means by a "fuller text," we can intuitively discern that it has to do with the rhetorical effect that allusions bring to a text. To dig deeper into the rhetorical value of allusions we will turn to the work of Carmela Perri.

In her piece entitled "On Alluding," Perri deals not just with what an allusion is but also with what it accomplishes in the literary text.[48] She, like Ben-Porat before, sees allusions as signs or markers that reference a source

---

Jakobson, "Two Aspects of Language and Two Types of Aphasic Disturbances," in *Fundamentals of Language* (The Hague: Mouton, 1956), 76.

46 For thorough discussions on these columns see: Philip R. Davies, *1QM, The War Scroll from Qumran: Its Structure and History* (Rome: Biblical Institute Press, 1977), 24–67. Brian Schultz, *Conquering the World: The War Scroll (1QM) Reconsidered* (Leiden: Brill, 2009), 245–254.

47 Ibid., 127.

48 Carmela Perri, "On Alluding," *Poetics* 7 (1978): 289–307.

text by echoing attributes in a way that are recognizable by an informed reader. Perri adds that allusions work on two spheres: denotation and connotation.[49] In the former, allusions are like "proper names" that evoke aspects of the source text just like names do of the individuals carrying them, while the connotation sphere consists of those aspects within the allusion that tacitly hint at the implications that this reference has for the alluding text. A good example of these two spheres happens in the Gospel of John.

John 1:1 begins with the phrase, "Ἐν ἀρχῇ ἦν ὁ λόγος" ("In the beginning was The Word"). This is a clear allusion to Gen 1:1 where we read, "ἐν ἀρχῇ ἐποίησεν ὁ θεός τὸν οὐρανὸν καὶ τὴν γῆν" ("In the beginning God made the heavens and the earth."). The use of the same introductory phrase ἐν ἀρχῇ ("in the beginning") denotes not only that John's gospel echoes the beginning of the creation narrative, but in doing so the allusion connotes that what is about to happen is the generation of something new. One of the more significant implications in the use of this allusion becomes apparent towards the tail end of this verse with the assertion, "καὶ ὁ λόγος ἦν πρὸς τὸν θεόν, καὶ θεὸς ἦν ὁ λόγος" ("and The Word was with God, and The Word was God"). The λόγος ("word") was part of the beginning not just as a spectator but as creator. Yet the creation that begins in verse 1 and beyond is not of the natural order but of a recontextualization of Israel back to God's original purpose.[50]

The previous example illustrates the denotations and connotations that come with an allusion. Perri notes that the power of allusions come at the exact moment when a reader crosses that initial stage of recognizing a reference and begins to draw out both inter and intra-textual connections with other sources.[51] For this to happen, she adds, a reader needs to be equipped with knowledge of the source text(s) to which the author is referring. Otherwise, allusions can be introduced and totally missed because the reader is not able to recognize the marker or the rhetorical purpose that the author pursues in introducing that reference. The reader's familiarity is the last critical aspect of allusions that we will cover in this discussion.

Gregory Machacek describes the reader's familiarity with the evoked

---

49 Ibid., 289–291.

50 Elaine Pagels, "Exegesis of Genesis 1 in the Gospels of Thomas and John," *JBL* 118 (1999): 477–496. Maarten Menken, "Genesis in John's Gospel and 1 John," in *Genesis in the New Testament,* ed. Maarten Menken and Steve Moyise (New York: T&T Clark, 2012), 83–98.

51 Ibid., 295–299. These notions are key for our study, because for every allusion that we identify in 1QM we will proceed to draw out the intra-textual relations (i.e. those within 1QM) and the intertextual relations. The intertextual relations will be further broken down into two intertextualities, which we illustrated above: Scriptural intertextuality (i.e. 1QM and other Jewish texts of like Scripture) and sectarian intertextuality (i.e. 1QM and other sectarian texts within the DSS library).

Methodology   37

sources as "scholarly annotation." By this he means that a reader must possess a type of advanced literacy that enables her/him to partake of the shared tradition, and ultimately be able to recognize the references that the author taps into. Further, this scholarly annotation underscores that the shared tradition must be valued enough that it moves the reader to pay close attention to every detail and to draw out from it the subtle nuances that the writer makes by using such a device. Another aspect of this scholarly annotation that we must consider is that it tends to separate readers into those who share the author's tradition and those who do not.[52]

Machacek divides allusion in two broad categories: learned references and phraseological appropriations. The former are subtle insertions into the alluding text that could be little-known details or roundabout references to a well-known fact from a particular text or tradition, while phraseological appropriations are short phrases that are cut and pasted from other sources into the text.[53] For the purpose of this study we will refer to both of these categories as allusions, and we will add further clarification when an allusion falls within either of these categories. In essence, the concept of scholarly annotation highlights the importance of the reader's familiarity with a tradition, which ultimately allows a reader to intuitively perceive an allusion and draw from it the rhetorical purpose that the author conveys.

The concept of scholarly annotation becomes especially important when assessing the DSS. The highly allusive character of these manuscripts suggests that the readers must have possessed the type of erudition and familiarity with the Scriptural traditions that the scrolls use. We can glean from manuscripts like 1QS, CD, and the Pesharim, that the readers needed to be well-acquainted with the prophecies of Scripture and the details that were to be fulfilled through the sectarians. The continuous use of traditions within the scrolls also highlights another aspect from Machacek's discussion regarding the division between informed and uninformed readers. In particular we can notice within the sectarian texts that the readers must have been well informed not just of the traditions of the Scriptures, but on a particular way of interpreting them. This last point is particular to sectarian groups that split from the general population, in order to live according to a set of beliefs and aspirations that they themselves believe will come true in their own community and timeframe. This separatist attitude is what distinguishes sectarian groups from other peoples, since they are the informed and enlightened

---

52 Gregory Machacek, "Allusion," *PMLA* 122 (2007): 526.

53 Ibid., 527–528. Machacek comments that phraseological appropriations can be "cut, reworked, and incorporated into a new setting - like scraps of paper glued to a collage or fragments of stone set into a mosaic."

readers for whom these promises were preserved.[54]

The preceding discussion sets the stage for how we will identify and explain the use of allusions within 1QM 10–12. Before we proceed in our own study it will behoove us to look back at the work of some DSS scholars that have taken on this issue. This brief survey will particularly consider the contributions that are applicable to 1QM and to our methodology. The reason for this narrow scope is the breadth of available material on Scriptural references in the scrolls and our limited space to address them all.

Jean Carmignac was one of the first scholars to publish regarding the presence of allusions in 1QM.[55] Carmignac labeled all references to Scripture as "citations." He differentiated between two broad categories of citations: one is *citations explicites* which are direct references to Scriptural passages introduced by formulaic language, which we will see in more detail below. The other category is *citations implicites* which are allusions that are spread out throughout the scroll. Different from the explicit citations, these allusions are more difficult to identify because they are not introduced by a formula but are triggered by a set of words or a "marker" that recall another passage.

Before Carmignac delves into analyzing each of the references that he identified, he notes that 1QM betrays much of the content and thought found within the Old Testament. He supports this assertion by citing the opinions of other scholars like Tournay who categorizes 1QM as a specimen of the *style anthologique,* where the Scriptural texts form *une mosaique de texts bibliques,* and Dupont-Sommer who describes 1QM 12 as a *tout tissu de textes bibliques.*[56] The curious aspect of these opinions is that they are very similar to the concepts that literary critics like Kristeva and Barthes would later use to explain intertextuality. These qualities of texts as anthologies and mosaics underscore, in our opinion, the dialogical essence of texts and their capacity to establish a connection with other works. Although Carmignac's work provides one of the very first substantial discussions of allusions in 1QM, we will focus primarily on his remarks regarding 1QM 1.[57]

Carmignac starts off with a broad statement about the author of 1QM and his use of the language of Scripture.[58] He suggests that the sectarian author must have been used to expressing himself with the help of what he labels as

---

54 Stephen L. Cook, *The Apocalyptic Literature* (Nashville: Abingdon Press, 2003), 79–83.

55 Jean Carmignac, "Les Citation de l'Ancien Testament dans la 'Guerre des Fils de Lumière Contre des Fils de Ténèbres,'" *RB* 63 (1956): 234–260.

56 Ibid., 234. Raymond Tournay, "Les anciens manuscrits hébreux récemment découverts," *RB* 56 (1949): 218. André Dupont-Sommer, *Aperçus préliminaires sur les manuscrits de la Mer Morte* (Paris: Librairie Maisonneuve, 1950), 102.

57 Our exegesis will consider Carmignac's work on allusions in columns 10–12 as well.

58 Carmignac, "Les Citation de l'Ancien Testament," 239.

Methodology 39

"biblical formulas." He adds that these formulas would have sprung from the author's memory and familiarity with the Scriptures. Plus, they compensated for the author's lack of creative imagination. Carmignac proposes that a study of these biblical formulas will provide valuable information about the state of biblical texts during 1QM's time and will allow us to discern more about the author's psychology.

In 1QM 1 Carmignac identifies six different allusions. His treatment of each of these instances is not thorough enough, but he rather focuses on pointing out the main passages that the writer evokes and in describing the main editorial decisions. Carmignac takes for granted that each of these instances reveals an allusion and explains the editorial decisions as changes to Scripture. For instance, 1QM 1.1–2 describes the enemy army as made up of Edom, Moab, Ammon, Philistia, and Asshur. Carmignac intuitively recognizes that the author is careful not to use the real names of the enemies during that particular time, but he replaces them with the names of Israel's traditional enemies. Despite the fact that Carmignac identifies these names as allegorical references, he still feels compelled to identify a specific Scriptural passage and uses Ps 83:7–9 as the source of this allusion, where the names of each of these nations appear in the same order. The reference to the enemies by name and in the same order is enough for Carmignac to consider that this psalm is the source for the allusion in 1QM 1.[59]

Furthermore, in terms of lines 2–6 Carmignac states that the author used Daniel 11 and describes the different editorial moves. For instance, the description of the מרשיעי ברית ("violators of the covenant") comes from Dan 11:32, יצא בחמה גדולה ("he shall go with great wrath") is a copy of Dan 11:44, להלחם במלכי הצפון ("to fight against the kings of the north") is an adaptation of Dan 11:11, ואפו להשמיד ("and his anger to destroy") alludes to Dan 11:44, ואין עוזר לו ("no one to help him") is borrowed word for word from Dan 11:45, and ופלטה לוא תהיה ("there will be no salvation") modifies the order of Dan 11:42 and supersedes an attributive ל. In 1QM 1.8 Carmignac is not clear, however, whether the phrase הלוך ואור ("to walk and shine") is an allusion of Prov 4:18 or if it is a mere coincidence. As for the benediction in 1QM 1.9, Carmignac sees a connection with Sirach 1:11–13 and with 1QS 4.7. He goes on to explain that most likely 1QM is dependent on 1QS. Also, the phrase קול המון גדול ("the voice of a great multitude") in 1QM 1.11 alludes to Isa 13:4, Ezek 23:42, Dan 10:6, and 1 Macc 6:41, although the word גדל ("great") is missing in these references. Lastly, Carmignac suggests that the phrase in line 12 ובכול צרותמה לוא נהיתה כמוה מחושה עד תומה לפדות עולמים ("in all

---

59 Ibid., 240.

their afflictions none will be like this, hastening until the completion of the eternal redemption") depends on Dan 12:1, but it was also influenced by Joel 2:2. Carmignac concludes that Daniel 11 is the main chapter that the author of 1QM draws from, although he acknowledges that other Scriptural passages play a significant role in this column.

Overall Carmignac's work, which covered the entire scroll, was a pioneer contribution to the study of traditions in 1QM. His identification of Scriptural references and some of the editorial moves that the author of this scroll made were important for subsequent conversations about the presence of Scripture, not just in 1QM, but in other scrolls. Nevertheless, Carmignac's initial statement about the author of 1QM is something we must deal with. For instance, does the use of allusions (what Carmignac labels as biblical formulas) demonstrate the author's lack of creativity as he proposes, or does the fact that these references sprung from the author's memory contradict this purported lack of creativity? And how much can we say about the author's psychology based on the use of these references? It is our assertion that the writer of 1QM demonstrates a creative approach in the way the Scriptural traditions were chosen and organized throughout this scroll. With that in mind we are also careful not to make definite statements regarding the author's thought at the moment. All we can say is that based on the choice, placement, editing, and combination of the Scriptural references, the author of 1QM creatively reinterprets the sacred traditions and creates a new testimony for the community. To say anything beyond this is pure speculation.

The next major work that deals with allusions in 1QM is that of Gregory K. Beale.[60] Beale's discussion of 1QM is grounded on his overall investigation of how the book of Daniel was interpreted among the sectarians specifically in their use of רז ("mystery") and פשר ("interpretation") to untangle the meaning of Scripture. In the book of Daniel, a cryptic message appears in the form of a vision or a dream, which is then followed by an interpretive formula that functions as a transitional mark that leads into the interpretation. Beale argues that this same pattern appears in Qumran, where the original word was not deciphered but it needed a subsequent divine intervention for it to be explained. Further, there is a parallel experience that happens in Qumran that was seen in Daniel. That is, just as the kings in Daniel are not able to decipher the mysteries conveyed in their dreams and they needed further revelation, the prophets also did not possess the full understanding of their revelations and needed the Pesherists to untangle the meaning of their prophecies.

---

60 Gregory K. Beale, *The Use of Daniel in Jewish Apocalyptic Literature and in the Revelation of St. John* (New York: University Press of America, 1984).

Methodology 41

Beale adds that the Teacher of Righteousness plays the role of Daniel as the sapiential figure: the interpreter of the mysterious prophetic message.[61]

Following this discussion, Beale illustrates the links between Daniel and 1QM. He asserts that there are more allusions from Daniel in 1QM 1 than in any other scroll. He begins his analysis of 1QM 1 by establishing the criteria that will guide his work. He establishes three different criteria for the type of allusions he observes. These are: clear allusions, probable allusions, and possible allusions or echoes, although it is not entirely clear what qualifies an allusion to fall in either of these categories. Nevertheless, in Beale's opinion the extent to which a phrase in 1QM is similar both in the number of words and syntactical order to a Scriptural text, the more it can be labeled as a clear allusion. 1QM 1 therefore has clear allusions to Dan 11:32–34 in line 2 with the mention of the wicked of the covenant and the role of the Kittim of Asshur, to Ezek 20:35 in line 3 with the use of the מדבר העמים ("desert of the people"), to Dan 11:44 in line 4 with the fight against the Kings of the North, to Zech 14:13 in line 5 with the picture of confusion upon the land, and to Isa 31:8 in line 6 with the reference to Asshur falling by the sword of no man, which also appears in 1QM 11.11–12. The rest of the lines in 1QM 1 have probable or possible allusions or echoes that point to other passages but primarily to Daniel 12.[62]

The many references to the Scriptures mentioned above suggest to Beale that 1QM 1 is an eschatological midrash of Daniel. In it the author of 1QM 1 organized this column with the structure of Daniel 11–12 in mind, while at the same time adding other ideas from various Scriptural sources. These allusions not only came about as a result of the common key words that the context of Daniel and 1QM shared, but they were incorporated into 1QM's conceptual framework, to supplement and amplify the deliverance of Israel per Dan 12:1–3.[63] Thus, 1QM 1 is a continuation of the deliverance that Daniel 12 envisions.

The last example we will consider is an article written by Dean O. Wenthe entitled "The Use of the Hebrew Scriptures in 1QM" where he picks up the discussion that Carmignac started regarding allusions and quotations in 1QM.[64] Different from the seminal works by Carmignac, Yadin, and Davies that deal mainly with the presence of Scriptural references in this scroll and how they compare to their sources, Wenthe goes a step further by asking questions about hermeneutics. His aim in approaching this question is to determine the importance that both the placement of the citations/allusions

---

61 Ibid., 38–39.

62 Beale, *The Use of Daniel*, 42–59.

63 Ibid., 60–66.

64 Dean O. Wenthe, "The Use of the Hebrew Scriptures in 1QM," *DSD* 5 (1998): 290–319. Russell Gmirkin, "Historical Allusions in the War Scroll," *DSD* 5 (1998): 172–214.

and their frequency have for the structure and the development of an ideology within 1QM. To do so he compares each citation/allusion with its original meaning in the Hebrew Scriptures, so that he can draw out possible indications not just of the redactional moves but more importantly of any hermeneutical assumptions by the 1QM author.

In the case of 1QM 1, Wenthe draws out the allusions not only from the book of Daniel but also from texts like Numbers, Ezra, and Chronicles. These allusions, he adds, serve to set the stage for the eschatological conflict that the sectarians were about to engage. From the introduction of the enemy nations to the descriptions of how the skirmish was to take place, these allusions fall within this "weak anthological style" which is a term that Wenthe borrows from Daniel Patte and that Joseph Fitzmyer also uses to describe the gathering and organization of Scriptural passages that revisit the historical moments in Israel's past.[65] The use of this style reveals to Wenthe a move on the part of the author of 1QM in trying to depict that the Sons of Light will: a) experience an analogous experience to the one described by book of Daniel, and b) that the Sons of Light would have followed a similar direction to the one Israel opted at many points in its history from Numbers to Nehemiah. Wenthe concludes from these observations that the anthological style highlights that 1QM is a theological collage rather than an exposition of each allusion *vis-à-vis* its original setting.[66] Essentially, Wenthe recognizes that the author of 1QM adapts each passage to fit a particular Scriptural interpretation, and in this process the author creates a new vision that it is informed both by Scripture but it also sensitive to the realities of the community and what it believes and aspires for the future.

These brief descriptions demonstrate that from Carmignac to Beale to Wenthe there is a transition in the study of allusions in 1QM from: the identification of the sources alluded to in 1QM, the qualification of these allusions into different types, and the possible hermeneutical payoff of using these sources. These efforts, therefore, have set the stage for a new analysis that will consider some of the new available interpretive approaches to allusions. Our work seeks to fill in that gap, although it must be said that other scholars of the DSS in particular George Brooke and Julie Hughes have already begun to use concepts of literary criticism and comparative literature to read these manuscripts.[67] We will refer to Brooke's work throughout our work, but for

---

65 Daniel Patte, *Early Jewish Hermeneutics in Palestine* (Missoula: Scholars Press, 1971). Joseph Fitzmyer, "The Use of Explicit OT Quotations in the Qumran Literature and in the NT," in *Essays on the Semitic Background of the NT* (London: Geoffrey Chapman, 1971), 3–58.

66 Wenthe, "The Use of the Hebrew Scriptures in 1QM," 295–300.

67 For Brooke's use of intertextuality, see: George J. Brooke, "Hypertextuality and the

Methodology 43

the time being our focus will turn to Hughes' contribution.

In her recent monograph *Scriptural Allusions and Exegesis in the Hodayot*, Hughes uses the theoretical work of literary experts, such as Carmela Perri, to exegete some of the poems in 1QHa.[68] Hughes first lays out a methodology for her study where she begins by asking questions about Hebrew poetry and parallelism, metre, and other structural indicators. She is quick to point out, that while she appreciates the contribution of scholars like Dennis Pardee, who have done significant comparative work on matters of syntax and parallelism within Hebrew and Ugaritic poetry, her work is geared towards interpretation rather than in setting up a formal approach to her close reading. She attributes part of this direction to Robert Alter's influential study on biblical poetry.[69] Once she lays out her methodology and her biases, Hughes proceeds to deal with the literary features in the Hodayot and how comparative literature can inform her reading of these poems.

The thrust of these questions is to come up with a working methodology by which she can retrieve the exegetical payoff in the use of Scriptural allusions. First, she engages with Carmela Perri's theory of allusion, which we have analyzed above. Hughes recognizes that a Scriptural reference (i.e. allusion) within the Hodayot indirectly engages other texts and creates a degree of verbal parallel.[70] These allusions in the Hodayot, she adds, suggest that the "implied reader" was an informed reader; someone who knew the Scriptures and could ably recognize when a reference is introduced. In addition, this implied reader would be someone who was familiar with biblical Hebrew, the Scriptural texts, and had knowledge of and in principle agreed with the beliefs presented by the author. Hughes also astutely recognizes that the more distance exists between the critic (i.e. the modern reader of the text) and the "implied reader" of the text, the less certain any claim made about this reader becomes. With this statement Hughes is making her audience aware of the inescapable tension that exists when modern readers, who on the one hand use notions like the "original" author and readers of the text, try to understand from their own vantage point the dynamics that existed between these original readers and the text. She concedes that regardless of the meth-

---

'Parabiblical' Dead Sea Scrolls," in *Reading the Dead Sea Scrolls*, ed. George J. Brooke (Atlanta: Society of Biblical Literature, 2013), 67–84; and George Brooke, "Controlling Intertexts and Hierarchies of Echo in Two thematic Eschatological Commentaries from Qumran," in *Reading the Dead Sea Scrolls*, ed. George J. Brooke (Atlanta: Society of Biblical Literature, 2013), 85–98.

68 Julie A. Hughes, *Scriptural Allusions and Exegesis in the Hodayot* (Leiden: Brill, 2006).

69 Ibid., 36–40. For two different approaches to the study of Hebrew poetry, see: Dennis Pardee, *Ugaritic and Hebrew Poetic Parallelism* (Leiden: Brill, 1988); Robert Alter, *The Art of Biblical Poetry* (Edinburgh: T&T Clark, 1990).

70 Hughes, 45–46.

44   INTERTEXTUALITY AND PROPHETIC EXEGESIS IN THE WAR SCROLL OF QUMRAN

od, there will always be the reality that our conclusions are provisional until the next time someone else comes and reads these passages again. From this point, Hughes proceeds to delineate the criteria that she will implement in her literary reading of the Hodayot.

She first presents a working definition of allusion as "a reference which is recognized by a reader as referring to a textual source, knowledge of which contributes to the meaning for the reader."[71] To recognize allusions Hughes sets the following steps. First a reader must establish if an allusion has a correspondence with a *hapax legomenon*, a group of words with similar syntactical order, and/or a recurring phrase that appears in more than one Scriptural passage. Another cue is if the marker brings forth awareness to the context of another passage, and if there is a poetic device such as word play, irony, variation and/or juxtaposition of another text and its context. Hughes warns that these principles are supposed to aid in the recognition of a possible allusion, but they are not to be held tightly since the artistic goal of poetry often times is to surprise a reader.[72] From this point forward, Hughes proceeds from the premise that the Hodayot is an anthology drawn from other sources (i.e. sectarian manuscripts or other pieces of Second Temple Literature), and that these sources or "intertexts" are in continuous dialogue with one another.[73] Her analysis of 1QHa 11.20–37 shall display how her approach works.[74]

Hughes provides the background information of the poem before she delves into the close reading of the text. She lays out the structural limits of this poem, as it follows a gap in the manuscript after line 19 and begins with the formula אודכה אדוני ("I thank you my Lord"). The end in line 37 shows a similar structure as it ends with a gap in the manuscript and proceeds with the same thanksgiving formula that introduces the next poem. Once she sets the limits of the text in question, Hughes presents an annotated translation of the poem laying it out with the poetic structure that she recognizes in the text. She then comments on the structure of the poem and the logical flow of each of the main parts. Finally, Hughes begins her close reading of the allusions and other intertexts within this poem after she has provided a substantial delineation of these background elements.

Specifically, Hughes asserts that 1QHa 11.20–37 contains two unmistakable allusions from Ps 18:4 in lines 28–29 with the references to the "cords of death" (Hebrew) and the "torrents of Belial" ("Hebrew"). Lines 20–29 use expressions seen in Scripture to describe the heavenly beings, the wicked, and

---

71   Ibid., 52.

72   Ibid., 52–53.

73   Ibid., 58–62.

74   Ibid., 207–228.

Methodology   45

the traps set by the evil ones. From lines 30–37 Hughes recognizes the use of
eschatological and holy war language that comes partly from 1 *Enoch* 17–18
and other parts of Scripture that connote images of a theophany, like Sinai,
and God's fiery judgment from Psalm 18. Likewise, she proposes that the use
of Belial in this poem is different from other texts, where Belial is represented as a spiritual being that opposes God, but instead it is an epithet for the
realms of evil and the underworld. Hughes concludes her analysis of 1QHa
11.20–37 by asserting that the poem does not refer to individual passages of
Scripture but to a complex set of ideas regarding the universe. The poem assumes the reader's familiarity with these views, which she identifies from the
common currency of ancient Near Eastern mythology and exegesis seen in
different extra-biblical texts like the DSS.[75]

Hughes proceeds to compare this poem and its ideas with other sectarian
texts (what she would label as intertexts). She observes the similarities with
other Hodayot that use the same language of communion with angels like
1QHa 19.13–17. Also, there is language of membership that this poem evokes
from 1QS when it alludes to the liturgical and covenantal renewal as seen
in 1QS 1.16–2.12. Finally, there are similarities of this poem in its description
of the mobilization of the royal army as it appears in 1QM 12.1–4.[76] Hughes
concludes by addressing the issues of classification and theology; mainly, she
questions the approach by other scholars that label this poem as a Teacher or
pseudo-Teacher hymn on the one hand or as a Community Hymn. She suggests, rather, to look beyond the perceived format of this poem and to appre-
ciate it for its artistic style, for the poem leads the reader to participate and
have communion with the heavenly realm in the final triumph.

For the purpose of this chapter and for that matter of this study as a
whole, Hughes' methodology illustrates what we will try to accomplish. On
the one hand is to study allusions by asking questions of how the text at hand
evokes the language of Scripture and what implications can be drawn from
the allusion, whether it follows the Scriptural reference or goes on a different
direction. The other aspect to consider is the comparison with fellow sectarian texts. We will establish a dialogue between our text and other DSS that
speak to the ideas depicted in the text at hand. This two-pronged approach,
which Hughes demonstrated in her work, is what we have identified as the
Scriptural and Sectarian axes of intertextuality.

Our discussion of allusions has yielded important findings that we need
to keep in the forefront of our analysis as we proceed. The first aspect to

---

75 Ibid., 223.
76 Ibid., 226–228.

consider when determining if we are dealing with an allusion is if there is a recognizable "marker", whether that is a historical character, similar context, use of a well-known theme, the repetition of religious term, or the insertion of a syntactical phrase that evokes another text. This marker needs to be clear enough that an informed reader can distinguish it. The other aspect to consider when dealing with an allusion is if it appears in other witnesses approximate to the context of 1QM. Once the marker (allusion proper) has been identified and compared with the immediate context, the next questions to consider are: what direction does the allusion take in relation to the evoked text? And what connotations does the allusion raise by how it is used within 1QM? Once these issues have been dealt with, we will be in much better grounding to begin positing possible interpretations of the passage at hand.

Our close reading of 1QM 10–12 will be the result of the gradual process, where we will compare an allusion with the evoked tradition as well as other witnesses that tap into that reference. Because allusions are not always clear cut in their identification, we will be careful not to make rushed leap from reading to interpretation without doing our due diligence in setting up the background of these references. As we turn our attention to textual citations, the identification of these references becomes easier because there are specific aspects that demonstrate that we are dealing with another text. However, citations, like allusions, require that we engage in the same process of researching and comparing.

ii.   Citations

Citations, or quotations as some may refer to, are some of the most straightforward examples of intertextual references found in a work of literature. We say that they are straightforward in the sense that they provide the reader with clear markers that the text at hand is using another source. These markers may include an introductory phrase, the mention of a saying attributed to a special figure, and in modern texts they are introduced by quotation marks and in some cases they are followed by footnotes or endnotes. Although these markers help in recognizing a citation, the reader still needs to have familiarity with the cited text for the rhetorical purpose of this literary feature to be fully accomplished. Informed readers can identify a citation and notice whether such a reference follows the content and context of the original source or if it reveals certain editorial liberties that will affect the meaning and application of such text. Literary theorists have studied some of the nuances of citations that will be helpful for our study of 1QM.

Methodology   47

Stefan Morawski has provided a comprehensive classification of quotations.[77] In his opinion schools of thought throughout history have tended to approach their heritage with new lines of inquiry. This phenomenon can be seen in the way later generations reorganize and reinterpret traditions, thus revealing a development in thought and a transition from one epoch to the other. In each historical stage an inherited tradition evolves and takes on a different meaning and application for the community that upholds it. A quotation, therefore, is not just a reference to a distant tradition but it is a continuation or a breach to that tradition. It is a renewed reflection of the principles of the past and how they apply to the current situation.

For his part Robert Sokolowski describes quotation as the repetition of something said by another source.[78] He holds that the difference between a quotation and the original statement is not the content of the words but their presentation. A quotation may recite the original statement verbatim, but the manner in which it repeats these words and where it appears in the dialogue of the alluding text changes the effect of the original statement. In his words a quotation is "as though we no longer saw an object directly but now only in a mirror."[79] He adds that quoting another source is never a neutral exercise; it is a communication laden with the intention to persuade the hearer that what is being conveyed is important and that it needs careful attention. Sokolowski describes this more eloquently when he states:

> The speeches of others who are quoted but who are not now themselves speaking are woven into our referential continuity: sometimes as authoritative statements, sometimes as things to be merely entertained, sometimes as positions to be destroyed, sometimes just as dicta to be noted. The thing to be studied when we study quotation is not a single mind, nor is it a single sentence that happens to have a quotation inside itself; it is rather the complex pattern of discussion, argument, and discourse with its plasticity, its capacity to include so many different voices, so many different assertions, even those of speakers who are not with us while we speak. The whole is the conversational setting, not the relationship of a single mind or a single sentence to an object.[80]

The works of Morawski and Sokolowski highlight the importance of

---

77 Stefan Morawski, "The Basic Functions of Quotation," in *Sign, Language, Culture*, ed. Greimas et al. (The Hague: Mouton, 1970), 694.

78 Robert Sokolowski, "Quotation," *The Review of Metaphysics* 37 (1984): 699–723.

79 Ibid., 701.

80 Ibid., 708.

quotations and more importantly the dialogical dimensions that happen when an author quotes another source. This will become a point of emphasis in our work as we seek to understand how the writer of 1QM uses Scriptural references and what these textual snippets disclose about the author's rhetorical agenda. Before we delve into that analysis, we will look at what scholars of the DSS have developed regarding Scriptural quotations.

Moshe Gottstein was one of the first scholars to publish on the importance of quotations within the DSS.[81] In this very brief journal article Gottstein raises key questions regarding textual variance in the quotations from the sectarian scrolls (i.e. 1QS and CD) that would later be taken in subsequent works. He notices that some quotations in these scrolls have a different wording from the MT. This fact, he adds, makes it difficult to ascertain whether the author of the scroll used a written biblical text or "wrote according to the custom of his day."[82] What exactly he means by "custom of his day" is not exactly clear, but he goes on to say that the writer of CD, for instance, "quoted always by heart or intended to change the verse in order to suit the context."[83] With this statement Gottstein demonstrates that citing a source was done for a particular purpose where the author using that source relied on the tradition to make a point applicable to her/his time. Decades later Moshe Bernstein dealt with the issue of the accuracy of Scriptural citations in the sectarian scrolls. In his work Bernstein states that there should not be any assumption that these references need to conform to the MT, LXX, or other recension of the Scriptures. In fact, he argues, that this variance within these Scriptural references "may be exegetically, rather than textually, based, and even the word-play or punning on the biblical text (analogous to the rabbinic *al tiqrei*) might be looked for and found in the citation of the text and not only in the comment on it."[84] These two previous discussions highlight that in citing the Scriptural texts, the writers of some of the scrolls were not just repeating a text verbatim but were approaching the text freely from the standpoint of using it to make a point that was based on their interpretive approach. In this way, as we shall see in more detail, they were in line with tradition by relying on its testimony and at the same time they were asserting their own beliefs of what that particular tradition meant for their communities.

Joseph A. Fitzmyer has provided perhaps one of the most comprehensive

---

81 Moshe Gottstein, "Bible Quotations in the Sectarian Dead Sea Scrolls," *VT* 3 (1953): 89–92.

82 Ibid., 80.

83 Ibid.,82.

84 Moshe J. Bernstein, "Scriptures: Quotation and Use," in *Encyclopedia of the Dead Sea Scrolls*, ed. Lawrence H. Schiffman and James C. VanderKam (Oxford: Oxford University Press, 2000), 841–842.

Methodology 49

discussions of the use of explicit Scriptural quotations in the sectarian scrolls outside of the Pesharim.[85] Fitzmyer points out that these references are introduced by special formulas and used to bolster an argument or to make an illustration; they are the starting point that work as proof-texts. From this point he proceeds with an analysis of the introduction formulas used in these quotations and proposes different classes into which quotations fall.[86] There are forty-two explicit quotations in the sectarian texts outside of the Pesharim: three in 1QS, thirty in CD, five in 1QM, and four in 4Q174. Fitzmyer argues that the introductory formulas reveal the fundamental attitude of the sectarians, much like their NT counterparts, towards the Old Testament as Scripture. The use of the verbs כתב ("write") and אמר ("say") within these formulas further displays the belief among the sectarians that Scripture was the collection of normative traditions, and also the commentary of what had once been "said" about these traditions whose closest point of comparison happens in the NT.[87]

After dealing with the introductory formulae Fitzmyer proceeds to qualify the different types of quotations in these manuscripts. He is interested in addressing some of the questions that have vexed scholars for some time like: if the Scriptural passage is understood in its original context, or if it is adopted to a new situation, or if it is twisted for the purpose of the one quoting.[88] In studying all forty-two quotations, Fitzmyer brackets them into four categories, which are for the most part distinct one from the other. First, there is the "historical class" of quotation where the Scriptural passage is actually cited in the same sense as it was intended by the original writer.[89] Also, there is the "modernization class" where a Scriptural text is applied to a new event in the context of the sectarian group.[90] Related to this modernization class, the "accommodation class" modifies and deliberately changes the content of the passage in question to fit a new situation or purpose on behalf of the sectarian group.[91] The last category is the "eschatological class" where a promise

---

85 Fitzmyer, "The Use of Explicit OT Quotations in the Qumran Literature and in the NT," 3–58. Fitzmyer explains his reasoning for leaving out the quotations within the Pesharim. He explains that the references to Scripture in the sectarian scrolls (such as: 1QS, CD, 1QM, and the thematic Pesharim) are closer in their use to those found in the New Testament. Plus, the exegesis seen in these scrolls furnish a more valid comparison to that found in the New Testament.

86 Ibid., 6–7.

87 Ibid., 10–16. Bruce Metzger makes a similar point and he adds that the DSS citations also have close similarities to those of the Mishnah. See: Bruce Metzger, "The Formulas Introducing Quotations of Scripture in the NT and the Mishnah," *JBL* 70 (1951): 297–307.

88 Fitzmyer, "The Use of Explicit OT Quotations in the Qumran Literature and in the NT," 16.

89 Ibid., 17–21.

90 Ibid., 21–33.

91 Ibid., 33–45.

or a threat contained within Scripture is taken to be fulfilled in the coming eschaton.[92] Regarding the eschatological class, Fitzmyer comments that these quotations cite the original sense of the Scriptural passages and extend it to a new situation of what is hoped for. There are ten quotations that fall within this category: CD 7.10–12, 19.7–9, 19.11–12, 19.15–16, 20.15–17; 1QM 10.1–2, 10.2–5, 10.6–8, 11.11–12; and 4Q174 1–3 2.11–13.

In terms of the citations in 1QM 10, Fitzmyer observes that they are part of the High Priest exhortation where the priest uses the words of Moses for instruction and exhortation to the combatants prior to the eschatological battle. He notes that 1QM 10.2–5 also appears in 1QM 15.8–9 but without being introduced as an explicit citation. As for the citation in 1QM 11.11–12, he comments that this text modernizes the ancient promise given to Isaiah by applying the fall of Assyria and projecting it to the Kittim. The connection of the Kittim to the Assyrians appears also in 1QM 1.2. Fitzmyer intuitively recognizes that the quotations in 1QM interpret the passages of Scripture as directly applying to the new eschaton that will benefit the sectarians.[93]

Besides Fitzmyer, Jean Carmignac also dealt with the citations to Scripture in 1QM. He notes that the sectarian author uses the references to Scripture to reanimate the courage of the combatants, by appealing to the promises made in the past to the Jewish people and by selecting the texts that support this purpose.[94] He goes on to analyze each of the five quotations found in columns 10–12. Different from Fitzmyer, Carmignac devotes his attention to point to the orthographic adjustments that the sectarian author makes of the Scriptural text. He pays careful attention to changes, such as in 10.1–2 where יהוה ("Lord") is substituted for אתה ("you") *par respect pour le nom divin*. He goes on to assess whether 1QM agrees or goes on a different direction from the MT, the Samaritan Pentateuch, the Targum, or the Peshitta (1QM 10.2–5 cf. 15.8). He describes when major characters are introduced, like Moses whom he labels as *l'intermédiaire* and whose *paternite est bien affirmée* (10.6–8) over Israel. Lastly, he also notices when the sectarian author makes explicit changes to the Scriptural text, either to emphasize God's powerful

---

92 Ibid., 46–52.

93 Ibid., 51–52. At this junction Fitzmyer contrasts the eschatological quotations in Qumran with those in the NT. He proposes that this type of quotation in the NT is far less frequent than in Qumran, because NT writers were more concerned in looking back at the salvation event, presumably the crucifixion of Jesus, rather than looking forward to the future deliverance.

94 Carmignac, "Les Citation de l'Ancien Testament," 235. As we will note, the use of these passages falls within the categories of modernization, accommodation, and eschatological fulfillment illustrated by Fitzmyer above. Although we will deal with each of these quotations in more detail later in our work, it suffices for now to provide a broad summary of how Carmignac interpreted these quotations.

Methodology 51

acts through Israel (1QM 11.5–7) or to show that the ruin of the Kittim is actually the final ruin of all Israel's enemies (1QM 11.11–12). These last examples are important ones because Carmignac deals with issues of exegesis and textual moves rather than orthography and manuscript comparison. He states that in 1QM 11.11–12 the sectarian author might be engaging in a type of *d'exégèse extensive qui depasse le sens litteral.*[95] With this statement Carmignac recognizes what Gottstein and Bernstein argue in that the cited text transcends an exact comparison *vis-à-vis* its source but merges into a specific didactic purpose where the strict adherence to the wording in the tradition is not the most critical point.

Like Carmignac, Wenthe also devotes a specific section on the five citations in 1QM. He notices that the first three are placed within the context of the priestly exhortation in 1QM 10, where the language of Deuteronomy is used to exhort the combatants prior to the eschatological battle. As for the citations in column 11, he sides with Carmignac in stating that they display an implicit exegesis that he labels as "typology;" where the events in Israel's history serve as a type that defines the sectarian community and its eschatological mission.[96] This combination of the citations and the typological illustrations give the impression that the author is relaying that the sectarians are the true Israel. Further, Wenthe believes that the author not only uses the typological hermeneutic but also the pesher hermeneutic, to define both the present and the future in terms of the past.[97]

Aside from these scholars others have used the findings of Fitzmyer to deal with the different categories of quotations in the DSS.[98] Some of these recent studies have used the presence of citations to begin asking questions about the redactional history of particular scrolls. One particular study is from Sarianna Metso who uses the recent publications of manuscripts from Cave 4 (i.e. 4QSb and 4QSd) to deal with questions regarding the redaction of the Community Rule.[99] Specifically, Metso wants to use the presence of

---

95 Ibid., 239.

96 Ibid., 307–309.

97 Ibid., 319.

98 Devorah Dimant, "The Hebrew Bible in the Dead Sea Scrolls: Torah quotations in the Damascus Covenant," in *'Sha'arei Talmon': studies in the Bible, Qumran, and the ancient Near East presented to Shemaryahu Talmon*, ed. Michael Fishbane, Emanuel Tov, and Weston W. Fields (Winona Lake: Eisenbrauns, 1992), 113–122. Johan Lust, "Quotation Formulae and Canon in Qumran," in *Canonization and Decanonization: Papers Presented to the International Conference of the Leiden Institute for the Study of Religions*, ed. A. Van der Kooij and K. Van der Toorn (Leiden: Brill, 1998), 67–77.

99 Sarianna Metso, "The Use of Old Testament Quotations in the Qumran Community Rule," in *Qumran between the Old and New Testaments*, ed. Frederick H. Cryer and Thomas L. Thompson (Sheffield: Sheffield Academic Press, 1998), 217–231.

citations within 1QS in conversation with the Cave 4 witnesses to suggest that 1QS represents a later redaction of the rule. She observes that 1QS has three citations of the Scriptures (i.e. Exod 23:7; Isa 2:22, 40:3) that are completely absent from 4QSb–d. After going through the analysis of each of the citations, Metso addresses the question dealing with the more "original" version of the Community Rule.[100] She observes that not only are the citations from 1QS missing in 4QSb–d but that the wording of both textual witnesses differs in several places. In particular, 4QSb–d lacks key words like יחד ("community") and ברית עולם ("everlasting covenant") which are charged with religious meaning for the sectarians.

The previous evidence moves Metso to propose, by following classic principles of textual criticism, that the shorter version is the more original. Although 1QS has been dated to the Hasmonean period (ca. 100–75 BCE) and 4QSb–d are dated to the Herodian period (ca. 30–1BCE), Metso explains that both texts are part of parallel textual traditions. In addition, the fact that 4QSb-d lack the references to the community and the covenant suggests that these witnesses represent the more original version, because it is more probable that these key terms were added at a later point than removed from the manuscript. Metso concludes that the Scriptural citations in 1QS provide legitimacy to the regulations and justification for the community's self-understanding. These proof-texts were added at a time when the community's enthusiasm and need to separate began to wane, thus the reference to Scripture justified the stricter rules and motivated the people to obey these teachings.[101]

The use of citations in the DSS require careful attention. Different from allusions, citations have specific markers that call the attention to the reader that another text is about to be introduced. As we have seen, the use of this feature follows a rhetorical purpose in that it provides an ideological foundation to what the text at hand tries to convey to its audience. By referencing to a known fact from the Scriptures or to a famous leader like Moses, the citation becomes a credential that the writer uses to validate the teaching that she/he tries to convey. Our study of 1QM 10–12 will explore how the citations to the Scriptures work as well as how they in of themselves reveal something about the ideology of the sectarians. Also, we will highlight that these citations appear in a section of 1QM that scholars have identified as a liturgical piece, which most likely was added to the other columns.[102] This is an import-

---

100 Ibid., 226–228.

101 Ibid., 228. Metso also uses the example of the relationship between the gospel of Mark and Matthew. Just like Matthew added more Scriptural basis to Mark's accounts, 1QS added the Scriptural citations to further the teachings for the community that appear in 4QSb–d.

102 Yadin, *The Scroll of the War of the Sons of Light Against the Sons of Darkness*, 208–216.

Methodology 53

ant aspect to consider, because it gives us additional questions regarding the reasons behind the use of the citation, the state of affairs for the sectarians, and what do these citations accomplish from a rhetorical standpoint. It may also show, like Sarianna Metso's study did, that Scripture citations became a way to call the people to believe in a time when they needed encouragement and a firm foundation for their faith. Thus, as we engage with the citations in 1QM 10–12 we will adopt the same process we posited for the study of allusions. We will first identify the Scriptural reference introduced by the citation, we will inquire if this reference appears elsewhere in the DSS, and then we will compare it with the Scriptural passage. After this initial analysis we will proceed with the introduction of new questions that seek not just to describe what the citation does but what it implies for the overall context of the passage at hand.

c.   Summary

This chapter has introduced the methodology that we will follow to study the passages in 1QM 10–12. We have labeled this approach intertextuality, because 1QM is an allusive text that continually appeals to various passages of the Scriptures to depict its vision of the future. Likewise, as we shall see in our exegesis, 1QM is a text that fits within the category of sectarian texts like some of the Rule Books. These two fundamental aspects require us as readers to continually ask questions that pertain to the mutual dialogue that 1QM establishes with other sources, mainly through the use of allusion and citations. These two literary features are the markers that link 1QM to the Scriptures and to other textual witnesses. In addition, they are windows from where we can peek into the ideological makeup of the sectarian author and the community that received this text. Our process, which we have identified as a two-pronged approach will take the following steps.

Initially we will introduce the passage at hand and identify the markers. These can be a reference or an explicit phrase that evokes another text. Once we have confidently identified the markers, we will ask if such references appear in other manuscripts, whether they are sectarian texts or other manuscripts from the DSS. This initial step seeks to gather as much evidence as possible about the alluded text prior to taking the comparative effort much further. Afterwards, we will analyze the evolution of such a tradition as it can be traced from the Scriptures and other witnesses. This trajectory would undoubtedly complicate matters to some extent, but it is a necessary step as we

---

Davies, *1QM, The War Scroll from Qumran*, 91–92, 121–124.

try to gather not just how the tradition evolved but how that tradition is handled within 1QM. This leads into the last phase of our analysis which posits questions that will get us closer to an interpretation and the implications of the passage at hand. We believe that the gathering of the evidence sets the analysis on solid ground where we can then come to the text with additional questions. Without this foundational work we run the risk of either asking the wrong questions of our text or asking too few questions that do not go far enough in analyzing the rhetorical effect that such an allusion or citation makes on the reader.

This last point leads into the next chapter that deals with how the sectarian author taps into the arsenal of Scriptural references to persuade the audience. As we shall see the author asserts herself/himself as an interpreter of Scripture by engaging on what we will refer as "prophetic exegesis." By this we mean that the different poetic decisions that the author makes, whether in the referencing a particular Scriptural text, to the positioning of that text at a particular junction of 1QM, to using that reference as evidence of its fulfillment on behalf of the community, are all part of this type of exegesis that is both foretelling as well as forthtelling.

CHAPTER 2

PROPHETIC EXEGESIS

THE INTRODUCTION LAID OUT the main thesis of this work regarding the prophetic interpretation of Scripture in 1QM. This interpretive approach labeled as "prophetic exegesis" comprises a two-pronged approach that foresees the fulfillment of Scriptural teachings in the immediate future through the life of the sectarians, and it calls these believers to align their lives according to these aspirations. Scripture in 1QM, and for that matter in many of the DSS, is both predictive and prescriptive. The current chapter will review and analyze with specific examples the background that sets the stage for the flourishing of this type of exegetical tradition.

The goal of the present chapter is to gather enough evidence from the primary sources to demonstrate that exegesis became a mode of prophetic teaching. To develop this argument, we will briefly explore some of the key factors that led into the formation of interpretive traditions and the beginning of prophetic exegesis. This discussion will feed into a close reading of some of the most salient examples of "prophetic exegesis" in the scrolls that have ideological and/or thematic affinities with 1QM. The Thematic Pesharim (i.e. 4QFlorelegium and 11QMelchizedek) and the Rule Books (i.e. 1QS and CD) will provide good examples, because they have a similar type of interpretation of Scripture that appears in 1QM.[1] Specifically, in these scrolls we will find passages that demonstrate how allusions and citations of the sacred traditions were used to establish the teaching and formation of the sectarians.

For instance, the Thematic Pesharim adopt a significant number of passages that speak about the fulfillment of prophecy to the benefit of the

---

1 Although we could draw from other examples of prophetic exegesis in texts like the Continuous Pesharim (e.g. 1QpHab), Parabiblical books (e.g. 1QapGen) or Pseudo-prophetic books (e.g. 4QApocryphon of Jeremiah), none of these provide the clear connection that the Thematic Pesharim and the Rule Books have with 1QM.

sectarians. Similarly, 1QM develops the theme of the eschatological war, to underscore that all that was predicted will be fulfilled in the upcoming conflict. As for the Rule Books, they use Scripture to guide the community in light of the eschatological times. In addition, they develop their teachings to foment the idea that the sectarians are the true remnant of Israel. 1QM as well is prescriptive as it calls the sectarians to carefully consider the laws and prophecies in preparation for their skirmish against their enemies, and it illustrates with a mix of poetry and prophecy the reconstitution of Israel and the conquest of Zion (cf. 1QM 12; 19). In essence, the Thematic Pesharim and the Rule Books provide the closest and clearest evidence of the type of prophetic teaching that happens in 1QM.

After the close readings of these manuscripts, a final statement will summarize the findings and provide specific considerations that will be used in our study of 1QM 10–12.

a.   Prophetic Exegesis in Post-Exilic Times

i.   Interpretation of Scripture Traditions

The interpretation of Scripture evinced in the DSS has its roots in the historical vicissitudes of the Jewish people following the exile to Babylon in the sixth century BCE. The absence of the Temple and the possibility to exercise many of the cultic customs and traditions created a vacuum for a centralized source of religious authority and communal gathering.[2] These social realities led to the cultivation of traditions, and the methodical proliferation of interpretive works that looked to the past to derive insight for the present. Scripture essentially became the locus of authority that steered the people in their daily lives in matters of ethics and cultic observance, but it also gave them a sense of community. The centrality of Scripture paved the way for the formation of established communities of study, whose primary purpose was to discern the will of God through the careful analysis of these traditions. The other significant factor to consider is that within these groups grew a specialized class of sapiential leaders and teachers that were endowed with the wisdom and knowledge to teach the people.[3] One of the earliest accounts that illustrate the role of these teachers happens in Nehemiah 8:1–8 where

---

2 James L. Kugel, "The Beginnings of Biblical Interpretation," in *A Companion to Biblical Interpretation in Early Judaism,* ed. Matthias Henze (Grand Rapids: Eerdmans, 2012), 3–27.

3 Leo Perdue, "Sages, Scribes, and Seers in Israel and the Ancient Near East: An Introduction," in *Scribes, Sages, and Seers: The Sage in the Eastern Mediterranean World* (Göttingen: Vandenhoeck & Ruprecht, 2008), 1–34. Arie van der Kooij, "Authoritative Scriptures and Scrib-

Prophetic Exegesis   57

the scribe Ezra read the "book of the Torah of Moses" (ספר תורת משה) before the "assembly" (קהל) that was comprised of men and women alike. Verses 7–8 are key because they indicate that along with Ezra there were other
scribes and Levites who went around explaining (מבינים) and providing an
interpretation/translation (מפרש) of the reading of Torah.[4] This brief passage illustrates some of the core elements that took place during this period,
as Scripture takes center stage and is expounded by a specialized group of
leaders who mediate God's will to Israel.

In addition to the historical circumstances, other factors propelled the
rise in the study of Scripture. In his work entitled *The Bible As It Was*, James
L. Kugel describes some of the most widely held values or assumptions that
Jewish interpreters had about Scripture.[5] He recognizes that these interpreters consistently viewed Torah as a source of divine instruction that was perfectly harmonious and relevant for daily living.[6] This divine instruction, however, was not easily understood and was often seen as a cryptic message that
possessed several layers of meaning that the common person could not decipher alone but needed the assistance of an expert; that is, a knowledgeable
teacher who would decode the mystery and reveal through analysis of the
text what the naked eye could not perceive. The argument can be made that
1QM demonstrates all of these assumptions, but we will particularly focus on
the notions of relevance and mystery associated with Scripture.

Kugel explains the belief in mystery by recalling that behind the overt
teaching of a Scriptural passage stood a secret meaning that needed to be ex-
trapolated. Whereas a text might denote a particular lesson, its true meaning
was something hidden that needed to be explained often times by bringing
up another text into the conversation.[7] The pairing of different passages set
up a dialogical dimension, whereby each text would converse and/or develop the concept introduced by the first text. This is the case, for instance, in
the Pesharim where a prophetic verse is explained often times by citing other passages that would speak on that topic.[8] Kugel also points out that the

---

al Culture," in *Authoritative Scriptures in Ancient Judaism,* ed. Mladen Popovic (Boston: Brill,
2010), 55–71.

4 As we shall see in our discussion of the DSS, the concepts of understanding and coming up with an interpretation become key components of the interpretive practices of the
sectarians.

5 James L. Kugel, *The Bible as It Was* (Cambridge, MA: Belknap Press, 1997), 1–42.

6 Ibid, 17–23.

7 Ibid, 18.

8 Rabbinic Midrash is another example of this web of meaning that Scriptural texts establish once they are put in conversation. Daniel Boyarin, *Intertextuality and the Reading of
Midrash* (Bloomington: Indiana University Press, 1994), 11–19. In this work Boyarin uses the
concept of intertextuality (from a literary critical standpoint) to propose a new theory of mid-

mysterious nature of Scripture vouchsafed for the need of study and interpretation that was often led by a class of specialists. The belief among the faith communities, he adds, was that these traditions were relevant for everyday life and needed to be carefully considered for the health of the community.[9] In 1QM the assumptions of mystery and relevance play out in very distinctive ways. For instance, 1QM describes in imaginative way the events of the future eschatological battle. This fantastic view of the future is loaded with the ideas of revelation often times through the continuous repetition of key concepts that imply that these hidden things were kept from prior generations but that they found their ultimate fulfillment in the life of the sectarians. The depth of this revelation also presents a big responsibility for the warriors who consequently must vow to follow Torah faithfully (as evinced in 1QM 2–9).[10]

The interpretive assumptions drawn out by Kugel are helpful for beginning to sketch a picture of how the Jewish people perceived Scripture in post-exilic times. An issue that must be addressed deals with the relationship between Scripture and other traditions. This is a key question because 1QM builds its account by taking the content of these other texts into new hermeneutical horizons. 1QM evinces a mutual connection with Scripture, where it exists because of Scripture, and Scripture itself is recontextualized and applied in creative ways in 1QM. The field of tradition-history can explain this mutuality.

In his seminal work *Biblical Interpretation in Ancient Israel* Michael Fishbane provides the most thorough treatment of the different types of exegesis found in the biblical texts.[11] He begins his work by suggesting that early Judaism believed that the central task of exegesis was to demonstrate the capacity of Scripture to regulate all matters of life and thought. This essential task, he adds, was accomplished by deriving new teachings or by legitimating existing religious norms by association with these texts. Tradition and Scripture balance each other and exist for the sake of the other. To explain this relationship Fishbane uses the concepts of *traditum* and *traditio*.[12] The former is an established text that is often based on the testimony of another source whether

---

rash. Here he establishes the three foundations by which his new reading of midrash, informed by intertextuality, will stand: a) midrash is made up of a mosaic of conscious and unconscious citations of earlier discourse; b) midrash is dialogical in nature; and c) midrash is comprised of cultural codes that constrain but also allow the production of new texts.

9 Kugel, *The Bible as It Was,* 19.

10 The War of Divisions in 1QM 2–9 lays out many of the stipulations that the warriors must meet prior to enlisting and engaging in the battle.

11 Michael Fishbane, *Biblical Interpretation in Ancient Israel* (Oxford: Clarendon Press, 1985).

12 Ibid, 5–8.

written or oral, while the latter is the trajectory of subsequent interpretations that result from the continuous interactions of interpreters with this established testimony. However, Fishbane is careful to point out that these two concepts have been typically used by tradition-history experts in a different way than what he proposes. For instance, whereas tradition-history begins from the standpoint of the written source and moves back in time to recover the traces of older traditions (whether oral or written), his approach takes the Scriptural text (i.e. the verse of Scripture) and moves forward in time to analyze the derived interpretations of this passage. He adds that when the nexus between *traditum* and *traditio* can be recovered and demonstrated, that is where "inner-biblical exegesis takes place."[13]

The concept of inner-biblical exegesis steers Fishbane's work throughout, and it is helpful that he mainly deals with the question of exegesis within the Hebrew Bible. However, when the relationship of *traditum* and *traditio* goes beyond the "canonical" texts and includes other traditions (i.e. *traditio*) such as the DSS, then we are not talking about inner-biblical exegesis anymore. Nevertheless, with the relationship between *traditum* and *traditio* Fishbane laid out a blueprint by which we can see the impact that Scriptural texts made on subsequent interpreters. His work also highlights how exegetical traditions relied on Scripture and in turn how Scripture was revitalized by exegesis. More recent works, however, have taken Fishbane's model and asked additional questions about interpretation as well as the issue of canonicity.

Yair Zakovitch widens the scope of inner-biblical exegesis and problematizes the boundary between "inner" and "extra" biblical interpretation as he recalls that several Jewish groups used different canons of Scripture, such as: the Samaritan Pentateuch, the Septuagint, and the Christian canon. He goes on to describe specific instances from these texts where we can see their particular assumptions and interpretations about God's revelation. In addition, he cites other texts like Ben Sira and Jubilees and their popularity among Jewish groups.[14] The case of Jubilees (and of 1 Enoch as well) is an important one to consider, because its cultic, legal, and calendrical concerns were of special relevance to the sectarians of the DSS.[15]

---

13 Our methodology of sectarian and Scriptural intertextuality points to a similar intersection, where the tradition of Scripture meets the use of this text among several manuscripts in the DSS.

14 Yair Zakovitch, "Inner-biblical Interpretation," in *A Companion to Biblical Interpretation in Early Judaism*, ed. Matthias Henze (Grand Rapids: Eerdmans, 2012), 29–35

15 Manuscripts of Jubilees were found in Caves 1, 2, 3, 4 and 11 (1Q17–18; 2Q19–20; 3Q5; 4Q176, 216, 219, 220, 227; 11Q12). For discussions on Jubilees and its importance on matters of cult and calendar in Qumran, see: Lawrence Schiffman, "The Sacrificial System of the Temple Scroll and the Book of Jubilees," *SBLSP* 24 (1985): 217–233. Joseph Baumgartner, "The Calendars

The mention of these textual traditions serves Zakovitch to posit a fundamental question: Is exegesis that takes place outside of the canonical text of Scripture (e.g. the Masoretic Text) inner- or extra-biblical exegesis?[16] He begins to address this question by asserting that interpretive traditions (i.e. what Fishbane labeled as *traditio*) were not written *ex nihilo*, but they were deliberate works of pre-existent traditions (*traditum*) that were codified from their oral existence. The evolution of these textual traditions was not always without problems. In fact, he adds, there are many passages that posit problems to the interpretive communities.[17] One example takes place in Sir 46:4 and its treatment of the story in Josh 10:12–14, where the sun and the moon stood still until the Amorites were defeated. Ben Sira provides a mythological interpretation of this account suggesting that Joshua had a particular relationship with the sun and was able to stop it. With this example Zakovitch highlights the evolution of this tradition and suggests that in general traditions become normalized once new nuances of meaning are acceptable to the beliefs and ideologies of the reading community. Likewise, he notices that the divide between inner- and extra-biblical exegesis is blurry, and argues that extrabiblical literature helps us to discover the more ancient stages of the exegetical process.[18] Zakovitch concludes that extrabiblical articulations constitute *midrash*, for they are textual approaches that allow and even encourage the search for multiple meanings; that is, the filling of the gaps within the original traditions. Zakovitch holds that *midrash* derives from the study of Scripture, but it was also present at the moment of Scripture's inception.[19]

The previous discussion touches on some of the concepts that will be helpful for our study. As we will observe, 1QM shows a negotiation between the source of authority (i.e. Scripture) and the interpretive tradition. The way this scroll not only adopts the words and images of the Scriptural traditions, but also claims to be *the* revelation preserved for this time, underscores the back and forth between *traditum* and *traditio* that Fishbane describes. 1QM also retrieves from Scripture the promises that God will act in the near future according to prophecy, and it interprets how these promises will be fulfilled. In referencing the promises of Scripture, 1QM does not copy the texts verbatim without engaging with them, as it adjusts the chronology, identifies who the actors will be by linking them to ancient figures, and ultimately identifies who will be the chosen remnant. In essence, tradition feeds the ideology in

---

of the Book of Jubilees and the Temple Scroll," *VT* 37 (1987): 71–78.

16 Zakovitch, "Inner-biblical Interpretation," 35.

17 Ibid, 37.

18 Ibid, 38.

19 Ibid, 61.

Prophetic Exegesis 61

1QM just as much as 1QM uses these traditions to meet its own agenda. 1QM 1 is an illustrative example as it adopts the prophecies of Daniel 11–12 to draw the new chronology of the battle between the forces of light and darkness. Whereas the מַשְׂכִּלִים in Daniel are the recipients of God's deliverances, 1QM 1 holds that the "Sons of Light" (בני אור) are not just the people that receive God's help, but they are co-participants in bringing this victory in the eschatological skirmish. This passage brings up a fundamental aspect of 1QM as a text that engages in prophecy through the analysis of the Scriptural texts, what we label as "prophetic exegesis."

   ii.   Beginnings of Prophetic Exegesis

There are several passages where God commands that his words be inscribed prior to their proclamation to the people. One of these instances happens in Jeremiah 36, where God tells the prophet to write in a scroll all the prophecies that he has uttered since the beginning of his ministry. Jeremiah's mission was to go to the Temple and read these prophecies (דברים), so that when the people would hear them they would turn to be forgiven (Jer 36:3; למען ישובו...סלחתי). The statement in verse three highlights the critical nature of Jeremiah's mission, but it also shows something that will be repeated in Jewish history: God's teachings will be recorded and continuously recited for the purpose of eliciting obedience from the people. Jeremiah 29 provides another example of this phenomenon. This chapter describes that the prophet's letters to the exiles become a source of direction, as Jeremiah explicitly provides instructions on how they should live in Babylon in light of the seventy-year prophecy. The codification of the prophetic words also happens in Ezekiel (Ezek 3:1–4), Zechariah (Zech 5:1–4), and Daniel (Dan 12:1–4) were the prophetic word transitioned from an oral source to a written text, therefore, demonstrating that these utterances were preserved and became through time one of the main sources of communal study along with Torah of Moses. In addition, the preservation of the prophecies attests to a change that takes place in post-exilic times, where the in-depth study and interpretation of prophecy became a form of prophecy itself.[20]

In *The Word of God in Transition: From Prophet to Exegete in the Second Temple Period,* William M. Schniedewind deals with the transition from oral

_____

20 Joseph Blenkinsopp, *Prophecy and Canon* (Notre Dame: University of Notre Dame Press, 1977), 71. Joachim Schaper, "The Death of the Prophet: The Transition from the Spoken to the Written Word of God in the Book of Ezekiel," in *Prophets, Prophecy and Prophetic Texts in Second Temple Judaism,* ed. Michael H. Floyd and Robert D. Haak (New York: T&T Clark, 2006), 63–79.

to scribal prophecy in the book of Chronicles.[21] His analysis consists of a two-pronged approach: first, he deals with the technical terms that are associated with prophetic figures such as: נביא, חזה, ראה, איש האלהים, and עבד האלהים and how Chronicles uses them.[22] The second part of his study deals with the different introductory formulae by which the prophets in Chronicles relay the words of God.[23] Schniedewind observes that the Chronicler makes a clear distinction by the way these technical terms are carefully used between those individuals who exercised the prophetic office (i.e. the נביא) and other inspired messengers (i.e. the מלאכים). He adds that whereas the former operated as interpreters of the words and acts of God, whether in the royal court or in the periphery, the latter were individuals whom God raised spontaneously at different times.[24] A couple of examples will illustrate this distinction.

In 2 Chr 12:1–8 the prophet Shemaiah acts as traditional נביא in that he interprets for Rehoboam and his officials that Shishak's invasion is the result of Judah abandoning God. The account proceeds following the repentance of the people with Shemaiah ushering an encouraging word announcing God's favor to Judah. On the other hand, 2 Chr 20 recounts the occasion when Jahaziel, a Levite, was endowed with a prophetic word. The account describes that following Jehoshaphat's prayer the Spirit of God came upon Jahaziel, to exhort the people in the face of a looming danger. Jahaziel, however, does not offer a revelation but rather provides an encouraging word based on his familiarity with God's actions in the past.[25] These examples among others serve Schniedewind to illustrate the distinction between Shemaiah's role as a נביא and Jahaziel as an inspired messenger, and they allow him to begin drawing a picture of the changes in the prophetic ministry after the exile. He asserts that with the end of the Judahite monarchy the office of the נביא begins to cease and transitions into the inspired messenger. For that matter, he adds, in post-exilic times the term נביאים will become a reference either to the pre-exilic prophets or to the texts that bear their name, while the inspired messengers take over the role of teachers of Scripture. Furthermore, these inspired teachers were individuals trained and endowed with the gift to discern

---

21 William Schniedewind, *The Word of God in Transition: From Prophet to Exegete in the Second Temple Period* (Sheffield: Sheffield Academic Press, 1995).

22 Ibid, 31–53.

23 Ibid, 55–79.

24 Yairah Amit, "The Role of Prophecy and Prophets in the Chronicler's World," in *Prophets, Prophecy and Prophetic Texts in Second Temple Judaism,* ed. Michael H. Floyd and Robert D. Haak (New York: T&T Clark, 2006), 80–101.

25 Ibid, 236. Schniedewind sees in Jahaziel's passage a recontextualization of Moses' injunction to Israel in Exodus 14.

God's mysteries from the written word, and to illuminate them to their communities. Examples of these kind of teachers include Ezra (Ezra 7:6) and the Teacher of Righteousness.

In terms of the Teacher of Righteousness, Schniedewind observes that he is never called a נביא in the scrolls. However, in 1QpHab 2.8–9, the Teacher is attributed with the ability to explain or interpret (לפשור) the words of the prophets. He is an inspired instructor who has a special "prophetic" status even if he is not considered a prophet per se. Schniedewind also notes that Josephus described the Essenes (*War* 12.259) as individuals who were able to predict future events through the study of the holy books and the sayings of the prophets. Schniedewind concludes that the picture in Qumran is one where revelation and prophecy went hand in hand. The study of Scripture in particular that of prophetic writings as exemplified by texts like 11Q13 2.18, shows that "prophecy was thus no longer an enterprise which could be done independently of the Scriptures, but was an interpretation and elaboration of Scripture."[26]

Schniedewind's work is helpful to begin delineating the trajectory from oral to scribal prophecy, and how the in-depth study of Scripture (i.e. exegesis) becomes a type of prophetic teaching. Other scholars have picked up on this discussion and used different terms like "inspired eschatological exposition" and "charismatic exegesis" in their attempts to explain the interpretive works of the inspired messengers.[27] To some extent each of these terms covers many of the same aspects like the rise and study of interpretive traditions and the transition from oral to written prophecy. In particular, the notion of charismatic exegesis is especially helpful because of the explicit, and sometimes implicit, claim to divine revelation made by Jewish interpreters.

In his essay entitled "Charismatic Exegesis in Early Judaism and Early Christianity," David E. Aune unpacks this term and explores some of its methodological complexities.[28] Aune begins by describing the four major qualities

---

26 Ibid, 242–243.

27 Edward Ellis, *Prophecy and Hermeneutic in Early Christianity* (Grand Rapids: Eerdmans, 1978), 26. David E. Aune, *Prophecy in Early Christianity and the Ancient Mediterranean World* (Grand Rapids: Eerdmans, 1983), 339–346. Ellis coins the first term as part of his discussion regarding the spiritual gifts in the Pauline community. Aune on the other hand uses "charismatic exegesis" as a broad concept that deals with exegesis of Scripture in the Greco-Roman and Early Christian times. He establishes this concept on two presuppositions that appear in the historical sources: 1) Scripture contains hidden or symbolic meanings which can only be deciphered by an inspired interpreter, and 2) The true meaning of the text at hand concerns eschatological prophecies being fulfilled during the exegete's time.

28 David E. Aune, "Charismatic Exegesis in Early Judaism and Early Christianity," in *The Pseudepigrapha and Early Biblical Interpretation,* ed. James H. Charlesworth and Craig A. Evans (Sheffield: Sheffield Academic Press, 1993), 126–150.

of charismatic exegesis. He observes that interpreters in early Judaism engaged in a continuous conversation with the sacred texts that resulted in the production of works that covered all the genres of Scripture. The main assumption that these authors held was the belief that a person needs a special type of insight to sort out the mysteries of Scripture. This type of wisdom, however, was not available to everyone, but it was reserved for a select few who had acquired enough training to be able to discern God's ways. These interpreters would also believe that they were living in the latter days, and that the ancient prophecies were being fulfilled in their own lifetime. The balance between divine wisdom and the proximity of the end of history gave rise to a prophetic strand that was based on the meticulous study of traditions that would shape the communities.[29] After he has established the main characteristics of charismatic exegesis (which correlate with the assumptions that Kugel introduced above), Aune analyzes specific examples from the Pesharim, the writings of Josephus, the apocalypses, and other early Christian writings.

In terms of the Pesharim, Aune describes some of the presuppositions and interpretive moves that are characteristic of this type of literature. He notes among other things that 1QpHab 2.7–10 and 7.1–5 describe that Scripture, in particular the prophetic texts, contained predictions about the events of the final generation. The pesher assumes that these moments described in the text relate not to Israel as a nation, but they focus exclusively on the sectarians and their future as the mysteries from the words of the prophets came to the Teacher of Righteousness for the sake of the community. These passages underscore not just an isolationist orientation but also highlight the exclusive revelation that was given to this prophetic figure on behalf of the sectarians. Although Aune does not see a predetermined set of exegetical techniques within the Pesharim, he does believe that they are heavily influenced by the conviction that this special insight came through revelation to the prophets (e.g. 1QS 8–9).[30] He adds that charismatic exegesis is essentially a hermeneutical ideology that legitimates a particular interpretation that is rooted on the belief that Scripture can be properly understood through divine insight that is vested on a particular leader or group. The exclusivity of revelation within the Pesharim reveals the sectarian orientation, and it legitimates not just a way of interpreting a text but also the very existence of the group's identity and its plans for the future.[31]

---

29 Ibid, 126–129.

30 Ibid, 133–137. We also note that in 1QS 8.15 the מדרש התורה is the foundation of the revelation. This further supports the claim, made by Aune, that revelation did not come at a moment's instance, but that it was gradually disclosed to the sectarians.

31 Ibid, 149–150.

Prophetic Exegesis 65

One of the most recent contributions that deals with the topic of exegesis in the DSS is by Alex Jassen. In his study entitled *Mediating the Divine: Prophecy and Revelation in the Dead Sea Scrolls and Second Temple Judaism,* Jassen adopts a tripartite approach that starts from a set of manifestations that can be gathered from the DSS.[32] These include: a) the rewriting of the prophetic experience and how prophetic/revelatory models were received and transformed by the sectarians; b) the sectarian belief that they were living in an eschatological age that would usher a new time of prophetic experience; and c) the sectarian belief that they were the heirs of the prophetic tradition.[33]

Following these remarks, Jassen briefly deals with the difficult issue regarding the purported cessation of prophecy in the Second Temple period.[34] He recognizes that although there are references to an apparent end of prophecy in works that span from the Persian period up to the Rabbinic era (e.g. Zech 13:2–3; 1 Macc 9:27; t. *Sot* 13.3), he holds that these passages reflect the views of the groups associated with these works and proposes, in agreement with Schniedewind, that prophecy takes on a different form during the post-exilic period. In fact, he adds, Josephus himself points to this difference by the way he distinguishes between the prophets in Scripture (i.e. προφήτης) and the contemporary figures that function in prophetic manner (i.e. μάντις). Jassen pushes forth the argument that any attempt to understand how the prophetic traditions evolved during the Second Temple period must account for the new "language of prophecy."

As we proceed in this work we will see that Jassen's perspective is helpful because of his assessment of the evidence within the DSS, as the scrolls bear witness to an interpretive approach that uses Scripture to provide a "prophetic" teaching. Likewise, his proposal to a new type of prophecy in the DSS concurs with the evidence laid out by Schniedewind and Aune above, who believe that the careful engagement with the Scriptural texts became the main conduit by which the revelatory message of God, both predictive and prescriptive, came to the sectarians.

The previous discussion demonstrated that during post-exilic times there was a shift in prophetic teaching, where the text of Scripture seen through the lens of interpretive traditions became the source of guidance and revelation

---

32 Alex P. Jassen, *Mediating the Divine: Prophecy and Revelation in the Dead Sea Scrolls and Second Temple Judaism* (Boston: Brill, 2007).

33 Ibid, 4–7.

34 Ibid, 11–18. For a recent work that deals with the question regarding the apparent cessation of prophecy in Jewish circles, see: Stephen L. Cook, *On the Question of the "Cessation of Prophecy" in Ancient Judaism* (Tübingen: Mohr Siebeck, 2011). Especially, the sections that review the ancient sources (pp. 5–9) and summarize the approaches to deal with this question prove to be helpful (pp. 181–191).

to the people. The words that are explicitly quoted or alluded to within these interpretive works, become the snippets of revelation that were entrusted to a group of endowed teachers (or charismatic exegetes) who possessed the knowledge and wisdom to discern the mysteries of God. As we shall see in the case of the DSS, the words of Scripture become the *traditum* that the sectarians adopt to draw the principles by which they established the different communities and steered their members to believe in the new age (i.e. *traditio*).

b.   Prophetic Exegesis in the Dead Sea Scrolls

The preceding discussion covered in broad strokes some of the factors that will be fundamental in our study of prophetic exegesis in the DSS. We noticed that the study of Scripture during the Second Temple period became the locus of authority and direction for the life of the Jewish people. This surge propelled a paradigm, where the prophetic proclamation veered from a hortatory activity of relaying the words of God to an interpretive exercise of traditions. This interpretation, however, was not just a gathering of facts from the past, but it was believed to be God's revelation for this new place and time in history. This was particularly the case among the sectarians of the DSS.[35]

As we analyze how prophetic exegesis took place in Qumran, we will explore specific examples where we can witness this sectarian interpretation not just of texts of the Torah but also of other passages from the Scriptures. Our main argument is that the sectarians viewed their own genesis and communal existence as a type of prophetic activity. This underlying assumption will be explained from various texts, where the sectarians reveal their eschatological ideology and how they were waiting for God's redemption. Prophetic exegesis happened among them as a predictive and formative enterprise, thus creating a type of catechetical blueprint for the present in preparation for the future deliverance.

i.   Thematic Pesharim

The Pesharim are one of the prime examples of prophetic exegesis in the DSS. Since the work of Jean Carmignac, scholars have recognized two categories of Pesharim.[36] The first is the continuous pesher (*pesher continu*) which consists of a running commentary of a text of Scripture that follows a sequence

---

35 George J. Brooke, "Prophecy and Prophets in the Dead Sea Scrolls: Looking Backwards and Forwards," in *Prophets, Prophecy and Prophetic Texts in Second Temple Judaism*, ed. Michael H. Floyd and Robert D. Haak (New York: T & T Clark, 2006), 151–165.

36 Jean Carmignac, "Le document de Qumrân sur Melkisédeq," *RevQ* 7 (1970): 343–78.

Prophetic Exegesis   67

from verse to verse. Examples of this type of pesher include commentaries of texts in Habakkuk (1QpHab), Micah (1QpMic) and Psalms (1QpPs). The other category is the thematic pesher (*pesher thématique*), which follows a different pattern than the continuous pesher. Instead of doing a running commentary the thematic Pesharim typically proceed from the standpoint of developing a theme, although the organizational principle is not always clear as they introduce different texts that support the main theme. Recently, scholars like George Brooke have questioned these two distinct categories. He holds that there are many varieties of exegesis within the continuous Pesharim and that the thematic Pesharim are not always based on unfulfilled prophecies.[37] Brooke's proposals alert us to not place these texts within tight genre categories that did not exist at the time of their composition or that they would not be flexible enough to account for their variety. In addition, at the root of Brooke's questioning is the difficulty of deciphering what the Pesharim are and how they compare to other Jewish literature. Our goal at this junction is not to land on any particular definition but to explore some of the work surrounding the genre of the Pesharim and to highlight some of the extant texts that will be most useful for our study.

In 1981 Brooke established three factors to define the genre of Pesher: a) form and content, b) method, and c) history of literary traditions.[38] He observes in texts like CD 7:13–18 and 4Q174 1.1–13 the presence of midrashic techniques, which he compares with pesher texts from 1QpHab (i.e. 6.2–5; 6.8–12; 12.1–10). In this comparison Brooke notices a shared approach of Scriptural citation followed by an interpretation of the passage. The main difference between 1QpHab and CD is the explicit use that the former makes of the word "pesher" (פשר). However, he lessens the relevance that use of pesher has in defining the genre, because of the many ways that this word appears in the scrolls.[39] In the end Brooke relies heavily on the midrashic techniques that he observes in both the Pesharim and in the other non-pesher texts, and proposes that the Pesharim should be classified as Qumran "midrash," and that the category of pesher only complicates matters. He concedes, however, that pesher can be useful to the extent that it is an interpretation of a prophetic text, although he goes only far enough as to identify the Pesharim as a subgenre of midrash.[40]

---

37 George J. Brooke, "Thematic Commentaries on Prophetic Scriptures," in *Biblical Interpretation at Qumran*, ed. Matthias Henze (Grand Rapids: Eerdmans, 2005), 134–157.

38 George J. Brooke, "Qumran Pesher: Towards the Redefinition of a Genre," *RevQ* 10 (1981): 491–494.

39 Ibid, 501.

40 Ibid, 502–503. Brooke was not the first one to make this argument. William H. Brownlee labeled his commentary on Habakkuk as midrash and in an earlier paper in 1953 he com-

Robert Williamson Jr. takes on a different approach and notices two tendencies among past proposals.[41] On the one hand there is the tendency to subsume pesher under the genre of midrash as in the case of Brooke above. On the other hand, there is a doubt that pesher is a genre at all due to its lack of common features shared across the member texts. Williamson believes that by using cognitive genre theory he can mediate both extremes. This theory holds that the mind organizes and categorizes information in a type of radial structure, that starts at the center with a prototype that meets expectations and it moves outward to other types whose membership in this radial category is more debatable.[42] Thus, in this cognitive model texts like the continuous Pesharim would be at the center, because they meet what he labels as the "compulsory" elements of this genre, which include: a) the continuous quotation of Scriptural texts, b) the use of pesher in the introductory formula, and c) the identification of a Scriptural figure with a contemporary one.[43] Texts like the thematic Pesharim (e.g. 4Q174 and 11Q13) and the isolated Pesharim (e.g. CD 7.14–19 and 1QS 8.13–15) stand on the periphery of this genre circle; although in the case of the latter they are part of this genre only to the extent that they use pesher as a mode of interpretation.[44] This last point on pesher as a mode of interpretation is an important one, because it permeates across different texts among the DSS.

Timothy Lim believes that pesher is best seen as a distinct type of exegesis.[45] As such it stands in a continuum that spans from innerbiblical exegesis that Fishbane illustrated above to Rabbinic midrash.[46] He adds that in of itself pesher exegesis is not totally unique although he concedes that the content of the exegesis, its eschatological orientation, contemporizing tendencies, and special role to revelation sets it apart. Lim suggests rather that pesher as a genre of Scriptural interpretation is a scholarly construct, since there is no ancient list of texts labeled "Pesharim".[47] He adds that pesher as

pared the relationship of pesher to midrash as that one between halakha and haggadah. His 1953 paper was entitled "The Dead Sea Habakkuk Midrash" which is cited on page 25 in his own commentary of Habakkuk. See: William H. Brownlee, *The Midrash Pesher Habakkuk* (Atlanta: Scholars Press, 1979).

41 Robert Williamson Jr. "Pesher: A Cognitive Model of the Genre," *DSD* 17 (2010): 307–331.

42 Ibid, 312–315.

43 Ibid, 318–319.

44 Ibid, 328–330.

45 Timothy Lim, *Pesharim* (Sheffield: Sheffield Academic Press, 2002), 52–53. Timothy Lim, "Midrash Pesher in the Pauline Letters," in *The Scrolls and the Scriptures: Qumran Fifty Years After*, ed. Stanley Porter and Craig Evans (Sheffield: Sheffield Academic Press, 1997), 280–292.

46 Shani Berrin (Tzoref), "Qumran Pesharim," in *Biblical Interpretation at Qumran*, ed. Matthias Henze (Grand Rapids: Eerdmans, 2005), 134–157.

47 Lim, *Pesharim*, 53.

Prophetic Exegesis 69

a method of exegesis appears in non-Pesharim texts like CD and 1QS and in other texts like 4Q180 (to explicate the ages of creation), 4Q159 (to expound on law) and 4Q464 (to describe the promise to Abraham). In essence, rather than focusing on a set of texts that are established as Pesharim, Lim prefers to focus on the type of exegesis that is shared among these texts, which coincides with Williamson when he says: "Pesher is a genre of biblical interpretation in which the prophetic passages of the Bible are viewed as mysteries of God (רזין) concerning history contemporary to the author of the pesher; as such, the biblical text is understood to be properly interpreted only by one specially endowed by God to unravel (פשר) its meaning."[48]

In any case, the Pesharim adopt in various ways the type of exegesis that is prophetic in nature. By prophetic we mean that they interpret Scripture, both prophetic and non-prophetic passages, to disclose a vision of the future that was hidden to previous generations and to shape the communities in light of this revelation. As such, the Pesharim carry a word of encouragement to those in the inner circle but also of doom for those outside of the favored people. No one pesher exhibits all aspects of this type of exegesis, but the relevance of Scripture to establish the interpretation is an essential feature across the board. For our purposes the ensuing discussion will focus on two thematic Pesharim, namely 4Q174 (Florilegium) and 11Q13 (11QMelchizedek), because their form and content as they adapt the sacred texts to a new context are similar to 1QM. These texts develop an eschatological theme and Scripture provides the supporting evidence. Likewise, 1QM deals with the theme of an eschatological skirmish that comes as the fulfillment of prophecy. It is not our contention that 1QM should be classified as a thematic Pesher, but we are simply drawing a comparison and identifying by virtue of a close reading, how these Pesharim in their exegesis organize the different themes and supporting Scriptural texts in a manner that is comparable to what we will encounter in 1QM.

4Q174 Frg. 1–2 Col. i–ii[49]

1 [ולוא ירגז ע[ו]ד אויב[ולוא יוסי]ף בן עולֿהֿ[ן לענות]וֿ כאשר בראישונה ולמן היום אשר	1 ['And no] enemy [will oppress him an]y more, [and no] son of deceit [shall afflict] him [agai]n, as formerly, from the day that

---

48 Williamson, "Pesher," 327. Marti Nissinen, "Pesharim as Divination: Qumran Exegesis, Omen Interpretation and Literary Prophecy," in *Prophecy after the Prophets?* (Leuven: Peeters, 2009), 43–60.

49 Block texts from the DSS and their translations are from: Emanuel Tov et al, *The Dead Sea Scrolls Electronic Library* (Leiden: Brill, 2006).

2 [צוייתי שופטים] עَל עמי ישראל הואה הבית אשר[יבנה] ל[וא]ב[אَחרית הימים כאשר כתוב בספר	2 [I appointed judges] over my people Israel' (2 Sam 7:10–11). This is the house which [he will build] for [him] in the latter days, as it is written in the book of
3 'משה מקדש יהוה כَ[וَnנו ידיכה יהוה ימלוך עולَם וَעד הואה הבית אשר לוא יבוא שمה	3 [Moses, 'The sanctuary,] O Yahweh, which your hands have fashioned. Yahweh will reign for ever and ever.' (Exod 15:17–18) This (is) the house which these will not enter
4 [עד] עَולם וَעَמَوני ומואבי וממזר ובן נכר וגר עד עולם כיא קדושי שם	4 [for]ever, nor an Ammonite, a Moabite, a bastard, a foreigner, or a proselyte forever, for his holy ones (are) there.
5 יَגَל[וَה]ן כבודו ל[עَولם עליו תמיד יראה ולוא ישמוהו עוד זרים כאשר השמו בראَישונה	5 [His glory shall] be revealed for[ev]er; it shall appear over it perpetually. And strangers shall lay it waste no more, as they formerly laid waste
6 את מקדَ[ש י]שראל בחטאתמה ויואמר לבנות לוא מקדש אדם להיות מקטירים בוא לוא	6 the sanctua[ry of I]srael because of their sin. And he has commanded that a sanctuary of human(s) be built for him, so that they may offer incense in it to him,
7 לפניו מَעَשׂَי תורה ואשר אמר לדויד וَ[הניחו]תَי לכה מכול אויביכה אשר יניח להמה מכَ[ו]ל]	7 before him, works of Torah. And (that) which he said to David, 'And I [shall give] you [rest] from all your enemies' (2 Sam 7:11) that (is) he will give them rest from a[ll]
8 בני בליעל הَמכשילים אותמה לכلותمَ[ה]مה כאשר באו במחשבת בَ[لَי]ע[ל להכשיل בَ[ני]	8 the Sons of Belial who cause them to stumble in order to destroy th[em]mh just as they came with a plan of [Be]lial to cause to stumble the S[ons of]
9 אَו[ר] ולַחשוב עליהמה מחשבות און לَמَ[ع]ן יתَ[פשו לבליעל במשגת אَ[ו]נَמה vacat	9 Ligh[t] and to devise against them evil plans so t[hat th]ey might be cau[ght] by Belial through their ini[quit]ous error. *vacat*
10 [והגَ]י̇ד לכה יהוה כיא בית יבנה לכה והקימותי את זרעכה אחריכה והכינותי את כסא ממלכתו	10 'And Yahweh [decl]ares to you that he will build you a house. And I will raise up your offspring after you, and I will establish his royal throne
11 [לעَו]לَם אני אَהَיَה לוא לאב והוא יהיה לי לבן הואה צמח דויד העומד עם דורש התורה אשר	11 [fore]ver. I will be a father to him, and he shall be a son to me.' (2 Sam 7:13–14) He (is) the Shoot of David who will arise with the interpreter of the Torah who
12 [ ]בَצَי̇[ון ב]אَחרית הימים כאשר כתוב והקימותי את סוכת דויד הנופלת היאה סוכת	12 [ ] in Zi[on in the] latter days, as it is written, 'And I will raise up the booth of David that is fallen.' (Amos 9:11) He (is) the Booth of
13 דויד הנופלَ[ת א]שֹׁר יעמוד להושיע את ישראל vacat	13 David that is falle[n w]ho will arise to save Israel. *vacat*

מִדְרֵשׁ מאשרי [ה]איש אשר לוא הָלַךְ בעצת רשעים פשר הדבָ[ר עָ]לֹ [ ] סרי מדרָךְׂ 14	14 Midrash of 'Happy is [the] man who has not followed the counsel of the wicked.' (Ps 1:1) The interpretation of the passa[ge conc] erns those who turn aside from the way [ ]
אשר כתוב בספר ישעיה הנביא לֹאֹ־ חֲרִית הֹימִים ויהי כחזקתָ[ן היד ויסרני מלכת בדרך] 15	15 which is written in the book of Isaiah the prophet concerning the latter days, 'And it was as with a strong [hand that he turned me aside from walking in the path of]
העָם הזה והמה אשר כתוב עליהָמָה בסֹפָ[ר יחן] [זֹקֵאל הנביא אשר לוֹ]אֹ יטמאו עוד בכוֹל] 16	16 this people.' (Isa 8:11) And they (are) the ones about whom it is written in the book of Ezekiel the prophet, who ['shall] ne[ver defile themselves with all]
גֹּלֹ[וֹ]לִיהָמה המה בני צדוק וֹאָ[נֹ]שי עצֹ[תמ]הֹ רוח[קים מרע] אֹהֲריהָמֹה [בעצתׂ] הֹיחד 17	17 their id[o]ls.' (Ezek 37:23) They (are) the Sons of Zadok and the m[e]n of [the] Council who ke[ep (far) from evil] after them [in the Council of] the Community.
[לׁמה רגשׁ]וֹ גויים ולאומים יהגֹּ[וֹ] ריק יתֹ]יׂצבון מלכי ארץ ורֹ[וזנים נוסדו בִּיחד על יהוה ועל 18	18 ['Why] do the nations [rag]e and the peo- ples plo[t in vain? Kings of the earth r]ise up [and r]egents intrigue together against Yahweh and against
[מׁשׁיחו פ]שׂר הדבר [גוֹ]יׂים וֹהֹ[ ] בחירי ישראל באחרית הימים 19	19 [his anointed.' (Ps 2:1–2) The in]terpreta- tion of the passage [nati]ons and the [ ] chosen ones of Israel in the latter days.
היאה עת המצרף הבָ[א]ה על בית יהודה להתם 1	1 This (is) the time of refining com[ing on the house of J]udah to perfect[ ]
בליעל ונשאר שֹאֹרֹ [העָ]ם [ישרֹ]אֹל ועשו את כול התורֹה 2	2 Belial and a remnant of [the peo]ple of [Isra]el will remain and they will observe the entire Torah[ ]
מושה היאה הֹ[דבר אשׂ]ר כתוב בספר דניאל הנביא להרשׂיֹ[ע רשעים ולוא יבינו] 3	3 Moses. This is the [passage tha]t is written in the book of Daniel the prophet, ['For the wicked] to act wickedly [but they do not discern,]
וצדיקים יֹתֹ[בררו ויתלב]נׂו ויצטרפו [ ]וֹעם יודעי אלוה יחזיקו הֹמֹ[ה] הֹ אֹחֲרי הֹן]אשר אליהמה יורֹ[ד [4	4 but the righteous shall [purify themselves and make] themselves [white] and refine themselves' (Dan 12:10) and 'a people that know God will be strong' (Dan 11:32) The[y after the[ ]whose God will come do[wn]
[ ]הֹ ברדתו מן [ ] 5	5 [ ]h in his descent m[ ]
[ ]אֹ [ ] 6	6 [ ] '[ ]

There are twenty-six fragments identified under 4Q174. Columns 1–2 of the first fragment are the best-preserved texts where we glean the exegesis of pro- phetic texts that is characteristic of the Pesharim. Because of the fragmentary

72   INTERTEXTUALITY AND PROPHETIC EXEGESIS IN THE WAR SCROLL OF QUMRAN

nature of this scroll, it is hard to determine with complete certainty where the text starts and ends beyond what scholars were able to reconstruct.[50] Nevertheless, we can divide this reconstructed fragment in two major parts with different topics and Scriptural sources: Part I (col. 1.1–13) represents an interpretation of Nathan's prophecy recorded in 2 Samuel 7, and Part II (cols. 1.14–2.6) consists of a midrash of sayings that appear in Psalms 1 and 2. Despite their thematic difference both parts showcase the use of prophetic teachings to illustrate the promise and future fulfillment of God's will for the sectarians.[51]

Part I starts with a partial citation of 2 Sam 7:10–11 that picks up at the point where Nathan's prophecy guarantees relief from the "enemy" (אויב).[52] Line 2 explains this prophecy as the construction of the "house" (בית), which suggests that the citation of Samuel might have started with 2 Sam 7:10. In this prophecy Nathan predicts that God will establish a "place" (מקום) for Israel, which the Pesher interprets as the house that will be constructed "in the latter days" (באחרית הימים). Line 3 supports this interpretation by citing Exodus 15:17–18 where we read about the edification of the "sanctuary" (מקדש) of God, which lines 3–4 interpret as the eternal "house" that no foreigner shall enter. In these first three lines we can gather the strategic substitution of "place" and "sanctuary" for "house", which denotes temple but can also connote a messianic expectation. The references to David and the citation of Amos' prophecy in line 13, which has typically been interpreted as a messianic promise, suggest that the pesher is envisioning something more than just the reconstitution of a new temple but the consecration of a future house where God will inhabit and nothing prohibited can enter. Likewise, we can assert that the rhetorical effect of these exegetical moves is that they bring the reader back to nostalgic moments in Israel's history that depict the essence of what the temple should be, as the place where God dwells amidst the people without the blemish of the enemy. The ensuing lines will continue to drill down with additional descriptions of this future house.

Line 4 continues with the restrictions that will characterize this future house. It will be a place where no "Ammonite, Moabite, a bastard, a foreigner, or a proselyte" (ועמוני ומואבי וממזר ובן נכר וגר) will enter. The consecutive

---

50 John M. Allegro and Arnold Anderson, *Qumrân Cave 4.I (4Q158–4Q186)*, DJD V (Oxford: Clarendon Press, 1968), 53–56.

51 For a thorough discussion of this text, see: George J. Brooke, *Exegesis at Qumran: 4QFlorilegium in its Jewish Context* (Sheffield: JSOT Press, 1985), 80–160. George J. Brooke, "Controlling Intertexts and Hierarchies of Echo in Two Thematic Eschatological Commentaries from Qumran," in *Reading the Dead Sea Scrolls,* ed. George J. Brooke and Nathalie LaCoste (Atlanta: Society of Biblical Literature, 2013), 86–92.

52 The other significant aspect of this citation is the inclusion of אויב, which does not appear in the text of Samuel.

Prophetic Exegesis 73

mention of the Ammonite, Moabite, and bastard alludes to Deut 23:3–4 where Moses includes them as the people who cannot have access to the "assembly" (קהל) of God. Differently from Deut 23:8 and 24:17 where Moses advocates justice for the גר ("proselyte," 4Q174), includes them among those ostracized from the assembly. As for the phrase "foreigner" (בן נכר) it appears in Gen 17:12, 27, Exod 12:43, and Lev 22:25, but the strongest connection with 4Q174 is in Ezek 44:9 where God states that no bastard shall enter the sanctuary. Lines 4–6 explain that these restrictions will be imposed because "holy ones" (קדו־שי) are already in the sanctuary. These lines also predict that the new sanctuary will not be destroyed as the former Temple was at the hands of foreigners. We notice in these lines the interpretation that the fall of the first Temple was the by-product of foreign influence and the easing up of the restrictions that were once established in the Law of Moses. In the same manner as in the preceding lines, here 4Q174 uses Scriptural traditions to establish the future aspirations. Just like the former house was supposed to be for Israel, 4Q174 argues that the new abode that God will raise will be reserved for the holy ones. At this point we do not know yet who these holy ones are, but the subsequent lines will elaborate on their identity.

Line 7 quotes 2 Sam 7:11 where God promises David relief from his enemies. The next two lines add details to who the enemy is and who is its target. Twice we are told with the use of the verb "to stumble" (כשל) that the "Sons of Belial" (בני בליעל) seek the destruction of the "Sons of Light (בני אור). The verb כשל is used elsewhere in the scrolls to denote "stumbling" as in relinquishing the path of obedience in the observance of Torah, but specifically in connection with Sons of Light it appears in our text as well as in 1QS and 4Q177. 1QS 3.24 describes that the whole purpose of the Angel of Darkness and all these spirits of his lot is to cause the Sons of Light to stumble and deviate from the path of obedience. This passage also adds the conviction that God ultimately assists the Sons of Light in delivering them from the oppression of these forces (1QS 3.25–26). For its part 4Q177 Frg. 10–11.7 describes the stumbling at the hands of the "men of Belial" (אנשי בליעל) within the context of God's promises for salvation to the people. These examples underscore that along with the challenge of living in the face of oppression, the Sons of Light also have the promise of deliverance as it was originally given to David. They are the ones who will receive the promise of respite from the plans of Belial, whose purpose is to make them stray from the path of obedience and trap them in his plans. These lines continue with the theme of deliverance from enemy forces that we saw previously.

Lines 10–13 depict God's plan to counter the enemy by introducing the citation of 2 Sam 7:12–14. Like the citation in line 1 this reference also shows some adjustments. One major difference in line 10 is the change from "he will build a house for my name" (יבנה בית לשמי) in Samuel to "he will build you a house" (בית יבנה לכה). With this change the subject of the action changes; whereas in Samuel the prophesied king is the one who will build the Temple to God, in our text God will build the Temple and establish the kingdom of this future king. Lines 11–12 set the citation to an eschatological time and in the process, they introduce the mysterious identity of this future king "the Shoot of David" (צמח דויד) and of his main helper "the interpreter of the Torah" (דורש התורה). The reference to a shoot (צמח) has its background in passages like Isa 4:2, where it appears as a metaphor for Jerusalem in the prophet's vision of restoration. The prophet Jeremiah also envisions the rise of the Shoot of David who will rule in righteousness following the exile (Jer 23:5; 33:15). But the closest link to our context appears in Zech 3:8, where Joshua the High Priest receives a word that reveals to him that God will raise his servant the shoot. Further in Zech 6:12 the prophet Zechariah is charged to crown Joshua and to announce that he will be the one who will re-build the Temple. In addition, the ensuing verse states that there shall be a "priest" (כהן) who will associate with him in peace. These verses in Zechariah match with the interpretation in 4Q174 where a royal and a priestly figure are predicted and to some extent consolidated in a shared mission.

Lastly, lines 12–13 cite Amos 9:11 to provide further evidence of the Shoot of David. In this reference God predicts the restoration of the "booth of David" (סכת דויד), which traditionally has been interpreted to represent the Davidic monarchy.[53] 4Q174, however, equates the "booth" (סכת) with the "shoot" (צמח) and describes that the shoot will deliver Israel; thus, turning a monarchic prophecy into a messianic one. This type of interpretative move also appears in the book of Acts (Acts 15:15–16), where the apostles believe that the resurrection of Jesus is the fulfillment of the words of the prophets regarding the rise of the "tent of David" (σκηνὴν Δαυίδ) and the inclusion of the Gentiles in the apostolic mission. The presence of the shoot and the interpreter of the Torah in 4Q174 suggests the vision of a future where the offices of ruler and interpreter of the commandments are closely aligned. A similar type of vision appears in 1QS 9.11 where it describes the coming of the "messiah of Aaron and Israel" (משיחי אהרון וישראל) and it correlates with the

---

53 Frank Moore Cross, "The Priestly Tabernacle in the Light of Recent Research," in *Temples and High Places in Biblical Times*, ed. Avraham Biran (Jerusalem: Keter, 1981), 177. Shalom Paul, *Amos* (Minneapolis: Fortress Press, 1991), 288–290. Shalom Paul describes the last pericope in Amos "as a return to the halcyon golden age of David and Solomon."

Prophetic Exegesis   75

vision laid out in Chronicles, where the Davidic rulers are also cultic/priestly figures. Hence, lines 1–13 in this pesher interpret the promises to David as promises to the holy ones and predict the return of Israel to an ideal place, where intimacy with God and protection from the enemies is guaranteed as the monarchic ruler and priestly authority play a fundamental partnership in God's will.

As we turn to lines 14–19, we are dealing with a different topic. Despite the fact that the main topic of these lines differs from the previous ones, we still notice the presence of prophetic exegesis. Line 14 begins with a "midrash" (מדרש) of Ps 1:1. Subsequently this same line offers the interpretation that equates the man in the psalm with those who turn from the path of the wicked. The intriguing part of this interpretation is that it follows the word pesher, which is the first instance that it appears in this manuscript. Further, the consecutive use of midrash and persher has prompted some scholars to inquire if this instance suggests a rethinking of the genre pesher.[54] However, this might not be necessary considering that this is the only time where both of these terms occur simultaneously. Also, the evidence in the use of midrash in Qumran has many connotations that does not point to a specific type of literature but to an exercise of scrutinizing the Scriptures.[55] The suggestion that pesher as a genre has to be reconsidered based on these passages seems unnecessary, and it further underscores that scholars have used this notion of "genre" probably too rigidly, as a template that demands that different pieces of literature need to fit into. In any case, this saying from Psalms is used prophetically not as prediction but as prescription.

Michael Knibb has suggested that there is an interesting connection between the interpretation of Ps 1:1 in our text and similar language in both CD (CD 8.16, 19.29) and 1QSa (1.2b–3).[56] The former describes the sectarian community and the latter the eschatological congregation. Interestingly enough the reference in 1QSa also talks about the Sons of Zadok, which appear in line 17 of our text. Knibb's findings point to the use of midrash as tradition that was held regarding the sectarian community as the ones who, like the figure

---

54 Aharon Shemesh, "Biblical Exegesis and Interpretations from Qumran to the Rabbis," in *A Companion to Biblical Interpretation in Early Judaism,* ed. Matthias Henze (Grand Rapids: Eerdmans, 2012), 469–470. Shemesh makes a similar argument using the examples of 4Q174 and 4Q249 with its apparent title (מדרש ספר משה), to suggest that pesher should be substituted for midrash when referring to the scrolls that have commonly been labeled as Pesharim.

55 מדרש can denote the following: a) Study and interpretation of Torah (CD 20.6; 1QS 8.15; 4Q249 1.1; 4Q258 6.7; 4Q259 3.6; 4Q266 5i.17, 11.20; 4Q269 16.19; and 4Q270 7ii.15); b) Community Inquiry to decide internal matters (1QS 6.24, 8.26; 4Q258 7.1); or c) Teaching for the משכיל (4Q256 9.1; 4Q258 1.1).

56 Michael A. Knibb, *The Qumran Community* (Cambridge: Cambridge University Press, 1987), 257–263.

in Psalms 1, ceased to walk in the path of wicked. This interpretation is confirmed by lines 15–17 where the pesher uses Isa 8:11 to confirm that the community, like the prophet Isaiah, has been called in these last days to separate from the rest of the people, and also in Ezek 37:23 where both the Sons of Zadok and the rest of the community shall not be defiled by the surrounding idolatry. Column 1 ends in lines 18–19 with a fragmentary quote from Ps 2:1–2 that mentions the "chosen ones of Israel" (בחירי ישראל) which is another way of referring to the sectarians.[57]

The second column of 4Q174 consists of six lines. These lines apparently continue the discussion from the previous column as they describe a time of trial and refining over the house of Judah. Here we are told that this will be a time of refining and that the "remnant of the people of Israel" (שאר העם ישראל) will obey the Torah of Moses. To support this description the pesher cites Dan 12:10 that describes that those who know God will remain strong in this time of trial. The reference to the prophet Daniel is important, because here he is cited along Isaiah and Ezekiel. This also happens in 11Q13 2.18 where the pesher interprets the messenger in Isa 52:7 as the "anointed of the spirit" according to Daniel 9:25 and the "anointed prince", and adds further detail by citing the words of Isa 61:2–3 where this messenger will bring comfort to the needy.[58] Daniel is not mentioned explicitly in 1QM, but the descriptions in Daniel 11–12 set the stage for the eschatological war in column 1, and much of the angelology that we see in Daniel appears throughout 1QM.

4Q174 Frg. 1–3 Col. i–ii is a composite text that brings references from all genres within Scripture to advance the interpretation that the Sons of Light are the recipients of God's promises. The vision that this pesher paints is of restoration of something that has been defiled, that is, the temple in Jerusalem. It pictures a new order where the house will be pure and where God will be manifest to the holy ones. It is also a house that has both monarchic and priestly servants that steer the people in the direction of obedience to the words and works of Torah.

11Q13 2.1–25

] ֯מ ֯ע ֯ל [ ] 1	

---

57 See: 1Q37 1.3; 4Q165 6.1, 4Q171 11.2.

58 To a lesser extent Daniel's prophetic relevance also appears in the very fragmentary parabiblical texts of 4Q243–245. This type of parabiblical texts is also seen for Moses (4Q374–375; 4Q387–389), Jeremiah (4Q385b–387b), and Ezekiel (4Q385).

‫[ל] ואשר אמר בשנת היובל [הזואת‬ ‫תשובו איש אל אחוזתו ועליו אמר וז]ה‬	2 [ ] and as for what he said: 'In [this] year of jubilee [each of you shall return to his property,' (Lev 25:13) concerning it he said: 'And th]is is
‫[ ]דבר השמטה] שמוט כול בעל‬ ‫משה יד אשר ישה]ן ברעהו לוא יגוש‬ ‫את רעהו ואת אחיו כיא קרא [שמטה‬	3 [the manner of the remission:] every creditor shall remit what he has lent [his neighbor. He shall not press his neighbor or his brother for it has been proclaimed] a remission
‫ל[א]ל פשרו [ל]אחרית הימים על‬ ‫השבויים אשר] [ואשׁר‬	4 of Go[d.' (Deut 15:2) Its interpretation] for the final days concerns the captives, who [ ] and whose
‫מור[י]המה התבאו ו]סתרו]ן ומנחלת‬ ‫מלכי צדק כי]א [ו]המה נחל]ת מלכי‬ ‫צ[דק אשר‬	5 teachers have been hidden and kept secret, and from the inheritance of Melchizedek, fo[r] and they are the inheritan[ce of Melchize]dek who
‫ישיבמה אליהמה וקרא להמה דרור‬ ‫לעזוב להמה] משא [כול עוונותיהמה‬ ‫ו]כן יהי]ה הדבר הזה‬	6 will make them return. And liberty shall be proclaimed to them, to free them from [the debt of] all their iniquities. And this [wil]l [happen]
‫בש[ב]וע היובל הראישון אחר תש]עה‬ ‫ה]יובלים וי]ום הכפ]ורים ה]וא]ה ס]וף‬ ‫ה]יו]בל העשירי‬	7 in the first week of the jubilee (that occurs) after [the] ni[ne] jubilees. And the D[ay of Atone]ment i[s] the e[nd of] the tenth [ju]bilee,
‫לכפר בו על כול בני [אור ו]אנש]י [‬ ‫גורל מל]כי [צדק]ן [ם עלי]המ]ה התן [‬ ‫לפ]י [כ]ול עש]ותמה כיא‬	8 in which atonement shall be made for all the sons of [light and for] the men [of] the lot of Mel[chi]zedek[ ] over [th]em [ ] accor[ding to] a[ll] their [doing]s, for
‫הואה הקץ לשנת הרצון למלכי צדק‬ ‫ולצב]איו ע]ם קדושי אל לממשלת‬ ‫משפט כאשר כתוב‬	9 it is the time for the year of grace of Melchizedek and of [his] arm[ies, the nati]on [of] the holy ones of God, of the administration of justice, as is written
‫עליו בשירי דויד אשר אמר אלוהים‬ ‫נ]צב בע]דת אל [בקורב‬ ‫אלוהים ישפוט ועליו אמ]ר ו]על]י]ו]ה‬	10 about him in the songs of David, who said: 'Elohim shall [st]and in the ass[embly of God]; in the midst of the gods he shall judge.' (Ps 82:1) And about him he sa[id: 'And] above [it,]
‫למרום שובה אל ידין עמים ואשר‬ ‫א]מר עד מתי ת]שפוטו עוול ופני‬ ‫רשע]י]ם תשאו ס]לה‬	11 to the heights, return: God shall judge the nations.' (Ps 7:8–9) And as for what he s[aid: 'How long will you] judge unjustly, and be par[tial] to the wick[e]d? [Se]lah,' (Ps 82:2)
‫פשרו על בליעל ועל רוחי גורלו‬ ‫אש]ר [ ]ם בסו]רמ]ה מחוקי אל‬ ‫ל]הרשיע]‬	12 the interpretation of it concerns Belial and the spirits of his lot wh[o], in [the]ir tur[ning] away from God's commandments to [commit evil].

13 ומלכי צדק יקום נקֹם משפֹּטֵי אֵל וביום ההואה יצי[ל]מה מיד בליעל ומיד כול ר[וחי גורלו]	13 And Melchizedek will carry out the vengeance of Go[d]'s judgments [and on that day he will f]r[ee them from the hand of] Belial and from the hand of all the s[pirits of his lot.]
14 ובעזרו כול אלי [הצדק וה]וֹאה אֵ[שר]כֹול[בני אל והפן	14 And all the gods [of justice] are to his help; [and h]e is (the one) wh[o] all the sons of God, and he will [
15 הזואת הואה יום ה[ן]שלום אֵ[שר אמֹר] ביד ישע[יה הנביא אשר אמר]מה [נֹאוו	15 This [ ] is the day of the [peace ab]out which he said[through Isa]iah the prophet who said: ['How] beautiful
16 על הרים רגל[י]ן מבש[ר מ]שמיע שלום מב[שר טוב משמיע ישוע]ֹה [אֹ] ומר לציון [מלך אֹ]לוהיך	16 upon (the) mountains are the feet [of] the messen[ger who an]nounces peace, the mes[senger of good who announces salvati]on, [sa]ying to Zion: your God [is king'] (Isa 52:7)
17 פֹּשרו ההרֹי[ם] המה[ן הנביא[ים המה אֹ[ן]מֹן[ ]לכול]	17 Its interpretation: the 'mountains' [are] the prophet[s]; they [ ] every [
18 והמבשר הו[אה]מֹשיח הרוֹ[ח] כֹאשר אמר דנ[יאל עליו עד משיח נגיד שבועים שבעה ומבשר]	18 And the 'messenger' i[s] the anointed of the spir[it], as Dan[iel] said [about him: 'Until an anointed, a prince, it is seven weeks.' (Dan 9:25) And the messenger of]
19 טוֹב משמי[ע ישועה]הואה הֹב תוב עליו אשר]	19 good who announ[ces salvation] is the one about whom it is written [
20 לנחֹ[ם] הֹ[אבלים פשרו]ל[ה]שֹכיל־ מֹה בכול קצי העֹ[ולם	20 'To comfo[rt] the [afflicted,' (Isa 61:2) its interpretation:] to [in]struct them in all the ages of the w[orld
21 יֹ באמת לֹמֹן[ ]מֹה אֹ[ן]	21 in truth [ ] [
22 יֹ ר הוסרה מבליעל ותשֹׁ[וב]נֹ[קֹ]]	22 [ ] has turned away from Belial and shall retu[rn to] [
23 במשפטֹ[י]ן אל כאשר כתֹוב עליון אומר לציֹ[ו]ן מלך אלוהיך [צי]וֹן הֹ[יֹאה]	23 [ ]in the judgement[s of] God, as is written about him: '[saying to Zi]on: your God is king.' (Isa 52:7) '[Zi]on' i[s]
24 עדת כול בני הצדק המה [מקימ]יֹ[ן הברית הסרים מלכת [בד]רֹךֹ העם ואל[ו]היך הֹואה	24 [the congregation of all the sons of justice, who] establish the covenant, who avoid walking [on the p]ath of the people. And 'your G[o]d' is
25 מלכי צדק אשר יצי[ל]מה מי]ֹדֹ בליעל ואשר אמר והעברתמה שו[פר ב]כֹוֹ[א]רֹץ	25 [Melchizedek who will fr]ee [them from the han]d of Belial. And as for what he said: 'And you shall blow the ho[rn in] all the [l] and (of)...' (Lev 25:9)

Prophetic Exegesis

The other thematic pesher that we will address is 11Q13.[59] This manuscript has a total of eight fragments, with column two being the one that is most legible. In this column the text describes the deliverance that Melchizedek will bring to the captives of Israel. The identity of Melchizedek is a question that has caught the attention of scholars. Some have argued that Melchizedek is an intermediary, like the angel Michael, while others have instead proposed that Melchizedek represents another title for Yahweh.[60] More recently, Rick Van de Water has tried to mediate both of these positions by positing that the role of Melchizedek represents an earlier version of what the rabbis believed to be the "two powers in heaven."[61] The precise identity of Melchizedek is not our main focus, but rather how prophetic exegesis happens in this text. Whether Melchizedek is an angel or Yahweh, the use of Scripture is explicit in describing that the deliverance of the captives will happen as the fulfillment of prophecy.[62] Just like 4Q174, this pesher gathers passages from not only the Prophets, but also from Torah and Psalms to illustrate how they all point to this eschatological deliverance.

Our text establishes the redemptive vision beginning in lines 2–3 with two passages from Torah that deal with economic justice. Lev 25:13 introduces the "Year of Jubilee" (שנת היובל) when each person returns to his property as a sign of release of duties. For its part Deut 15:2 contextualizes this jubilee with the remission of debts and the fair treatment that the creditor needs to give to his neighbor. The pesher imaginatively transforms this socio-economic context into a word for the last days, where the "neighbor" becomes the "captives" (השבויים).[63] The concept of the "captives" appears in the DSS to refer to Israel (4Q385a 18.3), to the spoils of wars (1Q20 22.4–25; 1QM 12.10), but more importantly it denotes the "captives of Israel" (שבי ישראל) which is a

---

59 Florentino García Martínez, Eibert J.C. Tigchelaar, and Adam S. van der Woude, *Qumran Cave 11.II (11Q2–18, 11Q20–31)*, DJD XXIII (Oxford: Clarendon Press, 1998), 221–242.

60 For those who argue that Melchizedek represents an angelic figure see: F. Garcia Martinez, *Qumran and Apocalyptic* (Leiden: Brill, 1992), 176; James VanderKam, *The Dead Sea Scrolls Today* (Grand Rapids: Eerdmans, 1994), 171. On the other hand, for those who hold that Melchizedek is a reference to God, see: Franco Manzi, *Melchisedek e l'angelologia nell'epistola agli Ebrei e a Qumran* (Rome: Pontifical Biblical Institute, 1997), 67–96.

61 Rick Van de Water, "Michael or Yhwh? Toward Identifying Melchizedek in 11Q13," *JSP* 16 (2006): 75–86.

62 In taking this approach I am siding with Jean Carmignac who was more concerned with the theme of deliverance described in this pesher. For Carmignac Melchizedek does play an important redeeming role, but the center of this text lies in the deliverance of the captives from the dominion of Belial. For Carmignac's approach see: Carmignac, "Le Document de Qumrân," 343–78.

63 In its translation of 11Q13, Florentino Garcia Martinez reconstructs this line and cites the prophecy of Isaiah 61:1. See: Florentino Garcia Martinez, *The Dead Sea Scrolls Translated: The Qumran Texts in English* (Grand Rapids: Eerdmans, 1996), 139.

representation that the sectarians use in CD 6:5. In these initial lines we have a prediction of deliverance for the sectarians, where they see the words of Torah representing a time when they will experience liberty from their captivity. The following lines add further details on how this deliverance will take place.

Lines 4–9 clarify two main points: first, who will bring forth this deliverance and second, how will it take place. Following the interpretation of "captives", the pesher introduces the figure of Melchizedek as the one who will bring them back. With a language reminiscent of the prophecy in Isa 61, here Melchizedek takes on the role of God's herald. He is the one who will release the captives from their debts, which the pesher identifies as "their iniquities" (עוונותיהמה). In addition, lines 6–8 show that this release will follow the chronology of the weeks of jubilees, which ends with the "Day of Atonement" (יום כפורים) for the Sons of Light and for the men of the lot of Melchizedek.[64] Line 9 culminates with the proclamation of the "year of grace" (שנת הרצון) and the exaltation of the "holy ones of God" (קדושי אל). In these lines we have a creative interpretation that mixes legal and prophetic language from Isa 61 to describe a future event. In employing this exegetical strategy the text uses prior actors from Scripture and assigns them new roles. The captives become the sectarians as it is explained by the inclusion of different titles that metaphorically refer to this group, and Melchizedek takes on the role of deliverer that the herald in Isaiah attributes to God. In addition, the pesher confirms the heavenly identity of Melchizedek in lines 10–11 by introducing three consecutive passages from Psalms that describe God establishing his supremacy and justice (Ps 82:1, 7:8–9, 82:2). With the last citation and the question regarding injustice, the pesher transitions to describe the manner of the deliverance.

Lines 12–14 confirm that Melchizedek will indeed carry out the vengeance of God against Belial and the spirits of his lot. The intriguing part happens in line 14 when the pesher describes that Melchizedek will receive help from "all the gods" (כול אלי). The manuscript cuts off at this junction and we do not know exactly who these "gods" are or what their relationship is to the "sons of God" (בני אל) that appear at the tail end of this line. Florentino Garcia Martinez restores this line as follows: "to his aid shall come all the gods of justice; he is the one who will prevail on this day over all the sons of God, and he will preside over this assembly."[65] According to this restoration Melchizedek along with these other heavenly beings will bring deliverance

---

64 Ibid, 140. Garcia Martinez translates "sons of God" instead of Sons of Light in line 8.
65 Ibid, 140.

Prophetic Exegesis 81

to the sectarians. The end result of this victory is that he will preside over the
assembly of the gods. This picture is comparable with the descriptions that
we will see in 1QM, where God along with angelic beings plays a key role in
bringing forth the victory for the Sons of Light. Plus, in the end God is the one
crowned in a procession toward Zion (1QM 19.1–11). The similarity with 1QM
would suggest that Melchizedek in 11Q13 represents God, but again we are
working with a reconstructed text and there is not much more that can be
said besides the obvious that Melchizedek along with these heavenly beings
will fight on behalf of the sectarians.

Lines 15–25 mainly deal with the prophecy of Isa 52:7 and add supporting material from Daniel and Isa 61:2. Line 15 begins by elaborating on the
"day of peace" (יום השלום) that line 14 introduced. To do so it cites Isa 52:7,
which describes the appearance of a "messenger" (מבשר) who announces
peace, salvation, and God's reign over Zion. From this point forward the pesher breaks down what each of the constituent parts of this passage denotes.
First off, the "mountains" (הרים) and the messenger represent prophetic figures that will appear during this time. Differently from other passages that
we see in the DSS, the designation of the prophets here is not preceded by either the title "servants" (עבדי) or "books" (ספרי), which would indicate that
it is talking either about the historical prophets, like Isaiah or Jeremiah, or
the prophetic books. Perhaps what we have here is a reference to prophets
in a generic sense that will be intermediaries between God and the people.[66]
The legislative material in the Temple Scroll regarding prophets (11Q19 51.1–5;
54.8–18) and the attitudes toward false prophecy that we see in CD 5.20–6.3
and 1QHa 12.13–17 support that the sectarians did not believe that prophecy
was dead, but that it was part of their future destiny.[67] As for the messenger
the pesher interprets it as the "anointed" (משיח) predicted in Daniel. In Dan
9:25 Gabriel announces in his explanation of Jeremiah's seventy-year prophecy that a future anointed prince will appear to bring forth the restoration of
Jerusalem.

Line 19 continues by describing the work of the messenger in announcing salvation, by linking it with the prophecy of Isa 61:2 where the messenger
of God announces comfort to the afflicted. The forthcoming deliverance will
be one where the messenger instructs the afflicted in to the "age of the world
in truth" (קצי העולם באמת) which echoes Daniel's penitent prayer in 9:13

---

66 Jassen, *Mediating the Divine*, 179. Here Jassen states that "the eschatological context
of the text as a whole, and this passage in particular suggests that the classical biblical prophets are not in view. Rather, 'prophets' here refers to those who will appear in the eschatological age."

67 Ibid., 300.

when he recollects Israel's failure to reflect in God's truth. Thus, what Israel could not accomplish in the past, the future eschatological community will be able to fulfill.

From lines 21–22 the condition of the text contains many gaps that prevent us from properly interpreting how each of these fragments interconnects. It is not until line 23 when the pesher picks up the end of the prophecy in Isa 52:7 that deals with the word to Zion that God reigns. Although there are gaps in the text, one possibility is that Zion represents the congregation of "sons of justice" (בני הצדק), which is another way of referring to the sectarians (cf. 4Q259 3.10). We also learn that this congregation will establish the covenant and turn from the ways of the people, which goes back to the beginning of our text where it describes how the community was steered away from its contemporaries. Line 24 begins to clarify who "your God" (אלוהיך) is, but the ensuing line contains gaps that prevent us from ascertaining what the original subject was. A plausible explanation is that "your God" represents Melchizedek. Now this brings us back to the issue above about Melchizedek's identity: Is Melchizedek another way of referring to God by creatively combining the words מלך and צדק? Or is he a type of messianic intermediary like Michael is in the book of Daniel? 1QM 17.7 provides an intriguing example where it states that Michael is exalted among the "gods" (אלים). Perhaps Melchizedek is seen in the same light as an intermediary or an angelical figure who has access to God and engages in the mission of deliverance of the faithful.

In any case, these latter lines demonstrate that the messenger represents an individual who brings forth awareness that delivers the community. This messenger is one who along with the other prophets will be part of the future. Who this messenger is precisely cannot be ascertained, but what is amply clear is that the future of the sectarians was seen as one where prophecy, truth, and intimacy with the divine were all anticipated. 11Q13, like 4Q174, is a prophetic text in the sense that it foretells what will happen in the eschaton while also guaranteeing that the holy ones will be exalted from their captivities. 11Q13 adopts different passages from the prophets as signs of God's actions that were predicted by these servants. The holy ones in both 4Q174 and in 11Q13 can, therefore, trust that their current trials and challenges at the hand of Belial and his spirits will come to an end when the jubilee comes and brings forth an intimacy with God that cannot be broken.

In many respects both Pesharim echo what 1QM describes, where the future is anticipated by a prophetic interpretation of Scripture where God and the divine beings participate in bringing to fruition a new hope. This vision

Prophetic Exegesis 83

is also attested in the Rule Books where the sectarians are instructed to abide to a set of ordinances in order to enter and maintain their place among the chosen ones.

ii. Rule Books

In this section we will deal with two passages from the Rule Books. These books are a special type of texts because they develop many topics that work together to establish the identity of the groups that they address. Some of these topics include: reflections on the community's origin, hierarchical structure of its membership, purity and ethical norms that the members must follow, and teachings on the relationship that the members must have with one another and with the outside world.[68] Despite the fact that other texts in the DSS deal with many of these aspects, the Rule Books are particularly geared towards providing this type of training that its members must adhere to if they are going to be part of this group.

We must also mention that the evidence from the DSS attests to the presence of other instructional books. For instance, CD 16.3–4 mentions the "Book of the Time Divisions by Jubilees and Weeks" (ספר מחלקות העתים ליובליהם ובשבועותיהם), which purportedly contains all the specifics of the times when Israel was blind to the precepts of Torah. 1QM 15.5 introduces a prayer book labeled the "Book of the Rule of Its Time" (ספר סרך עתו), which contains the prayer for the appointed time of the battle that the Chief Priest along with the priests and Levites shall read aloud before the Sons of Light. CD 10.6 and 14.7 also mention the "Book of Meditation" (ספר ההגי), which along with the Torah is one of the mandatory texts that priests and judges alike should be well versed before they can lead the people.[69] It is also a text that every Israelite shall be instructed in from early childhood according to 1QSa 1.7. Also, 1QS 6.7–8 describes a time when the sectarian community will read aloud together from the "Book," and they will seek justice and bless the community. The references to these books point to the instructional nature of these communities where not only the Torah but also these other texts played a role in forming the beliefs of this people.[70] However, 1QS (Rule of the Com-

---

68 For in-depth introduction of the Rule Texts and the nature of the communities behind them, see: Charlotte Hempel, *The Qumran Rule Texts in Context* (Tübingen: Mohr Siebeck, 2013), 1–20.

69 4Q265 7.6 also mentions the ספר ההגי as something that a priest shall be well versed, so as not to depart from the community.

70 Lawrence Schiffman, "The Dead Sea Scrolls and the History of the Jewish Book," *AJS Review* 34 (2010): 359–365.

munity), CD (Damascus Document), 1QSa (Rule of the Congregation), and their respective parallels from Caves 4 to 6 are the only extant manuscripts at our disposal. Specifically, in the case of 1QS and CD, they have been instrumental in piecing together a model to discern the genesis of their respective communities and their religious/ideological presuppositions in relation to the Scriptures and their surrounding sociological context in Israel.[71] These Rule Books along with the references to other books have allowed scholars to reconstruct a picture of these communities that based much of its constitution, teaching, and celebration of the communal gatherings on these codified texts along with the Scriptures. As we shall see in our analysis, prophetic exegesis happens within these books in accounts that reflect on that particular community's birth and their role in the fulfillment of prophecy.

Rule for the Community (1QS 8.1–16)

בעצת היחד שנים עשר איש וכוהנים 1 שלושה תמימים בכול הנגלה מכול	1 In the party of the *Yahad* there shall be twelve laymen and three priests who are blameless in the light of all that has been revealed from the whole
התורה לעשות אמת וצדקה ומשפט 2 ואהבת חסד והצנע לכת איש אם רעהו	2 Law, so as to work truth, righteousness, justice, lovingkindness and humility, one with another.
לשמור אמונה בארץ ביצר סמוך 3 ורוח נשברה ולרצת עוון בעושי משפט	3 They are to preserve faith in the land with self-control and a broken spirit, atoning for sin by working justice and
וצרת מצרף ולהתהלכ עם כול ב{} 4 מדת האמת ובתכון העת בהיות אלה בישראל	4 suffering affliction. They are to walk with all by the standard of truth and the dictates proper to the age. When such men as these come to be in Israel,
נכונה {ה}עצת היחד באמת 5 למטעת עולם בית {ל} vacat קודש לישראל וסוד קודש	5 then shall the party of the *Yahad* truly be established, *vacat* an 'eternal planting' (Jub. 16:26), a temple for Israel, and-mystery!-a Holy
קודשים לאהרון עדי אמת למשפט 6 ובכ{}°חירי רצון לכפר בעד הארץ ולהשב	6 of Holies for Aaron; true witnesses to justice, chosen by God's will to atone for the land and to recompense
לרשעים גמולם vacat היאה 7 חומת הבחן פנת יקר בל vacat	7 the wicked their due. *vacat* They will be 'the tested wall, the precious cornerstone' (Isa 28:16) whose *vacat*

---

71 Hempel, *The Qumran Rule Texts*, 65–105. Maxine L. Grossman, *Reading for History in the Damascus Document* (Leiden: Brill, 2002), 1–37.

8 יזדעזעו יסודותיהו ובל יחישו ממקומם vacat מעון קודש קודשים	8 foundations shall neither be shaken nor swayed, *vacat* a fortress, a Holy of Holies
9 לאהרון בדעת כולם לברית משפט ולקריב ריח ניחוח ובית תמים ואמת בישראל	9 for Aaron, all of them knowing the Covenant of Justice and thereby offering a sweet savor. They shall be a blameless and true house in Israel,
10 להקם {} ברית לחו}{קות עולם והיו לרצון לכפר בעד הארץ ולחרוץ משפט רשעה {בّתّمّیّם דّרّךّ} ואין עולה בהכון אלה ביסוד היחד שנתים ימים בתמים דרך	10 upholding { } the covenant of eternal statutes. They shall be an acceptable sacrifice, atoning for the land and ringing in the verdict against evil, so that perversity ceases to exist. When these men have been grounded in the instruction of the *Yahad* for two years-provided they be blameless in their conduct-
11 יבדלו קודש בתוכ עצת אנשי היחד וכול דבר הנסתר מישראל ונמ־צאו לאיש	11 they shall be set apart as holy in the midst of the men of the *Yahad*. No biblical doctrine concealed from Israel but discovered by the
12 הדורש אל יסתרהו מאלה מיראת רוח נסוגה ובהיות אלה ליחד בישראל	12 Interpreter is to be hidden from these men out of fear that they might backslide. When such men as these come to be in Israel,
13 בתכונים האלה יבדלו מתוך מושב הנשי העול ללכת למדבר לפנות שם את דרכ הואהא	13 conforming to these doctrines, they shall separate from the session of perverse men to go to the wilderness, there to prepare the way of truth/ the Lord,
14 כאשר כתוב במדבר פנו דרך ישרו בערבה מסלה לאלוהינו	14 as it is written, 'In the wilderness prepare the way of the Lord, make straight in the desert a highway for our God' (Isa 40:3).
15 היאה מדרש התורה אֹ[ש]רֹ צוה ביד מושה לעשות ככול הנגלה עת בעת	15 This means the expounding of the Law, decreed by God through Moses for obedience, that being defined by what has been revealed for each age,
16 וכֹאשר גלו הנביאים ברוח קודשו וכול איש מאנשי היחד ברית...	16 and by what the prophets have revealed by His holy spirit. No man belonging to the Covenant of the Community...

From the outset, the "Rule of the Yahad" (סרך היחד) establishes its purpose to guide the readers to fulfill everything taught by Moses and the Prophets (1QS 1.1–3). The introduction proceeds by describing the mission for the Yahad as a community that follows God's precepts and vows to love the Sons of Light and detest the Sons of Darkness (1.7–11) while living under the dominion of Belial (1.16–23). The concepts that we see in this introduction will

86 INTERTEXTUALITY AND PROPHETIC EXEGESIS IN THE WAR SCROLL OF QUMRAN

appear in column 8 where we encounter the clearest example of prophetic exegesis.

Column 8 starts by providing a description of the number and qualities of the individuals that make up the "party of the Yahad" (עצת היחד). Line 1 states that the council shall be made up of twelve men and three priests. The symbolism of the number twelve is important, because of its connections to the tribes of Israel. Several passages also describe the summoning and appointment of twelve men who would represent the twelve tribes of Israel in different situations (Num 1:44, Deut 1:23, Josh 3:12, 4:2–20; Ezra 8:24; Sir 49:10).[72] The number twelve in 1QS 8.1 is one of two references that provides a specific description of the membership number of this council. The other reference happens in 4Q265 Frg. 7.7 where it describes that according to the revelation given to the prophets, the council shall be made up of fifteen men twelve laymen and three priests in agreement with 1QS 8.

Although we do not exactly know if the actual number of the council was either twelve or fifteen, what is clear from these texts is that this was a mixed group of lay people and priests who were to be blameless in everything that was revealed in the Torah (תמימים בכול הנגלה מכול התורה).[73] This standard of perfection appears several times in 1QS and in the other Rule Books, but the use of "blameless" (תמים) in conjunction with "revealed" (הנגלה) appears in 1QS 1.8 and 9.19. In each of these references the revelations consists of the teachings that the Yahad has received from the Torah and the Prophets. For instance, 1QS 8.15–16 emphasize this point when it describes that the study (מדרש) of Torah and the Prophets is the council's main mission. We will deal with this reference below, but for now it suffices to say that Torah and the Prophets are the revelation that the council shall be perfect in observing, which lines 2–4 expound by listing the different attributes that the members must possess.

The end of line 4 introduces a fulfillment formula that leads into a deeper description of the council and its mission. It asserts that the fulfillment of "these" (אלה) will establish the council in truth. The question is: What is the referent of "these"? Is it the men of the council? Or is it the list of attributes of justice recounted in lines 1–4?

One possible explanation comes from 1QS 9.3 where the same line appears. Here seems to refer to the rules that the Yahad will fulfill in accordance with the regulations. 1QS 9.6 adds that once this list has been fulfilled the

---

72 Also, Acts refers to the twelve apostles as the pillars of the Church in Acts 1:15–26.

73 In 4Q174 Frgs. 1–2 Col. i.17 where it cites that the Sons of Zadok and the men of the council are the ones called to distance themselves from the idols according to the prophecy in Ezek 37:23.

Prophetic Exegesis

Yahad shall separate themselves and become a holy house for Aaron. 1QS 9.3–6 essentially uses the same formula as in 8.4 to underscore that the fulfillment of these deeds will establish the community. We can suggest, therefore, that 1QS 8.4 has a similar expectation; that is, when the deeds of Torah are a reality in Israel then the council of the Yahad will be established in truth.[74]

Lines 5–7 continue by describing that the council shall become an "Eternal Plant" (מטעת עולם) and "the tested wall the precious cornerstone" (הבחן פנת יקר חומת). The image of the Eternal Plant appears five times in the DSS (1QS 11.8; 1QHa 16.6; 4Q265 Frg. 7.8; 4Q418 Frg. 81.13). In all these references the metaphor represents a Qumran community. Prior use of this metaphor comes from the prophecy of Isa 61:3, where the "Plant of the Yahweh" (מטע יהוה) refers to the people who will experience the deliverance that God's herald brings. The interesting point to highlight is that at several points in the DSS, the sectarians adopt some of the lowly titles from Isaiah 61 as a representation of themselves.[75] The other two sources for this metaphor come in Jubilees (4Q216–4Q222) and 1 Enoch. Jub. 4Q219 2.30 and 4Q221 1.8 (cf. Jub. 21.24) describe the "plant of truth" (האמת מטעת) as Abraham's descendants who will bring blessing to all the generations of eternity (4Q219 2.33). In the case of 1 En. 10.16, part of God's commission to Michael was not only to imprison Shemihazah and destroy the giants, but to usher in a new era where the "plant of righteousness and truth" will appear and the people will worship God. Also, 1 En. 93:5, 10 describe that the "plant of righteousness" will rise both at the end of the third week as well as at the conclusion of the seventh week. In the last week, this "plant of righteousness" represents the chosen ones to whom will be given sevenfold wisdom and knowledge, in order to uproot violence and deceit as well as to execute judgment among the people (93.11). These concepts of being chosen and able to render judgments appear in 1QS 8.6–7, where it states that the council shall "atone for the land and to recompense the wicked their due" (לכפר בעד הארץ ולהשב לרשע־ים גמולם).

The reference to the "tested wall the precious cornerstone" (הבחן פנת יקר חומת) in 8.7 is the only instance that appears in the DSS. The source of this image is the prophecy of Isa 28:16, where God predicts the establishment of this sure foundation which verse seventeen explains by stating that

---

74 This interpretation goes against the translation that we have used for this line. The end of 8.4 should be translated: "when these things happen in Israel..."

75 For the most representative uses of ענוים in the DSS, see: 1QHa 13.21, 1QHa 19.25, 1QHa 23.14, 4Q88 9.14, 4Q163 19.1, 4Q165 6.5, 4Q171 2.9, 4Q434 1.3. For the most representative uses of שבוים (i.e. captives) in the DSS, see: CD 6.5 (שבי ישראל), 11Q13 2.4 (השבויים). For the most representative uses of פקח־קוח in the DSS, see: 4Q434 1.2. For the most representative uses of אבלים in the DSS, see: 1QHa 19.22a; 4Q177 1.9; 4Q427 1.3–4.

"justice" and "righteousness" will be the instruments that will lay this foundation. The cornerstone appears elsewhere in Scripture. Ps 118:22 describes that the stone that the builders rejected actually became the cornerstone. Zech 10:4 describes God's angers towards the leaders of Judah and predicts that from the flock of Judah will come both the instruments of war (קשת מלח־ מזה) and also the instruments of construction (פנה and יתד). The metaphors of the "eternal plant" and the "tested wall the precious cornerstone" echo the language of Scripture to describe how the council of the Yahad will become this important piece to accomplish God's will, which lines 6 and 10 describe as atoning for the land. It will also be a holy dwelling for Aaron, which underscores that the council shall be place of justice and teaching. Therefore, the council is a critical piece in the eschatological destiny of Israel, which 1QS as well as other sectarian documents assert.

The next prophetic interpretation comes in lines 14–16 with the citation and explanation of another word from Isaiah. After the men of the council had been in the Yahad for two years they shall be consecrated and privy with every teaching from the "Interpreter" (לאיש הדורש). At that moment they shall withdraw to the desert and begin their ultimate mission. Line 12 introduces this mission with a temporal clause, which is similar to the one in line 4. Because the temporal clause is ambiguous, the question that emerges is about the antecedent that "these" (אלה) refers to. In line 4 we proposed that the antecedent refers to the deeds of justice that the men of the council shall observe. In line 12 we propose that the consecration and separation of the men of the council (יבדלו) is the antecedent of the אלה. Plus, line 13 introduces another אלה, although this time it refers to the men of the council who will separate (יבדלו) from the rest of the population. The purpose of this separation is presented with two infinitival constructions "to walk" and "to prepare" (ללכת and לפנות) that denote the mission of the men, which is to fulfill the prophecy of Isaiah 40:3 in preparing the way of Yahweh. Line 15 immediately explains that "the way" is the "study of Torah" (מדרש התורה) that was commanded through Moses to do everything that was revealed for each age.

In 1QS, מדרש appears in 1QS 6.24, 8.15, and 8.26 where it denotes "to study," whether it be the inquiry among the community in matters of communal regulation or in matters of study when the council of the Yahad meets. These uses clarify that the council is to study the Torah of Moses, which has been revealed from age to age. Line 15 repeats the belief that the Torah is revelation which was initially introduced in lines 1–2, and it adds the revelation by the Prophets. Consequently, the council of the Yahad and its followers shall

Prophetic Exegesis   89

devote themselves to the study of Torah as expounded by the Interpreter. This means that for this programmatic vision of the future to take place and for the council and the sectarians to be included into what will happen, the devotion to the study of the Torah has to be a central part for their daily living. Failure to do so, as lines 17–26 describes, creates the risk of a person being shunned from the gathering of the community. Returning to the prophecy of Isaiah in line 14, we must compare this use with other uses elsewhere.

For instance, outside of the DSS the prophecy of Isa 40:3 appears prominently in the gospel accounts in the New Testament. The Synoptic Gospels as well as the gospel of John cite the word of Isaiah as being directly fulfilled in the ministry of John the Baptizer (Mark 1:1–3; Matt 3:1–3; Luke 3:1–4; John 1:23). He is identified as the "voice" that calls the people to draw near to their God. Whereas the Hebrew in Isaiah denotes that the voice calls for the preparation of God's way "in the desert," the gospels point out that the voice (e.g. John himself) was "in the desert" calling the people to his baptism of repentance. The interpretation of John of being in the desert discloses the social reality, where charismatic movements took place in the wilderness. Consequently, we see in the gospels that John causes the people to wonder if he is the prophet or future messiah, which the New Testament associates with Jesus of Nazareth. For our purposes, however, it is important to draw out particular nuances that each of the gospel passages has in depicting John as a prophetic voice that called the people in Judea to draw near to God.

Mark 1:2–4 introduces John as the fulfillment of Isaiah's prophecy. The quote that Mark uses, however, is not just of Isa 40:3 but of Mal 3:1. By using the passage of Malachi, John is identified as "the messenger" (τὸν ἄγγελόν) who will prepare the way of God. Luke 3:2–6 introduces the ministry of John with an interesting description that places John as a prophetic figure. Luke 3:2 states that "the word of God came to John son of Zechariah in the desert" (ἐγένετο ῥῆμα θεοῦ ἐπὶ Ἰωάννην τὸν Ζαχαρίου υἱὸν ἐν τῇ ἐρήμῳ). The phrase "the word of God came to" (ἐγένετο ῥῆμα θεοῦ ἐπὶ) is similar to the phrase "the word of the Lord came" (ἐγένετο ῥῆμα κυρίου) that appears in several prophetic passages in the Septuagint, specifically in the stories of the prophet Elijah (3 Kgdms 17:2–8). The connection with Elijah is something that the gospel accounts make clear as they describe John in his attire and diet in the same light as the prophet Elijah (Mark 1:6; Matt 3:4; John 1:21–23; cf. 2 Kgs 1:8). The last significant aspect to raise is that Matt 3:2 describes that John preached repentance because "the kingdom of heaven has drawn near" (ἤγγικεν γὰρ ἡ βασιλεία τῶν οὐρανῶν).

The reference to the dawn of God's kingdom is an important aspect that we also note in the descriptions of the DSS, where eschatological language is used to depict the coming of a new age. Therefore, the use of the prophecy of Isa 40:3 in the gospels demonstrates that John is represented as a prophet and a messenger who is endowed with the word of God to announce the coming of God's kingdom. He is the fulfillment of the prophecy of Isaiah. Similarly, the establishment of the council and the "study of Torah" (מדרש התורה) in 1QS 8 becomes the fulfillment of Isaiah's prophecy. This becomes more apparent by the continuous repetition of the line "when these happen in Israel" (בהיות אלה בישראל) and the reiteration of its purpose "to atone for the land" (לכפר בעד הארץ) which appear here and in column 9. Furthermore, 1QS 9.11 describes that the council of the Yahad shall do all of this labor "until the Prophet and the Messiahs of Aaron and Israel come" (עד בוא נביא ומשיחי אהרון וישראל). This means that the mission of the council is in of itself a prelude to the mission of these messianic and prophetic figures which correlates with the gospel interpretation of John's mission preceding the ministry of Jesus of Nazareth. The prophecy of Isa 40:3, therefore, is a key text to not just understand the aspiration of a future messianic figure, but more importantly the preparatory efforts that Israel as a people had to do. In the case of 1QS 8 the "study of Torah" prepared the way, while in the New Testament repentance followed by baptism, which one could argue is an act of obedience to Torah, set the stage for the messianic leader.

Damascus Document (CD 1.1–11)

1 [ ] ועתה שמעו כל יודעי צדק ובינו במעשי	1 Listen, all you who recognize righteousness, and consider the deeds of
2 אל כי ריב לו עם כל בשר ומשפט יעשה בכל מנאציו	2 God; for He has a suit against every mortal and He executes judgment upon all who despise him.
3 כי במועלם אשר עזבוהו הסתיר פניו מישראל וממקדשו	3 When in their treachery they abandoned him He turned away from Israel and from His sanctuary
4 ויתנם לחרב ובזכרו ברית ראשנים השאיר שאירית	4 and gave them up to the sword; but when He remembered the covenant of the forefathers, He left a remnant
5 לישראל ולא נתנם לכלה ובקץ חרון שנים שלוש מאות	5 to Israel and did not allow them to be totally destroyed, but in a time of wrath three hundred
6 ותשעים לתיתו אותם ביד נבוכדנאצר מלך בבל	6 and ninety years when He put them into the power of Nebuchadnezzar, king of Babylon

Prophetic Exegesis 91

7 פקדם ויצמח מישראל ומאהרן שורש מטעת לירוש	7 he took care of them and caused to grow from Israel and from Aaron a root of planting to inherit
8 את ארצו ולדשן בטוב אדמתו ויבינו בעונם וידעו כי	8 His land and to grow fat on the good produce of His soil. They considered their iniquity and they knew that
9 אנשים אשימים הם ויהיו כעורים וכימגששים דרך	9 they were guilty men, and had been like the blind and like those groping for the way
10 שנים עשרים ויבן אל אל מעשיהם כי בלב שלם דרשוהו	10 twenty years. But God considered their deeds, that they had sought Him with a whole heart.
11 ויקם להם מורה צדק להדריכם בדרך לבו	11 And He raised up for them a teacher of righteousness to guide them in the way of His heart

The last example of prophetic exegesis that we will deal with comes in CD 1.1–11.[76] This passage like 1QS 8 relays information about the origin of the sect, and it does so by interpreting it as a fulfillment of prophecy. The start of our passage follows a gap in the manuscript with the abrupt command "and now listen!" (ועתה שמעו). The evidence from the Cave 4 manuscripts gives us additional information about what may have preceded this initial command. In 4Q266 Frg. 1.1–4 there is an extended introduction where we find a first person call presumably by a sage or teacher that warns the Sons of Light to separate from the path of the wicked until the appointed time when God will destroy their evil deeds.[77] Immediately after this warning the teacher draws the attention of the readers through the refrain "and now listen to me and I will instruct you" (ועתה שמעו לי ואודיעה) as he is about to disclose God's "plans" (מחשבות) which are kept hidden from the outsiders. This is an important line because it describes that the teacher is about to impart Torah and uncover mysteries; it is both a legal and sapiential line. After several gaps in the manuscript the next critical statement comes in Frg. 2i.1–6, where the teacher draws a stark contrast through a play on words between those who do not know God and those who do. Line 3 states that God ordained a "time of wrath" (קץ הרון) for the people who do not know God, while for those who

---

76 Jonathan Campbell, *The Use of Scripture in the Damascus Document 1–8, 19–20* (New York: De Gruyter, 1995). Charlotte Hempel, *The Laws of the Damascus Document* (Leiden: Brill, 1998). Charlotte Hempel, *The Damascus Texts* (Sheffield, England: Sheffield Academic Press, 2000).

77 4Q266 Frg. 1a–b lines 3–4 introduce some of the characters it identifies as wicked. One particular case worth mentioning is the מסיני גבול, which appear in CD 5.20 as the מסיני הג־ בול that is the false prophets.

seek the commandments they will have "appointed times of favor" (מועדי רצון) when they understand the "deep things" (עמוקות).[78] The evidence from 4Q266 helps to gather that the teacher is setting up the stage for the rest of his work. From the outset the aim of this text is to establish a threshold that separates the insiders from those outside. The use of dualistic concepts reveals the nature of this teacher's ideology as well as the belief that the community was living in the latter times. As we shall see below this dualism will become very important to assess how CD 1 interprets the community's origin as the fulfillment of prophecy; a word that originally applied for all Israel, but that CD interprets as directly impacting the sectarians as the remnant of Israel.

CD 1.1 addresses the reader and introduces the main topic of this section with the refrain "and now listen" (ועתה שמעו), which we saw in 4Q266. This refrain appears nine times throughout the scrolls: seven in CD and in the Cave 4 manuscripts (CD 1.1, 2.2, 2.14; 4Q266 2i.6, 2ii.2; 4Q268 1.9; 4Q270 2ii.19) and twice in other texts like 4Q185 and 4Q525. In all of these instances there is a component of instruction that the addresser is about to convey, and in CD 2.2 and 2.14 there is also an element of revelation as the teacher is about to uncover (גלה) wisdom to the addressees. CD 1.1 identifies these recipients as those who have "knowledge" (יודעי) and "understanding" (בינו) of God's righteous deeds. The use of these two verbs is significant, because it underscores that the sectarians were endowed with a special knowledge that allowed them to perceive and understand God's deeds.

Once we know who the addressees are, line 2 introduces the main topic of this section with a prophetic announcement. The use of the collocation "for a suit" (כי ריב) recalls prophetic passages where the prophets introduce God's complaint against the people. A particular connection exists with Jer 25:31 where a similar indictment happens against all flesh with a prediction of judgment by sword. Lines 3–4 proceed from this complaint to recollect the history of Israel and how God abandoned the nation. The descriptions of God hiding his face and giving the nation to the sword allude to Ezek 39.23–24, where it describes how Israel was abandoned and handed over to the adversaries. It is also worth mentioning that line 3 adds that God hid from his sanctuary, which supports the interpretation that what was happening in the Temple was consequential to the exile. Plus, by bringing up this interpretation our text hints at the displeasure that the sectarians had with their current sanctuary.[79] After setting the stage for God's suit against the people, our

---

78 Notice the use of מועדי, which denotes an appointment time but is also used for festivals (CD 3.14, 12.4; 1QS 1.15; 1QSb 3.2; 1QHa 12.12; and 4Q216 2.8, 6.8).

79 These references describe the aspiration of a new and consecrated מקדש: 1QpHab 12.9;

Prophetic Exegesis   93

text briefly describes the condemnation of Israel and proceeds on a much different direction. Rather than elaborating on the judgment of Israel, the teacher introduces how God preserved a remnant.

CD 1.4b–8a describe that God remembered the covenant with Israel's ancestors and kept a "remnant" (שארית) away from judgment. The exact identity of the remnant is not clear at this point. The context suggests that this group had a direct bearing on the rise of the "plant" (מטעת) which 1QS 8.5 refers as the Yahad. Elsewhere in the DSS the remnant refers to the eschatological group that God will preserve.[80] Also, the fact that the plant comes from Aaron may suggest that this remnant was either a priestly group or a people whose cultic concerns gave rise to the sect. Lines 5–7 continue by describing that in a "time of wrath" (קץ חרון) exactly "three hundred and ninety years" after Israel was handed to Nebuchadrezzar, God caused the growth of the root of planting, which alludes to Ezek 4:5 where the prophet bears the punishment of Judah for "three hundred and ninety" days.[81] This chronological change from days to years shows an interpretive move like the one we see in Dan 9:23–27, where Jeremiah's seventy-year prophecy turns into seventy weeks. It also points perhaps to the symbolic nature of this number or more persuasively, to how CD interprets Israel's history as being directly fulfilled in the formation of the sect. These lines culminate in 8a with the promise that the sect will inherit the land and produce riches, which follows a prophetic

---

4Q174 Frg. 1–2 Col. i.21.6; 11Q19 35.7, 46.10. For a discussion on the sectarians and their stance regarding the Temple in Jerusalem, see: Craig A. Evans, *Opposition to the Temple: Jesus and the Dead Sea Scrolls* (New York: Doubleday, 1992), 235–253. Eyal Regev, "Abominated Temple and a Holy Community: The Formation of the Notions of Purity and Impurity in Qumran," *DSD* 10 (2003): 243– 278. Hilary Evans Kapfer, "The Relationship Between the Damascus Document and the Community Rule: Attitudes Toward the Temple as a Test Case," *DSD* 14 (2007): 152–177. Hanne von Weissenberg, "The Centrality of the Temple in 4QMMT," in *Dead Sea Scrolls: Texts and Context* (Leiden: Brill, 2010), 293–305. Martin Goodman, "The Qumran Sectarians and the Temple in Jerusalem," in *Dead Sea Scrolls: Texts and Context* (Leiden: Brill, 2010): 263–273. Cecilia Wassen, "Visions of the Temple: Conflicting Images of the Eschaton," *Svensk exegetisk årsbok* 76 (2011): 41–59. Eileen M. Schuller, "Worship, Temple, and Prayer in the Dead Sea Scrolls," in *Judaism in Late Antiquity: A Systemic Reading of the Dead Sea Scrolls* (Leiden: Brill, 2001), 125–143.

80 For the most representative references and uses of שאר in the sectarian documents, see: a) For the eschatological remnant (CD 1.4; 1QM 13.8, 14.5–9, 1QHa 14.8); b) For those who will not have a remnant (CD 2.6; 1QS 4.14, 5.13; 1QSb 1.7; 1QM 1.6, 4.2, 1QHa 14.32 15.22, 27.2). For a discussion on the sectarians representation of themselves as the eschatological remnant, see: Philip R Davies, "'Old' and 'new' Israel in the Bible and the Qumran scrolls: Identity and Difference," in *Defining Identities: We, You, and the Other in the Dead Sea Scrolls* (Leiden: Brill, 2008), 33–42. John S. Bergsma, "Qumran Self-Identity: 'Israel' or 'Judah'?" *DSD* 15 (2008): 172–189. James C. VanderKam, "The Pre-history of the Qumran Community with a Reassessment of CD 1:5–11," in *Dead Sea Scrolls and Contemporary Culture* (Leiden: Brill, 2011), 59–76.

81 The combination שורש מטעת happens only in CD 1 and in the Cave 4 parallels (4Q266 2.11–12; 4Q268 1.14).

pattern of illustrating the blessing that will come to those whom God favors (Amos 9:1–15; Ezek 40–48; and Dan 12).

After introducing the plant as the fulfillment of prophecy, CD 1.8–11 relay the coming of the Teacher of Righteousness. The latter part of line 8 uses the same verbs that appear in line 1 (i.e. ידע/בין). In this line the verbs describe the awareness that the sectarian people had that in spite of their willingness to please God they still needed direction, for they had been "like the blind and those groping for the way for twenty years" (ויהיו כעורים וכימגששים דרך שנים עשרים). This situation leads into God discerning the situation and raising a leader. The Teacher of Righteousness is to be the one to guide the sectarians in the path of his heart (להדריכם בדרך לבו). The Hiphil use of "path" (דרך) appears in Scripture in passages like Isa 42:16, 48:17, Hab 3:19, and Ps 25:5, where God acts as a shepherd who steers the people in the right direction. The Teacher of Righteousness likewise is the one who will act as a sapiential and prophetic figure that will guide the sect and teach them in the right path as they learn from the fate of the evil generation. In line 12 our text transitions into describing the evil generation as the opposite of the righteous remnant, and in line 14 it introduces the "Man of Mockery" (איש הלצון) who stands in stark contrast to the Teacher of Righteousness.

Line 13 refers to the "company of traitors" (בוגדים) originally introduced in line 12 as a "rebellious cow" (כפרה סוררה), which is an expression that appears in Hos 4:6. The representation of Israel as a confounded people appears also in line 9 where the plant is described as a blind people. The difference, however, is that the plant acknowledges its confusion and accepts to be guided by the righteous teacher, whereas the company of traitors does not realize its situation and is misled by the Man of Mockery. Further, lines 14–15 depict that this false teacher "sprayed on Israel the waters of deceit and caused them to wander in the wasteland without a path" (הטיף ליש־ ראל מימי כזב ויתעם בתוהו לא דרך). The first description uses the verb נטף, which typically means to flow or drip (e.g. Judg 5:4; Amos 9:13; and Joel 3:18) but is also used metaphorically in the Hiphil for the flowing of words as it happens in prophecy (e.g. Amos 7:16; Ezek 20:46; Mic 2:11). In the second description the false teacher steers Israel through the wasteland, which is a phrase that appears in Job 12: and Ps 107:40. The intriguing aspect is that in both of these references God is the one who leads the people in that path, whereas CD ascribes that role to the Man of Mockery. This description also contrasts with the work of the Teacher of Righteousness who will properly lead the sectarians in the righteous way. The dualism in this text is obvious with the assertion of two paths, two teachers, and therefore two distinct

Prophetic Exegesis

destinies for the followers.

With line 16 we begin to glean more about this Man of Mockery. For instance, we see that he "tore the boundary marker" (לסיע גבול). CD 5.20 uses a similar expression for the false prophets who are referred as the "Boundary Shifters" (מסיגי הגבול). The notion of boundary (גבול) happens in the scrolls as the precepts from Torah or wisdom that Israel was bound to follow (cf. CD 1.16, 20.25; 1QS 10.25; 4Q416 2.6). The "shifters" (מסיגי), on the other hand, are those individuals whose teachings turned Israel away from the proper interpretation of the covenant. A possible candidate for this title is the Pharisees who were seen by many groups, including the sectarians, as rivals because of their particular interpretation of Torah.[82] Also, the phrase "sought flattery (smooth things)" (דרשו בחלקות) in line 18 which is typically linked with the Pharisees, points at least to the possibility that the Man of Mockery was associated with a movement that became the Pharisees.[83] Elsewhere in the scrolls the Man of Mockery is referred to as the "Man of Deceit" (איש הכזב). In Pesher Habakkuk this man (1QpHab 2.1, 5.1) is the rival of the Teacher of Righteousness and the one who led Israel astray. This point is also made in 4Q171 1.26 where it depicts that the Man of Deceipt led the people to listen to the deceptions and empty words instead of the words of the "Interpreter of Knowledge" (מליץ דעת), which could potentially be another way of depicting the Teacher of Righteousness. These lines in CD 1 culminate with the Man of Mockery and the destiny that came to those who heeded his words, which CD 2.1 describes as the annihilation of their impure deeds.

Scholars have used CD 1 to posit theories about the birth of the sect following a split among the Essenes.[84] The evidence in these lines suggests that it was not necessarily a split within a group that prompted the formation of the sectarian groups, but rather a split with the rest of the Israel following matters of proper interpretation of Torah. CD 1 can be interpreted as a coming out of exile passage, as an exodus, where the Teacher of Righteousness represents

---

82 Lawrence Schiffman, "The Pharisees and Their Legal Traditions According to the Dead Sea Scrolls," *DSD* 8 (2001): 262–277. James VanderKam, "Those Who Look for Smooth Things, Pharisees, and Oral Law," in *Emanuel: Studies in Hebrew Bible, Septuagint, and Dead Sea Scrolls in Honor of Emanuel Tov* (Leiden: Brill, 2003), 465–477.

83 John Collins, *Beyond the Qumran Community* (Grand Rapids: Eerdmans, 2010), 48–50. In this analysis Collins is open to the position originally proposed by Hartmut Stegemann (cf. Harmut Stegemann, *Die Entstehung der Qumrangemeinde* (Bonn: Univ zu Bonn, 1971), 227–228) that the איש הלצון led a breakaway group that eventually became the Pharisees. See also Baumgarten analysis of the phrase דרשו בחלקות and how CD uses it to designate the Pharisees (Albert I. Baumgarten, "The Name of the Pharisees," *JBL* 102 (1983): 420–422).

84 Florentino Garcia Martinez, "A 'Groningen' Hypothesis of Qumran Origins and Early History," *RevQ* 14 (1990): 521–541. Lawrence Schiffman, "Origin and Early History of the Qumran Sect," *BA* 58 (1995): 37–48.

a type of Moses, in that he is the righteous leader full of wisdom in order to direct Israel in the right path. The use of the refrain "and now listen" (ועתה שמעו) echoes passages in Deuteronomy where Moses, as a preacher, calls the people to heed the words of Yahweh. In the same fashion the teacher in CD is calling the readers to heed this interpretation of their history, which goes back to God's plan to preserve a remnant following the exile. The ideas of a plan and God's systematic revelation to the remnant are key themes throughout the Damascus Document, as the sectarians believe per the teaching of Scripture that they are the new Israel and the recipients of God's revelation.

The main contribution that this passage provides to our argument is that Scripture was used in a prophetic manner, to explain history and to contextualize it to predict the future of the latter generations. The combination of wisdom and halakhic terminology as well as the periodization of history evinces a type of exegesis reminiscent of other texts of early Judaism that combine prophecy, wisdom, and law such as the apocalypses.

c. Summary

In this chapter we have developed the concept of prophetic exegesis from the standpoint of how it is used in the DSS. We noticed prior to analyzing the examples in the Qumran scrolls that there occurred a transition in prophetic teaching from an oral to a scribal enterprise as evinced by the prophet Jeremiah and his use of textual material to convey his prophecies. Although we acknowledge that all we know about these prophetic figures in Israel comes from the scribal record of these characters' stories, we assert that what was a mainly oral teaching later became a codified mode of study that saw in the words of these servants the revelation of God. In addition, we gleaned from Fishbane's work that the root of this pedagogical model can be seen already in Scripture itself as the traditions become the object of study in subsequent works.

The concepts of *traditio* and *traditum* have helped us to be able to encapsulate this process by which a sacred text continues to be in continuous dialog with subsequent traditions that engage with it as they look back to the past to gain revelation for the present. The example of Daniel 9 is one of the clearest instances in the continuum of a *traditum* that converses with the *traditio* of the seventy-year prophecy in Jeremiah. This example is exactly what happens in Scripture itself but also what predominates in the writings of the Second Temple period, where revelation is never static but is constantly assessed from different vantage points. We agree with scholars like Kugel,

Prophetic Exegesis

Schniedewind, and Aune who assert that following the exile to Babylon there is an explosion of interpretive works that look back to Scripture for models and direction for both the present and the future.

This phenomenon, therefore, has a direct correlation in how we assess the DSS as several exegetical works try to make sense of history in light of what Scripture has already revealed but also in light of how it can be applied to new circumstances. The examples from the Thematic Pesharim, as well as the selected passages from the Rule Texts, underscore that prophetic exegesis became the model by which the sectarians viewed the past and were inspired for the future. Prophetic exegesis, therefore, becomes in the sectarian writings a model by which the authors can align their texts by gathering snippets of revelation from Scripture. These Scriptural passages become not just "proof-texts" or tokens of "implied" or "explicit" exegesis, but rather they are dialogical engagements where the author(s) converses with the words (whether it be metaphors, predictions, and/or descriptions) of these texts and introduces new windows into the past that can both explain and construct the future. The cryptic ideas that appear in the Scriptural passages become in the hand of the sectarian authors revelations that came by the instruction of the Teacher of Righteousness or by means of study (i.e. מדרש), to form the groups that would separate from what they believed to be a corrupt environment that was irredeemable. As we turn to 1QM, we will adopt prophetic exegesis as both a Scriptural and a sectarian dialog. It will be a sectarian analysis as we engage with other scrolls and works like 1 Enoch and Jubilees that are closer in time, and it will be Scriptural as we look back at passages, that is, traditions that evolved and were used in prophetic manner both in predicting and prescribing a teaching to the sectarians.

CHAPTER 3

PROPHETIC EXEGESIS IN 1QM 10

Preliminary Considerations

1QM 10 BEGINS A SET OF LITURGIES that are a transition point between the War of Divisions (1QM 2–9) and the War against the Kittim (1QM 15–19). 1QM 10 contains two distinct pieces: lines 1–8a include a priestly speech to encourage the warriors prior to the war, and lines 8b–18 consist of a song that celebrates God and Israel as the chosen people. Throughout this chapter, we will notice that both of these pieces have different styles and use various passages and themes from the Scriptures. This diversity of styles and themes confirms what we will see throughout these columns, mainly, that the liturgies do not follow a chronological order. One probable reason that was originally proposed by Yigael Yadin is that these columns were part of a liturgical book mentioned in 1QM 15.4–5 as the "Book of the Rule of its Time" (ספר סרך עתו).[1] Other scholars have taken different approaches in an attempt to explain the placement of these liturgies, and the fact that they contain elements from both the War of Divisions and the War Against the Kittim.

Jean Carmignac proposes that in column 10 the scroll transitions into a series of speeches. He adds that the author follows a hierarchical order in the arrangement of the speeches: first is the discourse of the Chief Priest (1QM 10–12), followed by the speeches of other leaders (1QM 13–14.1), and concluding with the troops' thanksgivings (1QM 14). This hierarchical order is then changed for a chronological one that begins with a speech to the first troop of fighters 1QM 15–16, a discourse to the second troop in 1QM 16–17, and finally a speech of thanksgiving in column 18.[2] On a similar trajectory, Bastian

---

1 Yigael Yadin, *The Scroll of the War of the Sons of Light Against The Sons of Darkness*, trans. Batya Rabin and Chaim Rabin (London: Oxford University Press, 1962), 210–212.

2 Jean Carmignac, *La Règle de la Guerre: Des Fils de Lumière contre Les Fils de Ténèbres*

Jongeling observes that in column 10 the sequence of the scroll changes and the content varies from the preceding passages. He notes that the theme of holy war continues to resonate in this column but without the explicit descriptions of military affairs. In addition, Jongeling observes that these liturgies actually begin in 1QM 9, since column 10 starts with a reference to the "camp" (מחנה) and continues the discussion that takes place beginning in column 7.[3]

For his part, Yadin offers a more comprehensive analysis of columns 10–12.[4] Like Carmignac and Jongeling above, he holds that the liturgies are part of a different section which he labels as "Ritual Serekh." Yadin noted an interesting connection between the Ritual Serekh and 1QM 15.4–5, where the chief priest stands before the army and reads aloud the "prayer for the appointed time of the war" (תפלת מועד המלחמה) contained in the "Book of the Rule of its Time." He goes on to argue that columns 10–12 are the "Prayer for the Appointed time of the War" and compares it with Jehoshaphat's prayer in 2 Chr 20 and other passages in Maccabees (1 Macc 4:9, 30; 7:41; 2 Macc 12:15) and in Sotah 8. Yadin concludes that the prayer is an "introductory prayer" that stresses God's assistance because Israel is the chosen people.

Lastly, Philip R. Davies argues that the liturgies in columns 10–14 were added at a subsequent stage of the redactional process of the scroll, especially since the War of Divisions (1QM 2–9) and the War against the Kittim (1QM 15–19) present a coherent structure and purpose. In his view, columns 10–14 are merely a series of hymns and prayers that deal with war in some way. He, therefore, proposes that these liturgies are from a different source, and concurs with Yadin that the probable source is the "Book of the Rule of its Time."[5] Like Davies, Brian Schultz discerns that the relation of columns 10–14 to either of the two main parts of the scroll is ambiguous. On the one hand he observes that the Kittim are mentioned in column 11, which points to a connection with the War against the Kittim. Conversely, Jerusalem appears in column 12, thus pointing to a connection to the War of Divisions. Schultz believes that these columns cannot be interpreted as a single unit, and instead focuses on retrieving any element within the prayers that could point to either stage of the war in which they were supposed to take place.[6]

(Paris: Letouzey et Ané, 1958), 138.

3 Bastiaan Jongeling, *Le rouleau de la guerre des manuscrits de Qumrân* (Assen: Van Gorcum, 1962), 240.

4 Yadin, *The Scroll of the War,* 212–214.

5 Philip R. Davies, *1QM, the War Scroll From Qumran: Its Structure and History* (Rome: Biblical Institute Press, 1977), 91–90.

6 Brian Schultz, *Conquering the World: The War Scroll (1QM) Reconsidered* (Leiden: Brill, 2009), 255–258.

The previous proposals offer important insights as the placement of these liturgies in 1QM remains an open question. Likewise, the fragmentary nature of the end of column 9 prevents us from ascertaining any link between this column and what follows. Regardless of this limitation, it is clear that columns 10–14 (more specifically columns 10–12) are different compositions possibly from a later stage in the redactional process. The main aspect that supports this assertion is that columns 10–12 are the only parts in the entire scroll where explicit citations to the Scriptures occur. Yadin is right in that these liturgies were recited for the occasion of war, and that they are not meant to be read chronologically. This also gives credence to his proposal that the "Book of the Rule of its Time" in 1QM 15.4–5 is the source of these prayers. In addition, columns 10–14 represent a nexus between the Wars of Divisions and the War Against the Kittim, as they refer to passages that point to both stages of the eschatological war, and in the process they create a collage of images of the past for the purpose of reinforcing the faith of the sectarians.[7] The effect of culling together these texts is that it opens up a window to the reader regarding the ideology and aspirations of the sectarians as the true Israel; the one that waits for God's promises to be fulfilled in this final battle. 1QM 10.1–8a starts by citing the teachings of Moses that guide the army to maintain the sanctity of the camp and reinforces the faith of the combatants on God's promises.

a.   1QM 10.1–8a: God Fighting for the Sectarian Army

i.   Text and Translation

<table>
<tr><td style="text-align:center">1QM 10.1–8a</td><td style="text-align:center">1QM 10.1–8a</td></tr>
<tr><td style="text-align:right" dir="rtl">1 מחנינו ולהשמר מכול ערות דבר רע
ואשר הגיד לנו כיא אתה בקרבנו אל
גדול ונורא לשול את כול</td><td>1 ...our camps and to be careful from any shameful nakedness, for he told us that you were in our midst great and awesome God, to drive away all</td></tr>
<tr><td style="text-align:right" dir="rtl">2 אויבינו לפנינו[וילמדנו מאז לדורו־
תינו לאמור בקרבכם למלחמה ועמד
הכוהן ודבר אל העם</td><td>2 our enemies before us. (Deut 7:21–22) And he taught us from ancient times to our generations, saying: "When you draw near to war, the priest shall stand and speak to the people</td></tr>
</table>

---

7 Todd Scacewater, "The Literary Unity of 1QM and its Three-Stage War," *RevQ* 27 (2015): 242–246. Scacewater's approach is to read the prayers in column 10–14 as both a continuation of the instructions in the War of Divisions (columns 2–9) and prayers intended for the War Against the Kittim. He argues that there is no need to "dichotomize" these prayers from either part of the scroll, since they have elements that link to both parts.

לאמור שמעה ישראל אתמה קרבים ₃ היום למלחמה על אויביכמה אל תיראו ואל ירך לבבכמה	3 saying: 'Hear, Israel! Today you are drawing near to fight against your enemies. Do not fear and do not let your heart decline,
ואל תחפן[ז]ו וא[ן]ל תערוצו מפניהם ₄ כיא אלוהיכם הולך עמכם להלחם לכם עם אויביכם להושיע	4 and do not tremble or be terrified before them, for your God walks with you to fight for you against your enemies, to save
אתכמה ון[ש]וטרינו ידברו לכול ₅ עתודי המלחמה נדיבי לב להחזיק בגבורת אל ולשוב כול	5 you.'" (Deut 20:2–5) And our officers shall speak to all who are prepared for battle, those of willing heart, to strengthen them in God's might and to return any
מסי לבב ולחזיק יחד בכול גבורי ₆ חיל ואשר ד[ב]ר[ת]ה ביד מושה לאמור כיא תבוא מלחמה	6 whose heart faints and to strengthen together all the valiant combatants, for your said by the hand of Moses saying: "When you go to war
בארצכמה על הצר הצורר אתכמה ₇ והריעות[מה] בחצוצרות ונזכרתמה לפני אלוהיכם	7 in your land against the oppressor who oppresses you, you shall sound the alarm of the trumpets that you may be remembered before your God and
ונושעתם מאויביכם _{8a}	8a be delivered from your enemies." (Num 10:9)

ii.   Content

The following is the content of 1QM 10.1–8a:

- 10.1–2a
  1. Remarks about purity in the camp: מחנינו ולהשמר מכול ערות דבר רע
  2. Introduction of a Scriptural teaching with the collocation: אשר הגיד לנו
  3. Content of the Scriptural teaching. Citation of Deuteronomy 7:21–22.
- 10.2b–5a
  1. Remarks about the received teachings: וילמדנו מאז לדורותינו
  2. Introduction of a Scriptural teaching with the collocation: לאמור
  3. Content of the Scriptural teaching. Citation of Deuteronomy 20:2–5
- 10.5b–8a
  1. Remarks about the Officers' duties prior to the skirmish: השוטרינו ידברו

2. Introduction of a Scriptural teaching with the collocation: ואשר
   דברתה ביד מושה לאמור
3. Content of the Scriptural teaching. Citation of Numbers 10:9

The beginning of this column shows that line one continues with a discussion that began in the previous column as indicated by the random reference to "our camps" (מחנינו). Unfortunately, the fragmentary end of 1QM 9 following line 14 does not allow us to know exactly how the preceding lines connect with the start of column 10. However, we can gather that 1QM 9.10 introduces the "Rule for changing the order of the battle divisions" (סרך לשנות סדר דגלי המלחמה), which is followed by a description of the maneuvers of the towers, the shields, and the setup of an ambush for the battle line. This rule presumably continues until the bottom of the manuscript that was not recovered, and 1QM 10.1 immediately starts with the command to not have any nakedness in the camps. Another important aspect to consider is that 1QM 10.1–8a continue with themes like the role of priests and officers in encouraging the troops and the use of trumpets prior to the battle, which we see in the War of Divisions in 1QM 2–9. This connection with the War of Divisions is an important one that we need to explore in more detail beginning in column 7.

In 1QM 7 we have the stipulations for the men who should be part of the army. Not only does this column describe matters of age and who can and cannot be part of the army (lines 1–5), but it also emphasizes that the "holy angels" (מלאכי קודש) are in the midst of the army. Lines 6–7 warn that there should not be impurity among the combatants and that there should be a considerable distance between them and these heavenly beings.[8] The end of line 7 explicitly states "and no shameful nakedness shall be seen in the surroundings of all their camps" (וכול ערות דבר רע לוא יראה סביבות כול מחניהם) which resembles the command in 1QM 10.1. In addition, 1QM 10.2 recalls the instruction given to the priest to stand before the army to exhort them before the battle. A similar description happens in 1QM 7.10–12, where the sons of Aaron shall stand before the army. Line 12 describes that the first priest shall walk before the army to strengthen the hands of the combatants,

---

8 Saul Olyan, "The Exegetical Dimensions of Restrictions on the Blind and the Lame in Texts from Qumran," *DSD* 8 (2001): 46–50. Olyan observes that texts like 1QM 7 elaborate on existing Scriptural traditions and increase the range of restriction and severity of these traditions. He adds that the presence of the angels has an effect on how the traditions like Deut 23:10–15 influence the restrictions imposed in 1QM 7. For a similar discussion about the ritual restrictions because of the presence of angels, see: Aharon Shemesh, "The Holy Angels are in their Council: The Exclusion of Deformed Persons from Holy Places in Qumranic and Rabbinic Literature," *DSD* 4 (1997): 179–206.

which resembles the description in 1QM 10.5–6 where the "officers" (שוטרים) shall walk before the lines to strengthen the soldiers and send away any who are not ready for the conflict. Also, 1QM 10.7 cites Num 10:9 and the reference of the sounding of the "trumpets" (חצוצרות). In the same manner, 1QM 7.13 describes that the priests shall go with the trumpets in their hands and blow them as they march in the midst of the military lines.

These thematic links support that 1QM 10.1–8a fits with the content of 1QM 7. Also, because line 10.1 clearly continues with a preceding discussion, we argue that these lines are the culmination of the War of Divisions and more specifically the end of the Rule in 1QM 9.10. Hence, the integration of 1QM 10.1–8a to the War of Divisions brings up additional questions. At what point were these citations added? And what is the rhetorical purpose of adding these traditions?

As we saw before both Davies and more recently Schultz proposed that columns 10–14 represent a subsequent redactional stage of 1QM. In their perspective, the topics that covered in these columns and their lack of chronological order do not match with either 1QM 2–9 or 1QM 15–19, which have been identified as self-contained pieces. The position adopted by both Davies and Schultz is further corroborated by the fact that columns 10–11 are the only places in the entire scroll where explicit citations of the Scriptures appear. This fact suggests a later redactional stage, since it is more plausible that Scripture passages were added for didactic purposes rather than they were removed from the text. Sarianna Metso takes a similar approach in her analysis of the redactional history of the Community Rule.[9]

Metso observes that 1QS has three citations to the Scriptures in 1QS 5.13b–16a (Exod 23:7), 5.16b–19a (Isa 2:22), and 8.12b–16a (Isa 40:3) that are completely absent from the Cave 4 manuscripts (4QS). After going through the analysis of each of the citations, Metso approaches the question of the more "original" version of the Community Rule. She notes that not only are the citations from 1QS missing in 4QS but that the wording of the Cave 1 and Cave 4 manuscripts differ in several places. For instance, 4QS lacks key words like "community" (Yahad; היחד) and "everlasting covenant" (ברית עולם) which are charged with meaning for the sectarians. Metso, therefore, proposes that the shorter version (i.e. 4QS) is the more original, because it is unlikely that these words were added to the text later. Metso concludes with a proposal for the rhetorical purpose of these passages, as the citations in 1QS

---

9 Sarianna Metso, "The Use of Old Testament Quotations in the Qumran Community Rule," in *Qumran between the Old and New Testaments*, ed. Frederick Cryer and Thomas Thompson (Sheffield: Sheffield Academic Press, 1998), 217–231.

Prophetic Exegesis in 1QM 10

provide legitimacy to the regulations and justification for the Yahad's self-understanding. These "proof-texts," she adds, were inserted at a time when the sectarians' enthusiasm and need to separate began to wane. The references to Scripture justified the stricter rules and motivated the sectarians to continue to obey these sacred teachings.[10]

If we use Metso's insights, we can see how a similar logic applies to 1QM 10–11 as later compositions. We can also glean that the citations from Deuteronomy and Numbers in 1QM 10.1–8a were added with a rhetorical purpose in mind, as the themes that these lines share with 1QM 7 suggest that they were added to provide a capstone to the War of Divisions. The specific purpose in adding these passages will be the topic of our close reading below, but we posit at this point that these passages not only establish the teachings of purity within the camp but make it clear to the priests what their role is in reminding the troops about God's presence and faithfulness. The final citation provides the foundation of faith that the readers of the scroll can hold on to in the face of danger; the trumpets not only trigger God's memory, but they are reminders to the soldiers that the same deliverance effected in ancient times will also take place now. Essentially, the citations serve to reenact in a prophetic fashion the victories of God recorded in Scripture.

iii. Sectarian Intertextuality

In this section we will be looking at how the content in 1QM 10.1–8a appears elsewhere within the scrolls. In particular, we will be looking for terms and expressions that potentially evince a sectarian ideology. From the beginning of 1QM 10 we begin to see traces of a particular way of interpreting and adopting the commands of Torah.

1QM 10.1 starts with the command "to be careful from any shameful nakedness" (להשמר מכול ערות דבר רע). This same charge appears in 1QM 7 where we find the stipulations and functions that the men of the camp shall fulfill. Specifically, in line 7 we learn that there shall be a distance between the camp and the "place of the hand" and that "no shameful nakedness shall be seen in the surroundings of all their camps" (וכול ערות דבר רע לוא יראה סביבות כול מחניהם). These two mandates come after a series of ordinances that the warriors need to follow. 1QM 7.1–3 states that men of a certain age will be responsible for the main duties of the camp and that women and

---

10 Ibid., 228. Metso also uses the example of the relationship between the gospel of Mark and Matthew. Just like Matthew added more Scriptural basis to Mark's accounts, 1QS added the Scriptural citations to further the teachings for the community that appear in 4QSb–d.

children are prevented from entering the camp until the warriors return from Jerusalem. This column also restricts participation in the battle to only men who are blameless in spirit and flesh (1QM 7.5); thus, anyone who experiences any sort of inability cannot be part of the army (1QM 7.4–6a).[11] The tail end of line 6 along with line 7 explain that these restrictions are because the "holy angels are with the armies."

The presence of the angels also demands that there would be a distance between the camps and the place of the hand of two-thousand cubits. What exactly is the place of the hand is not entirely clear from the text. This place also appears in 4Q491 1–3.7, where it establishes similar restrictions as 1QM 7. Yadin explains "the hand" by referencing Deut 23:13, where it describes it as the place where members of the camp should go for easement. Through the passage of time, Yadin adds, that "the hand" became a euphemism for that place.[12] Another important point for Yadin is the distance between the camp and the hand. He posits that the two-thousand cubit distance may have been borrowed from the language in Josh 3:4, where the same distance of is used for the space between the people and the Ark of the Covenant. Another option is that this could be linked to the Sabbath boundary, which Rabbinic Judaism places at two-thousand cubits (Sotah 5.3).[13] Yadin acknowledges that we cannot assume that the rulings for Rabbinic Judaism applied for the sectarians, and adds evidence from Josephus who describes the Essenes and their strict observance of the Sabbath (Jewish War 2.147–149). Josephus describes that prior to the Sabbath the Essenes would dig a small pit in desolate places that they would later use for easement. Although this easement was originally considered natural, the Essenes would need to wash themselves because they thought of it as defilement. Interestingly, Yadin uses the evidence from Josephus to identify the warriors in 1QM with the Essenes.[14] At any rate, 1QM 7 clearly describes the camp as a sacred place that was to be kept pure according to the standards from Deuteronomy 23 because of the presence of the angels. The concern for the sacredness of the camp continues with the command to keep away any nakedness.

The reference to "nakedness" (ערות) not only appears in 1QM 7.7 and 10.1, but it is also addressed in other manuscripts.[15] CD 5.10 (cf. 4Q251 17.4–6) comments on the prescription recorded in Lev 18:13. Following a discussion on the

---

11 Yadin, *The Scroll of the War*, 70–79.

12 Ibid., 73.

13 We also notice that CD 11.5–6 and 4Q265 7.5 use two thousand cubits as the distance that a person should walk to graze an animal.

14 Yadin, *The Scroll of the War*, 75.

15 Other places where ערות appears include: 1QHa 5.21; 4Q251 17.4–6; 4Q512 36–38.17.

Prophetic Exegesis in 1QM 10

defilement of the Temple by those who took the daughters of their brother or sister as wives, the passage from Leviticus is quoted as evidence that incestuous relationships were forbidden in Israel. Line 10 explicitly states that this law applies to both men and women and to the daughter that uncovers her nakedness to her father's brother. 1QS 7 lists out many of the fines and disciplinary actions that would be handed to those who violate the statutes of the Yahad. Among these sanctions, lines 12–15 (cf. 4Q259 1.12; 4Q261 5a–c.9; 4Q266 10ii.11; 4Q270 7i.3) describe the penalty for those who expose their nakedness. Anyone who walks naked in the presence of another member of the Yahad will suffer six months of reduced meal rations. Also, a man who "brings out his penis from under his garment" (יוציא ידו מתוחת בגדו) and exposes his nakedness will be punished with thirty days of reduced rations. These examples evince the influence that Deut 23:10–15 exerted on these sectarian texts, and they underscore that this type of exposure was deemed to be a punishable offense.

The next evidence of a sectarian ideology comes in 1QM 10.2 with the statement "and he taught us from ancient times to our generations" (וילמד־ נו מאז לדורותינו). This line precedes the citation of Deut 20:2–5 that deals with the teachings of Moses. By adding the suffix "our" (נו) to both the verb "to teach" (למד) and the direct object "generation" (דור) 1QM adopts these teachings and connects its audience with ancient Israel; that is, the sectarians are the recipients of the same teachings that were previously imparted to their ancestors. We will comment on the rhetorical effect of this phrase below in our close reading, but in the meantime, we need to break down this statement into its constituent parts to decipher what it tells us about the sectarians and their beliefs.

The verb למד in its most basic use means "to learn" and in the Piel it conveys the idea of teaching. It can also appear in the Pual as someone who is "well-versed." In 1QM 6.12–13, 10.10 the participle מלומדים denotes that the combatants are trained in the art of battle and in the statutes of the covenant. 1QM 14.6 also uses this verb to describe how God teaches the feeble the art of war. Outside of 1QM, this verb appears in CD 15.14 where the "Overseer" (מבקר) commands the postulant who wants to enter the covenant to turn to the law and to study it for a full year prior to gaining access. Also, CD 20.4 uses למד to describe those who are disciples of God and in 1QS 3.13 to describe the duties of the "wise" (משכיל) who is responsible for instructing the sectarians. According to 1QS 9.13 the wise must study every teaching that has been revealed in prior times and conduct herself/himself according to these precepts until the Messiah of Aaron and Israel comes. Lastly, 1QSa 1.1–7 (cf.

4Q249a 1.5) provides a description of the responsibilities of the Yahad to live by the precepts of the Covenant and to instruct their youth from the "Book of Meditation" (ספר ההגי).

From this brief survey we can gather that למד was used for training, like in the art of war, and most importantly in the instruction of the sectarians to follow the precepts of Torah. The presence of the "Book of Meditation" co-incides with the use of the "Book of the Rule of its time" as another textual source the sectarians used to impart training to their members.[16]

The word מאז is a temporal adverb that can refer to either the distant past or in some contexts to the future. In the DSS, מאז appears 15 times with eight of these references in 1QM alone. 1QM 1.10 (cf. 1QM 13.14) introduces the final battle between the sectarians and the army of Belial as something that God appointed from ancient times (מאז) 1QM 11.6 quotes Balaam's oracle de-clared in ancient times as a prediction of the new Israel's future success in the battle. 1QM 13.10 (cf. 4Q495 2.1) uses מאז to describe God's appointing of the Prince of Light to help the army of the Sons of Light. And 1QM 16.15 and 18.7 use מאז in relation to the covenantal relationship between God and Isra-el. Other war texts like 4Q491 11i.10 use מאז to deal with God establishing "his truth" (אמתו), and in 4Q491 11ii.13 to describe how Israel has obeyed the mys-teries of God from ancient times. These uses confirm not only the temporal aspect of this adverb, but they also confirm what Bilhan Nitzan has described about the prophetic use of מאז.[17] That is, מאז not only acts as marker of time but also as a marker of something that was appointed to become a reality. The preceding examples convey both the temporal and the imminent aspect of what God established and ordained since ages past.

As for דור it denotes a period of time or age that reflects on the past, but it can also account for the future. Often times the future can be described as an endless time. דור can also mean a "generation" as a group of people like Israel's ancestors. In 1QM 10.2 we see this latter use as it references a teaching given to a past generation. 1QM 14.9 also carries this perspective of genera-tions and how God has continuously favored Israel. The interesting part of both of these uses is that they attach the suffix נו-, which gives the impression that דור not only points to past generations (the ancestors) but that it in-cludes the present generation as well; that is, the sectarians as the generation being addressed.

The Rule Books use דור to: a) describe what past generations did or failed to do, and how God is raising a new people, and b) demonstrate how

---

16 Other passages include: CD 16.4 where it references the ספר מחלקות העתים when all Israel will be blind to the rules of Torah, and 1QS 1.1 where it introduces the ספר סרך היחד.

17 Bilhan Nitzan, *Qumran Prayer and Religious Poetry* (Leiden: Brill, 1994), 216–217.

Prophetic Exegesis in 1QM 10

the sectarians are to be instructed throughout their generations. In these books דור definitely functions in a dualistic way by differentiating the sectarians from either the past ancestors or the contemporaries who do not acknowledge God. For instance, CD 1.12 interprets the raising of a new generation as part of the ministry of the Teacher of Righteousness, where he should guide the new disciples on a path different from the previous generation that incurred God's wrath. CD 2.8 also describes how God rejected the generations of old, because they forsook the Torah and strayed from the path. This same picture emerges in CD 19.1–4 (cf. CD 20.22) where God's covenant promises prosperity to a "thousand generations" of those who keep the covenant, but wrath to those that stray. 1QS 3.14 cites דור as part of the teaching ministry of the wise who is to instruct the sectarians in the deeds of the past generations and their failure to meet God's standard of conduct. 1QS 4.13–15 echoes this teaching as it depicts the failure of past generations and their pending punishment.[18]

The evidence regarding each of the constituent parts of the statement ילמדנו מאז לדורותינו (1QM 10.2) underscores its sectarian influence, and it reflects the interpretation that the teachings given from ancient times were applicable to the current generation. The use of למד demonstrates that the instruction stemming from the Scriptures was something that was part of the pedigree of the sectarians. Also, מאז highlights not just that the teaching happened in a distant past, but that it was something that God deliberately prepared to be used for the current time. This brings a sense of predetermination to מאז that is also seen in the use of דור. The use of "our generations" (דורו־ תינו), therefore, indicates that Israel's ancestors as well as the sectarians, are the recipients and direct beneficiaries of the teaching that comes from the citation of Scripture. Essentially, 1QM 10.2 claims that the words of Moses recorded in Deuteronomy were prepared on behalf of the current generation. This interpretation hints at what we will learn in more detail in the song in 1QM 10.8b–18, and that is that the sectarians are the true Israel who are endowed with the teachings and mystery of God's revelation.

---

18 1QpHab describes דור as the "latter generation" who are the recipients of God's wrath (1QHa 1.1–4; 2.7; 5.2). 4Q395–399 consists of a composite halakhic letter written presumably by a group that separated from the rest of Judaism disgruntled about the lack of observance in matters pertaining to the Torah. In 4Q397 4.11 we encounter an appeal to authoritative books as it talks about the ספר מושה, ספר הנביאים ודויד and to the מעשי דור ודור. The exact same reference appears in 4Q398 14–17i:3. What exactly is this מעשי דור ודור is not clear from these references, but we can discern that it was included among authoritative works along with the Torah of Moses and the Prophets. For a discussion on 4QMMT and Scripture, see: George Brooke, "The Explicit Presentation of Scripture in 4QMMT," in *Legal Texts and Legal Issues: Proceedings of the Second Meeting of the International Organization for Qumran Studies*, ed. John Kampen, Moshe Bernstein, and Florentino García Martínez (Leiden: Brill, 1997), 67–88.

iv. Scriptural Intertextuality

The goal of this section is to explore the trajectory of Scriptural traditions within 1QM 10.1–8a. There are three explicit citations to the Scriptures: Deut 7:21–22, Deut 20:2–5, and Num 10:9. In addition, there are other more subtle themes that shape the overall rhetoric of the passage.

God is in the Midst of the Camp

<table>
<tr><td>1QM 10.1–2a</td><td>Deut 23:15</td></tr>
</table>

Deut 23:15

כי יהוה אלהיך מתהלך בקרב מחנך
להצילך ולתת איביך לפניך והיה
מחניך קדוש ולא־יראה בך ערות דבר
ושב מאחריך:

מחנינו ולהשמר מכול ערות דבר
רע ואשר הגיד לנו כיא אתה בקרבנו
אל גדול ונורא לשול את כול אויבינו
לפ[נינ]ו

Deut 7:21–22

לא תערץ מפניהם כי־יהוה אלהיך בק־
רבך אל גדול ונורא ונשל יהוה אלהיך
את־הגוים האל מפניך מעט מעט לא
תוכל כלתם מהר פן־תרבה עליך
חית השדה:

As we pointed out above, 1QM 10.1 continues the discussion that starts in 1QM 9.10 with the "Rule for changing the order of the battle divisions" (סרך לשנות סדר דגלי המלחמה). The command to keep the camp free from any shameful nakedness echoes the language of Deuteronomy 23. In this chapter, Moses establishes the restrictions on who can have access to the "assembly" (קהל) as well as other sanitary, ritual, and humanitarian precepts that Israel shall follow. In particular, 1QM 10.1 has similarities with Deut 23:15 that require our attention. There are distinct markers in the form of key words and expressions that create a textual connection between these passages. The mention of the "camp" (מחנה), the assertion that God is in the midst of the camp, and the command to keep the camp free of any "shameful nakedness" (ערות דבר) are the main links. Also, the reference to God protecting Israel from the "enemy" (אויב) adds to the evidence that Deut 23:15 is within the scope of 1QM 10.1. In addition, 1QM 10.1 introduces the testimony of Moses through the collocation "which he told to us" (אשר הגיד לנו).[19] The description of God as "great and awesome" (גדול ונורא) and the promise of deliverance from

---

19 The line ואשר הגיד לנו appears only in 1QM 10.1 and in 4Q378 26.2, which details how the עדה of Israel gave ear to what Moses declared.

Prophetic Exegesis in 1QM 10

Israel's enemies point to Deut 7:21–22, where the same expressions appear. Taken together this evidence suggests that 1QM 10.1 uses language reminiscent to Deut 23:15 to conclude the requirement for the purity of the camp and it introduces via the line אשר הגיד לנו the Scriptural basis for this position.

Before we address the use of Deut 7:21–22 a comment about the introductory line is needed. The use of נגד in 1QM 10.1 is different from the other citations in this column. Line 2 introduces Deut 20:2–5 with למד/לאמור while line 6 references Num 7:9 with דבר/לאמור. In his analysis of line 1, Yadin distinguishes the use of נגד and למד in that the former conveys a religious instruction while the latter provides a legal ordinance.[20] This distinction, however, is not sufficiently clear. Based on the evidence from other manuscripts נגד appears in different contexts like visions, prophecy, proclamation, and praise of God, while למד is used specifically for instruction as we saw before.[21] The difference that Yadin points, however, may not be a precise distinction. Rather, 1QM 10.1 uses נגד to convey an interpretation of a tradition, and through the relative clause אשר the subject matter transitions from the rules of the camp to the basis for all these rules. Therefore, נגד refers to a tradition that is taken as a matter of fact and that it is applied to the current circumstance. 1QM 10.1 underscores that God lives in the midst of Israel and will protect them from all their enemies. The Scriptural citation establishes the prophetic foundation that the remaining two citations will elaborate, by giving additional instructions to the priests/officers (lines 2–6a) and by invoking God's promise (lines 6b–8a). The purpose of this reference is to conclude the discussion about the purity within the camp and introduce the basis for the confidence that the combatants should have about God's support.[22] There are three key concepts or expressions within Deut 7:21–22 that have a significant influence across Scripture.

The notion that God is in the "midst" (קרב) of the people is paramount to the relationship between Israel and God. The other two include the assertion of God as "great and awesome" (גדול ונורא) and God driving away Israel's enemies. The perspective of God "great and awesome" is expressed in Deuteronomy, but we can see echoes across Scripture. Nehemiah uses this expression twice: once during his prayer after he learns of the current state of the Jewish people back in the land (Neh 1:5), and another time when he

---

20 Yadin, *The Scroll of the War*, 303.

21 נגד: Visions: 4Q158 1–2.6; 4Q160 1.4; Declaration: 4Q171 Frg. 1–10 4.5; Prophecy 4Q174 Frg. 1–2i. 21.10, 4Q177 1–4.10; Praise: 11Q5 19.9, 11Q6 4–5.10.

22 Jean Carmignac, "Les Citation de l'Ancien Testament dans la 'Guerre des Fils de Lumière Contre des Fils de Ténèbres'," *RB* 63 (1956): 235–236. Dean Wenthe, "The Use of the Hebrew Scriptures in 1QM," *DSD* 5 (1998): 290–319. Russell Gmirkin, "Historical Allusions in the War Scroll," *DSD* 5 (1998): 306–307.

encourages the troops to believe in God and to continue building the wall (Neh 4:8). Daniel echoes this sentiment during his prayer, when he seeks to understand Jeremiah's seventy–year prophecy (Dan 9:4). Likewise, it is also used in songs to God. Ps 99:3 describes God's great and awesome name as well as the kingship over the peoples of the world. The same refrain appears in Chronicles when the Ark of the Covenant was brought to the city of David (1 Chr 16:25). In a different vein Joel uses this same expression to describe the "day of the Lord" (יום יהוה) and the chaos that will come upon those who need to repent (Joel 2:11; 3:4; Mal 3:23).

The LXX renders this phrase from Deuteronomy as μέγας καὶ κραταιός. In 2 Esd 19:32 (Neh 9:32) Ezra culminates his prayer during the people's fasting with the proclamation "our God, the powerful, the great, and mighty" (ὁ θεὸς ἡμῶν ὁ ἰσχυρὸς ὁ μέγας ὁ κραταιός) as he recollects God's deeds and covenant with Israel. For his part Job 9:4 describes God's mind as wise and his character as "might and great" (κραταιός τε καὶ μέγας). Psalms of Solomon 2:29 describes the arrogance of the dragon in failing to recognize the majesty of God, which it describes "God who is great, powerful in his strength". Lastly, Psalms of Solomon 4:24 finishes the imprecation on the wicked with the psalmist calling out God as the righteous judge with the line "for the Lord our God is a great and powerful judge in righteousness" (κριτὴς μέγας καὶ κραταιὸς κύριος ὁ θεὸς ἡμῶν ἐν δικαιοσύνῃ). In essence, the reference to God as גדול ונורא (μέγας καὶ κραταιός) is often used in the context of an individual reflecting on God's character, in order to impress on the audience the magnitude of God. Often this assertion appears in passages that not only deal with God's character as warrior, but also as creator and the source of wisdom. The most obvious connection in 1QM 10.1 is to God as the warrior, but as we proceed to the song in 1QM 10.8b–18 we will begin to notice that descriptions of God's wisdom and favor towards the sectarians begin to take place.

The other connection between 1QM 10.1–2a and Deut 7:21–22 happens in the description "to drive away all our enemies before us" (לשול את כול אויבינו לפנינו). At first, we want to highlight the use of the verb "to drive away" (נשל) to express God's handling of Israel's enemies. This type of action first appears in Deut 7:1 when Moses describes how God will bring the Israelites into the land and drive away the other peoples that live in the land as well as the other seven nations mightier than Israel. 1QM 1.1–2 also uses a similar description, albeit with the verb "to undertake or to profane" (חלל), when it lists out all the enemies (i.e. the Edomites, Moabites, Ammonites, and Philistines) that the sectarians will fight in the eschatological battle. נשל is also used in 2 Kgs 16:6 when Rezin, king of Aram, removed the Judeans from Elath

Prophetic Exegesis in 1QM 10

and allowed the Arameans to return to Elath.

When it comes to the "enemies" (אויבים), Scriptural tradition represents them as people outside of the confines of Israel and the covenant that God established with them. These peoples were deemed enemies, because they did not know God and exerted their influence on Israel not just on the po-litical and military contexts, but they also blemished the cult of God. The first significant reference to the enemy happens in the song of Moses in Exod 15:6–9, where the Israelites celebrate God's defeat of Pharaoh. A similar use takes place in Deut 32, in a song that deals with how God dealt with Israel and their enemies. Interestingly both verses 27 and 42 describe how God spared judgment on Israel lest the enemies think that it was them and not God's hand that was in control. The prayer of Solomon also uses references to the enemy to plead with God to forgive Israel of their sin and deliver them from the enemy. Both Kings and Chronicles (1 Kgs 8:33, 46 // 2 Chr 6:24, 36) inter-pret that the sin of Israel causes the nation to succumb to the enemy.

The Greek texts render אויב as ἐχθρός (e.g. 1 Macc 4:18; 9:46). 1 Macc 2:7 relays the moment when Mattathias mourns that the holy city has fallen in the "hand of the enemies and the sanctuary in the hands of foreigners" (χειρὶ ἐχθρῶν τὸ ἁγίασμα ἐν χειρὶ ἀλλοτρίων). Notice that this description lists out "en-emy" (ἐχθρός) and "foreigner" (ἀλλότριος) in the same sentence. Ironically, in 1 Maccabees 12 Jonathan sends emissaries to renew their friendship with for-eign nations including Rome and Sparta. And in 1 Macc 12:15 he interprets the success of the revolution on God's help and how God humbled all their ene-mies. Lastly, in 1 Macc 15:33 Simon describes how God returned the lands to his people that were unjustly taken by their enemies.

The references to the enemy in Scripture underscore that throughout their history Israel dealt with foreign influence that often brought existential crises. Across Scripture, the interpretation is that as long as Israel remains faithful to the precepts of Torah, success over the enemy shall come. On the other hand, failure to meet the standards of the covenant meant that the na-tion would suffer under the hands of their enemies. The question as to how this belief shaped the rhetoric of 1QM is something that we will deal in our next section. Suffice to say at this moment that 1QM 10.1 demonstrates the conviction that the army of the Sons of Light should trust, as their ancestors in Deuteronomy did, that their enemies will be handed over to them. This as-surance comes from the conviction that they have maintained the purity of the camp, and thus God's presence guarantees victory. The ensuing lines pro-ceed from this prophetic conviction to describe what the priests need to do in order to prepare the combatants to take this victory.

God Marches Against Israel's Enemies

1QM 10.2b–5a	Deut 20:2–5
2b וילמדנו מאז לדורותינו לאמור בקרבכם למלחמה ועמד הכוהן ודבר אל העם	2 והיה כקרבכם אל־המלחמה ונגש הכהן ודבר אל־העם:
3 לאמור שמעה ישראל אתמה קרבים היום למלחמה על אויביכמה אל תיראו ואל ירך לבבכמה	3 ואמר אלהם שמע ישראל אתם קרבים היום למלחמה על־איביכם אל־ירך לבבכם אל־תיראו ואל־תחפזו ואל־תערצו מפניהם:
4 ואל תחפן[זו וא]ל תערוצו מפניהם כיא אלוהיכם הולך עמכם להלחם לכם עם אויביכם להושיע	4 כי יהוה אלהיכם ההלך עמכם להלחם לכם עם־איביכם להושיע אתכם:
5a אתכמה	5a ודברו השטרים אל־העם לאמר מי־האיש אשר בנה בית־חדש ולא חנכו ילך וישב לביתו פן־ימות במלח־מה ואיש אחר יחנכנו:

Line 2b starts with the preparation that the army needs to make prior to the battle. The use of "teach" (למד) in the collocation "and he taught us from ancient times to our generations, saying" (וילמדנו מאז לדורותינו לאמור) denotes that what follows is a teaching that the sectarians must follow according to the customs of their ancestors. The quotation of Deut 20:2–4 is for the most part identical to the version in the MT with slight variations. The following table illustrates some of these differences between 1QM 10.2b–5a and Deut 20:2–4:

1QM 10.2b–5a	Deut 20:2–4
בקרבכם	כקרבכם
למלחמה	אל־המלחמה
ועמד	ונגש
לאמור	ואמר אלהם
אל תיראו ואל ירך לבבכמה	אל־ירך לבבכם אל־תיראו
כיא אלוהיכם הולך	כי יהוה אלהיכם ההלך

Deut 20:2–4 illustrates the protocol that the army of God shall follow before

Prophetic Exegesis in 1QM 10

engaging in battle. The interesting feature about this protocol is that it is not a military leader who is to address the army, but rather a priest. We are told that a priest will "draw near" (נגש) and speak to the people, whereas 1QM uses "stand" (עמד).[23] The difference might not be significant, although in several passages the scrolls describe how priests stood in position of authority before the sectarians. For instance, in CD 13.5 a priest shall stand and decide matters relating to skin diseases and how to isolate the person suffering this condition. 1QM also uses עמד to describe the actions of the priests. First in 1QM 15.4 the chief priest and his brothers shall stand in front of the combatants to read the "prayer for the appointed time of the war" (תפלת מועד המל־ חמה). And in 16.3 when the call is made for the combatants to return, the Chief Priest shall stand in front of the battle line and encourage the warriors (4Q491 11ii.11). A similar description happens in 4Q491 Frg. 1–3.17 where the Chief Priest stands along with his brothers and the Levites while the different attacks on the enemy take place. The use of עמד instead of נגש reveals not necessarily a purposeful change of the Scriptural passage, but rather a way that 1QM and other manuscripts depict the position of authority that priests often enjoyed within the sectarians.[24] As for the content of the priestly exhortation, we can divide it in two tiers: the exhortation and the evidence to believe in this word.

The exhortation begins in a fashion that is used across Deuteronomy. The opening "listen, Israel," (שמע ישראל) happens every time Moses conveys a teaching (Deut 5:1, 6:4, 9:1). Deut 20:3 is similar in that Moses prescribes what the priest should say prior to the battle. This command also demonstrates that the priest should act in the same fashion as Moses, as a leader who reminds the nation of God's support and the promise for success. Therefore, by citing this passage and keeping the call "listen, Israel," 1QM demonstrates that the priest (like his counterpart in the Scriptures) should continue with the tradition and act as a type of Moses. The priest should play the intermediary role between God and the army and encourage the combatants with the testimony of what God promised in the past.

---

23 Yadin, *The Scroll of the War*, 212. Yadin interprets that the priest is given by the chief priest. He comes to this conclusion, because he identifies the prayers in 1QM 10 with the תפלת מועד המלחמה in 1QM 15.

24 For a recent discussion regarding priests in the context of the DSS, see: Heinz-Josef Fabry, "Priests at Qumran - A Reassessment," in *The Dead Sea Scrolls: Texts and Context*, ed. Charlotte Hempel (Leiden: Brill, 2010), 243–262. Christophe Batsch, "Priests in Warfare in Second Temple Judaism: 1QM, or the Anti-Phinehas," *Qumran Cave 1 Revisited: Texts from Cave 1 Sixty Years After Their Discovery*, ed. Daniel Falk et al. (Leiden: Brill, 2010), 165–178. Charlotte Hempel, "Do the Scrolls Suggest Rivalry Between the Sons of Aaron and the Sons of Zadok and If So Was It Mutual?," *RevQ* 24 (2009): 135–153.

Following the call to Israel the priest shall deliver his message. The priest describes in 1QM 10.3 that Israel is about to engage in a battle against the enemy (אויב). Notice that the marker אויב appears here as it did in lines 1–2a, as a key concept that Israel is to confront and defeat. Once the priest sets the stage, he goes on to provide four directives to the warriors preceded by the prohibitive particle "do not" (אל): "do not fear" (אל תיראו), "do not let your heart decline" (אל ירך לבבכם), "do not tremble" (אל תחפזו), and "do not be terrified" (אל תערצו). The first directive appears in Deut 20:3, and it also in Isa 7:4 and Jer 51:46. In Isaiah the prophet gives Ahaz the word "do not fear and do not let your heart decline" (אל תירא ולבבך אל ירך) when the king faces the threat from Aram and Ephraim. As for Jeremiah 51:46 the exhortation comes at a point when God calls the people of Israel to leave Babylon, because of the coming destruction that will fall upon the city. In Jeremiah as in Deuteronomy and Isaiah the verbs "to faint" (רכך) and "to fear" (ירא) appear as part of the call to the people. The only instance when the softening of the heart comes in a positive light happens in 2 Kgs 22:19 when God proclaims via the prophetess Huldah that Josiah will be spared because his heart was contrite (יען רך לבבך).

The call "do not fear" (אל תיראו) echoes instances when Moses called the people to trust in God. The most prominent of these instances happens in Exod 14:3 when he emboldens the people to not fear and wait for the deliverance of God. The other reference happens in Deut 31:6 when Moses finishes his mission and exhorts the people to cross the Jordan led by Joshua. The significance of this reference is that it echoes the sentiment from the priestly exhortation in that the Israelites should not be frightened by their enemies (אל תערצו מפניהם), because God walks with them.

The phrase "do not tremble" (אל תחפזו) happens only in Deut 20:3. Elsewhere in Scripture, חפז appears in the context of escaping from an enemy, like in 1 Sam 23:26 when David escapes from Saul. Also, in 2 Kgs 7:15 the same word happens when messengers come to see what happened to the Aramean camp after these had left it out of fear of God's army. The priestly exhortation, especially its call to not fear, happens in the Maccabean wars. In 1 Macc 3:22 Judas commands the Jewish army μὴ φοβεῖσθε as they are about to clash with the Syrian army. Likewise, in 1 Macc 4:8 Judas uses the same expression to encourage the army. Further, in this exhortation Judas reminds the army of what God did on behalf of their ancestors when they fled from Egypt. This historical event and others will be referenced in 1QM 11 as evidence of what God did in the past and how it will happen in the future. The call to not fear the threat of the enemy armies is a theme that surfaces as

Israel fights for its existence. The priestly encouragement is based mainly on the belief that the God who established a covenant with the nation partners with them to face this treat. The latter part of line 4 introduces the testimony for why Israel shall take on this challenge without fear. Following the demonstrative particle כי, this line uses the verbs "to walk" (הלך), "to fight" (לחם), and "to deliver" (ישע) to describe the intimate relation between God and Israel.

The phrase "for the Lord your God walks with you" (כי יהוה אלהיכם ההלך עמכם) in Deuteronomy 20:4 has antecedents in other parts of Scripture. The earliest reference to this type of connection comes in Exod 14:19 when the Angel of God walks both ahead and in the back of the camp of Israel. Deut 1:30–33 alludes to the fact that Israel did not consider the evidence of how God walked with them and protected them when they left Egypt as enough proof for future success. Following this failure, Moses describes how God granted the next generation of Israelites to be the ones to see the promised land. Thus, Deut 31:6–8 ends with Moses encouraging Joshua and the Israelites with the word that God walks with them as they go and possess the land. Further, evidence that God fights against Israel's enemies is spread throughout Scripture. One important example takes place in 2 Chr 20:17 where Jahaziel proclaims in a prophetic fashion that the pending conflict is not for them to resolve. With the assertion "is not for you to fight" (לא לכם להלחם) Jahaziel echoes the sentiment in Deut 20:4 where God is the one fighting for Israel.[25] This passage will have significant implications for 1QM 11, where the hymn continuously uses the refrain "yours is the battle" (לכה המ־ לחמה) to assert that the battle is God's.

Lastly, the notion that God delivers Israel appears in several passages of Scripture. Many of the references use the passive form of "to deliver" (ישע) to describe how Israel was delivered by God (e.g. Deut 33:29; 2 Sam 22:4; Isa 45:22). On the other hand, this same verb is also used to denote the active giving of help or deliverance like in Judg 10:1, 13:5 where God raises Judges to deliver Israel. Also, in 1 Sam 17:47 David challenges the Philistines by stating "the Lord delivers not by sword or spear, for the battle is the Lord's, and he will hand you in our hand" (כי לא בחרב ובחנית יהוה יהושיע כי ליהוה המלחמה ונתן אתכם בידנו). The claim of deliverance that David makes also appears in 1QM 11, where the hymn echoes this statement as evidence that Israel's battles are not theirs but God's. Thus, the notion of God fighting and delivering

---

25 Schniedewind also points out that, "Jahaziel's exhortation is an inspired recontextualization of Moses' injunction to the children of Israel at the Red Sea." William Schniedewind, *The Word of God in Transition: From Prophet to Exegete in the Second Temple Period* (Sheffield: Sheffield Academic Press, 1995), 236.

Israel seen in the priestly exhortation will resurface in 1QM 11. This evidence shows the intersection within columns 10–12 of different themes that create for us a full picture of the type of faith that the Sons of Light display in these liturgies. Following the priestly address, 1QM 10.5b–8b describe the officers' encouragement to the combatants and add the quote of Num 10:9.

God Remembers and Delivers Israel

1QM 10.5b–8a	Num 10:9
5b ו[ש]וטרינו ידברו לכול עתודי המלחמה נדיבי לב להחזיק בגבורת אל ולשוב כול 6 מסי לבב ולחזיק יחד בכול גבורי חיל ואשר ד[בר]תה ביד מושה לאמור כיא תבוא מלחמה 7 בארצכמה על הצר הצורר אתכמה והריעות[מה] בחצוצרות ונזכרתמה לפני אלוהיכם 8a ונושעתם מאויביכם	9 כי־תבאו מלחמה בארצכם על־הצר הצרר אתכם והרעתם בחצצרות ונזכרתם לפני יהוה אלהיכם ונושעתם מאיביכם:

The image of the "officers" (שוטרים) addressing the combatants echoes the discourse in Deut 20. Yadin points out that this passage is based on Deut 20:8, although he acknowledges that both discourses are different.[26] Whereas in Deuteronomy the officers address the combatants prior to the battle and give them ways to be discharged honorably, 1QM mentions that only those who have lost valor will be sent back (לשוב כול מסי לבב). Yadin, Davies, and Schultz have addressed this difference with each taking a different approach.

Yadin explains that every exemption except for fear was handled prior to leaving the camp. He posits that since the prayer takes place in the battlefield, it would be superfluous to bring to the fight those who had been exempted. He cites the passage in 1 Macc 3:46–56, to show that the army handled these exemptions before heading to war. He also observes that in Gideon's war (Judg 7:3) those who were fearful were removed from the battle at the very moment when they faced the enemy. These examples suggest to Yadin that the author of 1QM did not deviate from Deuteronomy.[27]

Schultz, on the other hand, takes a different approach. He notices that

---

26 Yadin, *The Scroll of the War*, 304.
27 Yadin, *The Scroll of the War*, 69–70.

Prophetic Exegesis in 1QM 10

the phrase לשוב כול מסי לבב happens right between the descriptions that
the officers shall strengthen the army. For Schultz, it is illogical to think that
the officers are to encourage the soldiers while at the same time they are to
exclude the fearful. He proposes that instead of preserving the Qal of the
verb "to turn" (שוב) the most plausible application is that those with melt-
ing hearts needed to repent or be restored (e.g. Hiphil of שוב). This explains
why the author did not mention any of the other exemptions from the text
of Deuteronomy.[28]

For his part, Davies agrees with Yadin that the most logical explanation
is that each member of the army has already committed to the cause and left
everything to partake in the war. He proposes that the army handled the exemptions during the enlistment of the soldiers in 1QM 2. Yadin and Davies
provide the more plausible explanation for this discrepancy. Since the soldiers had already committed to the cause, the only thing that can affect them
at the time when they face the enemy is fear.[29] Also, by sending these combatants away 1QM 10.5–6 reinforce the logic of Deut 20:8, where it describes that
it is better for a soldier who is afraid to leave than to stay and affect the rest of
the troops. Once the officers encourage the troops and send back those who
have lost valor, 1QM wraps up with the quote of Numbers.

1QM 10.6 introduces Num 10:9 with a reference to the "hand of Moses"
(ביד מושה). Whereas the citations of Deuteronomy 7 and 20 lack a specific
mention of the speaking subject, the citation of Numbers mentions Moses.
In Scripture the phrase "by hand of Moses" is used to denote how God's communication to the people happens through Moses. For example, Exod 9:35
recalls the word that God gave through Moses about Pharaoh's reluctance
to let Israel leave Egypt. Lev 26:46 introduces the statutes and recalls that
these were given at Sinai through Moses. In Num 4:37–49 the different clans
of Israel enroll in the service according to everything that God commanded through Moses. In the DSS this phrase carries the same meaning of God
teaching through Moses, but it also points specifically to the Torah.[30]

The citation of Num 10:9 can be divided into three parts: a) the setting,
which Numbers describes as the moment when Israel goes to battle; b) the

---

28 Schultz, *Conquering the World*, 262–263.

29 Davies, *1QM, the War Scroll*, 94.

30 CD 5.21 describes how the מסיני הנבול led the people of Israel astray and spoke rebel-
lion משה על מצות אל ביד. For its part, 1QS 1.3 starts with the call that the teacher of the community should abide with everything that was צוה ביד מושה וביד כול עבדיו הנביאים. 1QS
8.15 interprets the prophecy of Isa 40:3 as the expounding of the Torah commanded by God
through Moses, and to do everything that was revealed by the prophets. In 1QHa 4.12 the prayer
gives thanks to God for being spared of the judgment and for the compassion and forgiveness
of sins that God spoke through Moses.

command that Israel shall follow; and c) the promise that God gives to Israel. The setting is the conflict against "the oppressor who oppresses" (הצר הצר רר). We also notice that the end of this verse mentions that God will deliver Israel from their enemies (מאויביכם). The phrase הצר הצורר appears only in this verse in Numbers. The צר represents an adversary or enemy, and often it is translated as oppressor. The verbal form of צר is צרר, which means to be hostile or in a state of conflict. In Num 24:8 Balaam describes that Israel will "devour the nations that are his foes" (יאכל גוים צריו). Deut 32:27 recalls how God considered destroying Israel but relented because their "foes" (צרימו) might think that it was not God who had accomplished everything on Israel's behalf. Lastly, beginning in verse 6 Ezra describes how God handed the Israelites to their "oppressors" (צריהם) and how in their "oppression" (צרתם) Israel called out to God to be delivered from their enemies (Neh 9:27). These references indicate that the צר represents an enemy that oppressed Israel. However, the immediate context in Num 10:9 does not indicate whether the צר was necessarily oppressing Israel. Rather, the verse states what Israel shall do when they face their צר in battle. The reason for clarifying this point is because Davies uses the traditional interpretation of צר as "oppressor," to question the presence of this verse in 1QM 10.7–8a. In his opinion, the presence of הצר הצרר indicates that the context of this verse refers to a defensive response to enemy attacks rather than an offensive encounter. For this reason, he questions the connection between 1QM 10.1–8a and the War of Divisions.[31] We have already addressed why these lines fit with the War of Divisions, and we do not need to rehearse it at this point. In any case, the setting of Num 10:9 is the ensuing conflict with Israel's enemies.

The next important part of this verse is the command that Israel shall follow. God commands Israel that at the moment of their skirmish they should sound the battle signal with their trumpets. The חצצרה is a trumpet that not only signals a battle cry but is also used in other instances. Num 10:1–10 provides the initial descriptions of what these instruments were used for and who was responsible for their use. These verses indicate that the trumpets were used to gather the people, to call the leaders to assemble, to sound an alarm to alert the people in moments of war, and also to celebrate their festivals. An important point within these descriptions comes in verse 8, where it explicitly states that the sounding of the trumpets is a perpetual ordinance (חקת עולם לדרתיכם) that the Sons of Aaron, the priests, shall fulfill. Num 31:6 highlights this priestly role as Moses sends Phinehas the priest (with

---

31 Instead, he sees these lines as part of a self-contained section that neither fits the War of Divisions or the War against the Kittim (1QM 15–19). Davies, *1QM, the War Scroll*, 94–95.

Prophetic Exegesis in 1QM 10

the vessels of the sanctuary and the trumpets) to accompany the warriors in their clash against Midian. Outside of Numbers, the חצצרות mostly appear in the book of Chronicles with a couple of other instances in Nehemiah and Ezra (cf. Ezra 3:10; Neh 12:35, 41). 2 Chr 13:12–15 describes the moment when Jeroboam and his troops surrounded Judah. Verse 15 adds that the priests sounded the trumpets and Judah raised the battle cry, which is the same verb that Num 10:9 uses. In addition, 2 Chr 20:20–28 describes the moment when worshippers call on God to ambush the enemy armies that had surrounded Judah. The account ends with a procession to the house of God with lyres and trumpets. This passage is an important one for our work, because of the conflation of military and worship themes that we find in 1QM.[32]

The Hebrew word "trumpets" (חצצרה) is sometimes rendered as σάλπιγξ. In the Maccabean wars the "trumpet" (σάλπιγξ) is continuously used prior to the military encounters against the enemies.[33] 1 Macc 3:46–60 describe the moment when Judas assembles his army and appoints leaders responsible for sending back the would-be soldiers that could not engage in the battle because of prior commitments (cf. Deuteronomy 23). Verse 54 describes that they sounded the trumpets prior to marching against the Gentiles in Emmaus. 1 Macc 4:36–43 also describes how the trumpets were used to rally the troops after they ascended to Mount Zion and witnessed the state of the sanctuary. An interesting aspect about these references is that none of them describe that the descendants from Aaron sounded the trumpets, which is a command explicitly stated in Num 10:8. Sir 50:1–16, on the other hand, clearly states that in the days of Simon son of Onias the sons of Aaron played a key role in the service and in rallying the congregation with the sounding of the trumpets. The importance of the sons of Aaron is something that 1QM meticulously describes in 1QM 7.9–18. The detailed description of their garments and the use of the חצצרות suggests that in the perspective of 1QM this was something that needed to be observed for the eschatological fight.[34]

---

32 John Endres has described 2 Chr 20 as a type of worship service with the singers taking a lead role in the battle against enemy forces. 2 Chr 20 is comparable to other communal celebrations in Israel, such as 1 Chr 15–16 in the bringing of the Ark of the Covenant to Jerusalem and 2 Chr 5–7 in Solomon's dedication of the Temple. However, he differentiates this event from these other accounts, since fear instead of joy is what causes the congregation to gather. John Endres, "Theology of Worship in Chronicles," in *The Chronicler as Theologian: Essays in Honor of Ralph W. Klein*, ed. M. Patrick Graham, Steven L. McKenzie, and Gary N. Knoppers (New York: T&T Clark, 2003), 177–180.

33 σάλπιγξ appears in Maccabees, see: 1 Macc 3:54, 4:40, 5:31–33; 6:33; 7:45; 9:12; 16:8. It is also used in the Sibylline Oracles in the context of eschatology, see: Sib 4:174; 5:253; 7:116; 8:117; 8:239.

34 The importance of the sons of Aaron is evident from 1QM and other sectarian texts like

Lastly, the citation of Num 10:9 contains the promise that Israel will be delivered from their enemies when they sound the trumpets. This promise takes place in several passages of Scripture; sometimes it focuses on individuals like Noah and Abraham, and other times on the nation of Israel. Exod 2:24 is a classic example where God hears "their groaning" (נאקתם) and remembered the covenant with Abraham, Isaac, and Jacob (cf. Exod 6:5). Also, in Moses' final blessing he describes how God has favored Israel and become their shield and sword who will overcome their enemies (Deut 33:29). The combination of being remembered and saved plays a significant role in Israel's relationship with God.

On the other hand, the loss of a nation's name means its dismay. Isa 23:15–18 calls for Tyre to play instruments and sing songs so that their name will be remembered. Also, Ezek 25:10 describes the judgment that will come upon Ammon as they will be remembered no more. Essentially, the traditions from Scripture attest that to be remembered means that a nation has God's favor. Musical instruments, like the חצצרות, trigger God's memory so that the nation will be delivered. The continuous use of the חצצרות in 1QM underscores the belief that the sounding of the trumpets invokes God's memory and ultimately leads to the nation's victory.

All of this evidence demonstrates that the sectarians adopted the traditions in Numbers and Deuteronomy to re-enact the wars of God recorded in these Scriptural traditions. The implications of this belief are that the sectarians visualized the war against Belial in the same light as Israel's war against the nations. Plus, it underscores the ideology that in fighting the war against Belial, the sectarians were fighting for the purpose of establishing a new Israel.[35] Our exploration of the intertextuality in 1QM 10.1–8a has demonstrated a web of Scriptural themes that 1QM uses to describe the looming

---

1QS 5.21, 9.7; 1Q28a 1.23–24, 2.13; 4Q396 4.8 and 4Q397 2.14. However, several questions are still open regarding the sons of Aaron and the sons of Zadok and their relation as well as their roles within the community. One approach by Charlotte Hempel is to distinguish the references of these priestly lineages and their authority. Hempel sees that the references to the sons of Aaron point to their authority over Israel, while the texts that mention the sons of Zadok are a subsequent textual stage that point to their authority over the sectarians (Hempel, "Do the Scrolls Suggest," 135–153). Another approach is to see both the Aaronides and Zadokites as mutual partners in the formation and functionality of the sectarian community. Fabry analyzes the references to the priestly lineages and concludes that the sons of Aaron were responsible with cultic functions, while the sons of Zadok with official and administrative duties (Heinz-Josef Fabry, "Priests at Qumran," 243–262).

35 Dean Wenthe devotes his study to the use of Scripture in 1QM and in his analysis of 1QM 2–9 he concedes that the Scriptural themes and purity standards point to the army of the בני אור vis-à-vis Israel in Numbers, and to portray the army in priestly terms. Wenthe, "The Use of the Hebrew Scriptures in 1QM," 302–307.

eschatological battle. By alluding to the passages in Deuteronomy and Numbers, 1QM adopts the promises within these passages to its own context. In the following section we will describe how these promises are used prophetically to encourage the warriors to believe that they, like the Israel of old, will be the recipients of God's protection.

v. Prophetic Exegesis

The analysis of 1QM 10.1–8a has focused on the intertextual connections that this passage has with both the immediate context in the DSS and the wider world of Scriptural tradition. At this junction we will use these findings to provide a close reading of this passage.

We observed that these lines pick up a discussion that begins in 1QM 9.10 with the "Rule for changing the order of the battle divisions" (סרך לשנות סדר דגלי המלחמה). The סרך delineates the instructions and maneuvers that the army shall follow to discourage the enemy and set an ambush in the battle line (1QM 9.17). As we shall see below the threat of the enemy and his looming end is a constant theme in 1QM 10.1–8a, but the key that develops this theme is the prophetic interpretation of Scripture.

Peter von der Osten-Sacken originally labeled these lines as a florilegium and a collection of proof-texts.[36] He observed that these texts are the "kernel" of the instructions and rules of war in 1QM 7–9 and in 15–19. Davies agrees with Osten-Sacken that these Scriptural texts provide the blueprint for the war, and labels this passage as a combination of prayer and Mishnah because it contains law code accompanied by commentary.[37] Yadin interprets that this passage is the prayer for the appointed time of war, and he further labels it as a "survey of the laws of warfare in the Bible."[38] Rather than proposing another label for these lines we argue that 1QM 10.1–8a uses the passages of Scripture "prophetically," to encourage the army to believe that God's presence will bring the end of the enemy.

These lines are knit together via three passages of Scripture (Deut 7:21–22; 20:2–5; Num 10:9) to convey eternal principles to the sectarians. These principles are: Prophetic Testimony, God's Presence and Promise of Deliverance, and the End of Israel's Enemies. The chart below illustrates the repetition of key terms that link these lines and how they fit within these principles.

---

36 Peter von der Osten Sacken, *Gott und Belial: Traditionsgeschichtliche Untersuchungen zum Dualismus in den Texten aus Qumran* (Gottingen: Vandenhoeck & Ruprecht, 1969), 60–61.

37 Davies, *1QM, the War Scroll*, 92–93.

38 Yadin, *The Scroll of the War*, 66.

1QM 10	Prophetic Testimony	God's Presence and Promise of Deliverance	End of Israel's Enemies
1–2	ואשר הגיד לנו כיא	אתה בקרבנו אל גדול ונורא	לשול את כול אויבינו לפ[נינ]ו
2–5	וילמדנו מאז לדורותינו לאמור	כיא אלוהיכם הולך עמכם להלחם לכם... להושיע אתכמה	היום למלחמה על אויבכמה...עם אויבכם
6–8a	ואשר ד[ן]בר[תה ביד מושה לאמור	והריעות[מה] בחצוצרות ונזכרתמה ונושעתם לפני אלוהיכם	על הצר הצורר... מאויביכם

We have used the label Prophetic Testimony, because there is a continuous reflection on the teachings of the past. The use of the verbs נגה ,למד, and דבר all convey that a teaching given a long time ago (denoted by the reference of מאז לדורותינו) is directly applicable to the current circumstance. Even though the subject of each of the prophetic words is not mentioned, we know from the context of Deuteronomy and Numbers that Moses was imparting these instructions. The implications of the use of these passages are that the sectarians are constituted in the light of the armies of God in the past. This is something that we can observe through the continuous allusions to Deuteronomy and Numbers in columns 2–9, and in the explicit citation of the Scriptures in lines 1–8a. Furthermore, the citations are not just "proof-texts" as Osten-Sacken observed, but they are also windows that allow us to peek into the sectarian faith and how the sectarians view themselves in light of the past.[39] The descriptions in columns 2–9 along with the citations in column 10 seal the image of the sectarians as the new army of Israel. The Prophetic Testimony of these passages points to the sectarians as the current day recipients of the favor and deliverance that God gave to Israel's past generations (לדורותינו). For that very reason the sectarians follow every instruction literally; whether it is to keep the camp pure from any shameful nakedness, or for the priest and officers to encourage the combatants, or for the army to sound the trumpets in the midst of the fight, every instruction is a

---

39 Schultz, *Conquering the World*, 274. Schultz argues that lines 1–8a are not sectarian. He makes reference to Yadin's comparison of this passage with other prayers before the battle in the Second Temple Period, to support the assertion that there is nothing distinctively sectarian within these lines. See Yadin, *The Scroll of the War*, 212–214.

Prophetic Exegesis in 1QM 10

re-enactment of the past. As such, each re-enactment follows the conviction that all that was applicable in the past will also be experienced in the future war as God is with them in their midst.

This promise has two sides. There is the promise itself that God is in the camp and that God will act on behalf of the army to defeat the enemy. We have broken this promise in two, but they essentially constitute two sides of the same promise. They are in essence the result of what God, through the prophets like Moses, promised and will accomplish for the sectarians. This we have demonstrated in the chart above by pairing each description; that is, God is in the קרב of army to לשול את כול אויבינו (lines 1–2), God walks (הולך) with the army to fight (להלחם) and deliver them (להושיע) from the אויבכם (lines 2–5), and God remembers and delivers (נזכרתמה, נושעתם) the soldiers from the oppressor and enemy (הצר הצורר, מאויביכם) (lines 7–8). The repetition of these themes and the organization of these passages demonstrate that these texts were carefully considered, to recap what the War of Divisions has already described in the processions, formations of the army, and purity teachings, which is that God walks with Israel to provide the final blow to the enemy forces.

This brings us to the end of Israel's enemies which is one of the main themes of these lines. As we have observed the citations refer to the enemy (אויב). The repetition of this term not only emphasizes that God will act against the forces that threaten Israel, but it also highlights the fact that the terms אויבים or הצר have a life beyond the passages of Scriptures. By using these terms 1QM contextualizes its current realities according to the language and images of Scriptures. Therefore, the enemies that threatened the identity of ancient Israel appear in this scroll as the antagonist force that the new Israel must overcome. This aspect will become more apparent in 1QM 11 where the scroll mentions specific examples from history (including Goliath, Pharaoh, and Gog of Magog), to depict how God will defeat the new enemies in Belial and the seven nations.

b.   1QM 10.8b–18: God the Sovereign Teacher

    i.   Text and Translation

1QM 10.8b–18	1QM 10.8b–18
8b מיא כמוכה אל ישראל בש[מי]ם ובארץ אשר יעשה כמעשיכה הגדולים	8b Who is like you, God of Israel in the heavens and on earth who does like your great deeds,

וכגבורתכה החזקה ומיא ____ כע־ 9
מכה ישראל אשר בחרתה לכה מכול
עמי הארצות

9 and as your great strength? And who____ is like your people Israel, whom you chose for yourself from all the peoples of the earth,

עם קדושי ברית ומלומדי חוק מש־ 10
כילי בינ[ה]|] ושומעי קול נכבד ורואי

10 a people of the holy covenant, learned in the statutes, wise in knowledge and who hear the voice of glory, seers of

מלאכי קודש מגולי אוזן ושומעי עמו־ 11
קות [ ]|] מפרש שחקים צבא מאורות

11 the holy angels, with open ears, and hearers of deep things ... the expanse of the skies, the host of luminaries

ומשא רוחות וממשלת קדושים אוצ־ 12
רות כב[ו]ד | עבים הבורא ארץ וחוקי
מפלגיה

12 the task of the spirits and the dominion of the holy ones, treasures of glory [ ] of clouds. The one who created the earth and limits of its divisions

למדבר וארץ ערבה וכול צאצאיה 13
עם פר[י]ם]ה חוג ימים ומקוי נהרות
ומבקע תהומות

13 for the wilderness and the dry land, and all its products, its fruit and seeds, the circle of the seas, the source of the rivers, and the chasm of the abyss,

מעשי חיה ובני כנף תבנית אדם 14
ותול[ ]עו בלת לשון ומפרד עמים
מושב משפחות

14 the deeds of wild beasts and winged creatures, the form of humanity and gen-erations, the division of tongues, and the separation of the peoples, of the dwelling of the clans,

ונחלת ארצות |]מועדי קודש ותקו־ 15
פות שנים וקצי

15 and the inheritance of the lands, of the holy festivals, of cycles of the years and times of

עד [ ]ה אלה ידענו מבינתכה אשר 16
[ ] ס

16 eternity. These things we have known through your knowledge that...

[אוזנ]כה אל שועתנו כיא [ ] 17

17 your ear to our cry, for ....

[ ]ל ביתו הכו[ן] 18

18 his house.

ii.   Content

The following is the content of 1QM 8b–18

- · 10.8b–9a - Celebration of God
   1. Introductory question: מיא כמוכה אל ישראל בשמים ובארץ (line 8b)
   2. Description of God's deeds and Power (lines 8b–9a)
- · 10.9b–12a - Celebration of Israel's favor
   1. Introductory question: מיא כעמכה ישראל (line 9b)
   2. Remark about of Israel's favor: בחרתה לכה מכול עמי הארצות

Prophetic Exegesis in 1QM 10

(line 9b)
3. Description of Israel's special place (lines 10–12a)
- 10.12b–18 - Celebration of God's Creation
  1. Listing of God's creative acts (lines 12b–16a)
  2. Remark about Israel knowing God's mysteries (line 16b)
  3. Remark about God hearing Israel's cry (line 17)

Scholars have recognized that beginning in line 8b 1QM 10 transitions into a new type of composition. Yadin observes that this prayer is influenced by the language of Deut 3:24 with similar language from Pss 113:5–6; 92:6; and 71:19. He also points out similarities with 1QHa 15.28 and 1QM 13.13.[40] Davies also sees a connection between this hymn and the *Hodayot*. In particular, he agrees with Osten-Sacken that 1QM 10.8b–18 is a creation hymn which is comparable to 1QHa 9.1–37. Both hymns praise God's attributes (1QM 10.8b–9a; 1QHa 9.1–9a) and God's heavenly and earthly creation (1QM 10.9b–12a; 1QHa 9.13b–20), and both conclude with the assertion that mysteries were revealed through God's wisdom (1QM 10.16b; 1QHa 9.21). Davies adds that both of these texts can be categorized as "generations" (תולדות) and are alternative accounts of the subject of creation. He concludes that the hymn in 1QM has nothing to do with war, but it is a creation hymn.[41]

While the previous comparison is informative in that it offers categories for the genre of 1QM 10.8b–18, we are not convinced that this is a creation hymn. Moreover, Davies' assertion that this creation hymn has nothing to do with war ignores how the question in 8b–9a "Who is like you, God of Israel in the heavens and on earth who does like your great deeds, and as your great strength?" (מיא כמוכה אל ישראל בשמים ובארץ אשר יעשה כמעשיכה הג־ דולים וכגבורתכה החזקה) recalls passages like the Song of the Sea in Exodus 15. The descriptions of God's dealing against the enemy in lines 1–8a and the sudden introduction of this question only reinforces that the song in lines 8b–18 continues with the theme of war. Plus, the language of creation within this hymn is directly connected to wisdom. Thus, it is not creation that takes center stage in this song, but rather that the same God who is supreme over creation has vested knowledge of the mysteries on the new Israel.

iii. Sectarian Intertextuality

The main concern for this section is to draw out any information that can

---

40 Yadin, *The Scroll of the War*, 305.
41 Davies, *1QM, the War Scroll*, 95–96.

elucidate the presence of this song in 1QM. We will proceed by exploring how the language of this song appears elsewhere in the DSS. The main questions that we want to ask are: is this a sectarian song? A subsequent question is who is the Israel that this song refers to? Our tentative answer is that this represents a sectarian song mainly because of its wisdom themes and its use of language that connotes that Israel is an insider group.

The descriptions of Israel in lines 9–11 support the argument that Israel is a chosen people that has the knowledge and access to God's wisdom. Likewise, the references in lines 15–16 to the "holy festivals" (מועדי קודש) emphasize the importance that these festivities have among God's creative acts. Taken together lines 9–11 and 15–16 support that Israel refers to an specific group that observes the statutes and wisdom of God and for whom the festivals are an important part of God's creative acts. Line 16, therefore, closes with the speaker acknowledging that these things have been manifested to them by God's knowledge. In essence, 1QM 10.8b–18 is a song that celebrates God as the sovereign teacher and the sectarians as the chosen people – the new Israel. The ensuing discussion will focus on the main markers within this song and how these suggest that the sectarians are the recipients of God's wisdom. Initially, we will focus on the descriptions in lines 10–11 of an insider group who is privy to the mysteries of God. Then we will cover lines 15–16 to explore how these festivals point to a sectarian source.

Lines 10–11 list out attributes that Israel possesses as the chosen people. These attributes combine a sensorial verb and with an object of that verb. For instance, Israel as a people are "learned in the statutes" (מלומדי חוק), "who hear the voice of glory" (שומעי קול נכבד), and are "seers of the holy angels" (רואי מלאכי קודש). Moreover, they have open ears to hear "deep things" (מגולי אוזן ושומעי עמוקות). This Israel is, therefore, not only a chosen people, but they are those who are attuned to God's mysteries and will, which many sectarian texts interpret as part of their own ethos.

For instance, the phrase "learned in the statutes" (מלומדי חוק) appears in 1QM 10.10 as well as in the parallel version in 4Q495 1.2. Also, מלומדים is used in 1QM 7.12–13 to describe the soldiers who are trained in battle and in the use of horses. Elsewhere the sectarians are described as "disciples" (למודים). CD 20.4 states that the person who wanders away from following the virtuous rules shall be removed and shall not have part of the "disciples of God" (למודי אל). In 1QHa 15.10–14 the speaker reflects on being appointed to comfort the weary and vows that her/his tongue remains as one of the למודים.[42] Also, 1QS 9.12–14 lists out that the duties of the "Instructor"

---

42 Further, in 4Q428 10.7 we find that the speaker was established on the righteous path

Prophetic Exegesis in 1QM 10

(משכיל) who is not only responsible to adopt a proper conduct of a leader, but is to study the wise sayings and "statutes of the time" (חוק העת). The Instructor is also in charge of discerning who is a true Son of Righteousness and to sustain the "chosen ones" (בחירי), which 1QM 12.1 describes as the "chosen of the holy people" (בחירי עם קודש).

On a parallel vein the phrase משכילי בינה from 1QM 10.10 denotes the wisdom that Israel possesses. CD 12.21–23 describes the statutes that the מש־כיל shall live by and adds that if the seed of Israel lives by these precepts, they will not see condemnation. The passage ends with the provision of the Rule, which is a standard that everyone who dwells in the camp shall follow. 1QS also captures the same essence when it describes that the Instructor shall "enlighten" (להבין) and "teach" (ללמד) the sectarians (1QS 3.13; cf. 9.12–21). Other passages like 1Q28b 1.1, 3.22, and 5.20 emphasize the blessing that the Instructor shall provide to the sectarians by teaching and reminding them about God's precepts.[43]

As for the phrase "seers of the holy angels" (רואי מלאכי קודש) the scrolls provide ample evidence of the sectarians' belief that divine beings were in their midst. We saw in 1QM 7.6 that the מלאכי קודש are in the camp and the command to observe strict purity (cf. 4Q491 Frg. 1–3.10). The same type of restriction appears in 4Q266 8i.9 (cf. CD 15.17) where it restricts access to the "congregation" (עדה), because the מלאכי קודש are in their midst. And the prayer in 4Q289 1a–b.5 mentions the priestly duties of the one who is in charge and adds a description about the מלאכי קודש in the congregation. The fragmentary nature of this manuscript prevents us from saying more, but we posit nonetheless that part of the priestly duties was to maintain purity because of the divine presence within the community.[44]

Lastly, when it comes to the description of Israel as having "open ears and hearers of deep things" (מגולי אוזן ושומעי עמוקות) 4Q266 2i.3–6 (cf. 4Q268 1.5–8) provides the most complete evidence of sectarian influence. Like we

---

and that her/his אוזן are open to God's teachings. This line captures some of the sense from 1QM 10.11 where the sectarians are described as מגולי אוזן ושמעי עמוקות. In 4Q435 Frg. 1 col. 1.3–4 we find this line that echoes the sentiment of 1QM and the 1QHa when it states: ויפקח עיניהם לראות את דרכיו ואזניהם לשמוע למודו.

43 Other passages with a similar theme include: 1QHa 20.4, 20.11; 4Q417 1i.25; 4Q418 81a.17; 4Q421 1a ii–b.10.

44 For a discussion about angels and the sectarian identity, see David Larsen, "Angels Among Us: the use of Old Testament Passages as Inspiration for Temple Themes in the Dead Sea," *Studies in the Bible and Antiquity* 5 (2013): 91–110. Esther Chazon, "Liturgical Communion with the Angels at Qumran," in *Sapiential, Liturgical and Poetical Texts from Qumran*, ed. Daniel Falk, Florentino García Martínez (Leiden: Brill, 2000), 95–105. Devorah Dimant, "Men as Angels: The Self-Image of the Qumran Community," in *Religion and Politics in the Ancient Near East*, ed. Adele Berlin (Bethesda: University of Maryland Press, 1996), 93–103.

mentioned above, 4Q266 contains the teachings of the Instructor to the sectarians. The material in this manuscript pre-dates CD and along with manuscripts 4Q267–272 it provides substantial information that parallels some of the content in CD.[45] Because of the fragmentary nature of 4Q266 2i.3–6 we need to pair it with 4Q268 1.5–8 to capture the essence of the passage.

4Q266 2i.3–6 (4Q268 1.5–8)	Translation
‏[והו]א חקוק קץ חרון לעם לא ידעהו	[H]e decreed times of anger for the people that do not know him,
‏[והוא הכין מועדי רצון לדור[שי מצוותיו ולהולכים בתמים דרך	[but he established times of favor for those who se]ek his commandments and walk on the path of integrity.
‏[ויגל עיניה מה בנסתרות וא[וזנמה פתחו וישמעו עמוקות	[He uncovered their eyes to hidden things and] opened their ears, and they heard deep things,
‏ויבינו [בכול נהיות עד מה יבוא במה[	and they understood [all that is to happen until it comes upon them]

The preceding text describes in dualistic fashion the two outcomes that God has decreed. The explicit use of the same subject and words with similar sounds (i.e. ‏הכין/חקק‎, ‏מועדים/קצים‎, ‏רצון/חרון‎) provide a rhythmic tune to these descriptions that make them easier to remember. The key differentiation between both parties is knowledge; those who do not know God will experience tribulation, while those who seek the path of knowledge encapsulated in the commandments will have favor. The seeking of the commandments is what allows the chosen people to be able to walk on the path of integrity. Further, the last two lines provide the most important descriptions for our current question. In them we see the use of revelatory language where the barriers that prevented this people from understanding the mysteries of God were removed. The notions in these lines of having "opened eyes" (‏יגל עיניה‎) and "ears opened" (‏אוזנמה פתח‎) appear elsewhere in the scrolls.

In CD 2.2, 14 the Instructor continuously uses the refrain "listen Israel" (‏ועתה שמעו‎) followed by a lesson. The sage precedes the teachings claiming that he will/I will open the ears and eyes (‏אגלה אזנכם‎ and ‏אגלה עיניכם‎) of

---

45 For a study that deals with the Damascus Document from the standpoint of source and redaction criticism, see: Charlotte Hempel, *The Laws of the Damascus Document: Sources, Tradition and Redaction* (Leiden: Brill, 1998). Hempel sets the stage in her work by describing the scholarly discussion surrounding the 4Q material and CD. She, like many other scholars, sees a development in the traditions that include halakhah, community rules, and penal code, as well as liturgy.

Prophetic Exegesis in 1QM 10   131

the members of the covenant and his children. 1QS 1.9 complements this picture by stating that the teacher of the community must walk in integrity and relay all that has been revealed for the appointed times.[46] 1QS 8.1, 15–16 add that the members of the Council of the Yahad shall do everything that has been prescribed in the Torah and revealed age by age (עת בעת) according to the "prophets" (נביאים). This same standard applies in 1QS 9.13–14 to the Instructor who shall follow what has been revealed from age to age and apply the statute to his time. We can gather from these texts that revelation, represented as the opening of the eyes or ears, is something that happens as the leaders of the sect impart their teaching. By the same token, the revelation is something that has already been given through the Torah and the Prophets. Thus, the picture that emerges is of the sectarians as disciples, who must continue on the path of learning what God has already revealed to them. The *Hodayot* provide a similar picture.

1QHa 9 is a prayer that deals with God's wisdom and supremacy over creation. In it we gather that God has appointed the destinies of people. In lines 20–21 the speaker states that he knows these things because God has "uncover" (גלה) her/his ears. Because God has opened his ears, the speaker is able to discern the order of things and the destinies of peoples even though he is not worthy of this privilege. The same sense of being unworthy of revelation happens in 1QHa 21.4–5 (4Q427 10.1–5). In this passage the speaker acknowledges that God has opened his eyes and ears, which helped him receive a "revealed word" (נפתח דבר) despite the fact that his ears are uncircumcised (לערל אוזן; cf. 1QHa 4.7–12, 23.4).[47] Lastly, 1QHa 14.4 provides an interesting description where the speaker states that God has "opened my ears to the admonition of those who rebuke righteously" (גליתה אוזני [למו]סר מוכיחי צדק), which in turn gives him hope that humans can change despite their sin.

The previous texts demonstrate the presence in other sectarian texts of the themes of Israel as a chosen people, who are endowed with not only the ability to understand the mysteries of God but have access to see and hear divine things as depicted in 1QM 10.10–11. Furthermore, the juxtaposition of wisdom, knowledge, revelation, and access to the divine underscore that these are marks of the chosen ones, which the sectarians believed pointed to them as the true Israel. This last point is further emphasized in lines 15–16 where the speaker claims those truths for the group.

---

46   Other significant passages that deal with the topic of revelation in 1QS include: 1QS 5.9, 8.1, 8.15–16, 9.13, 19.

47   Revelation of hidden things happens also in 4Q427 i.19–21; 4Q434 Frg. 1.1–4; 4Q463 Frg. 1.1–4. Also regarding deep things (עמוקות), see: 1QS 11.19; 1QHa 5.8; 4Q440 3i.23 with רז 4Q463 1.4.

Following the depictions of Israel as those vested with the divine gifts, the song transitions into a listing that praises God and creation in lines 12b–18. In these lines we will find a pair of very important clues that solidify the interpretation of Israel as the sectarians. The first clue happens in the explicit reference in lines 15–16 to the "holy festivals, of cycles of the years and times of eternity" (מועדי קודש‎, תקופות שנים‎, and קצי עד‎). The second clue is the fact that in lines 16–17 the song transitions to a first-person plural subject where the speaker claims these truths for the group: "these things we have known through your knowledge" (אלה ידענו מבינתכה‎) and "your ear to our cry" (אוזנכה אל שועתנו‎). The sectarians, therefore, attest that they know the mysteries of creation because God has made it known to them. Plus, they express their conviction that God hears their cry. The significance of lines 16–17 will be dealt in the prophetic interpretation of this song below. At this junction we will focus on lines 15–16 and how these descriptions point to a sectarian influence.

The "holy festivals" (מועדי קודש‎) are the communal gatherings established from ancient times that became an important part of the teachings and overall ethos of the sectarians.[48] The Damascus Document contains one of the clearest examples of how important these times were for the sectarians. CD 3 recalls Israel's historical vicissitudes since the days of Noah. Lines 12–16 transition from the disappointments of the past, to describe that God had preserved a remnant, which is an idea that CD 1 had already introduced. We are also told that God revealed to this remnant "hidden things" (נסתרות‎) that Israel had not understood.[49] Among those hidden things CD 3.14–15 list out the "holy Sabbaths and the glorious festivals" (שבתות קדשו ומועדי כבו־‎ ‎דו), that are part of God's will. To emphasize this last point lines 15–16 close with a citation of Lev 18:5 where it states about God's desires that "a man who does them shall live in them" (יעשה האדם וחיה בהם‎).[50]

For its part the Rule of the Community provides a similar scenario about

---

48 James VanderKam, *Calendars in the Dead Sea Scrolls* (London: Routledge, 1998), 43–51. Daniel Falk, *Daily, Sabbath and Festival Prayers in the Dead Sea Scrolls* (Leiden: Brill, 1998); Jeremy Penner, "Mapping Fixed Prayers from the Dead Sea Scrolls onto Second Temple Period Judaism," *DSD* 21 (2014): 39–63. John Jarick, "The Bible's 'Festival Scrolls' Among the Dead Sea Scrolls," in *The Scrolls and the Scriptures: Qumran Fifty Years After*, ed. Stanley Porter and Craig Evans (Sheffield: Sheffield University Press, 1997), 170–182.

49 A similar indictment happens in Jub. 23:19 where Israel is guilty of abandoning the proper observance of the feasts, Sabbaths, and jubilees.

50 Charlotte Hempel, *The Laws of the Damascus Document,* 88–89. Maxine Grossman, *Reading for History in the Damascus Document* (Leiden: Brill, 2002), 81, 112. Devorah Dimant, *History, Ideology and Bible Interpretation in the Dead Sea Scrolls* (Tübingen: Mohr Siebeck, 2014), 467. Other passages in CD that highlight the importance of the מועדי‎, include: CD 6.18 and 12.4.

Prophetic Exegesis in 1QM 10

the importance of these holy times. 1QS 1.13–18 describes that all who join the Yahad shall be endowed with God's knowledge. Lines 14–15 command not to deviate from the laws, specifically "they shall not advance their times nor to postpone any of the appointed times" (לוא לקדם עתיהם ולוא להתא־ חר מכול מועדיהם). Consequently, line 16 states that they shall deviate neither from following these customs nor to the right or the left (cf. 1QS 3.10).[51] 1QS 10.1–8 provide an important description of the sectarian belief regarding the "appointed times" (מועדים). Following a discussion of the precepts that the Instructor shall follow the end of column 9 states that he shall bless the Creator. Column 10, therefore, continues with a description of how God has ordained the cycles of time when the new sun and moon arrive (lines 1–3). Line 4 beautifully states that the renewal of these cycles gives way to a special day in the Holy of Hollies, because the מועדים are a sign of God unlocking eternal love each time these cycles begin as ordained. Line 8 proceeds with a prayer where the speaker glorifies God and confesses that "while I live the statute will be engraved in my tongue" (היותי חוק חרות בלשוני).

In 1QM the מועדים appear in contexts of the religious cult and in times appointed by God. The introduction in 1QM 1 describes that the sectarians will shine at the end of the appointed times of darkness. Lines 1.8–9 use מועדים: one as the end of the time of darkness, and as the prelude to prosperous times when the sectarians shall shine. In the War of Divisions the מועדים appear as the sacred festivals of Israel. 1QM 2.4–7 describe the distribution of responsibilities among the different chiefs and heads in Israel. One of these leaders is the Chief of their Courses who along the Commissioners will take their stand during their "appointed times, the new moons and Sabbaths, and on every day of the year" (למועדיהם לחודשיהם ולשבתות ולכול ימי השנה). In addition, this passage reveals that the assignment of roles, especially surrounding the organization of the cult and the festivals were part of the responsibilities of older men. The other appearances of מועדים in 1QM take place in passages that describe the arrangement of times for the war and victory of the sectarians, such as: the "appointed times of eternity" (מועדי עולמים) as the time when the warriors will be written in the book of the armies of God (1QM 12.3), and the covenant that God made with Israel's ancestors in 1QM 13.8. There is also the "appointed times of eternal assembly" (מועדי תעודות עולמים) in 14.13 when the warriors shall praise God day and night, the "appointed time of vengeance" (מועד נקם) when the priest shall pray retribution on the enemies

---

51 Charlotte Hempel, *The Qumran Rule Texts in Context* (Tübingen: Mohr Siebeck, 2013), 320. Sacha Stern, "The 'Sectarian' Calendar of Qumran," in *Sects and Sectarianism in Jewish History,* ed. Sacha Stern (Leiden: Brill, 2011), 39–62.

(15.6), the מועדים to bring down the Prince of the realm of wickedness (17.5, 6), and the appointed time for God's will and reprisal (18.14).

As we can see from the prior descriptions the מועדים in 1QM consist of times that Israel shall observe their prescribed communal duties and they denote as well specific times that God has ordained for the sectarians to overtake their enemies. An important aspect of this latter use of מועדים is that it precedes celebrations depicted with language that is full of joy, blessing, and peace. Not only does the introduction to the scroll present this picture, but in the latter columns we have a procession to Zion (19.5–8). The combination of appointed times and the celebration of this victory gives us a strong sense not just of the type of literature that 1QM is but of the intimacy with God that the sectarians aspired to enjoy.

The other two memorials mentioned in 1QM 10.15 are the "courses of years" (תקופות שנים) and the "times of eternity" (קצי עד). The evidence on these times is not as extensive as with the מועדים, but they do appear in contexts where we can gather their relevance in matters of cultic observance. In 4Q216 6.2–8 (Jub. 2.7–12) we have part of the account of creation and how God made the sun, the moon, and the stars. The sun we are told was set as a sign above the earth for the Sabbaths, the מועדים, and for the תקופות שנים. Jub. 4.17–18 add that Enoch was the first man to learn writing and knowledge of wisdom. Enoch was also the one who wrote in a book all the signs in the heavens, in order that the people would know the תקופות שנים. 1En. 82.7 adds to this description by indicating that Uriel had revealed to Enoch the mysteries of the months and festivals. The link between the מועדים to the תקופות שנים happens also in 4Q286 2b.10, where the language of God's majesty and power over creation includes these sacred times.

In terms of the phrase "eternal times" (קצי עד), the scrolls provide evidence of the connection between God's supremacy and the looming judgment upon creation. An interesting connection appears in 1QS 4 where there is a distinction between those who live according to God's wisdom and those who do not. Lines 15–17 draw this stark contrast as two diametrically opposed paths that God has established until the latter times. The image that comes from these descriptions is that God is in control of good and evil. Lines 25–26 corroborate this notion by describing that the two ways walk on parallel until God decides in pre-ordained knowledge to bring things to an end. Thus, the eternal times have a dualistic tone in which God controls not just the paths of people but ultimately the time when each will be called to account for their deeds. The image of judgment also happens in 4Q416 1.12–14 (cf. 4Q418 2c.6), where the dualistic perspective of good and evil is contrasted. These lines

Prophetic Exegesis in 1QM 10   135

specifically state that the Sons of Heaven will rejoice when all iniquity shall come to an end and peace will endure for eternal times.

Our survey has demonstrated that the song in 1QM 10.8b–18 possesses terms that point to the sectarians and their ideology. The use of wisdom markers that depict Israel as a chosen people, wise in knowledge and privy of God's mysteries, suggests that the focus is not ancient Israel but a new Israel that has received the revelation via the opening of the eyes and ears. This sectarian picture is complemented by the mention of the קצי עד, מועדי קודש, and the תקופות שנים, which refer to times that the sectarians kept meticulously. These intertextual markers, therefore, support the fact that this song is of sectarian origin, and they also introduce new aspects about revelation and wisdom not seen in the rest of the scroll. The special relation between God and this new people is highlighted at the end of the song when it confirms that not only do the sectarians know the mysteries of creation, but they can trust that God hears their cry. Thus, just like the trumpets in 10.7 invoke God's memory, Israel's "cry" (שועה) in line 17 causes God's ear to listen. We will see how the intimate image of God and Israel depicted in these lines takes place in Scripture.

iv. Scriptural Intertextuality

The main focus as we deal with the Scriptural intertextuality of 1QM 10.8b–18 will be on the question "Who is like you, God of Israel? (מיא כמוכה אל יש־ ראל). The ensuing discussion will demonstrate that this question was a rhetorical device used in diverse contexts, including war, worship, and wisdom, as the speakers expressed their belief in God's supremacy over other "gods," creation, and the destinies of people. This set of ideas made their way into 1QM 10.8b–18 and can be categorized into three distinct yet mutually connected ways: God as warrior, God as deliverer of the weak, and God as wise teacher. From these different images, the sectarians made a new song that elevates God as the sovereign teacher, and they as the new Israel and recipients of God's favor and blessings.

God the Warrior

When 1QM 10.8 transitions from the descriptions of the sounding of the trumpets to the question מיא כמוכה אל ישראל, we notice a change that triggers the reader's memory. God is no longer addressed in the third person, but there is a switch where God is addressed in the second person "you".

This question is a marker that evokes several Scriptural passages where Israel celebrates God's might and favor. The abrupt introduction of this question indicates to the reader not just that there is a transition in subject and type of composition (i.e. from war to worship), but also that the promises of success illustrated in 1QM 10.1–8a can be counted on as fulfilled. A similar scenario happens in Scripture, where a celebratory song introduced by the question מיא כמוכה אל is interjected in the context of God's war.

Exodus 15 celebrates the redemption of Israel from the house of slavery.[52] In this chapter we have two songs: one by Moses (vv. 1–19) often referred to as the "Song of the Sea," and one by the prophetess Miriam (vv. 20–21). In the Song of the Sea we have the proclamation of God's victory over Egypt illustrated in awesome language that depicts God as the mighty warrior that controlled the sea and shattered the ambitions of Pharaoh (vv. 2–10). In verse 11, however, the song shifts into a different set of descriptions. We notice this change first by the insertion of the question "Who is like you Lord among the gods? Who is like you, glorious in holiness, to be feared in splendor, who does marvels?" (מי כמכה באלם יהוה מי כמכה נאדר בקדש נורא תהלת עשה פלא). The depiction of God also changes from the mighty warrior to the shepherd that leads Israel through safe pastures. Verses 13–16 specifically recall passages from Torah, where God walks with Israel through this procession that leads the nation to the holy sanctuary. The mention of the "mountain" (הר) and the "sanctuary" (מקדש) as well as the exaltation of God's eternal reign suggests a possible connection with worship material that appears in Psalms. If this is the case, perhaps vv. 11–18 were incorporated to the Song of the Sea at a later time.[53] In any case, the transition from God's exaltation to the procession happens with the introduction of מי־כמכה באלם יהוה.

Likewise, 1QM 10 uses the question מיא כמוכה אל ישראל to lead the reader into a different focus, from Israel's deliverance from their enemies via the sounding of the trumpets in line 8 to the praises of God's sovereignty. An interesting distinction is that in the Song of the Sea the end of the procession leads to the holy sanctuary, while in 1QM 10 creation is the sanctuary of God. Also, the remnant in Exod 15 is established in God's abode, while the remnant

---

52 Martin Brenner, *The Song of the Sea: Exodus 15:1–21* (Berlin: De Gruyter, 1991). Brian Russell, *The Song of the Sea: The Date of Composition and Influence of Exodus 15:1–21* (New York: Peter Lang, 2007).

53 Georg Fischer, "Das Schilfmeerlied Exodus 15 in Seinem Kontext" *Biblica*, 77 (1996): 32–47. Anja Klein, "Hymn and History in Ex 15: Observations on the Relationship between Temple Theology and Exodus Narrative in the Song of the Sea," *ZAW* 124 (2012): 516–527. Mark Smith, "The Poetics of Exodus 15 and Its Position in the Book," in *Imagery and Imagination in Biblical Literature: Essays in Honor of Aloysius Fitzgerald*, ed. Lawrence Boadt and Mark S. Smith (Washington: Catholic Biblical Association of America, 2001), 23–34.

Prophetic Exegesis in 1QM 10   137

in 1QM 10 is established in creation and in the wisdom that comes from God. This distinction is an important one to consider, especially since the absence of Temple language in 1QM 10 (as well as in the songs in 1QM 12 and 19) could be an indication of 1QM's attitude towards the Temple in Jerusalem.[54] Another relevant distinction is that in Exod 15:13 the Song of the Sea describes God's redemption of a people without going into specific detail of who this people were and what their merits were for being redeemed. For its part 1QM 10.9 explicitly identifies the chosen people as Israel. And as we saw in our previous analysis, 1QM 10.9–12 further narrows the scope of this chosen people by using specific expressions that point to the sectarians and their view of themselves as the chosen remnant. The last point of comparison that we want to draw our attention to deals with the introductory questions in these songs.

When Exod 15:11 asks מי כמכה באלם יהוה it gives the impression that in the singer's perspective there might be other "gods." 1QM 10.8b, on the other hand, does not leave room for that possibility as it specifically mentions the God of Israel. Other scrolls, however, do not seem to draw such a contrast. Instances like 1QHa 15.28 (cf. 4Q428 9.3) where the speaker asks "Who is like you Lord among the gods? And who is as your truth? And who can be justified before you in his judgment?" (מי כמוכה באלים אדוני ומי כאמתכה ומי יצדק לפניכה בהשפטו), and 4Q427 7i.8 (cf. 4Q431 1.4) where God asks the question "who is like me among the gods?" (מי כמוני באלים) indicate that the type of question seen in Exod 15:11 (and Jer 49:19; 50:44) was also part of the sectarian poetic and liturgical repertoire.[55] But what exactly are the אלים in the sectarian context?[56]

The word אלים appears in 1QM 1 and in columns 14–19, which scholars

---

54 The only instances in 1QM that describe the מקדש are: 1QM 2.3 and 7.11. Yadin compares the attitude in 1QM and CD towards the Temple sacrifices. He observes that while CD gives guidance to members as to the current state of affairs in the age of wickedness, 1QM describes the future service. He adds that originally the sect was forbidden to participate in the Temple rituals until the time to come when the service is conducted according to the spirit of the sect. Yadin, *The Scroll of the War*, 199–201.

55 Esther Chazon, "Lowly to Lofty: the Hodayot's use of Liturgical Traditions to Shape Sectarian Identity and Religious Experience," *RevQ* 26 (2013): 3–19.

56 For a discussion about this question, see: John Collins, "Powers in Heaven: God, Gods, and Angels in the Dead Sea Scrolls," in *Religion in the Dead Sea Scrolls*, ed. John J. Collins and Robert A. Kugler (Grand Rapids: Eerdmans, 2000), 9–28. Dennis Green, "Divine Names: Rabbinic and Qumran Scribal Techniques," in *The Dead Sea Scrolls Fifty Years After Their Discovery*, ed. Lawrence H. Schiffman, Emanual Tov, and James C. Vanderkam (Jerusalem: Israel Exploration Society, 2000), 497–511. Jonathan Ben-Dov, "The Elohistic Psalter and the Writing of Divine Names at Qumran," in *The Dead Sea Scrolls and Contemporary Culture: Proceedings of the International Conference Held at the Israel Museum, Jerusalem (July 6–8, 2008)*, ed. Adolfo D. Roitman, Lawrence H. Schiffman, and Shani Tzoref (Leiden: Boston: Brill, 2011), 79–104. Edward Cook, "What Did the Jews of Qumran Know about God and How Did They Know It?: Revelation and God in the Dead Sea Scrolls," in *Judaism in Late Antiquity: A Systemic Reading*

have identified as part of the Battle against the Kittim.[57] 1QM 1.9–11 predict a day when the Kittim shall fall during time of distress when the sectarians and the Lot of Darkness will fight for supremacy before the God of Israel. We are also told that this will be a time when the "congregation of the gods" (עדת אלים) and the assembly of men shall confront each other. These lines distinguish between the God of Israel and the אלים. This distinction is further corroborated in the battle against the Kittim. 1QM 14.1–4 relays that after the priests had left the battlefield and cleansed from the impurity of the corpses, they shall all sing to the God of Israel. This praise continues till the end of the column in line 16 where it specifically uses the refrain "Rise, rise, God of gods" (רומה רומה אל אלים). On a similar vein in 1QM 18.3–6 the Chief Priest along with other priests and Levites will bless the God of Israel as the combatants are about to take on the Kittim. Here again the priestly praise highlights the supremacy of God over other gods through the line "blessed is your name, God of gods" (ברוך שמכה אל אלים). The explicit references to the God of Israel and אל אלים draw a distinction with the אלים that clearly highlights that the God of Israel is supreme over these other gods.[58]

Like 1QM the Hodayot also illustrate the distinction between God and other gods. In 1QHa 15 the speaker recounts his struggles and in lines 26–29 she/he gives thanks to God for revealing the truth and the depth of God's mysteries. Lines 28–29 are particularly revealing because in them the speaker asks "who is like you among the god, Lord?" (מי כמוכה באלים אדוני) and emphasizes that none of the "spiritual hosts" (צבי רוח) are able to stand before God's anger.[59] Who these צבי רוח are is not clear, but it could perhaps point to other אלים which are introduced in the initial question.[60] 1QHa 18.10 makes the point of God's supremacy over other "spiritual beings" when it states that God is "Chief of the gods" (שר אלים) and "Lord of every spirit" (אדון לכול

---

of the Dead Sea Scrolls, ed. Alan Avery-Peck, Jacob Neusner, and Bruce D. Chilton (Leiden: Brill, 2001), 3–22.

57 אל ישראל appears in: 1QM 1.9; 6.6; 13.1–2, 13.13, 14.4, 15.13, 16.1, 18.3, 18.6. On the other hand, אלים appears in: 1QM 1.10–11; 14.15–16; 15.14; 17.7; 18.6 (4Q491 8–10i.13–14; 10ii.15; 11i.12–18; 13.1; 14–15.8–11; 24.3–4).

58 Furthermore, according to 1QM 17.5–8 not only is the God of Israel over other gods but has lifted the authority of Michael above the other אלים. Yadin deals extensively on the angelology within 1QM. In particular he has a discussion about the connection between archangels and the sectarian. Yadin, *The Scroll of the War*, 229–242. Other manuscripts like 4Q491 11i.12–18 (1QHa 3 Bottom.8) describe a head of the אלים. The question that comes up is if these texts refer to Michael or to another agent. John O'Neill takes the position that t4Q491 describes a human agent. See: John O'Neill, "'Who is Comparable to Me in My Glory?': 4Q491 Fragment 11 (4Q491C) and the New Testament," *NovT* 42 (2000): 24–38

59 The manuscript reveals that an editor of the manuscript added צבי to the text.

60 There are only two instances of צבי רוח in the DSS: 1QHa 15.29, which is the object of our analysis and 1QHa 11.22.

רוח). Also, 1QHa 24.10 mentions the "angels" (מלאכים) and it describes that God has humbled the אלים. And 1QHa 27.3 (cf. 4Q427 7 ii.9–10) describes how God along with the "gods in the congregation of the Yahad" (אלים בעדת יחד) brings the haughty to eternal destruction.[61] These two manuscripts in the Hodayot depict God's supremacy over the divine beings, and it distinguishes, at least in the case of 1QHa 24, between the מלאכים and the אלים.[62] Overall, the Hodayot along with the references in 1QM demonstrate that the אלים were perceived as divine beings of lesser stature than God. 1QM 10 makes this distinction clear by using the reference of the God of Israel, which appears mostly in 1QM and in other war texts from Caves 4 and 11.[63]

1QM 10.8b points to a switch in the narrative. More significantly the question "who is like you God of Israel" triggers the allusion of the song of the Sea in Exod 15, where the same question follows God's military victory and deliverance of Israel. In the same fashion, the question in 10.8b follows the triumph over the enemy in the previous lines, and begins to list out the attributes of God in the same manner that Exod 15:13 depict God as the loving shepherd that leads Israel to the holy abode.[64] This last depiction gives way to the other image of God that emerges from this song as the deliverer of the weak.

God the Deliverer of the Weak

The question מיא כמוכה אל ישראל also evokes the image of God as deliverer of the weak. 1QM 10.8a already begins to display this facet with the promise that the sounding of the trumpets would alert God and bring freedom to Israel. Israel's dependence on God is picked up in line 9 when it points out that God had chosen them from all the peoples of earth. Certainly, the expression "you chose for yourself" (בחרתה לכה) highlights the intimacy that God and Israel have, and it underscores the redemption of Israel as a people. The tail end of this song in lines 16–18 make this more apparent when it describes Israel's privilege in understanding God's ways, and how God turns the ear to their cry. Below we will focus on specific pieces where the rhetorical question

---

61 Other References of the congregation of the אלים includes: 1Q22 4.1.

62 Angela Harkins, "Elements of the Fallen Angels Traditions in the Qumran Hodayot," in *The Fallen Angels Traditions: Second Temple Developments and Reception History*, ed. Angela Kim Harkins, Kelley Coblentz Bautch, and John Endres (Washington: Catholic Biblical Association of America, 2014), 8–24.

63 References to אל ישראל in the 4Q War Texts, include: 4Q491 8–10i.0–2 (cf. 1QM 14.3–4), 11ii.16; 4Q492 1.12. In Cave 11, the only reference appears in 11Q14.1ii.

64 The connections between the liturgies in 1QM and Exodus 15 will resurface in column 11, where the account recalls the end of Pharaoh in the ים סוף.

מיא כמוכה ישראל appears and where the image of God as deliverer of the weak takes center stage.

Psalm 35 has a combination of the language of war and deliverance. In the opening verse, the psalmist calls on God to intervene on her/his behalf with the cry "Contend Lord with those who contend with me, fight against those who fight me" (ריבה יהוה את יריבי לחם את לחמי). Verses 2–3 continue with this request when the psalmist calls for God to use the shield and buckler, and to hurl the javelin and spear against the pursuers. The combination of these combative descriptions presents the image of God as the protector who is called upon to rise and assist the needy.

The psalmist's dependence on God is highlighted in verse 3 with the statement "say to my soul: 'I am your salvation'" (אמר לנפשי ישעתך אני). The mention of נפש also appears later in verse 9 when the psalmist rejoices in God. Essentially, prior to verse 10 the psalm has depicted God as the warrior who fights for the psalmist. Thus, by the time the question "who is like you"(מי כמוך) comes up in verse 10, we have a similar pattern as the one in Exod 15; that is, the representation of God as warrior, Israel's reliance on God, and the praise of God through this rhetorical question. Verse 10 further emphasizes the deliverance of the weak when it states "delivering the weak from those stronger than them, and the poor and needy from those who robbed them" (מציל עני מחזק ממנו ועני ואביון מגזלו). Likewise, Ps 71:19 makes this same point when it asks "God, who is like you" (אלהים מי כמוך) and follows this question with a description of redemption as the psalmist is brought up from the depths of the earth. The reference to the depths of the earth correlates to the depiction in 1QM 10.12–14 where God is sovereign over creation.

This same sovereignty appears in Ps 89:9, which asks "Lord God of hosts, who is like you" (יהוה אלהי צבאות מי כמוך). This question is preceded in verse 7 by another question where the psalmist asks "who in the clouds can be compared to the Lord, who is like the Lord among the sons of gods" (מי בשחק יערך ליהוה ידמה ליהוה בבני אלים). The point that these questions make is that God is sovereign over the heavenly beings. The psalm proceeds in verses 10–13 to complete the picture as it shows God's power over creation. The interesting aspect of these descriptions is that they illustrate creation as mythical figures; thus, God rules the raging of the sea and crushes Rahab like a carcass. Further, God's dominion over creation is complete. The heavens and earth, the north and south, and Tabor and Hermon all praise God's name. Verses 14–18 complete this picture by introducing images of blessing and praise of God, and in verses 21–27 with the promises to David. These depictions reiterate God's commitment to be the deliverer and protector from

Prophetic Exegesis in 1QM 10   141

the enemy's attack on David.[65]

This point brings us to the last passage that we will consider. In Micah 7, the prophet grieves for the condition of Israel. In verse 18 Micah asks "who is like you God who pardons iniquity" (מי אל כמוך נשא עון). Prior to this question vv. 14–17 describe that the deliverance from Egypt was going to be repeated. That is, God would act again as a shepherd who leads and feeds the flock in Bashan and Gilead. Like in the previous passages we have considered, Micah 7 uses the rhetorical question as a statement of God as the deliverer. The difference in this case, however, is that Israel is depicted as being blemished by iniquity. In fact, Micah emphasizes that God is sovereign to lift the thing that has brought the humiliation of the people. Even more Micah shows that God is faithful to remove the "iniquity" (עון) and "transgression" (פשע) for the sake of the "remnant of his inheritance" (שארית נחלתו). This last point is an important one because it demonstrates that God's favor, as implied by the rhetorical question מי כמוכה, is directly applicable to God's chosen remnant. 1QM 13.8 echoes Micah's sentiment in a prayer where the priests and Levites recall God's help to the remnant and survivors for the sake of the covenant. Likewise, in 1QM 14.6–9 the soldiers celebrate that God gives strength to the weak and poor in spirit, and that across the generations God has made wondrous works for the sake of the covenant with the remnant.

God the Wise Teacher

The last aspect of God that 1QM 10.8b–18 brings up is that of a wise teacher. Despite the fact that God is not specifically depicted as a teacher, the song in lines 10–11 indicates that Israel has learned the mysteries of God in the statutes and in the revelation of the "deep things" (עמוקות). The song goes a step further in ascribing the knowledge of these mysteries through God's dominion over creation. The combination of the question מיא כמוכה אל ישראל and the depictions of wisdom and the language of creation trigger Scriptural passages like Job 36.

In this chapter Elihu continues with an argument that began in chapter 32. After stating that God punishes the wicked and gives justice to the afflicted (Job 36:6), Elihu adds that God also gives an opportunity for people to turn

---

65 For a discussion on Psalm 89 and the topic of creation and chaos, see: Carly Crouch, "Made in the Image of God: The Creation of אדם the Commissioning of the King and the Chaoskampf of YHWH," *Journal of Ancient Near Eastern Religions* 16 (2016): 1–21. Knut Heim, "The (God-) Forsaken King of Psalm 89: A Historical and Intertextual Enquiry," in *King and Messiah in Israel and the Ancient Near East: Proceedings of the Oxford Old Testament Seminar*, ed. John Day (Sheffield: Sheffield University Press, 1998), 296–322.

from their ways (Job 36:8–12). Verses 9–10 use the language of revelation as they state that God "he declares their deeds to them" (יגד להם פעלם) and "he opens their ears to instruction" (יגל אזנם למוסר). The use of נגד and גלה implies a revelation or the uncovering of hidden things (e.g. Ezekiel 43:10; Num 22:31), and מוסר (e.g. Psalm 50:17; Prov 15:33) is the instruction that God gives. Verse 15 emphasizes this point when it describes that God "delivers the afflicted by their affliction and open their ears by adversity" (יחלץ עני בעניו ויגל בלחץ אזנם). The combination of the language of revelation, the opening of the ears and the deliverance of the afflicted are all concepts that 1QM 10.8b–18 describes. In addition, Job 36:22 introduces Elihu's question to Job regarding God, first by stating God's supremacy and then by asking "who is a teacher like him" (מי כמהו מורה). Obviously, the question is a rhetorical one, and Elihu makes the point that there is no one like God. This he does by listing how God controls the order of creation and everything that happens in it through wisdom (Job 36:26–33). The intriguing part of this passage is that from the end of chapter 36 all the way through 37 references to God's creation and order of things are highlighted. Also, spread out within these chapters are rhetorical questions (e.g. Job 36:29, 37:15–20) that emphasize the futility of trying to understand all of God's ways. Thus, Job 37:21 ends this argument by starting with "and now" (ועתה), which introduces a teaching, where Elihu concludes his argument with a sense of futility in trying to comprehend God's inscrutable ways (Job 37:23). Chapters 38–41 continue with God directly addressing Job and making the same point about the depth of wisdom and God's unsearchable ways.

When 1QM 10.16 states "these things we have known through your understanding" (אלה ידענו מבינתכה), the song emphasizes what Job 36 illustrated when it depicted God ushering revelation through the opening of the ears and eyes to the depths of justice and righteousness. By its use of wisdom and creation material that resembles the language of Job, 1QM 10.8b–18 demonstrates that this type of song encompasses not just war and deliverance language but also wisdom. More significantly, the song underscores that the sectarians used war, creation, wisdom, and deliverance as part of their Scriptural inheritance. And it evinces their ability to integrate what on the surface seem to be disjointed topics to paint a full picture of the sectarian hopes and aspirations, informed by the language of the Scriptures.

We recognized in the sectarian intertextuality that the song in 1QM 10.8b–18 displays the intimacy between God and the new Israel. To continue on this topic, the Scriptural intertextuality focuses on three aspects of God's relation to this people. The qualities of a warrior, deliverer of the weak, and

Prophetic Exegesis in 1QM 10   143

wise teacher all have a Scriptural basis that shaped the sectarian interpretation of God and of God's dealing with Israel. These images together demonstrate that the sectarians understood themselves and their closeness to God
in light of the sacred traditions. What is new about this song is that it specifically points to an inner group, a people that were specifically endowed with
this knowledge and access that is reserved to a few. To have access to this relation one must be open to hear and understand the mysteries of God revealed
in the commandments and the wisdom of creation. The following discussion
will provide a close reading that will address how this song uses the allusions
to Scriptures in a prophetic manner.

v. Prophetic Exegesis

The song in 1QM 10.8b–18 has been labeled by scholars like Davies as a creation song.[66] However, as we have observed in our analysis of the different
intertextual connections, this song is not so much a celebration of God's creation but of God's election of Israel. The content of the song highlights this
interpretation.

When line 8b–9a breaks in with the question מיא כמוכה אל ישראל
בשמים ובארץ, the text suddenly shifts from the military descriptions into a
celebration. This same turn happens in Exod 15 where after the song depicts
how God dealt a final blow to Israel's enemies, a question about God transitions into a tender depiction of God leading the nation to a place of rest and
peace (Exod 15:13). Just like Exod 15:11, 1QM 10.8–9 proceeds from the point
of praising God's splendor into a description of redemption, as it transitions
from God's strength into Israel's choice as the people of God. Different from
Exod 15, however, the song in 1QM spends more time depicting Israel's privilege as the chosen people. Whereas in Exod 15 the song sticks to describing
how God removed all barriers and enemies to bring this people to the holy
abode, 1QM depicts the qualities of this selected people.

The depictions in lines 10–11 point to the sectarians, because much of
what is depicted correlates with the descriptions in other scrolls.[67] The intriguing aspect of these descriptions is that none of them have to do with

---

66 Davies, *1QM, the War Scroll*, 95–96.

67 Schultz, *Conquering the World*, 274–275. Schultz agrees that this song reveals a sectarian provenance. He, however, pursues a different way of demonstrating it. He argues that this
song along with the first 12 lines of 1QM 11 are one piece, that he describes "a hymn of praise."
Besides using Davies' comparison of this song with 1QHa 1, he adds that the mention of Belial
and the seven nations of הבל in 1QM 11.8–9 as well as the mention of the Kittim demonstrate
the sectarian provenance.

144   Intertextuality and Prophetic Exegesis in the War Scroll of Qumran

military might. Rather, we see that this chosen people are well versed in matters of the covenant, the statutes, and wisdom. This discernment gives this new Israel the ability to hear, see, and understand the divine realm. In the same fashion ancient Israel was led to the holy abode, the new Israel is led to this new abode; one that is marked not by architectural structures but one that is structured on the foundation of Torah. Knowledge of Torah, therefore, provides the new Israel with access to God. Such knowledge and access to the divine remind us of Ezekiel's vision in Ezek 40–48 and Enoch's heavenly ascent (1 Enoch 1–36). Wenthe describes the depictions in these lines as evidence of how the sectarians viewed the process of revelation as having direct access to the mysteries of Scripture and the "divine economy."[68] Speaking of divine economy, Christopher Rowland comments that in this passage the sectarians "ascertained the true meaning of Scripture through the inspired interpretation" and direct access to hearing God's voice and seeing the angels. This sort of description, he adds: "looks remarkably like the kind of visions of the heavenly world familiar to us from the apocalypses."[69]

Lines 12–16 ascribe the source of knowledge to God. However, instead of explicitly stating that God gave the new Israel access to the divine, the song directs its attention to the "creator" (בורא). Following the introduction of the בורא, the song enlists all the creative acts. The creation of the earth alludes to Gen 1:1 and it also it recalls Isa 40:28 where the prophet proclaims that the Lord is the creator of the ends of the earth. It is worth mentioning that from verses 25–29, the prophet argues via a series of rhetorical questions that the Lord is incomparable and is the one who empowers the faint. While the reference to the "form of humanity" (תבנית אדם) may echo the formation of humans, specifically of the female, in Gen 2:22. However, the term "form" or "pattern" (תבנית) appears mainly in reference to patterns like the Tabernacle (Exod 25:9) and in Deut 4:16–18 in the command that forbids idols in the likeness of humans, birds, or any other animal. As for the "confusion of language and the separation of peoples" (בלת לשון ומפרד עמים) alludes to Gen 11:9 when God confused the language of the earth. And the mention of the "holy festivals" (מועדי קודש) and the "cycles of years" (תקופות שנים) alludes to passages in the Torah (i.e. Lev 23:2–4, 37; Exod 34:22) where God gave the instructions of when these festivals need to take place. In addition, the explicit

---

68 Wenthe, "The Use of the Hebrew Scriptures in 1QM," 309–310.

69 Christopher Rowland, *The Open Heaven* (New York: Crossroads, 1982), 116. In assessing 1QM and its apocalyptic themes, Jean Duhaime concludes that while not an "apocalypse" per se 1QM shows the appropriation of apocalyptic thought by the group behind this scroll. See: Jean Duhaime, "La Règle de la Guerre de Qumrân et l'Apocalyptiques," *Science et Esprit* 36 (1984): 82–88.

Prophetic Exegesis in 1QM 10

reference to these festivities gives us a clear indication of the sectarian perspective that God not only established creation but also gave instructions for these times. This indicates the importance that the sectarians placed on the proper observance of these sacred times. Essentially, in lines 12–16 the song creates a picture of God as the one who has organized the cosmos and has set it in place. Likewise, God controls the affairs of humanity and history and is the one who established these sacred times to be observed by the chosen people. In a few lines this song encapsulates much of Scriptural belief: the God who created the universe picked Israel as the chosen people. Thus, in the tail end of line 16 the song proceeds with a direct address.

From line 16 and into the initial lines of column 11 God will be addressed in the second person. The relation goes from God-Israel to you-we. God is no longer the creator but is the intimate "you," and Israel is the "we." Line 16 depicts that everything that was recited above "we" know because of "your" understanding. Further, a similar line is recited in 1QH-a 9.21 where the speaker claims knowing these things, because of God's understanding.[70] As for the statement in line 17 "your ear to our cry" (אוזנכה אל שועתנו), it recalls Psalm 34:16 when the psalmist proclaims that God turns to hear the cry of the righteous. A similar statements happens in 1QH-a 13.12 when the speaker proclaims that God heard her/his cry in the bitterness of the soul.

The intertextual quality of the song in 1QM 10.8b–18 shows a pattern where several moments in Israel's history point to the sectarians. The combination of Scriptural allusions with the use of sectarian depictions serve to create a song that prophetically claims that the God of the universe has chosen them as the new Israel via the revelation of wisdom in Torah and creation. While this song is a different piece from the preceding lines in column 10, the combination of the promises given to the army of the sectarians and the celebration of Israel as the chosen people create a powerful image that is reminiscent to passages like Exod 15.

This brings us to a question that we posited before regarding the presence of this song at this junction of the scroll. We believe that the song in lines 10b–18 represents a link between the War of Divisions and the War Against the Kittim. The song follows the depictions of war in lines 1–8a and it precedes the hymn where the Kittim will be mentioned. As an intersection point between the two phases of the war, the song reverberates themes that encapsulate God's sovereignty and election of the sectarians. In this process, the song begins to illustrate some of the themes that will be highlighted in the songs of celebration in columns 12 and 19. The effect of adding this

---

70 Davies, 95–96. In this section of his work Davies compares 1QM 10.8b-16 to 1QH-a 9.1–21.

song at this junction of the scroll creates the impression that the sectarians can count that the God of creation has favored them over the peoples of the world because they are the chosen remnant.

c. Summary

1QM 10 is a transition point in the War Scroll. In this column we have two distinct pieces: the first in lines 1–8a is the conclusion of the War of Divisions, where the priests and the officials encourage the army of the sectarians prior to the eschatological encounter. The second in lines 8b–18 is a song that celebrates God and the choice of Israel as God's people. Although both pieces are distinct in their approach and themes (one uses direct citations of the Scriptures while the other uses allusions), they were put together for the purpose of relaying prophetic testimonies. Together these pieces provide ample evidence, via the use of key words seen elsewhere in the scrolls and the way that Scripture was adopted in the life and future of the sectarians.

The prophetic testimony of Moses in the citations of Deuteronomy and Numbers in lines 1–8a demonstrate the re-enactment of these sacred passages with the conviction that the promises to ancient Israel applied to the sectarians. We also observed that the overarching promise within these citations is that God is with the army and is ready to deliver them from the enemy. The scope of the promise further gives us a window into the ideological perspective that the sectarians adopted in their belief that they were the inheritors of the promises of their ancestors. In addition, the references to the "enemy" (אויב) highlight that these texts are applicable to any circumstance; the same enemies that Israel faced in the past can be defeated in the age of the Sons of Light. Together these details underscore the power of Scriptural texts as they were used prophetically to contextualize the reality of the sectarians in light of their ancestors. It was a way by which they placed their hopes on Scripture, and Scripture itself became revitalized by their use of these traditions.

The sudden interjection of the questions מיא כמוכה אל ישראל and מיא כעמכה ישראל in lines 8b–18 veer the narrative away from the military context and into the sphere of describing the intimate relation that God has with Israel. The song is explicit to point out that this Israel is not just a people who have been delivered from the bondage of oppression, like their ancestors were in countless times, but they are a people endowed with the ability to perceive God's will. They are "seers" and "hearers" that have their "ears open" that allow them to "discern deep things." This people of God are sealed by the holy covenant and as such they are well equipped to learn the statutes

Prophetic Exegesis in 1QM 10

and understand wisdom (lines 10–11). But above all this chosen people can trust that the God who controls all aspects of creation and history (lines 12–15; cf. Genesis 1–11) is also the one who hears their "cry" (שׁוּעָה). Essentially, the combination of these references represents an affirmation that the sectarians are this people who have been favored and privileged to partake of the mysteries of God. They are not only the warriors of lines 1–8a, but in lines 8b–18 they are God's flock who have received the favor to not only be delivered from their enemies but ultimately partake of everything that God created, including the seasons, cycle of years, and appointed times. The prophetic use of Scripture in this song takes place in the way that the relation of God with the new Israel is depicted, by tapping into the language of wisdom and creation as well as mystery endowed to a selected group(s).

The change of topic and style in both compositions in 1QM 10 points to the composite nature of this column. However, the intertextual evidence highlights that the same God of history is the one who constitutes a new people, a wise and discerning flock who has their ears attuned to the mysteries and deep things that God reveals to them. The celebration of this intimate relation supports the inclusion of the song at this point in the scroll, and as we will see in the following columns, history will be continually revisited to depict God's faithfulness to Israel. For that matter, the army can trust the victories of the past will be experienced in the looming conflict.

CHAPTER 4

PROPHETIC EXEGESIS IN 1QM 11

Preliminary Considerations

1QM 11 RECALLS CRITICAL PASSAGES in Scripture to strengthen the faith of the combatants. The significance of history and prophecy in 1QM 11 has caught the attention of scholars who have come up with different ways of organizing its content and explaining the use of Scripture.

Yigael Yadin believes that 1QM 10 and 11 are one prayer that is part of the Serekh Series. He adds that 1QM 11.1–12 teaches that the present war is God's war and uses past deliverances as well as prophetic testimony to ground this faith. Yadin does not use a specific label for this kind of religious reflection. Rather, he is more interested in drawing a comparison between this prayer and others from Israel'fs history. He notices an important connection with the words of encouragement in Maccabees, where history is also used to empower the combatants. There is the reference to Pharaoh's fall in the Red Sea (1 Macc 4:9), David's defeat of Goliath (1 Macc 4:30), and Sennacherib's defeat (1 Macc 7:41) all of which are mentioned in column 11. Other similar prayers appear in 3 Macc 2:1–20 and Sotah 8. Yadin also groups 1QM 11.13–12.15 as part of a different section of the Serekh, where God's exaltation and the agency of the "weak ones" take center stage. Thus, Yadin splits 1QM 11 into two major parts: lines 1–12 as a continuation of 1QM 10 and lines 13–18 as the beginning of the descriptions of the eschatological battle that span to 1QM 12. Yadin's arrangement of 1QM 11 is different from what other scholars have proposed, however his observations about the connection between 1QM 11 and the Maccabean prayers are shared by others[1].

Philip R. Davies holds that 1QM 11.1–7 is a *Heilsgeschichte* that revisits

---

1 Yigael Yadin, *The Scroll of the War of the Sons of Light Against The Sons of Darkness*, trans. Batya Rabim and Chaim Rabim (London: Oxford University Press, 1962), 212–215.

past military victories. He proposes that the *Sitz im Leben* of this hymn is
the use of these moments prior to engaging in the battlefield. He, like Yadin,
draws heavily from the Maccabean prayers to assess these lines. However, different from Yadin, Davies uses the Maccabean prayers to draw out possible
compositional layers that point to "a plausible origin for this hymn."[2] This approach becomes apparent in how he handles the Scriptural citations in this
column. For instance, when dealing with the prophecy of Num 24:17–19 in
line 7, Davies has difficulty explaining the logic of this passage with the rest of
the hymn. He holds that if the prophecy is to make any sense in its immediate
context, the thrust of the citation is to focus on God rather than on a military
warrior. Also, the fact that the citation does not follow the same order as the
Scriptural text shows to Davies that the emphasis of the passage changed;
thus Israel's contribution to the success of the campaign is secondary to the
power of God. Further, he suggests that the reference to the destruction of the
"survivor of the city" (שריד מעיר) points to the expulsion of the Seleucids
from Jerusalem[3]. Concerning lines 7b–12, Davies believes that they represent
a separate composition with a different subject matter and terminology. Here
he focuses on the Scriptural citation from Isaiah in 1QM 11.11–12. He notes
that in line 8 we have the formula "you told us" (הגדתה לנו) that references
the prophetic testimony of the seers. Line 11b, on the other hand, describes a
similar reflection but it instead uses "ancient times" (מאז) and introduces the
Scriptural passage with the participle "saying" (לאמור). The difference in formulas as well as the interpretation of the Kittim as Assyria suggests to Davies
that the prophecy of Isaiah is an interpolation, although he does not provide
substantial discussion to defend his assertion.

Further, Davies goes on to compare 1QM 11.7b–12 with 1QM 14.4b–8. He
draws out the similar themes of God granting victory to the weak and the destruction of the wicked nations. Like in the preceding lines Davies proposes
a Maccabean origin for lines 7b–12 and recognizes the presence of dualistic elements like the conflict of good and evil with God intervening to break
the gridlock[4]. Davies wraps up his analysis of 1QM 11 by examining the influence of Ezekiel in lines 13–18. Although at first he sees these descriptions
as perhaps a separate composition, he concedes that some of the themes in
these latter section appear in the preceding lines. And following a side by side
comparison of lines 13–18 with Ezekiel 38–39, Davies observes that the concept of the nations gathering to destroy Israel happens in Ezekiel and also in

---

2 Philip R. Davies, *1QM, the War Scroll From Qumran: Its Structure and History* (Rome: Biblical Institute Press, 1977), 96.

3 Ibid., 97.

4 Ibid., 98–100.

Prophetic Exegesis in 1QM 11   151

Maccabees. Interestingly, Davies proposes that the reference to Gog in line 16
could be a roundabout way of referring to Antiochus IV[5].

For his part Brian Schultz links the song in 1QM 10.8bff with 1QM 11.1–12.
He asserts that this hymn of praise evinces sectarian qualities such as the eschatological orientation of Scripture and the mention of Belial and the Kittim. Schultz highlights that the citation to the prophecy in Num 24:17–19 carries an eschatological dimension that points to an immediate future. Also the
reference to Belial as well as the use of the prophecy of Isa 31:8, which is associated with the fall of the Kittim, echoes 1QM 1 and the prediction of the
eschatological battle between the forces of light and darkness. Schultz highlights that the use of the prophecies in Numbers and Isaiah demonstrates
that the sectarians believed in the imminent fulfillment of these words. He
adds that the mention of the Kittim in line 11 lends support to the position
that this prayer as well as the prayer in 1QM 10.1–8a were intended for the
War Against the Kittim in 1QM 15–19. He agrees with Yadin that these prayers
ultimately link back to the "prayer for the appointed time of the war" (תפלת
מועד המלחמה) in 1QM 15.5[6]. As for 1QM 11.13ff, Schultz integrates these lines
with 1QM 12.1– 5 as one prayer. Like Davies, Schultz also believes that the reference to Gog points to a key rhetorical feature of this prayer, although he
does not go as far as his predecessor in pointing out a particular historical
figure. He concedes, however, that the allusion to Gog and the descriptions in
lines 15–16 of a war against the nations introduce another dimension to the
eschatological war that 1QM 15–19 describe. For instance, in 1QM 15.10–11 and
19.10 the scroll describes that the war will be against the assembly of multi-
tudes and all the nations assembled against Israel. Schultz points to this evidence as the reason why 1QM 11.13–12.5 fits with the outlook in columns 15–19
and agrees with Davies that 1QM 11 along with 1QM 1 and 15–19 evince the
presence of subsequent redactional phases of the scroll[7].

As we can see from the previous survey there is a variety of approaches
in analyzing this column. Regardless of how the content of 1QM 11 is divided, what is clear from these discussions is the important role that prophecy,
specifically with the citations of Num 24:17–19 and Isa 31:8, has in shaping
this column. In our analysis we will divide 1QM 11 into two pieces. We propose that lines 1–7a consists of a hymn that alludes to David's duel against
Goliath and Israel's victories over the enemies. The thrust of this piece is to
inspire the combatants in the face of a powerful enemy by recalling history

---

5 Ibid., 100.

6 Brian Schultz, *Conquering the World: The War Scroll (1QM) Reconsidered* (Leiden: Brill,
2009), 274–275.

7 Ibid., 275–276.

and ascribing the conflict to God. The repeated use of the refrain "the battle is yours" (לכה המלחמה) echoes David's statement in 1 Samuel 17 and Jahaziel's prophecy in 2 Chronicles 20, where both of them proclaim that the looming conflict is God's. This hymn ends with an explicit citation of the prophecy in Num 24:17–19, where the oracle of the star and the scepter functions as a prediction of Israel's success against the enemy. The second piece in lines 7b–18 consists in a prediction about God's exaltation through this eschatological conflict. This piece like the previous hymn relies on the prophetic testimony of the "seers of decrees" (חוזי תעודות) who announced the times of war. This piece grounds the testimony of these prophetic figures, by referring to God's defeat over more powerful forces like Pharaoh and his army dying in the Sea of Reeds, Assyria being defeated by the "sword of no man" (חרב לא איש), and Gog and his hordes falling via God's attack from the heavens.

In both compositions the scroll imaginatively uses the past as evidence to guarantee the future, and there is the continuous thematic thread where those who are weak are suddenly emboldened to defeat their enemies by God's power. There are the instances of David's encounter versus Goliath as well as Israel versus Pharaoh, Assyria, and Gog. Plus, there is also the use of images that elevate the agency of the "oppressed" (אביונים) and those who are "prostrate in the dust" (כורעי עפר) to carry out God's judgment against the mighty. The combination of historical references as well as the use of key metaphors underscores that the different intertextual markers in 1QM 11 create a web of meaning, where prophecy emboldens the sectarians and guarantees the future promises based on Israel's past victories.

a.   1QM 11.1–7a: God's War (לכה המלחמה)

i.   Text and Translation

1QM 11.1–7a	1QM 11.1–7a
1 כיא אם לכה המלחמה ובכוח ידכה רוטשו פגריהם לאין קובר ואת גוליית הגתי איש גבור חיל	1 For indeed the battle is yours, With the strength of your hand their corpses have been torn to pieces without anyone to bury them. Goliath from Gath, a might man of valor,
2 הסגרתה ביד דויד עבדכה כיא בטח בשמכה הגדול ולוא בחרב וחנית כיא לכה המלחמה ואת	2 you delivered in the hand of your servant David, for he trusted in your name and not in a sword or spear. For the battle is yours, the

פלשתיים הכנ[י]ע פעמים רבות בשם 3 קודשכה וגם ביד מלכינו הושעתנו פעמים רבות	3 Philistines he humiliated many times by your holy name, and by the hand of our kings you delivered us many times
בעבור רחמיכה ולוא כמעשינו אשר 4 הרעונו ועלילות פשעינו לכה המלחמה ומאתכה הגבורה	4 because of your mercy, and not because of our deeds by which we did wrong, nor for our acts of rebelliousness. The Battle is yours, And the power comes from you
ולוא לנו ולוא כוחנו ועצום ידינו 5 עשה חיל כיא בכוחכה ובעוז חילכה הגדול כאשר הגדתה 6 לנו מאז למור דרך כוכב מיעקוב קם שבט מישראל ומחץ פאתי מואב וקרקר כול בני שית וירד מיעקוב והאביד שריד מעיר 7 והיה אויב ירשה וישראל עשה חיל	5 and not from us, it is not our strength nor the power of our hands that perform these marvels, but in your strength and your mighty deeds just as you told us 6 from ancient times, saying: "A star will come from Jacob, a scepter will rise from Israel and it will smash the temples of Moab, and it will destroy all the sons of Seth. 7 It will come down from Jacob and it will exterminate the survivor of the city and the enemy will be its possession, and Israel will do valiantly." (Num 24:17–19)

ii. Content

The following is the content of 1QM 11.1–7a

- 11.1–2a
  1. Refrain כיא אם לכה המלחמה
  2. Statement about God's Power
  3. Reference to David's Defeat of Goliath
  4. Reason behind this Triumph
- 11.2b–4a
  1. Refrain כיא לכה המלחמה
  2. Statement about God's Power
  3. Allusion to Triumphs in History
  4. Reason behind these Triumphs
- 11.4b–7a
  1. Refrain לכה המלחמה
  2. Statement about God's Power
  3. Reference to Israel's dependence on God for their strength

4. Reason behind Israel's strength
5. Prophetic Explanation of Israel's strength
6. Citation of Num 24:17–19

The hymn in lines 1–7a follows the song "Who is like you, God of Israel?" (מיא כמוכה אל ישראל) in 1QM 10.8b–18. The end of column 10 is fragmentary and prevents us from asserting any unity with the hymn in column 11. One possible connection is that towards the end of column 10, the subject changes from the third person (God/Israel) to the second and first person (you/we). 1QM 10.17 addresses God directly and states that you "turn your ear to our cry" (אוזנכה אל שועתנו) and column 11 begins with the refrain "the battle is yours" (לכה המלחמה), which ascribes the battle to God. The direct address to God in the language of prayer suggests that 1QM 10.8b and the beginning of 1QM 11 could potentially be one prayer. If that is the case, then one problem to consider is at what point does this prayer end; is the end of this prayer in 1QM 11.6–7 with the citation of the prophecy in Num 24:17–19? And if these lines are one prayer, how do the themes of wisdom, creation, and festivities in 1QM 10.8b–18 correlate with the themes of war in 1QM 11.1–7a? Neither of these questions suggest that these lines in columns 10–11 cannot be one prayer. However, in our work we will proceed from the standpoint that 1QM 11.1–7b is a separate hymn because of its structure with the repetition of "the battle is yours" (לכה המלחמה) and citation to the prophecy in Num 24:17–19, plus it describes different themes in comparison to the previous song.

We can see that following each of the refrains לכה המלחמה the hymn has three distinctive parts: a) a statement about God's strength, b) an allusion to a moment in Israel's history where this strength was manifested, and c) an interpretation for why Israel enjoyed God's favor. The last major section of the hymn contains a citation of Scripture that provides the prophetic foundation for all the historical successes. The oracle in Num 24:17–19 is one of five citations that appears in 1QM 10–11. Besides this citation, 1QM 11.1–7a contains an allusion to David's defeat of Goliath (1 Sam 17:46–47) as well as indirect references to other military victories won by Israel's kings. The overarching theme of this hymn is the total dependence that Israel has on God, which allowed the nation to win many military victories throughout its history[8]. The rhetorical purpose of this hymn is to reiterate that the same strength that allowed

---

8 Dean Wenthe, "The Use of the Hebrew Scriptures in 1QM," *DSD* 5 (1998): 309–310. Wenthe proposes that by using these passages of Israel's history, the author demonstrates a typological approach of implied exegesis. The events of the past are analogous to the current events. In addition, by using these moments of history and adopting them as theirs (via the use of the first-person plural suffix "us") the community view Israel's history as their history. Thus,

Prophetic Exegesis in 1QM 11

Israel to defeat its enemies in the past is available now for the sectarians to defeat their enemies[9]. The hymn strengthens the faith of the soldiers by ascribing the battle to God and by recalling these memorable moments as evidence of God's faithfulness, and the oracle in Numbers establishes the faith that the soldiers should have on the sure foundation of the prophetic word. The use of this oracle resembles what we observed in 1QM 10.1–8a, where the prophecies of Moses provided the structure and the foundation for the faith that the army should have in God. The ensuing discussion will deal with the intertextual markers in 1QM 11.1–7a by focusing on the person of David, the prophecy in Num 24:17–19, and the traditional belief of ascribing the battle to God.

iii. Sectarian Intertextuality

Prophetic David

The character of king David has an important role in Scriptural traditions and theology. In this part of our work we will focus on two facets of David as they are depicted in the DSS. The first one deals with David's gift of prophecy and wisdom, which enabled him not only to compose songs but ultimately be a type of priestly figure[10]. Although in 1QM 11 we encounter David the warrior, this discussion will help us understand why line 2 labels David as God's "servant" (עבד).

1QM 11.1 alludes to the encounter between David and Goliath (cf. 1 Sam 17)[11]. Line 2 specifically recalls that God delivered Goliath into the hand of David, because he trusted in God and not in weapons. This is a clear allusion to 1 Sam 17:46–47, where David taunts the giant with the prediction that "this

---

past, present, and future, he adds, are expressions of the fundamental truth about Yahweh's strength, which only the author and his associates know.

9 Jean Duhaime, *The War Texts: 1QM and Related Manuscripts* (London: T & T Clark, 2004), 106–110. Duhaime observes that 1QM 11.1–5a underscores that God's power and action are the exclusive source of Israel's salvation. He notes that the continuous repetition of the refrain לכה המלחמה and the emphasis on David's encounter with Goliath provide the essence of these lines.

10 For a good discussion about the most important descriptions of David in the DSS, see: Craig Evans, "David in the Dead Sea Scrolls," in *The Scrolls and the Scriptures: Qumran Fifty Years After,* ed. Stanley Porter and Craig Evans (Sheffield Academic Press, 1997), 183–197. Evans surveys the references of David across the scrolls. He divides his survey of the Davidic tradition into 1) the David of history, 2) David as an ideal figure, and 3) the use of the Davidic tradition for eschatology and messianism. Our study will touch on references that fall within each of these groups.

11 Historical references to David appear also in: 11Q5 28; 4Q457b 2.2; 4Q479 1.4–5; 4Q522 22–26.1, 4; 4Q177 12–13i.2.

day the Lord will hand you in my hand" (היום הזה יסגרך יהוה בידי) and asserts that God delivers not by sword or spear but by directly taking over the battle. Also, the depiction in line 1 with images of corpses without burial alludes to verse 45 where David describes that the bodies of the Philistines will be given to the birds and animals. These images also evoke other accounts where foreign armies are not buried or are food for animals like: 2 Kngs 19:35; Ezek 39:17–20; 2 Chr 20:24. The war text in 4Q492 1.9–10 also describes something similar when it states that the camp will go out to see all the dead that have not been buried; line 10 specifically states "the multitude of the slain are dead without anyone to bury them; those that fell by the sword of God" (מתו רוב חללים לאין מקבר אשר נפלו שם בחרב אל)[12]. Line 10 demonstrates the religious belief that a lack of a proper burial renders the dead "profaned" (חללים). This is something that 1QM also introduces when it depicts in the song of 1QM 12.11 that God will place "your foot on the back of the slain" (רגלכה על במותי חלל). The intertextual links between 1QM 11.1, 12.11 and 4Q492 1.10 evince a belief that the looming conflict is seen in light of Scriptural tradition, where the weak will defeat the stronger force via God's strength. This strength will not only defeat the enemy but ultimately render him profaned. The allusion to David and his defeat of Goliath, therefore, stamps in the minds of the combatants that they can trust that the same strength that helped David will help them. However, an interesting point about David's allusion is that 1QM 11.2 states that God handed Goliath in the hand of your servant David.

The representation of David as God's servant is intriguing because the DSS use the designation "servant" (עבד) primarily for figures like the "prophets" (נביאים e.g. 1QS 1.3; 1QpHab 2:9) as well as Moses (e.g. 4Q378 22i.2; 4Q504 3.12; 4Q456 8.3)[13]. There are other instances where עבד appears in matters of halakha in the discussion about the treatment of both male and female servants (CD 11.12; 4Q251 4–7i.5). Aside from these instances עבד is used in the language of prayer. The Hodayot are characteristic of this approach as the speaker adopts the posture of a servant while addressing God (e.g. 1QH–a 6.25). Another interesting aspect about עבד is that it is not used for any other king except for David. The reference to David as עבד in line 2 most likely stems from the Scriptural traditions where he is referred as God's servant. However, as we shall see below, David's role as servant as depicted in the DSS encompasses other attributes.

---

12 The reference to בחרב אל is an important concept that will resurface in 1QM 11.11–12 with the citation of Isa 31:8 and the reference to the חרב לוא איש.

13 4Q379 19.2 is a fragmentary manuscript that describes Jacob as a servant.

Prophetic Exegesis in 1QM 11   157

For instance, the *Damascus Document* mentions David both in CD 5.1–6 and in 7.16. The first passage deals with him from the standpoint of history while the latter deals with the messianic promise. CD 5.1–6 follows the teaching that the Instructor provides about the three traps of Belial in CD 4.14–21. For the Instructor these traps are fornication, wealth, and defilement of the sanctuary. Specifically, in the case of fornication, CD 5.1–2 states that it is written that the Prince shall not multiply wives for himself according to the teachings in Deuteronomy 17. However, the interesting detail about these lines is that it states that David had not read the "book of Torah" (ספר התו־ רה). In fact, lines 3–5 describe that this book was sealed from Israel until it was "revealed" (נגלה) to the priest Zadok[14]. For that matter lines 5–6 justify all of David's deeds except for Uriah's murder which God forgave him for.

We can observe in this passage the tension that existed between the reality of what David did and the ideal image that had been created about him. The Instructor as a good exegete uses his persuasive skills and knowledge of the historical record to explain why David had failed at this standard. However, in the case of Uriah the Instructor does not have a Scriptural basis to defend this action except for pointing out that God forgave David. The other important aspect about this account is the combination of Torah being both sealed and then revealed. CD evinces in these lines the same belief that we observed in the song in 1QM 10.8b–18, which is that the sectarians were recipients of God's hidden mysteries.

Another fascinating depiction of David happens in the 11Q5 27. According to this manuscript, David was a wise and enlightened man; a scribe with "discernment" (בין) who was blameless in all his ways. Line 4 is especially important because it states that God gave David "a brilliant and discerning spirit" (רוח נבונה ואורה), which allowed him to write psalms and songs. The manuscript goes on to provide a tally of these writings whose significance is that it not only included songs for every significant cultic celebration including: songs before the altar by the burnt offering for every day of year (364 days), 52 songs for the Sabbath offerings, 30 songs for the New Moon, the festivals, and the Day of Atonement. Also, the mention of David composing songs "to play by the possessed" (לנגן על הפגועים) reminisces texts like 1 Sam 16:18 where David ministers to Saul, and it also shows the interest among the sectarians for treating individuals who were oppressed by evil spirits[15]. All

---

14 Maxine Grossman, *Reading for History in the Damascus Document* (Leiden: Brill, 2002), 171–172. Grossman focuses on this passage mostly to highlight the interest in CD for the priestly transition from the sons of Eli to the priestly line of Zadok, and to point how the "covenanters" believed that the Torah had been hidden until the arrival of a truly righteous priest.

15 11Q11 5.4 is one of the best examples of this type of composition. The song begins by

158 INTERTEXTUALITY AND PROPHETIC EXEGESIS IN THE WAR SCROLL OF QUMRAN

of this evidence shows a unique take on David and how he met the wisdom and cultic standards set by God as interpreted by the composers of the psalm. For our purposes, one of the most important pieces of evidence comes in line 11, where we learn that David composed all of these pieces "through prophecy which it was given to him by the Most High" (בנבואה אשר נתן לו מלפני העליון). This last line brings up many questions like: how did this "prophetic" gift manifest itself? Were music and prophecy mixed while David delivered these words? Was some sort of trance experience associated with this prophecy? Context does not give us sufficient information to address these questions. We can gather, however, that this prophetic gift was associated with possessing knowledge and discernment to write for every sacred occasion.

In his essay on David and prophecy, Peter Flint points out that another association between David and prophecy is the fact that there are three Pesharim (1Q16, 4Q171, and 4Q173) written about the psalms of David. The Pesharim analyze prophetic passages and use the Scriptural verse as the locus for its interpretation (i.e. פשר). However, he adds, in the case of these texts, the Pesherists use the psalms as prophecies of the life of the sectarians, where the Yahad and the Teacher of Righteousness represent the righteous while the Wicked Priest and the Man of Lies represent the wicked. Flint argues that the use of psalms written by David underscores the sectarian belief that David was a prophet to whom God had revealed in ages past the events of the life of the sectarians.[16] The significance of Flint's point is twofold: one is that the psalms of David were considered authoritative Scripture, but also that they had among their many didactic purposes a prophetic component that the sectarians viewed as directly applicable to their communal lives. We find both of these aspects play out in 4Q397 4.10–15[17].

Following a series of halakhic recommendations, the text wraps up by restating that these principles are in the books of Moses, the Prophets, and David. What follows is a series of exhortations that exhort the readers to not veer away from these principles during these "latter days." The inclusion of the book of David confirms that he was seen in a similar light as other prophetic ministers. Furthermore, the traditions attributed to him were seen as authoritative and essential to keep the readers on the right path until the

---

attributing it to David and stating that its purpose is על לחש. The song continues with a depiction of how the one oppressed addresses this spirit directly when it comes at night. The one being oppressed faces the spirit by condemning it and claiming that God will deal with it directly (11Q11 5.5–14).

16 Peter Flint, "The Prophet David at Qumran," in *Biblical Interpretation at Qumran*, ed. Matthias Henze (Grand Rapids: Eerdmans, 2005), 158–167.

17 Other reference to the books of the prophets and David appear in 4Q398 14–17i.3. David is also referred as the pious one in 4Q398 14–17ii.1.

Prophetic Exegesis in 1QM 11

end of days. The formative and eschatological aspect of these exhortations further support what Flint suggested above and make it more apparent why subsequent traditions in the books of Acts and the Antiquities of Josephus associated David with a prophetic gift[18].

The reference to David as עבד in 1QM 11.2 does not point to him as a prophet *per se*, but as we have observed, David was seen in other sectarian texts as one endowed or associated with the gift of prophecy. It is, therefore, no coincidence that in this same passage the hymn will end with a citation of Num 24:17–19. The marker of David as an עבד and the later reference to a prophecy that traditionally has been interpreted as messianic triggers associations between prophecy, messianism, and David. This brings us to another quality of David in the DSS, and that is his role in the messianic expectation.

Messianic David

The other major discussion about David in the DSS deals with the prophecies regarding his dynasty and the messianic promise. Some of the manuscripts that deal with this topic unpack the metaphors that Scripture uses to represent the monarchy, in order to interpret them according to the anticipated messianic figure and the restoration of Israel. Although 1QM is silent about a future messianic leader, an exploration of some of these prophecies across the scrolls can shed some light on how the restoration of Israel was visualized in connection to David and his lineage. This is important for our study, because David and his lineage are directly linked to Israel's military victories and to the prophetic aspirations in 1QM 11.1–7a.

The manuscripts that deal with a messianic expectation include: 4Q161 8–10.15–29, 4Q174 1–2i. 21.7–13, 4Q252 6.2, 4Q285 7.3–5, 4Q504 17.7, and CD 7.16. These texts can be grouped in three categories. 4Q161, 4Q174, and 4Q252 are commentaries that provide an interpretation of Scriptural passages; the first two are Pesharim while the latter is a rewritten account of Genesis. The other two categories include war texts, like 4Q285 and 11Q14, and Rule Books like the Damascus Document. 4Q504 is a liturgical text that deals with the promises to David by alluding to the prophecy in 2 Sam 7:8–17.

A link that connects all of these manuscripts is their exegetical approach, where they refer to a Scriptural passage or a portion of that text, in order to provide an explanation to the fulfillment of that passage. In addition, we can

---

18 Acts 2:25–31 describes David as a "prophet" in verse 30 because he knew that one of his descendants would sit on the throne. Because of this knowledge, David is able to speak about the resurrection of the Messiah. Josephus also describes David "prophesying" in passages like *Antiquities* 6.166.

glean from these texts that their analysis of Scripture was meticulous in that they would focus on even the smallest detail of a passage, and extrapolate a meaning that was applicable to their readers' context. One particular feature of this exegetical approach is the focus and subsequent interpretation of metaphors, like the "Shoot of David" (צמח דויד) that the Scriptural passages use.

For instance, 4Q252 is a fragmentary manuscript that consists of a running commentary of different accounts from Genesis[19]. The significance of this manuscript is that it provides an early example of Jewish commentary on the Scriptures. This manuscript also deals with topics such as covenantal election, which becomes an important aspect of Jacob's blessing to Judah recorded in Genesis 49.

4Q252 5.1–7	4Q252 5.1–7
1 לו[א יסור שליט משבט יהודה בהיות לישראל ממשל	1 The scepter shall not depart from the tribe of Judah. When Israel rules
2 לוא י[כרת יושב כסא לדויד כי המחקק היא ברית המלכות	2 it will not be cutoff one who sits on the throne of David. For the scepter is the covenant of kingship
3 ואל[פי ישראל המה הדגלים עד בוא משיח הצדק צמח	3 and the thousands of Israel are the standards until the messiah of righteousness comes, the sprout
4 דויד כי לו ולזרעו נתנה ברית מל־כות עמו עד דורות עולם אשר	4 of David. For to him and his descendants he gave a covenant of kingship of his people for everlasting generations
5 שמר [ ] התורה עם אנשי היחד כי	5 which he kept [ ] the Torah with the men of the Yahad for
6 [ ] היא כנסת אנשי 7 [ ] נתן	6 [ ] it is the assembly of men 7 [ ] he gave

Line 1 quotes the beginning of Gen 49:10 when Jacob blesses Judah. The focus of this citation is on the promise that the "scepter" (שליט) will not depart from the tribe of Judah. Two interesting points can be recognized about this citation: one is that scepter does not appear in the MT version of this verse[20].

---

19 Émile Puech, "4Q252: ‹Commentaire de la Genèse A› ou ‹Bénédictions Patriarcles›?," *RevQ* 26 (2013): 227–251. Shani Tzoref, "Covenantal Election in 4Q252 and Jubilees' Heavenly Tablets," *DSD* 18 (2011): 74–89. Juhana Markus Saukkonen, "Selection, Election, and Rejection: Interpretation of Genesis in 4Q252," in *Northern Lights on the Dead Sea Scrolls: Proceedings of the Nordic Qumran Network 2003–2006*, ed. Anders Klostergaard Petersen et al. (Leiden: Brill, 2009), 63–81. Devorah Dimant, "The Blessing of Judah in 4Q252," in *Studies in the Hebrew Bible, Qumran, and the Septuagint presented to Eugene Ulrich*, ed. Peter W. Flint, Emanual Tov, and James C. VanderKam (Boston: Brill, 2006), 250–260.

20 Genesis 49:10 (MT): לא־יסור שבט מיהודה
Genesis 49:10 (DSS): לוא יסור שליט משבט יהודה

Prophetic Exegesis in 1QM 11

The other aspect is that scepter is an Aramaic term used primarily in Ezra and Daniel to convey the power and authority vested on a ruler (Ezra 7:24; Dan 4:14, 4:22, 4:29, 5:21, and 5:29)[21]. Elsewhere in the scrolls שליט appears in prayers to describe the authority of God (e.g. 1Q20 20.13, 4Q542 1i.2) or in visions (e.g. visions of Enoch 4Q530 2ii.20; visions of Amram 4Q543 5–9.3; 4Q544 1.12, 2.16) to depict the power of God or of other celestial beings. The insertion of שליט in line 1, therefore, reveals an interpretive move within the citation that emphasizes that the authority vested by God will not depart from the tribe of Judah[22].

The ensuing lines connect the promise in Genesis to the line of David via another Scriptural connection. Line 2 states that "it will not be cutoff one who sits on the throne of David" (לוא יכרת יושב כסא לדויד). This same phrase appears in several texts of Scripture that recall the promises to David and his lineage given in 2 Samuel 7 (e.g. 1 Kgs 2:4, 8:25; Jer 33:17; 2 Chr 6:16). The fact that this phrase appears in Scripture and is echoed in the scrolls underscores the significance of this promise for the future of Israel. 4Q504 17.3–16 echoes this notion as it illustrates a beautiful depiction of a procession to Zion. Lines 7–9 specifically recall the covenant that God made with David and how he will become a shepherd that sits on the throne eternally. Following the Scriptural echo, line 2 provides the interpretation of the promise following the demonstrative particle כי.

In the same manner that lines 1 and 2 anchor their presentation via the key words "scepter" (שליט) and "throne" (כסא), the interpretation is also grounded on the two metaphors used in Gen 49:10; that is, the "scepter" (מ־חקק) and the "feet" (רגלים). The scroll interprets in line 3 the scepter to represent the covenant of kingship, and the thousands of Israel represent the "standards" (הדגלים). However, Gen 49:10 describes that the scepter will be between "his feet" (מבין רגליו). The discrepancy between "foot" (רגל) and "standard" (דגל) potentially indicates a confusion on the part of the scribe who read a ד instead of a ר. A more persuasive argument, however, is that this was a conscious decision to describe the authority that David's lineage would have over the standards or banners (דגלים), which the book of

---

21 The last of the references in Daniel uses שליט to describe the moment when Daniel was appointed third in command in the court of Belshazzar.

22 Jub. 31:12–19 describes the blessing that Isaac gives to Levi and Judah. The intriguing part of this passage is that the "spirit of prophecy" comes to Isaac and gives an oracle to each of Jacob's children. The promise to Judah in verses 18–19 highlights the coming of a prince who will rule with strength and be in the eyes of the nations. This prince will be the salvation of Israel. Shani Tzoref, "Covenantal Election," 79–80. Shani Tzoref comments on this passage in Jubilees as well as 32:21 where Jacob receives the tablets from an angel regarding him and his sons was true.

Numbers represent as the tribes of Israel (cf. Num 2:3, 10:14).

Also, line 3 adds a temporal clause that introduces the time when these things shall happen. It announces the coming of the "Messiah of righteousness" (משיח הצדק) and links him to the lineage of David by using the metaphor צמח דויד. Previously we saw that 4Q174 uses this same metaphor to predict the messiah as it associates him with the prophecy in Amos 9 and the "booth of David that is fallen" (סוכת דויד הנופלת). The difference with 4Q174, however, is that it also anticipates the "Interpreter of the Torah" (דורש התורה), which raises the question about the kind of messiah or messiahs that the sectarians anticipated. In other words, did the sectarians anticipate one or two messiahs? And is the messiah only a royal authority or is he a priestly one as well? These questions lie beyond the scope of this investigation, but 4Q252 makes it clear that this royal figure will have an eternal power over the sectarians. Line 4 specifically makes clear the eternal aspect of the promise as the Messiah of Righteousness shall rule over Israel "for everlasting generations" (עד דורות עולם). The time reference and the subsequent mention of the "Men of the Yahad" (אנשי היחד) in line 5 may support a sectarian provenance of this prophecy. However, we should be cautious in making any generalizations about the messianic expectation among the sectarians, because there were various views about the messiah and the type of partnership he would have with other leaders in Israel[23].

4Q161 Frg. 8–10.1–29	4Q161 Frg. 8–10.1–29
1 [הנה האדון יהוה צבאות מסעף]	1 See, Yahweh the lord of hosts will lop
2 [פארה במערצה ורמי הקומה גדועים והגבורים ישפלו וינקפו]	2 the branches with terror and the lofty in stature will be broken in pieces and the mighty will be humbled. And the thickets of the forest
3 סובכי היער בברזל ולבנון בא־ דיר יפול	3 will be cut down with an ax and Lebanon with its might will fall down. (Isa 10:33–34)
4 vacat	4 vacat
5 [ ]ם[ ]	5 [ ] m [ ]
6 [וינקפו ס]ו[בכ]ין היער [בברזל ולבנון באדיר	6 And the thickets of the forest will be cut down with an ax and Lebanon with its might
7 [יפול המה ה]כ[ת]יאים אש[ר] יפ[ולו] ב[י]ד ישראל וענוי	7 will fall down. They are the Kittim who will fall by the hand of Israel and the afflicted

23 Other war texts, like 4Q285 7.3–4 and 11Q14 ii.7–13, anticipate the coming of the צמח דויד and his partnership with the נשיא העדה in defeating the Kittim.

8 [כּוֹל הגואים וגבן]ורים יחתו ונמס ל[בם]	8 [ ] all the nations and the mighty ones will be dismayed and their heart will melt.
9 ורמי]הקומה גדועים [ ]המה גבורי כת[ן]איאם	9 And the lofty in stature will be broken in pieces. They are the mighty of the Kittim
10 ד[ ] וניקפו סובכי [ה]יער בברזל ה[מ]ה vacat	10 [ ] d. And the thickets of the forest will be cut down with an ax. vacat. They
11]ם למלחמת כתיאים vacat [ ] ולבנון בא[דיר]	11 [ ] m for the battle of the Kittim. vacat And Lebanon with its might
12 יפול המה ה[כ]תיאים אשר ינתֹ[נו]ו ביד גדולי [ ]	12 will fall down. They are the Kittim who will be given in the hand of the great one
13]ים בברחו מלפ[ני יש]רֹֽ֫אֹל [ ]מֹ[ ]	13 [ ] ym when they flee before Israel
14 [ ] vacat [ ]	14 [ ] vacat [ ]
15]ויצא חוטר מגז[ע מ]ישי ונצר משו[רשיו יפרה ונח[ה עלו ר]וח[	15 A shoot from the stump of Jesse will come and a sprout will grow from its roots. Over him will rest the spirit
16]יהוה רוח [חוכמ]ה ובינה רוח עצ[ה וגבורה] רוח דע[ת]	16 of God, a spirit of wisdom and discernment, a spirit of counsel and might, a spirit of knowledge
17]ויראת יהוה והריחו ביראת יהוה [לוא]למראה עֹ[י]ניו	17 and fear of God. He will delight in the fear of God. He will not judge by what his eyes see
18]וישפוט ולוא למשמע אוזניו יוכי[ח ושפ[ט] בצדק דלים והוכיח[	18 or by what his ears hear. But he will judge the lowly in righteousness and he will decide
19]במישור לעניו ארץ והכה ארץ בשבט פיו וברוח שפתיו[	19 with fairness for the poor of the earth. He will strike the earth with the staff of his mouth and with the breath of his lips.
20]ימית רשע והיה צדק אזור מֹ[תניו ואֹ[מונה אזור חלציו]	20 He will slay the wicked and righteousness will be the belt around his waist, and faithfulness will be the belt around his loins. (Isa 11:1–5)
21 [ ] vacat [ ]	21 vacat
22]דויד העומד באחֹ[רית הימים]	22 David who will stand in the latter days
23]אוֹ[י]בו ואל יסומכנו בֹ[רוח ג]בֹורֹה[]	23 his enemy. God will sustain him with a mighty spirit
24]כֹ[ס]א כבוד נזר קֹ[ודש ו]בגדי ריקֹמֹוֹ[ת]	24 a throne of glory, a holy crown, and garments of various colors

[בידו ובכול הגו]ואי[ם ימשול ומגוג] 25	25 with his hand and over all nations he will rule, and Magog
[כו]ל העמים תשפוט חרבו ואשר אמר לוא 26	26 all the peoples his sword will judge and when it says
[למראה עיניו ישפוט]ולוא למשמע אוזניו יוכיח פשרו אשר 27	27 'He will not judge by what his eyes see or by what his ears hear,' its interpretation which
[וכאשר יורדהו כן ישפוט ועל פיהם 28	28 just as they teach him, thus he will judge, and according to their command
[עמו יצא אחד מכוהני השם ובידו בגדי 29	29 with him will come one of the renown priests and in his hand garments

The last messianic text that we will address is 4Q161 Frg. 8–10 which is a re-constructed manuscript that provides an interpretation of Isaiah 11[24]. This manuscript begins from the standpoint of predicting the fall of the Kittim. The Pesher follows the prophecy in Isa 10:33–34 that describes how God will bring down the lofty and Lebanon. Lines 7–13 identify the lofty with the Kittim and add that the Kittim will fall by the "hand of Israel and the afflicted" (ביד ישראל ועני). In these lines we see an interpretive move where the Pesher turns a prophecy that describes God as the agent of destruction and turns it into an interpretation where the poor ones in Israel will be the main actors. This description correlates with the images that we see in 1QM 11.7b–18 where the enemies will fall not just by the power of God, but Israel's agency will be directly involved.

After a gap in line 14, lines 15–20 continue with a citation of Isa 11:1–5 where the prophet describes the coming of the "shoot from the stump of Jesse" (חוטר מגזע ישי)[25]. The themes of wisdom and understanding play a significant role in these lines, as the pesher highlights the discernment by which this future monarch will rule. Line 16 states that this descendant from Jesse will have a "spirit of wisdom and a spirit of discernment, a spirit of counsel and might" (רוח חוכמה ובינה רוח עצה וגבורה רוח דעת).The tripartite description of a spirit of "wisdom" (חוכמה), "discernment" (בינה), and "knowledge" (דעת) reveals the completeness of wisdom that this descendant

---

24 Alex Jassen, "Re-reading 4QPesher Isaiah A (4Q161) Forty Years after DJD V," in *The Mermaid and the Partridge: Essays from the Copenhagen Conference on Revising Texts from Cave Four*, ed. George Brooke and Jesper Høgenhaven (Leiden: Brill, 2011), 57–90; Joel Willits, "The remnant of Israel in 4QpIsaiah (4Q161) and the Dead Sea Scrolls," *Journal of Jewish Studies* 57 (2006): 11–25.

25 Besides 4Q161 the metaphor of Jesse's lineage appears in 4Q285 7.2 and 11Q14 1i.10. Both of these passages are part of war texts that interpret Isaiah 10–11.

Prophetic Exegesis in 1QM 11

will have. The only other instance where someone was vested with this kind of wisdom happens in Exod 31:3 (cf. 35:30), where God empowers Bezalel to build the furnishings of the tabernacle[26]. Lines 18–20 add that this future ruler will provide justice for the poor and be sovereign over all the earth. The picture that emerges from this citation, therefore, is of a wise and just ruler that will bring justice to Israel.

The pesher continues in line 22 with the interpretation of the prophecy with the description that "David who will stand in the latter days" (דויד העמוד באחרית הימים). Since what precedes the name of David is missing from the manuscript, it is possible that the metaphor צמח preceded the mention of David; thus, lines 21–22 could potentially be an interpretation of the coming of the "Shoot of David" (צמח דויד). A similar description happens in 4Q174 Frg 1–2i 21.11 where צמח דויד will stand with the "Interpreter of the Torah" (דורש התורה). The partnership of the צמח דויד with the דורש התו־ רה that 4Q174 depicts echoes 4Q161; notice that line 29 mentions a prominent priestly figure who will come along with the messianic ruler. In any case, 4Q161, like 4Q174, envisions that the צמח דויד will work alongside a priestly ruler in bringing restoration to Israel.

Further, in lines 24–25 we have a description of the majesty of this future ruler with the description "a throne of glory, a holy crown, and garments of various colors" (כסא כבוד נזר קודש ובגדי ריקמות). Not only is the tripartite description significant in that it encompasses completeness as we saw in the prophecy of Isaiah, but each of these images has both royal and priestly nuances. נזר is a crown and its verbal form denotes consecration that is mostly used as a command or encouragement to be devoted to God[27]. On the other hand, ריקמה appears in several descriptions depicting multicolored vestments used by priestly figures[28].

In lines 25–27, we transition from the description of this king/priest to his deeds. Line 25 is explicit in depicting that this king will rule over the nations and Magog. The mention of Magog is an intriguing one. It only happens five times in the entire scrolls, three of which appear in 1Q20 in reference to Magog son of Japheth and one very fragmentary reference in 4Q523 1–2.5 to Gog of Magog. This evidence, albeit small, suggests that the Pesher interprets that the rule of the messianic king will be one that encompasses the nations and regions like Magog. In lines 27–29, we have possibly one of the

---

26 The DSS preserve the text of Exodus in 4Q365 10.4.

27 CD 6.15, 7.1, 8.8, 19.20; 4Q183 1ii.5; 4Q266 1a–b.1, 2ii.3, 3ii.21, 3iv.6, 4ii.5; 4Q418 81a.2; 4Q423 8.1; 4Q512 69.2; 6Q15 4.4.

28 1QM 5.6–14, 7.11; 4Q179 1ii.12; 4Q270 7i.14; 4Q287 2a–b.5; 4Q402 2.3; 4Q403 1ii.1; 4Q405 14–15i.3–6; 4Q405 16.4; 4Q405 19 a–d.5, 21–22.11, 23ii.7; 4Q462 1.5; 11Q17 4.10, 6.6, 7.13, 9.7.

most interesting aspects of this text. The Pesher picks up the reference of Isa 11:3 and expounds it by introducing its interpretation. Line 28 describes that this king will judge "as they teach him" (כאשר יורוהו), and line 29 describes that along the king will come "one of the renown priests" (אחד מכוהני השם). Taken together these lines correlate with the depictions in 4Q174 where we can see the anticipation of the צמח דויד who will partner with a priestly authority in ruling Israel and the nations.

In conclusion, the previous evidence confirms that there was a consistent aspiration for a messianic figure according to the promises of Scripture. In the sectarian perspective this future deliverer in the line of David would not only be a ruler who would restore Israel, but also bring the nation back to observe Torah by association to a priestly figure. The associations that different manuscripts make of this messianic figure with a priestly leader underscore that much of the sectarian thinking aspired for a religious renewal and a commitment back to the foundational principles of Israel as a people. For the purpose of our analysis of 1QM, the previous discussion serves to inform part of the religious imagination surrounding this scroll, where images of restoration and return to Torah abound even if a direct reference to a messianic leader is missing.

Prophecy of Balaam

The other important marker in this hymn is the citation of the prophecy in Num 24:17–19. 1QM 11.6b–8 includes this prophecy as evidence of the promise that Israel will defeat its enemy through the power of God. A comparison of this citation with the MT version shows differences that are worth mentioning. Line 6b and verse 17 are virtually identical with the pairing of the two main figures the "star from Jacob" (כוכב מיעקוב) and the "scepter from Israel" (שבט מישראל) with two actions, that is, the "smash the temples of Moab" (מחץ פאתי מואב) and "destroy all the sons of Seth" (וקרקר כול בני שית). The major differences appear in line 7, where it begins with the phrase in verse 19 about the extermination of the "survivor of the city" (שריד מעיר). In addition, line 7 focuses on the "enemy" (אויב) and removes the descriptions from verse 18 where the Edom and Seir shall be Israel's possession. Line 7 concludes with the key assertion that "Israel will do valiantly" (ישראל עשה חיל). Thus, by finishing with this last statement 1QM gives the impression that Israel, not a messianic figure, will be empowered to make the enemy its possession. Plus, as we saw with the citations in 1QM 10, the enemy is a key marker that continuously resurfaces to provide cohesion to

Prophetic Exegesis in 1QM 11   167

the argument, which is that Israel will overpower its enemies through the power of God.

Joseph Fitzmyer was the first one to propose that this citation in 1QM 11 focuses not on a messianic leader, but on Israel's ability, through the power of God, to overcome its enemies[29]. He notes that the citation takes place in the context of the priestly discourse, where the combatants shall remember that success in war will be not due to their strength but rather to the promise of victory found in Scripture. Fitzmyer adds that the promise of a messianic figure, which is the normal understanding of this oracle, is set aside in favor of the new context of encouragement. The ensuing discussion will, therefore, expound on the use of this oracle elsewhere in the scrolls and assess how this use compares with 1QM 11.

The prophecy in Num 24:17–19 appears both in 4Q175 1.9–13 and in CD 7.19 (cf. 4Q266 3iii.20 and 4269 5.3). 4Q175 is a list of Scriptural texts including: Deut 5:28–29 (lines 1–4), Deut 18:18–19 (lines 5–8), and Num 24:15–17 (lines 9–13). The first two consist of the promise of blessing that Israel will have if they follow the commandments and God's word to Moses about the future prophet who would act as an intermediary between God and the people. These citations set the stage for the oracle of Num 24:15–17 in lines 9–13. Different from the other uses of this prophecy, 4Q175 begins with the description of Balaam as one who hears the words of God and knows the "knowledge of the Most High" (דעת עליון). The significance of this description of Balaam cannot be underestimated considering that this same manuscript mentions God speaking to Moses. Also, Balaam's access to this knowledge resonates with the sectarian perspective, where being privy to God's mysteries was considered a sign of closeness to God (cf. 1QM 10.8b–18)[30]. This is not to suggest that Balaam was necessarily perceived on the same level as other prophetic figures like Moses, but in terms of the revelation with which he was entrusted this manuscript confirms that this was a trustworthy word. The question that emerges from this text is: What kind of connection does the prediction in Numbers have with the promise of a prophet like Moses in Deuteronomy?

---

29 Joseph Fitzmyer, *Essays on the Semitic Background of the New Testament* (London: Geoffrey Chapman, 1971), 43.

30 For studies that deal with the figure of Balaam in Qumran, see: Stefan Beyerle, "'A Star Shall Come Out of Jacob': A Critical Evaluation of the Balaam Oracle in the Context of Jewish Revolts in Roman Times," in *The Prestige of the Pagan Prophet Balaam in Judaism, Early Christianity and Islam*, ed. George H. van Kooten and Jacques van Ruiten (Leiden: Brill, 2008), 163–188. Eibert Tigchelaar, "Balaam and Enoch," in *The Prestige of the Pagan Prophet Balaam in Judaism, Early Christianity and Islam*, ed. George H. van Kooten and Jacques van Ruiten (Leiden: Brill, 2008), 87–99. Florentino García Martínez, "Balaam in the Dead Sea Scrolls," in *The Prestige of the Pagan Prophet Balaam in Judaism, Early Christianity and Islam*, ed. George H. van Kooten and Jacques van Ruiten (Leiden: Brill, 2008), 71–82.

It is clear from the listing of these texts that we have an anticipation for an intermediary; one that was predicted to Moses and confirmed to Balaam. Further, by associating the prophecies in Deuteronomy and Numbers, 4Q175 depicts not necessarily two leaders but rather two qualities: a prophetic and a military one[31]. Also, the catena shows a progression where one text illuminates the other. This means the original problem of bringing the nation to follow the מצות is addressed by the prophet like Moses, while the defeat of Israel's enemies will come via the messianic leader in Numbers. The intriguing part of this manuscript is that it ends with a citation of Deut 33:8–11, where Levi and his kindred were blessed by Moses. This passage is of great significant because it confirms Levi's lineage as the ones to teach Israel and minister to God. In the end, 4Q175 creates via the combination of Scriptural texts an image of the interrelated mission that these leaders will have in the future; they will teach Israel, defeat its enemies, and minister to God. It is a complete vision of closeness to God, which correlates with 1QS 9.11 where the Yahad anticipates the coming of the Prophet and Messiahs of Aaron and Israel[32].

On the other hand, CD 7.14–21 consists of a combination of Scriptural references that are interpreted by alluding to another text. Different from 4Q175 where the language of Scripture provides the structure and essence of the vision, CD 7 is an exegetical text which works as a type of pesher. Although there is no use of the term "interpretation" (פשר), the focus of this column is to extrapolate an aspect of the Scriptural text, like a metaphor, and interpreting it with another metaphor that points to something or someone that was anticipated. The metaphors work as markers that create associations in the reader's mind, which is something that only a familiar reader is able to draw. Thus, the connections that CD makes in these lines suggest not just that the Instructor is familiar with the Scriptures, but that his audience is well acquainted with both his teaching method and with these associations as fulfillment of prophecy[33]. A closer look at these lines will illustrate our argument.

---

31 David Katzin, "The Use of Scripture in 4Q175," *DSD* 20 (2013): 200–236. Émile Puech, "Les Manuscripts de Qumrân Inspirés du livre de Josué: 4Q378, 4Q379, 4Q175, 4Q522, 5Q9 et Mas1039–211," *RevQ* 28 (2016): 45–116.

32 Fitzmyer, *Essays on the Semitic Background*, 84.

33 The use of specific words and the connection of these words to other Scriptural references resemble the interpretive strategies of Rabbinic midrash. For a discussion of intertextuality and midrash, see: Daniel Boyarin, *Intertextuality and the Reading of Midrash* (Bloomington: Indiana University Press, 1990), 12–17. In Boyarin's reading Midrash is just like any other work of literature, as it is made up of conscious and unconscious traces of other discourse where each verse stands in a continuous conversation and contestation with one another. Because Midrash takes place in history, it reveals the cultural codes of its time as well as the ideology of the people associated with it. It is the portrayal of how the rabbis interpreted the sacred

Lines 11–14a describe via the prophecy of Isa 7:17 a moment of reckoning when Israel was split between those who "backslid" (הנסוגים) and those who "held fast" (המחזיקים). The former fell by the sword while the latter escaped to Damascus according to the prophecy in Amos 5:26–27. Although the oracle was originally a condemnation against Israel, CD takes on a different direction and uses it as a prophecy that ultimately brought about the existence of the sectarians. By focusing on the images of this prophecy, that is, the "tents of your Kings" (סכות מלככם) and the "foundation of your images" (כיון צלמיכם), CD makes an interesting set of connections. First, lines 15–17 interpret that the books of the Torah represent the סוכת המלך and use the prophecy in Amos 9:11 which predicts the rise of the "booth of David that is fallen" (סוכת דוד הנופלת). With this interpretive move we notice a change in scope, where CD interprets the metaphor "booth" (סכות) with the Davidic monarchy instead of referring to the Assyrian deity Sikkuth[34]. In addition, lines 17–18 depict that the "books of the Prophets" (ספרי הנביאים) represent the "foundation of your images" (כיון צלמיכם). Lines 18–20 retake the metaphor of the "star" (כוכב) in Amos 5:26 and interpret it with the prophecy in Numbers 24, where it expounds on the symbols of this prophecy; thus, the star represents the Interpreter of the Torah while the scepter represents the "Leader of the whole congregation" (נשא כל העדה). At the end of this passage we are left with two messianic figures, the star (interpreted as the דורש התורה) represents a priestly figure and the scepter (interpreted as the נשיא כל העדה) represents a military leader. Therefore, CD turns the prophecy upside down; what was originally delivered as a word of punishment for Israel, CD makes it into a prophecy that points to the ultimate restoration of Israel. Although the books of Torah and the Prophets went to exile, they will return as the messianic leaders appear. One last important aspect of this text is that by focusing on the exile to Damascus and the advent of the Interpreter of the Torah and Leader of the whole congregation, CD evinces the conviction that the sectarians would be fundamental in the appearance of the messianic figure and in the restoration of Israel.

4Q175 and CD 7 use the prophecy in Numbers 24 to anticipate messianic figures and the restoration of Israel. This is different from what we see in 1QM 11 where the messianic interpretation of the star and the scepter takes a secondary role to Israel's victory. However, as we have seen from the previous

---

texts through their own subjective assumptions. Therefore, Midrash is a development of the intertextual character of the Scriptures, and the rabbis' role was to fill in the gaps of these heterogeneous texts by being careful readers who would strive not for originality but to illuminate God's words to the people.

34 Shalom Paul, *Amos* (Minneapolis: Fortress Press, 1991), 290–291.

examples, there is a diversity of approaches in how the prophecy was interpreted even when the thrust of the interpretation was messianic. In addition, we need to keep in mind that while 1QM 11 interprets the prophecy from Numbers in a non-messianic way, that does not stop readers from inquiring and making associations in their mind about any messianic implication. The presence of militaristic images and the mention of David (and the kings of Israel) along with the prophecy of Numbers forces us to ask if there is a messianic interpretation that is looming in the background. Or at the very least it should force us to be open to the possibility that Scriptural prophecies like Num 24:17–19 (and Amos 5:26–27 as well) have many interpretive trajectories and possibilities in the minds of exegetes.

Our exploration of the sectarian intertextuality in 1QM 11.1–7a has taken us on avenues of inquiry regarding David and the prophecy of Numbers. We have discovered that David was seen not just as a military leader and king, but he was also a wise man who was endowed with a prophetic gift. In addition, David and the messianic figure who comes in his lineage were depicted as devoted to the principles and observant of the festivities and traditions of Torah. The image of David and his lineage from the scrolls resembles much of the depictions that we have from Chronicles, where the Davidic line not only represents a royal lineage but also cultic leaders[35]. In terms of the prophecy of Num 24:17–19 we have observed that some scrolls connect it to a messianic figure. This is different from what we notice in 1QM 11, where the prophecy takes on a different direction by emphasizing Israel's power to overcome the enemy rather than anticipating a military leader. The previous evidence demonstrates the diversity of interpretations regarding David and the prophecy of Numbers as well as the careful analysis of the different metaphors associated with these topics. As we proceed, we will observe how the traditions of ascribing the war to God play in shaping these lines in 1QM 11.

iv.   Scriptural Intertextuality

The markers in 1QM 11.1–7a are numerous and an exploration of any one of them would require an investigation of its own. Instead, we will focus on one of the most salient intertextual aspects of this piece. With the refrain "the battle is yours" (לכה המלחמה) the hymn conveys two things: one is the trust that the looming conflict is God's war, and also that liturgy is an adequate conduit to convey this faith statement. The ensuing discussion will be circumscribed

---

35   For a discussion of the relationship of kings and cult in Chronicles see: Jozef Tiňo, *King and Temple in Chronicles: A Contextual Approach to Their Relations* (Göttingen: Vandenhoeck & Ruprecht, 2010), 147–161.

in that it will focus on the intersection of war and liturgy, by tapping into the most salient examples from the Scriptures and how these traditions became templates to strengthen the faith of sectarians combatants. We will pay close attention to two strands of traditions that have direct influence on 1QM. The book of Chronicles and book of Maccabees provide the closest resemblance to 1QM in how war and liturgy are key motifs that are constantly used to depict God intervening on Israel's behalf.

The significance of the Maccabean tradition for the study of 1QM has already been covered by Yadin and Davies[36]. Yadin has demonstrated the close affinity that exists between 1QM and 1 Maccabees in the interpretation of Scriptural traditions, while Davies speaks to the influence that 1 Maccabees has on 1QM from a historical, ideological, and redactional standpoint. The objective of this part is, therefore, to build upon this foundation and ask further questions about prayer and its efficacy for battle. Undoubtedly there are older traditions where these themes are intertwined, but Chronicles and Maccabees provide the closest comparisons to what we encounter in 1QM. Because 1QM 10–12 depict war from the standpoint of a priestly and liturgical standpoint, the traditions of Chronicles and Maccabees provide important points of comparison and influence useful for our assessment. Just like lines 1–7a anchor the hymn through the refrain לכה המלחמה, our subsequent discussion will focus on how this belief becomes a conviction that shapes the ideology in 1QM.

לכה המלחמה in Chronicles

The belief of ascribing military conflicts to God has its roots in some of the oldest traditions in Scripture. Cases like Exodus 15 depict the threat of enemy forces against Israel as God's war. These same passages also portray Israel primarily as a passive witness who is the beneficiary of the power of God demonstrated through the destruction of the enemy. Likewise these traditions use liturgical expressions via prayers or songs to celebrate God's victory. In Ex 15:1 for instance we have both Moses and the Israelites declare "I will sing to the Lord, for he rose exceedingly; horse and its rider he cast in the sea" (אשירה ליהוה כי גאה גאה סוס ורכבו רמה בים). Later on in the same chapter Miriam leads a chorus with the women while repeating the same refrain. In Chronicles we see this phenomenon play out consistently, as war plays a critical role in asserting Israel's existence in the land and liturgy as the expression by which kings not only express their faith in God but also celebrate

---

36 Yadin, *The Scroll of the War*, 198–228. Davies, *1QM, the War Scroll*, 91–111.

God's military victories[37]. An issue that we want to address is if these traditions of war and liturgy in Chronicles have an effect on how 1QM 11 visualizes the eschatological conflict.

Early on in Chronicles we see that מלחמה is an important element in the formation of Israel. The genealogies account for the formation of the different tribes of Israel, and in each instance, we read about the number of warriors each tribe had and how they fought against the surrounding peoples. 1 Chronicles 5 is an important passage because it is one of the earliest statements in Chronicles that war belongs to God. Verses 18–22 describe the moment when the Reubenites, Gadites, and the half tribe of Manasseh overcame their enemies in battle. The statement in verse 22 explicitly describes that many warriors fell "because the battle is God's" (כי מהאלהים המלח־ מה). The only other time that such a statement takes place is in 2 Chronicles 20:15, when Jahaziel proclaims "for it is not your battle, it is God's" (כי לא לכם המלחמה כי לאלהים). We will deal with this important passage below. For the time being we can suggest that the rest of 1 Chronicles operates from the standpoint that God is in control of war as God favored Israel and established David as king. It is not until 2 Chronicles 6 that we begin to see a more conspicuous intersection of war, liturgy, and faith that God controls war.

Solomon's prayer is a key moment in the book of Chronicles[38]. This passage not only recounts the dedication of the Temple, but it contains, via this king's words, important religious themes that will reverberate in the following accounts. For one there is the continuous reference in this prayer to the promises made to David, and how God kept the covenant to this servant. Of particular importance to this prayer is the notion that Israel shall remain faithful to God, in order to overcome their enemies and remain in the land. 2 Chr 6:24 further illustrates this last point, as Solomon pleads with God that Israel will be redeemed if they are defeated by their enemies due to their

---

37 Troy Cudworth, *War in Chronicles: Temple Faithfulness and Israel's Place in the Land* (London: T&T Clark, 2016). Gérard Nissim Amzallag, "The Subversive Dimension of the Story of Jehoshaphat's War Against the Nations (2 Chron 20:1–30)," *Biblical Interpretation*, 24 (2016): 178–202. Gary Knoppers, "Jerusalem at Aar in Chronicles," in *Zion, City of Our God*, ed. Richard S. Hess and Gordon J. Wenham (Grand Rapids: Eerdmans, 1999), 57–76. Gary Knoppers, "Battling Against Yahweh': Israel's War Against Judah in 2 Chr 13:2–20," *RB* 100 (1993): 511–532. Pancratius Beentjes, "War Narratives in the Book of Chronicles: A New Proposal in Respect of Their Function," *Hervormde Teologiese Studies*, 59 (2003): 587–596.

38 For a discussion on this prayer, see: Ralph Klein, "Psalms in Chronicles," *Currents in Theology and Mission* 32 (2005): 264–275. Mark Throntveit, "The Idealization of Solomon as the Glorification of God in the Chronicler's Royal Speeches and Royal Prayers," in *The Age of Solomon: Scholarship at the Turn of the Millennium*, ed. Lowell K. Handy (Leiden: Brill, 1997), 411–427. Raymond Dillard, "The Literary Structure of the Chronicler's Solomon Narrative," *JSOT* 30 (1984): 85–93.

Prophetic Exegesis in 1QM 11

disobedience. Specifically, it states that if Israel confesses God's name and turns from their sin that God would forgive them. Thus, prayer has the efficacy not just to heal the relationship between God and Israel but also to restore them to their land. The efficacy of prayer is further highlighted in verses 34–35 when Solomon asks God to hear Israel's prayer during the מלחמה, as it is directed toward the city and Temple that God chose. Verse 35 closes this part of the prayer with the call to God to hear the prayer and grant justice to Israel.

A similar reflection happens when Abijah confronts Jeroboam in 2 Chronicles 13. In this passage Jeroboam's army comes against the army of Judah, and in verses 3–11 Abijah raises an indictment against Jeroboam. In this word Abijah argues that Judah, not Ephraim, has continued to minister to God via the priests and Levites and has taken care of the ritual duties in the house of God. Verse 12 reminisces the descriptions in Numbers and 1QM 10.1–6, as Abijah describes that God is in their midst and the priests are ready with their trumpets to call upon God. Like his father Abijah, king Asa also confronted a similar threat when the Ethiopian army came against him. The account in 2 Chronicles 14 describes that Asa's kingdom had enjoyed prosperity because of their faithfulness to God. Verse 6 provides an interesting interpretation when Asa describes that they have continued to be in the land "because we have sought the Lord our God; we have sought him and he has given us rest from all around" (כי דרשנו את יהוה אלהינו דרשנו וינח לנו מסביב). At the moment when the Ethiopian army attacks Asa lifts a prayer reminding God of the promise to protect Israel in the face of threat. The previous examples reveal on the one hand the thematic significance that war has for Israel's survival in Chronicles, and they also demonstrate an intersection between war and prayer. If Israel is to survive in the land that God has given them, they not only need to remain faithful to God in matters of the cult, but they must also exercise their faith through prayer and worship when faced with an existential threat[39].

The last passage that we will consider is 2 Chronicles 20. This is a significant account because in it we see the same combination of war, prayer, and

---

39 Cudworth, *War in Chronicles*, 1–8. Cudworth has explored the connection of war and faithfulness to the cult in detail. Cudworth's argument is not just that war is a key literary feature of the Chronicler's agenda, but that in depicting war the Chronicler also illustrated the benefits of cultic faithfulness. Cudworth divides his work between faithful and unfaithful kings. Thus, David is the ideal king (cf. 1 Chr 11–16; 17–29) and Solomon, Abijah, Jotham, and Hezekiah are the faithful kings (2 Chr 1–9; 13; 27; 29–32). On the other hand are the unfaithful kings from Saul to Zedekiah (1 Chr 10; 2 Chr 21–22; 28; 33; 36). There are also faithful kings who falter, like Jehoshaphat (2 Chr 14–16; 17–20; 23–24; 25; 26; 34–35) as well as unfaithful kings who repent like Manasseh (2 Chr 10–12; 33). For our purposes, the connection of a monarch and cultic observance will become more apparent in 2 Chronicles 20 in the narrative of Jehoshaphat's prayer.

prophecy that we find in 1QM. From the outset 2 Chr 20:1 relays that a massive army of Moabites, Ammonites, and Meunites came against Jehoshaphat. Interestingly, the War Scroll also begins with a depiction of the enemy armies, including the Moabites, Ammonites, Philistines, and the Kittim (1QM 1.1). Different from Chronicles, however, this line depicts that the sectarians will launch the first attack against these enemies; thus, 1QM turns the depictions in Chronicles from a defensive to an offensive standpoint.

Once Jehoshaphat receives the report of the looming threat, he decides to seek God and declare a fast in Judah. He proceeds with a prayer that raises important points about Israel's inheritance of the land (vv. 6–7), God's promise to answer the cry of Israel in front of the Temple (vv. 8–9), and justice to be executed upon these foreign fighters (vv. 10–12). Once the king has finished his prayer, the account abruptly transitions in verse 14 where it describes that the Spirit of God came upon the Levite Jahaziel. The exact wording is particularly interesting as it states that "the spirit of the Lord came over him" (היתה עליו רוח יהוה). This sort of depiction happens elsewhere in Scripture when God empowers the Judges to overcome their enemies (Judg 3:10; 14:6, 19; 15:14). Isa 11:2 also describes that the Spirit of God will rest on the messianic figure. Once the spirit has come upon Jahaziel he proceeds in a manner fitting of prophetic figures by introducing the word of God through the collocation "thus says the Lord" (כה אמר יהוה). Before we address the content of the oracle, the way Jahaziel is depicted presents important aspects. Here we have a priestly figure who experiences the overwhelming presence of God's spirit in the same fashion as military and charismatic leaders were empowered by God. This depiction, therefore, fits perfectly with what we see across Chronicles where priestly figures are part of war, and it also presents us an interesting clue to what the War Scroll depicts more conspicuously; that is, cultic and military leaders battling shoulder to shoulder for their place in the land.

The content of the oracle is important because in it Jahaziel encourages Israel with the word כי לא לכם המלחמה כי לאלהים, which is exactly what the refrain in 1QM 11.1–7a repeats. The ensuing verses describe that following the prophetic word the Levites, Kohathites, and Korahites praised God and the king encouraged the people to believe in God and the prophets[40]. Verses 21–23 introduce what seems to be a worship service where the singers lead a chorus with the words "give thanks to the Lord, for his everlasting faithfulness" (הודו ליהוה כי לעולם חסדו) and God sets an "ambush" (מארבים)

40 4Q491 Frg 1–3 begins with a reference to Korah and his congregation. This manuscript depicts with both prophetic and cultic language, similar to 1QM 2–9, how the hand of God will prevail in the eschatological war.

Prophetic Exegesis in 1QM 11

where the enemy armies destroy each other in a massive confusion. The mention of the ambush is an interesting one, because 1QM uses the word/term מארבים in the description of the formation of the army in the War of Divisions (1QM 3.2, 8). And it also describes the setting of the ambush immediately prior to the prayers in 1QM 10 (1QM 9.17).

2 Chronicles 20 provides important similarities that correlate to what we see in 1QM 10–11. Priestly figures acting in prophetic roles, the repetition of the refrain, and prayers remembering God's acts on Israel's behalf, the setting of the מארבים and the threat of enemy forces create interesting connections between this passage in Chronicles and the War Scroll. This does not necessarily mean that 1QM is dependent or builds upon what Chronicles describes. But there seems to be an interesting connection between 1QM and Chronicles, where priests become actors not just of the cult but of the survival of the people through war. And in the case of Jahaziel he is endowed with a prophetic word[41].

The fact that the Chronicler introduces Jahaziel as a Levite of the sons of Asaph makes it clear that he is not supposed to be seen as a "prophet" (נביא). The fact that he was overwhelmed by the Spirit of God and his word was interpreted as trustworthy underscores that he was indeed operating like a prophet. In his work on prophecy in Chronicles, Schniedewind made the argument that the "possession" that Jahaziel experienced is not exclusively associated with the prophets[42]. This is confirmed by what we observed before that the formula היתה עליו רוח יהוה appears in the context of military feats in Judges. Nevertheless, Schniedewind concedes that Jahaziel operated like a prophet, and observes that Jehoshaphat's ensuing exhortation to believe in the prophets points to the former prophets. Schniedewind believes that the Chronicler's audience would have understood this statement as one referring to the writings of the prophets. Our perspective, however, is that Jahaziel acts in a prophetic manner because he is inspired by the Spirit of God, but more significantly because he reiterates in his statement the core of what the Scriptures teach about God's relation to Israel.

In that sense, Jahaziel acts as a prophet who speaks to the people on God's behalf. On the other hand, Jehoshaphat's statement points to the prophets, not at the expense of what Jahaziel stated, but because of what this Levite forth-told. In other words, Jehoshaphat recognizes that Jahaziel's word lines

---

41 The conflation of worship themes and priestly figures leading the war with trumpets and chants are themes that Chronicles retakes, perhaps as a reenactment of the narratives in Numbers, and that reappear throughout 1QM.

42 Schniedewind, *The Word of God in Transition: From Prophet to Exegete in the Second Temple Period* (Sheffield: Sheffield Academic Press, 1995), 182–184.

up with Scriptural teaching and encourages Israel to act accordingly. Prior in his work Schniedewind presented Jahaziel as a type of Moses, because his statement alludes to Exod 14:13–14 when Moses urges Israel to believe and not fear[43]. Consequently, Jahaziel's "possession" is not the most important aspect of his speech. Rather, this account shows us, as Schniedewind himself would agree, that prophecy in Chronicles is about acting as an intermediary between God and the people, with the revelation of the written and spoken Scripture as the foundation of faith for the nation.

This brings us back to 1QM 11 and what it does with the statement that the war is God's. Does the refrain לכה המלחמה signal a type of prophetic word, and does the repetition of this statement communicate to the sectarians that this is not just a belief that past generations held but that it is a guarantee for the success in battle? The answer to both questions is positive because the refrain, along with the historical allusions, create a prophetic word that exhorts the warriors to believe that this is God's war by way of remembering the victories of the past and repeating the refrain exactly three times, thus confirming a guarantee of success. Finally, the prophecy of Num 24:17–19 caps the thrust of this hymn that the sectarians will crush the enemies and do mightily. As we turn to Maccabees, we will continue to see some of the same beliefs about God's war resurfacing across the narratives.

לכה המלחמה in Maccabees

In Maccabees the theme of war constitutes one of the main themes as the Jewish people fight for their survival in the land. Like Chronicles, Maccabees evinces the intersection of war with prayer and prophecy. A particular feature that we will notice in the ensuing examples is that prayer becomes the conduit that the warriors use to reminisce on past moments in Israel's history and put their faith in God. These prayers are used prophetically in that they encourage the warriors to believe in God, and they predict a successful outcome not because of their own strength but because the God of their ancestors delivered them before. Our analysis will, therefore, explore texts in Maccabees that coincide with what we observe in 1QM 11.1–7a.

For instance, 1 Maccabees 3–4 relays the account when Judas restored the sanctuary in Jerusalem. Faced with the threat of enemy forces, verses 44–47 describe that the congregation met with the purpose of seeking God in prayer. Not only that, but they declared a fast and adopted a mournful posture.

---

43 Ibid., 236. Schniedewind sees in Jahaziel's passage a recontextualization of Moses' injunction to Israel in Exodus 14.

Prophetic Exegesis in 1QM 11   177

Verses 48–49 add to this picture with some sort of mediation with the divine, as the people inquired of the book of the law, brought up the priestly vestments and tithes as well as stirred the Nazirites who had completed their days[44]. Further, in a curious fashion the account makes it very explicit that in seeking the direction from God's words, the people were inquiring about those matters in the same way that the Gentiles consulted their deities. The account therefore makes it apparent that whereas the Gentiles seek wisdom in their idols, the Jewish people seek revelation from their God through the words of the law. And with this contrast the account already hints at what the final outcome will be of the looming skirmish.

This narrative recalls in many respects 2 Chr 20, where many of the literary features like the threat to Israel's place in the land and their sanctuary calls for drastic measures. There is not only a communal gathering, but there is also the observance of a fast that would focus the people on seeking God. The picture that emerges from this passage is that of a congregation that is afraid and in their concern they tap into all sources of revelation at their disposal like prayer, Scripture, cultic observance, and prophecy. As the account proceeds we see an emboldened Judas who encourages the warriors and recalls two major moments in Israel's history: one is the deliverance from Egypt (1 Macc 4:9) and David's defeat of the Philistines (1 Macc 4:30), which 1QM 11 also uses as evidence of God's faithfulness to Israel[45].

Like the preceding example 2 Maccabees 15 also depicts the dangers that came to Israel and how Scripture, prayer, and prophecy empower the Jewish army. Faced with the looming encounter against Nicanor, Judas encourages the combatants by referencing Torah and the prophets and how help had come from heaven in former times (2 Macc 15:8–9). The account continues by depicting Judas' persuasive capabilities as he moves the army to trust not in shields and spears but in revelation (2 Macc 15:11). He goes on to relay a dream, a vision that was "trustworthy."[46] In this dream Judas sees Onias

---

44 The Greek word use for inquiring is ἐξεραυνάω, which is the same term that 1 Pet 1:10 uses in describing the careful inquiry that the prophets made about the coming salvation in Christ.

45 Yadin, *The Scroll of the War*, 214.

46 The exact phrase in this verse is: προσεξηγησάμενος ὄνειρον ἀξιόπιστον ὕπαρ τι πάντας ηὔφρανεν. Notice the use of two terms that denote a vision: ὄνειρος is a dream while ὕπαρ is a vision. Although the account makes it seem that these terms are equivalent, they can also be opposite. That is, while ὄνειρος happens asleep, ὕπαρ can also happen while a person is awake. In any case, the account relays that in Judas' dream Onias has a vision of Jeremiah the prophet. This is an interesting feature, because instead of depicting that the revelation came to Judas himself, the warrior relays that the vision came to the Priest. The fact that the account describes Onias as one who was trustworthy in v. 12 underscores the emphasis that the vision came to this honorable man.

praying for Israel and while the High Priest prays the prophet Jeremiah appears. The way the account turns its focus from Onias to the sudden appearance of Jeremiah resembles the vision in Dan 7:13 when the account shifts from the Ancient of Days to the Son of Man. Also, just like the Son of Man receives the authority from the Ancient of Days, Judas receives from Jeremiah the golden sword to overcome his enemies. Empowered by this vision, Judas prays to God by reciting Scripture in verse 22 as he recalls how Hezekiah was delivered from Assyria by an angel that God sent. The reference to the sword in the vision of Jeremiah and the recollection of the Assyrian defeat correlate to 1QM 11, where the "sword of no man" will bring down the Kittim. The account concludes with the direct encounter of these enemy armies where Israel overcomes the trumpets and battle songs of their enemies with prayers to God.

The examples of Chronicles and Maccabees demonstrate that throughout the narratives of Scripture war was one of the hardships that Israel would have to endure in order to survive in the land. The specific focus of our analysis underscores this reality, plus it highlights the intersection of different religious beliefs and traditions. The combination of war motifs along with liturgical expressions (i.e. prayer and hymns) in Chronicles and Maccabees evinces, if not a direct influence on 1QM 11, at least a context whereby these expressions would act prophetically to embolden the Jewish people as they survive in the land. Also, the interpretation of prior traditions as the hortatory call by Jahaziel and Judas' vision of Jeremiah demonstrate, correlates with how the hymn in 1QM 11.1–7a uses tradition to ground the faith of the sectarians. Thus, the combination of prayer, prophecy, worship, and war as depicted in Chronicles and Maccabees, becomes a consistent set of themes that 1QM brings to create an account where war is visualized not just as a bellicose encounter between light and darkness, but ultimately as a type of worship service where God will be magnified in the eyes of the people[47].

v.   Prophetic Exegesis

Our investigation thus far has shown that the hymn in lines 1–7a is established

---

47 Duhaime, *The War Texts*, 53–60. Duhaime provides a survey of the different proposals that have been made regarding the genre of 1QM. One of the proposals that scholars have made is that 1QM, especially columns 10–19, is a liturgical piece. Among those scholars who have proposed such a label for 1QM are: Jean Carmignac, *La Règle de la Guerre des Fils de Lumière contre les Fils des Ténèbres: Texte, Restauré, Traduit Et Commenté* (Paris: Letouzey & Ané, 1958); Robert North, "'Kittim' War or 'Sectaries' Liturgy?," *Bib* 39 (1958): 84–93; Matthias Krieg, "Mo'ed Naqam - ein Kulturdrama aus Qumran: Beobachtungen an der Kriegsrolle," *TZ* 41 (1985): 3–30.

Prophetic Exegesis in 1QM 11   179

on both the historical and prophetic testimony that Israel's wars are in the hands of God. The refrain לכה המלחמה not only alludes to texts like 1 Samuel 17 and 2 Chronicles 20, but it is the main marker that provides the hymn with its rhetorical and religious framework. We can observe that the hymn opens up with the emphatic assertion כיא אם לכה המלחמה, it continues with a less emphatic line כיא לכה המלחמה, and it ends with what seems to be a more matter of fact statement לכה המלחמה. Also, as the refrain becomes narrower the Scriptural example becomes bigger, or shall we say more explicit to the principle that the hymn wants to convey. The emphatic statement in line 1 is followed by an allusion to the story of David and Goliath, while the narrower refrain in line 4 leads to the explicit citation of Num 24:17–19. It is the citation of the oracle in Numbers that provides this hymn with the core principle that Israel will do mightily because God through prophecy has already guaranteed victory. Further down in this column the prophetic testimony will resurface in the reference to the "seers of things appointed" (חוזי תעודות) in line 8.

Also, following each of the refrains the hymn inserts a generic statement about God's victories and provides examples that substantiate the previous assertion. In this way the hymn goes from a generic axiom לכה המלחמה, to a truth about God's power, to specific examples of how these victories were accomplished. Further, mixed within these big descriptions of God, the hymn inserts humble images of Israel's dependence on God. Therefore, as the hymn proceeds two pictures emerge: one is that God is mighty and the other is that Israel is wholly dependent on God. The combination of the refrain לכה המל־חמה with a Scriptural testimony gives the hymn the foundation that we will analyze in further detail.

1QM 11.1–7a can be divided into three parts: a) lines 1–2a, b) lines 2b–4a, and c) lines 4b–7a. Part a alludes to the historical encounter between David and Goliath. Prior to the allusion line 1 inserts the statement "and with the strength of your hand their corpses have been torn to pieces without anyone to bury them" (ובכוח ידכה רוטשו פגריהם לאין קובר). The image of corpses without burial reminisces several passages in Scriptures where the armies of God defeat Israel's enemies. The eschatological context of 1QM, especially with its gory descriptions of slaughter and blood in columns 15–19, demonstrates that at this junction the hymn is tapping into Scriptural imagery to underscore that the looming battle will be a reenactment of David's defeat of Goliath. The allusion to this combat is used therefore to substantiate this conviction. In addition, line 1 emphasizes that the strength of God's hand and that this mighty enemy was delivered into the hands of David. The transfer of power from God to David illustrates a notion that will be repeated consistently across the hymn, which is that Israel can do mightily only as God allows it.

The use of the particle כיא in line 2 introduces a causal clause that provides the main reason for the success depicted in line 1. This is a feature that will be repeated in parts b and c, as the hymn explains why God granted victory to Israel. In part a the causal clause reiterates that David's faith in God rather than on his own weapons brought the victory. Part b reiterates that David had success against the Philistines because he trusted in God's holy name. Line 3 adds that by the "hand of our kings" (יד מלכינו) God delivered Israel many times. Like in part a God is the main force driving the success, but humans have the agency to be used by God to bring that victory. The reference to David and the success of the kings of Israel against the Philistines recalls accounts in the history of Israel recorded in Samuel-Kings as well as Chronicles. Like in part a, part b also uses a causal particle (בע־בור), to add the reason for Israel's success. This time rather than emphasizing David's faith, the hymn adopts the language used in confessional prayer. It is Israel's acknowledgment that success comes not because of their own merits, but because God has allowed for victory to come. This last statement leads into part c where the hymn continues with the acknowledgement that it is God whose strength has brought victory for Israel. Lines 4–5b highlight the previous statement by reiterating that it is not Israel's strength that has brought victory. Line 5a explains with כיא that it is God's power and strength (כוח, חילכה) that brings success. In 5b–6 we have the introduction of a prophetic testimony. Notice that the prophecy of Numbers is introduced by the phrase "just as you told us from ancient times, saying" (כאשר הגדתה לנו מאז לאמור), which resembles the introduction of prophecy in 1QM 10. In 1QM 10.1–2, נגד and מאז are important terms that indicate that the teachings of Scriptures, delivered a long time ago, are applicable to the current circumstance. Not only that, but this combination also supports the notion that the sectarians see their place in history as the continuation of the prophecies given to their ancestors. Thus, when 1QM uses the direct object לנו, the hymn appropriates this prophecy as one that is addressed to its own readers/hearers[48]. The prophetic interpretation of Scriptures in this hymn evinces the conviction that the prophecies to ancient Israel are applicable to the sectarians, because they are the new Israel, the ones for whom the oracles of the past apply now.

---

48 We will see in our analysis of lines 7b–18 that this same approach is used in reference to the prophecy of the חוזי תעודות.

Prophetic Exegesis in 1QM 11   181

In addition, the way this hymn cites Num 24:17–19 demonstrates that in
the context of 1QM this oracle points to Israel and not to a messianic leader.
First, the citation omits the line "I see him but not now; I behold him but not
near" (אראנו ולא עתה אשורנו ולא קרוב). This is the case because line 6 already interpreted that this prophecy comes from God. The omission of this
phrase leaves the agency of the prophet Balaam aside to highlight that this
word is from God. Further, the citation changes the order of the prophecy,
where the descriptions in v. 19 precede those from v. 18. And the citation removes the word about Edom from v. 18, and instead highlights that the אויב
will be defeated and become the possession of Israel. The citation, like its
Scriptural counterpart, ends with the assertion that "Israel will do valiantly"
(ישראל עשה היל). Hence, by the end of line 7 the hymn has already demonstrated that Israel can do mightily only as they are empowered by God's own
might. The oracle of Numbers articulates explicitly the essence of the promise, which is that the sectarians (as the new Israel) will do mightily and defeat the enemy because God has already proclaimed it; thus, the prophecy of
Numbers functions as the confirmation of something that was already guaranteed and that the combatants need to embrace.

1QM 11.1–7a provides a beautiful example of prophetic exegesis. The
combination of hymnic elements mixed with historiographical references is
a neat example of how liturgy can feed the imagination of the audience by
bringing the readers/listeners back to sacred moments in that nation's history. What sets this hymn apart from other examples, however, is its citation
of prophecy. Typically, liturgical pieces rely on allusions and echoes to evoke
the images of the past in order to strengthen the faith of the listeners. In this
case, the hymn concludes with prophecy, not in a way that it delivers a new
oracular material. Rather, it takes a well-known prophecy that has significant
ramifications for Israel and turns it into the main thesis for why the sectarians
can trust in God's deliverance. The citation provides therefore the evidence
that all the historical successes in the past took place because of the promise
that Israel would do mighty things. The rhetorical effect of adding this citation to the end of the hymn is that it becomes a concluding remark, a token of
faith that the warriors can repeat to themselves as they are about to encounter their enemy. The repetition of the refrain לכה המלחמה and the insertion
of the Scriptural promise provide a powerful mechanism that emboldens the
warriors. These rhetorical moves via the repetition of key intertextual markers demonstrate that the language of Scripture (through the ascribing of the
war to God and the repetition of the prophecies of the past) was essential to
the language and beliefs of the sectarians.

b. 1QM 11.7b–17: God's Future Exaltation

i. Text and Translation

1QM 11.7b–18	1QM 11.7b–18
וביד משיחיכה 7b	7b By the hand of your anointed
8 חוזי תעודות הגדתה לנו ק[צין] מל־חמות ידיכה לה{לחם}כבד באויבינו להפיל גדודי בליעל שבעת	8 seers of decrees, you told us about the times of the wars of your hands, to {fight} glorify yourself over our enemies, to bring down the hordes of Belial, the seven
9 גוי הבל ביד אביוני פדותכה [ ]חֹ ובשלום לגבורת פלא ולב נמס לפתח תקוה ותעש להמה כפרעוה	9 nations of futility by the hands of the poor whom you redeemed [ ] and in retribution to wondrous strength, and a heart that melts to a door of hope. You shall do to them as Pharaoh,
10 וכשלישי מרכבותיו בים סו[ף] ונכאי רוח תבעיר כלפיד אש בעמיר אוכלת רשעה לוא תשוב עד	10 and the officers of his chariots in the Sea of Reeds. You will ignite the broken of spirit like a fiery torch of fire in a sheaf that consumes wickedness. You will not withdraw until
11 כלות אשמה ומאז השמן [עד גבורת ידכה בכתיים לאמור ונפל אשור בחרב לוא איש וחרב	11 the annihilation of the guilty. In times past [ ] until your powerful hand against the Kittim, saying: 'Assyria shall fall by a sword not of man, and a sword,
12 לוא אדם תואכלנו vacat	12 not of man, shall consume it.' (Isa 31:8).
13 כיא ביד אביונים תסגיר [או]יבי כול הארצות וביד כורעי עפר להשפיל גבורי עמים להשיב גמול	13 For into the hand of the oppressed you will deliver the enemies of all the lands, and into the hands of those who are prostrate in the dust, to bring down the mighty people, to return the recompense
14 רשעים בראש אש[ן] ולהצדיק משפט אמתכה בכול בני איש ולעשות לכה שם עולם בעם	14 of the wicked on the head of [ ], to pronounce the justice of your truth over all sons of man, and to make for yourself an everlasting name among the people.
15 [ ]המלחמות ולהתגדל ולהתקדש לעיני שאר הגוים לדעתֿן [	15 [ ] the wars, to magnify and sanctify yourself to the eyes of the remnant of the nations, for knowledge [ ]
16 [ע]שותכה שפטים בגוג ובכול קהלו הנקֿ[ה]לֹ[י]ם ל[ ] [	16 [when you] carry out judgments over Gog and over all his assembly that are assembled
17 [ ] [כיא תלחם בם מן השמ]ים]	17 [ ], for you will do battle against them from the heavens
18 [ ][ליהם למהמה]ן [	18 [ ] upon them for confusion[ ]

Prophetic Exegesis in 1QM 11

ii. Content

The following is the content of 1QM 11.7b–9a

- 11.7b–9a
  1. Proclamation by the חוזי תעודות
  2. Reference to the times of war
  3. Defeat of Belial and שבעת גוי הבל
- 11.9b–12
  1. Allusion to Pharaoh's defeat in the סוף
  2. Annihilation of the Wicked by the רוח
  3. Citation of Isaiah 31:8
- 11.13–18
  1. Fall of the Wicked by the אביונים and the עפר
  2. God's exaltation over the nations
  3. Prediction of God's fight against Gog

Different from the preceding lines 1QM 11.7b–18 does not have the marks of a liturgical piece. Rather what we find in these lines is a reflection that arises from the prophecy in line 7a and goes into additional predictions about the times of war.

Line 7b introduces the testimony about the times of the wars given by the "seers of decrees" (חוזי תעודות). The reference to seers is a natural transition from line 7a where we have the prophecy of Balaam. We know from Scriptures that Balaam was able not just to see the Angel of Lord (Num 22:31) but he was also able to convey promises of blessings for Israel (Num 24:17–19). Line 11 introduces another prophetic word when it cites Isaiah's prediction of the fall of Assyria. We will see that this citation, as in the case of Num 24:17–19 above, was adopted to apply directly to the current situation. Whereas the prophecy in Numbers establishes Israel's future success, the prophecy of Isa 31:8 is used as an example that applies directly to the defeat of the Kittim. Thus, just as Assyria was defeated by the "sword of no man," the Kittim will fall by God acting through those who are humbled. In these lines prophecy serves a dual purpose, to lift up Israel and to bring down the enemies by the hand of those who are less favored.

As in the case of lines 1–7a, here we also see God empowering Israel to do mightily. The difference, however, is that lines 1–7a describe Israel's success in history, while lines 7b–18 depict what God will do in the future. In addition, whereas in the previous section kings earn the victories, here we have the lowly receiving the victory. Specifically, lines 9 and 13 depict that God will act through the hands of the "poor" (אביונים), while line 10 describes that God will ignite the "broken of spirit" (נכאי רוח). Line 13 also predicts that those who are "prostrate to the ground" (כורעי עפר) will assist in bringing down the mighty.

Essentially, lines 7b–18 continue with the prophetic argument presented in lines 1–7a, but this time the prophetic testimony of the seers and the citation of Isaiah point not to ancient Israel but to the future Israel. In addition, as we shall see in our analysis, the depictions of the lowly reveal the sectarian agency. For the sectarians, future success in battle pointed to a redemption and a turning of history, where the lowly will be favored over the mighty. And in terms of the Scriptural intertextuality we will focus on the notion depicted in line 7b about the times of the wars of God and the overarching belief that wars serve for the exaltation and glorification of God before the peoples of the earth.

iii. Sectarian Intertextuality

1QM 11.7b–18 has the characteristics of a dualistic composition with apocalyptic type overtones. From the outset this section pits the mighty against the lowly, as it continually uses the language of extermination not just of the enemies but of wickedness itself. Line 9 predicts that the poor will bring down Belial and the "Seven Nations of futility" (שבעת גוי הבל). Also, in line 10 the נכאי רוח will become like a fiery torch until wickedness is exterminated, and in lines 13–14 the כורעי עפר will defeat the "mighty people" (גברי עמים) and the "wicked" (רשעים). Taken together these descriptions evince a conflict between the lowly and the mighty who are associated with wickedness. The metaphors used to associate each of the conflicting parties are powerful images that evoke other texts and give us a hint at how the sectarians viewed this conflict. The key notion, however, that runs throughout these lines is that Israel will continue to struggle against wickedness, as it has always done throughout history, but that God will intervene and tilt the balance in their favor. These are dualistic and apocalyptic type ideas, but they do not in and of themselves justify the category of an apocalypse.

We will focus on the descriptions of the lowly and trace the connections that these references make with other scrolls. As we shall see, these images represent direct interpretations that the sectarians will be the recipients of God's favor. We argue, therefore, that the implication of using this language is that the sectarians view themselves as God's people - the true Israel.

The Agency of the אביונים

1QM 11.7b–18 has several descriptions where the less fortunate partner with God in bringing down the wicked. Although the extent of their involvement is not clear, these lines show that God will bring the enemies under the power of the poor whom God has redeemed (אביוני פדותכה). Line 9 continues by describing that the poor will receive wondrous strength and that those whose heart melts will come to a door of hope. These descriptions illustrate a contrast, the change of events when God will turn the tables on the wicked and empower the lowly; in essence, God will hand the wicked to the poor.

1QM 13.14–18 echo this sentiment as they describe that the mighty hand of God is with the poor, and that the wicked will ultimately be defeated[49]. The war text in 4Q491 11i.8–11 adds to this image by claiming that God has established the "council of the poor" (עצת אביונים) as an "eternal congregation" (עדת עולמים). These war texts demonstrate the conviction that the poor represent the faithful of God for whom eternal favor will be demonstrated. However, the representation of the poor goes beyond the war texts. As a matter of fact, the consistent use of אביונים in several manuscripts underscores that the Scriptural traditions that identify Israel as the needy were quite popular among the sectarians, and it demonstrates that they adopted these traditions to represent themselves as the inheritors of God's promises[50].

For instance, 4Q171 Frg. 1–10.2.10 interprets Psalm 37 and the promises that are prepared for those who turn to God[51]. The context of this psalm deals with the trust that the faithful should have that God will eventually overturn the fate of the wicked in favor of the afflicted. Line 10 explicitly cites Psa 37:11 where the psalmist foresees that the "afflicted" (ענוים) will take possession of the land and rejoice in abundant peace. The pesher identifies the ענוים with the "congregation of the poor ones" (עדת האביונים) and sets the timeframe when this promise will take place. First the עדת האביונים will need to accept that there will be an appointed period of humiliation (מועד התענית). But after they have been delivered from the snares of Belial, they will enjoy prosperity. The lines of this pesher are comparable to what we see in 1QM

---

49 The difference between these lines in column 13 and column 11 is that it uses dualistic language of darkness as it depicts the violent end of wickedness. Thus, we see that darkness will be brought low (להשפיל חושך) and that the Sons of Darkness will be exterminated (לכ־לות כול בני חושך).

50 Yadin, *The Scroll of the War*, 311. Davies, *1QM, the War Scroll*, 98–99.

51 David Katzin, "'The Time of Testing': The Use of Hebrew Scriptures in 4Q171's Pesher of Psalm 37," *Hebrew Studies* 45 (2004): 121–162. David Katzin, "A Paradigm for Identifying the Use of Scriptural Allusion in Lemma-Based Exegesis within the Qumran Library Using 4QpPsa (4Q171) As an Example," *Hebrew Union College Annual* 87 (2016): 61–92.

11.8–9, where the notions of "appointed times" and the overturn of the current events end up with Belial being delivered to the poor[52].

The next fragment in this pesher continues with the promises to the congregation of the poor ones. 4Q171 Frg. 1–10.9–11 cites Ps 37:21–22 where the psalmist describes the righteous as generous and foresees that they will inherent the land. The pesher again takes the metaphor that the psalmist uses and interprets it with the "congregation of the poor" (עדה האביונים). Line 11 is significant because it specifically predicts that they will inherent the high mountain and they will delight in "his holy mountain" (בהר קודשו). The hope to celebrate in the holy mountain evokes the Scriptural celebrations where God is glorified, which correlates to the processions to Zion contained in both 1QM 12.13–18 and 19.5–8. 1QM 11.14–18 also depict a celebration, but this one is not necessarily a procession to God's abode, but rather an exaltation of God before the remnant of the people. The mention of the holy mountain in 4Q171 and of Zion in 1QM provides an interesting take on the sectarian interpretation of Jerusalem. They suggest, at the very least, that in their aspirations for a renewed relationship with God, Zion as the place for God's abode and place of worship remained in line with Scriptural tradition.

Another manuscript that deals with the poor ones is the Pesher Habakkuk[53]. 1QpHab 12 is a significant passage not just because it mentions the אביונים and associates this metaphor with the sectarians, but it is also important because it provides a commentary of the conflict that the Yahad had with the Wicked Priest. Plus, it is a key text to discuss about the identity of the Wicked Priest, as either one of the Chief Priests or as a set of Chief Priests from a non Aaronide lineage.

1QpHab 12 begins with an interpretation of Hab 2:17. In this tradition, God tells the prophet that the wicked will be punished for their treatment of Lebanon and the violence they brought to the land. Lines 2–5 go on to interpret this prophecy as the future condemnation that will come upon the Wicked Priest because of his violence against the poor. Moreover, these lines, like 4Q171 above, adopt the Scriptural characters to refer to contemporary counterparts; thus, Lebanon is the "council of the Yahad" (עצת היחד) and the "animals" (בהמות) are the simple people of Judah who observe the Torah.

---

52 The difference, however, is that 1QM 11 talks about the אביונים in more general terms while 4Q171 (and 4Q491) talks about the congregation of the poor.

53 John Collins, *Beyond the Qumran Community* (Grand Rapids: Eerdmans, 2010), 103–113. In this section of his work Collins gives ample space to the Pesher Habakkuk. Although he does not deal specifically with column 12, because the allusion in line 2–3 is too general, he nevertheless recognizes the importance of the other columns to try to reconstruct the history of that time; namely the conflict between the Teacher of Righteousness and the Wicked Priest.

Prophetic Exegesis in 1QM 11

Line 6 adds that God will destroy the Wicked Priest just as he tried to destroy the poor. The pesher continues in line 6 with an interesting strategy. It introduces what seems to be a saying "blood in the city and violence in the land" (מדמי קריה וחמס ארץ) which sounds close to the wording in Hab 2:17 where it describes "human bloodshed and violence to the earth". This saying could potentially point to a different source or a tradition associated with that verse. Whatever the source of this saying may be, the pesher interprets that the "city" (קריה) is Jerusalem and that the violence committed against it is the defilement of the "sanctuary of God" (מקדש אל). Also, the injustice committed against the land represents the cities of Judah where the Wicked Priest stole the assets from the poor. Different from what we see in 1QM 11.7b–18 where the lines depict a turn of events in favor of the poor, the pesher Habakkuk aims at describing the condemnation that the Wicked Priest will suffer because of his actions. Also, whereas the poor in 1QM 11 represent the sectarians, in 1QpHab the metaphor is more generic. It can include the sectarians as the interpretation of Lebanon with the עצת היחד indicates, but it can also encompass the people of Judah as lines 9–10 suggest. What is clear, however, from 1QM 11 and 1QpHab is that the poor represent the people who are not in leadership but on whom God has placed a special favor.

Lastly, the Hodayot use אביונים to describe the current struggle[54]. In 1QHa 10 the speaker expresses gratitude because God has delivered her/him from the snares of the deceitful. Line 34 specifically describes that God "redeemed the life of the poor" (פדיתה נפש אביון). The interesting aspect of this line is that it is in the third person and the speaker effectively takes on the persona of an אביון. The statement, therefore, has two effects in that it expresses the conviction that God redeems the poor and that the speaker adopts this truth to her/his own persona. Plus, this line correlates with 1QM 11.9 where the hymn foresees that God will hand Belial into the hand of the poor whom God has redeemed. 1QHa 11.25–26 also expresses a similar sentiment where the speaker introduces the notion that the "poor soul" (נפש אביון) suffers immensely because the surrounding environment is full of wickedness. This hodayah goes on to describe in detail all the snares that Belial places on the speaker, but in lines 34–41 God intervenes on behalf of the speaker. Finally, 1QHa 13.16–18 depicts this same turn of events. The narrative leading up to these lines illustrates the difficult life that the speaker lives, but in lines 16–18 the tenor transitions from describing distress to proclaiming trust in God.

---

54 Carol Newsom, "Apocalyptic Subjects: Social Construction of the Self in the Qumran Hodayot," *JSP* 12 (2001): 3–35. Esther Chazon, "Lowly to Lofty: The Hodayot's Use of Liturgical Traditions to Shape Sectarian Identity and Religious Experience," *RevQ* 26 (2013): 3–19.

Here the speaker also introduces the threat on her/his life and how God constitutes the redemption and safety against the wicked. These hodayot like the pesher texts above paint a picture of adversity that אביונים must overcome. Whether it was the Wicked Priest or other enemies, these texts depict in a prototypical fashion the sectarian thinking that pits themselves against the other.

1QM 11.7b–18 resembles the previous texts in that it envisions a conflict between the humble against the more powerful adversaries. The use of this type of language raises a question considering that throughout 1QM the sectarians have been depicted as warriors rather than weak and poor. One possibility is that the use of these markers represents an attempt to tease out another aspect of this eschatological war, where those considered less or weak will ultimately be favored in the end. The notion that we see in line 13 is key because it predicts that God will deliver the enemies into the hands of the אביונים. It also underscores that the humble are not without agency, but they have a role to play in the war; they are the people to whom God will hand the more powerful and strong enemies.

iv. Scriptural Intertextuality

1QM 11.7b–18 is loaded with language and descriptions that evoke several Scriptural traditions. There are markers like allusions to historical events like Pharaoh's defeat in the Sea of Reeds and a citation of the prophecy in the book of Isaiah that predicts the fall of Sennacherib. In addition, there is the mention of Gog of Magog and the language of God's exaltation before the eyes of the nations are a clear allusion to Ezekiel 38–39. The references to these military victories are markers that evoke past times where God intervened in miraculous fashion to save Israel. We will notice that along these military victories there are prophetic descriptions of God acting on Israel's behalf. For that matter, the ensuing discussion will explore the influence that these military victories have on the scroll. One particular aspect to which we want to pay close attention to is how these military leaders become examples of God's power acting against Israel's enemies, which we argue is the key for interpreting what the scroll envisions against Belial and his hordes. Lines 7b–18, therefore, depict in prototypical fashion following the examples of Scripture, how God acts on behalf of the weak to bring down the mighty enemies. The defeat of these military leaders becomes markers stamped in the minds of Israel that underscore to the sectarians that the prophetic testimony from the "seers of decrees" (חוזי תעודות) is trustworthy.

Pharaoh's Defeat in the ים סוף

In lines 7b–8 we learn that God has revealed the times of the war to the seers. From this prediction the scroll goes on to announce the fall of Israel's enemies, namely Belial and the seven nations of futility. Lines 9–10 are key because they not only describe the defeat of the enemy, but they illustrate the deliverance of Israel as a "door of hope" (פתח תקוה)[55]. The description of a door of hope begins to hint at the type of liberation that Israel will experience. This becomes more apparent in the tail end of line 9 and the beginning of 10, which compare the fall of Belial with the defeat of Pharaoh and his chariots in the sea. 1QM 11.9–10 show that the testimony of the seers consists of a second Exodus, where this new Israel will be freed from the grasp of Belial as their ancestors were delivered from Pharaoh. Furthermore, by introducing Pharaoh the scroll emphasizes the end that Belial will suffer, which alludes specifically to Exod 15:19–21 where God turns the waters of the sea against Pharaoh and throws horse and chariot into the sea[56]. Essentially, lines 9–10 indicate that Belial and the enemy nations will be defeated in a cataclysmic fashion comparable to how God overwhelmed Pharaoh and his chariots in the sea.

The fascinating aspect about how 1QM uses this tradition from Exodus is that it not only highlights the power of God over the military might of Israel's enemies. But in doing so the scroll depicts these encounters as cosmic conflicts where God controls nature and uses it to favor Israel. Plus, the enemy takes on a different dimension as Pharaoh becomes a symbol of evil. The reference to Pharaoh demonstrates that this character has transcended the realm of history and entered into a realm as a representation of the evil that Belial brings upon the sectarians. The closest example of this interpretation happens in the book of Ezekiel, where the prophet is constantly charged to deliver oracles of doom against Pharaoh king of Egypt.

Ezekiel 29–32 consists of series of oracles where God targets Egypt[57].

---

55 The restoration of the לב נמס depicted in line 9 recalls passages like Psalm 136 where the psalmist gives thanks to God. Verses 13–15 are important because they recall Exodus 15, but they do so in the context of a song of praise that highlights God's עולם חסדו.

56 4Q365 6b preserve this part of the songs of Moses and Miriam. The books of Maccabees also recall this moment in Israel's history. 1 Macc 4:9 recall the time when Judas exhorts the combatants by reminding them of how their ancestors were saved at the time when Pharaoh pursued them in the θαλάσσῃ ἐρυθρᾷ. Also, in 3 Macc 2:6–7 Simon the High Priest recalls how God overwhelmed Pharaoh in the depths of the sea and led those who trusted in God safely. And in 3 Macc 6:4–5 Eleazar recalls how God dealt with Pharaoh and his army as well as Sennacherib and his countless forces. The passage also depicts that God shined his mercy upon Israel.

57 Ellen Davis, "'And Pharaoh Will Change His Mind...' (Ezekiel 32:31): Dismantling Myth-

These prophecies evince on the one hand the firm conviction that God is in control of political and military affairs, as Babylon is favored over Egypt. In addition, these passages depict how God will deal with Egypt, more specifically with Pharaoh, by using cosmic language that not only echoes the descriptions in Exodus, but ultimately make a statement about God's supremacy. For instance, in Ezek 29:3 God describes Pharaoh as the "great serpent" (תנים הגדול) that lies down in the Nile. This chapter continues with an illustration of how God will "put hooks on the jaws" of this serpent and lift it up with the fish of the Nile clinging to it. Verse 5 adds that God will hurl this serpent to the open field to be consumed by the animals of the field without proper burial[58]. The key statement comes in verse 6 where it states that the earth will know that God is Lord.

Ezek 30:21–26 repeat this assertion as the prophet describes how God will break the arm of Pharaoh. In a symbolic manner this oracle predicts that God will not only remove the strength of Egypt by wounding Pharaoh but will hand the sword to the king of Babylon as a sign of authority and power. Verses 25–26 reiterate the statement in Ezek 29:6, as Egypt and the nations will know that God is Lord. Lastly, Ezek 32 contains one last word against Egypt. This passage resembles Ezek 29 in that Pharaoh is depicted as a "serpent" (תנים). Also, the wrath that will come upon Pharaoh is depicted in cataclysmic language that resembles chapter 29, where his carcass will feed the animals and there will be darkness as the sun and the moon will not give light (Ezek 32:4–8). Following a litany of condemnations, Ezek 32:31–32 end with a last word where God states that in the same fashion that Pharaoh spreads terror in the land of the living, he and his hordes will lay with the uncircumcised that fell by the sword (cf. Ezek 31:18).

The reference to Pharaoh and his chariots in 1QM 11.9–10 points to the historical moment in Exodus. The allusion to this moment is significant in that it uses a tangible tradition as an example of what will happen to Belial and his hordes. The interesting aspect of this allusion is that Pharaoh and his chariots are associated with spiritual forces; thus, Pharaoh represents Belial and his chariots are the armies of the nations. The texts from Ezekiel above illustrate how Pharaoh was perceived as a mythical character. The value,

---

ical Discourse," in *Theological Exegesis: Essays in Honor of Brevard S. Childs*, ed. Christopher Seitz and Kathryn Greene-McCreight (Grand Rapids: Eerdmans, 1999), 224–239. John Strong, "Egypt's Shameful Death and the House of Israel's Exodus from Sheol (Ezekiel 32.17–32 and 37.1–14)," *JSOT* 34 (2010): 475–504. Safwat Marzouk, *Egypt as a Monster in the Book of Ezekiel* (Tübingen: Mohr Siebeck, 2015).

58 The imagery of putting hooks to the jaw of the serpent and offering it as for the animals and birds in the air correlate with Ezekiel 38–39, where God puts hooks in the jaw of Gog of Magog and celebrates the annihilation of this army with a feast for the animals and birds.

Prophetic Exegesis in 1QM 11

therefore, of exploring these accounts is that they demonstrate how the tradition of Pharaoh evolved, and he became the personification of everything that was antagonistic to God.

Assyria's Defeat by the חרב לוא איש

1QM 11.11–12 has a citation of Isa 31:8 that predicts the defeat of Assyria by a "sword of no man" (חרב לא איש). The scroll describes this prophecy as a word that was announced in ancient times (מאז) about God's hand working against the Kittim. The connection of the Kittim and Assyria is something that the scroll describes in other passages as well. For instance, in 1QM 1.2 the Kittim are identified as the "Kittim of Asshur" (כתיי אשור). Also, 1QM 19.10 describes the moment when the priests will come to the camp of the Kittim and Assyria to see how many soldiers fell by God's sword. Taken together these texts demonstrate the thematic link between Assyria, the Kittim, and God's sword acting against them. However, some scholars view the citation in column 11 as evidence of a later tradition. Davies believes that the mention of the Kittim in 1QM 11.11–12 is an interpolation, because the Kittim are mentioned in the Battle against the Kittim (columns 15–19) and the introduction to the war in 1QM 1[59]. For his part Schultz observes that this is the only instance where the Kittim are mentioned in the liturgies of columns 10–14, which gives credence to the proposal that this reference is part of the prayer before the battle mentioned in 1QM 15.4–5[60]. The identification of the Kittim with Assyria is an important one, especially as it relates to how the citation is employed and what it evokes from Scriptural tradition.

Isaiah 31 deals with an objection that God has against Israel[61]. Facing the threat from Assyria many of the people of Judah decided to leave Jerusalem instead of going down to Egypt. The prophet taunts Israel for trusting in the strength of Egypt's horses and chariots, rather than trusting in God. The reference to Egypt's horses and chariots clearly alludes to the passages in Exodus, where God overcame the power of these military forces. This perspective is further confirmed in verse 3 where God recalls that the Egyptians are humans and their horses are flesh. Further, in verses 4–8 the prophet describes what God will do for Israel if the people renounce their idols. The promise of deliv-

---

59 Davies, *1QM, the War Scroll*, 98–99.

60 Schultz, *Conquering the World*, 274–275.

61 Shawn Zelig Aster, "Isaiah 31 as a Response to Rebellions Against Assyria in Philistia," *JBL* 136 (2017): 347–361. Marvin Sweeney, "Parenetic Intent in Isaiah 31," in *Proceedings of the Eleventh World Congress of Jewish Studies* (Jerusalem: World Union of Jewish Studies, 1994), 99–106.

erance from Assyria comes in verse 8 with a cryptic description of a mighty force coming from the "sword of no man and the sword of no human" (חרב לא איש וחרב לא אדם). The descriptions of judgment as well as the addition of images of chaos and panic recall Scriptural passages where God inflicts pain on Israel's enemies. But what exactly is the חרב לא איש and the חרב לא אדם is not entirely clear. One possibility from the immediate context suggests that this is God's sword. Elsewhere in Scripture we have other accounts that depict God or divine beings bearing a sword and bringing forth chaos to Israel's enemies. The intriguing aspect about how the citation of Isa 31:8 is used in 1QM is that it does not specify if it is only God's sword doing the damage.

Following the allusion to Pharaoh's defeat, 1QM 11.10 has an enigmatic description. The scroll describes that God will ignite the "broken of spirit" (נכאי רוח) as a "fiery torch in a sheaf" (לפיד אש בעמיר) which precedes the citation of Isa 31:8. Further, the use of the verb "to consume" (אכל) demonstrates that both the "broken of spirit" (נכאי רוח) and the "sword of no man" (חרב לוא איש) are connected; thus, just as the fire in the sheaf will consume wickedness, the sword of no man will consume the Kittim. From a literary standpoint, these two lines create pairings: the broken of spirit and sword are agents of destruction, while wickedness and the Kittim are symbols to be eradicated. In addition, both pairings illustrate the type of conflict that the sectarians envision, where earthly actors (the broken in spirit and the Kittim) fight against spiritual forces (the "sword" and "wickedness"). This is something that 1QM continuously illustrates in its depictions of angels fighting next to the soldiers, and it is a significant transition from Scriptural traditions where God alone wins Israel's victories.

The implications of this direction are many, but one in particular is that the sectarians adopted the belief that they needed to be involved in effecting change. To what extent this vision of fighting against the Kittim (whether the Greeks or the Romans) was a feasible aspiration for the sectarians is not entirely clear. But what does become abundantly clear in this passage and in 1QM as a whole is that faith in God's intervention was enough for the sectarians to adopt this vision that would revolutionize their world. In this regard, 1QM does preserve the spirit of the citation of Isaiah 31:8 where the prophet called the people to believe that with God on their side, they could trust that Sennacherib was going to be defeated.

Gog's Defeat from the השמים

1QM 11.16 predicts that God will bring judgment against Gog and all his

Prophetic Exegesis in 1QM 11

assembly. The allusion to Gog is an interesting one because this is one of two instances in the entire DSS. The other allusion happens in 4Q523, but the fragmentary nature of this manuscript prevents us from asserting much about this reference. In 1QM, however, the reference to Gog comes loaded with language that evokes the eschatological imagery. Davies has convincingly shown the similarity of language and descriptions that 1QM 11.13–18 have with Ezekiel 38–39. Davies sees that these lines in column 11 illustrate in vivid language the ethical distinction between the parties in conflict, that is, the weak ones from Israel and Gog. He adds that if these lines are the product of the Maccabean period, then the reference to Gog is an indirect way to refer to Antiochus IV[62]. Schultz on the other hand uses the reference to Gog and the descriptions of war against the "assembly" (קהל) to connect this part of 1QM 11 to the descriptions in columns 15–19. Schultz argues that this connection demonstrates another dimension to the War against the Kittim; that is, the war becomes a universal and final encounter between Israel and its enemies[63].

We concur with Schultz that the language in lines 13–18 adds important descriptions about how this conflict will evolve. Line 13 provides an important description where God will bring the enemies and the mighty people into the hand of the lowly. These references echo the descriptions in Ezekiel 39:18, 27, where the mighty enemy that comes against Israel will be defeated. In a manner different from Ezekiel where Israel does not participate in bringing down the enemy, in 1QM God brings the enemies so Israel can defeat them by their hand. Further, lines 14–15 depict that God will do this marvelous feat to "make for yourself an everlasting name among the people" (לעשות לכה שם עולם בעם) and "to sanctify yourself to the eyes of the remnant of the nations" (להתקדש לעיני שאר הגוים). Both of these infinitive constructs show a purpose, which correlate with God's stated purpose in bringing judgment against Gog in Ezek 39:21–29. Also, lines 16–18 depict that God will carry out judgment on Gog and all his company from the heavens, thus bringing confusion on all of them. This description is a clear allusion to Ezek 38:21–23, where God brings confusion on the army and rains fire and sulfur. Notice also that verse 21 describes that God's sword will be summoned against Gog, which echoes the reference to the "sword of no man" (חרב לוא איש) from the prophecy of Isaiah 31 in lines 11–12. Lines 13–18 are crafted by alluding to the images presented in Ezekiel 38–39. Different from Ezekiel, however, 1QM 11 takes a slightly different direction, which bears results significant to our analysis.

---

62 Davies, *1QM, the War Scroll*, 100. He also believes that Ezekiel 38–39 plays an influential role in the hymn in 1QM 14.4b–8a, see Ibid., 85.

63 Schultz, *Conquering the World*, 277.

The tradition of Ezekiel highlights that Israel dwells in a setting without walls and unaware of the looming danger of Gog and his hordes (Ezek 38:11). Also, in Ezekiel 38–39 God is the main actor who controls the actions of Gog of Magog that ultimately lead to the destruction of his army. Israel is an observer who is only responsible for the clean-up duties. In 1QM 11.7b–18 God delivers the enemies into Israel's hands. Also, by depicting Israel with images of weakness and humbleness, these lines show the paradoxical nature of how the eschatological battle will evolve. That is, those who do not have power of their own will be the ones who will bring down the mighty forces via God's strength.

The allusion to Gog and the use of the language of Ezekiel 38–39 are significant in that they give us a view of how the sectarians viewed the ensuing conflict. Like the mention of Pharaoh and Assyria above, these lines evince that in fighting against Belial and the Kittim the new Israel will engage in an all-out conflict in a manner similar, yet different, from the Scriptural example. The consistent thrust of these lines is that God will ultimately win the battle for the sectarians. Lines 7b–18 consist of a reenactment of history that ultimately ends with Israel's victory and the glorification of God before the eyes of the people of the earth.

v. Prophetic Exegesis

1QM 11.7b–18 is a prime example of prophetic exegesis as the descriptions of the "times of the wars" (קצי מלחמות) are grounded on the testimony of the "seers of decrees" (תעודות חוזי). The reference to this prophetic testimony demonstrates that the sectarians interpreted the future as something that was established since ages past. This is in line with the descriptions in 1QM 10 where the priest refers to the teachings of Moses as something that God had ordained in ages past.

The other significant aspect of the prophetic testimony is that it discloses the purpose of the wars. Originally, the scroll stated in line 8 that God was to "fight" (לחם) against Israel's enemies. The manuscript, however, has a correction that substituted "to glorify" (כבד) for "to fight" (לחם). This emendation provides a different perspective as the wars were not just seen as conflicts against the forces that oppress the sectarians, but they are ultimately viewed as the means by which God would be exalted before the people. From a rhetorical standpoint the change aligns well with line 15, where it reiterates that the wars were for God "to magnify and sanctify yourself to the eyes of the remnant of the nations" (להתגדל ולהתקדש לעיני שאר הגוים). The change

Prophetic Exegesis in 1QM 11

in line 8, therefore, demonstrates that a subsequent editor reflected on these lines and made the change, to show that war will become the vehicle to shine God's supremacy over the world. To accomplish this objective the scroll revisits different miraculous events as evidence of what God will do to Belial.

Lines 9–12 take figures like Pharaoh and Assyria as illustrations of what is in store for Belial and the Kittim. From an intertextual standpoint these are markers that not only evoke images of the past, but they provide examples of redemption where the underdogs overcome their more powerful enemies. Pharaoh becomes an example of an oppressive force that God eliminated thus breaking the chains of slavery. Line 9 specifically makes this point twice when it depicts that God will empower the poor and will give hope to those whose heart melts (לב נמס)[64]. Assyria, on the other hand, becomes the example of a powerful army that was defeated by a miracle from God. The key marker in lines 11–12 is the "sword of no man" (חרב לא איש) cited from the prophecy of Isaiah. We saw from previous examples from the Scriptures that God's sword is the source of power that defeats Israel's enemies. In lines 10–11, however, the sword is a marker associated with what God will do in igniting the "broken of spirit" (נכאי רוח). Therefore, the prophecy of Isaiah 31:8 points to the anticipated miracle that those who are weak will consume the wicked by the power of God's sword. The examples of Pharaoh and Assyria are metaphors of the oppression and wickedness that the sectarians will defeat through God. The key for understanding how these victories will come appears in line 13.

Line 13 starts with the causal particle כיא, which from a grammatical standpoint explains the previous statements. In it we learn that God will "hand over" (סגר) all of Israel's enemies into the "hand of the poor" (יד אביונים) and the "hands of those who are prostrate in the dust" (יד כורעי עפר). The use of the Hiphil verb סגר recalls Deut 32:30 when Moses reminds Israel that the overcoming of the thousands of enemies could only happen because God "delivered them" (הסגירם). In the same fashion this line in 1QM recognizes that the future defeat of the enemies will happen only because God will deliver them. The distinctive aspect of this interpretation is that it does not leave room for doubt; the statement is a firm conviction that God will accomplish this victory. Thus, the recollection of past victories and the prophetic testimony are used on the one hand to provide tangible evidence that God did accomplish these victories in the past, but they are also used prophetically to guarantee that Belial and the Kittim will be delivered into

---

64 This line contrasts with 1QM 10.5–6 where the officers relieve the מסי לבב from their military duties.

their hands. The interpretation in line 13 therefore leads into the final descriptions and the reference to Gog.

Lines 14–18 allude to the descriptions in Ezekiel 38–39, where God brings Gog of Magog and his hordes to invade Israel. The key concept repeated in lines 14–15 is that God does all of this to be exalted before the eyes of the people. This is in line with the statement in Ezek 39:21–29, where God explains that the purpose of defeating Gog of Magog is so the nations will know that God accomplished this feat, and also for the house of Israel to know that God is their Lord. 1QM 11.14–18 does not have the language of redemption *per se*, but it does highlight that God accomplishes the victories to show sovereignty over the nations.

The last point to make about these lines is the fact that they are part of liturgies that illustrate the aspirations that the sectarians have for the eschatological war. Although lines 7b–18 do not show liturgical elements *per se*, the beginning of column 12 begins with a song of celebration. The images of Belial and the Kittim being defeated by the sword of God usher in a time of worship. A similar chronology happens in 1QM 19.9–13 (cf. 4Q492 1.9–13) where it describes that the soldiers shall sing praises to God after they have seen all the enemies that fell by the "sword of God" (חרב אל). 1QM 19 has similarities with 1QM 12 that we will cover in the next chapter. Suffice to say at this point that the worship of God is the ultimate purpose for why the war in 1QM exists, which is in line with the Scriptural traditions where war and deliverance happen[65].

c. Summary

Our discussion has yielded important results regarding the prophetic interpretation of Scripture in 1QM 11. In lines 1–7a we observed that the hymn ascribes the battle to God. The refrain "the battle is yours" (לכה המלחמה) and the references to past military victories are used to invoke God's memory. The effect of this hymn is that it not only reminds God about the promises given to Israel, but it empowers the faith of the warriors prior to the skirmish. As it is in the case of the war and prayer traditions in Chronicles and Maccabees, this hymn relies on the rehearsal of God's past victories as a mode of prophetic speech. This sort of speech seen in the examples of Jahaziel and Maccabees fits with the transition from oral to exegetical prophecy. Furthermore, the

---

65 In the next chapter the mention of the nations occurs again in the context of the restoration of Zion. At that point we will assess the significance of this reference along with the evidence in column 11 for the sectarian ideology in the restoration of Zion.

Prophetic Exegesis in 1QM 11

citation of the oracle from Num 24:17–19 in lines 6–7 confirms that prophetic promise is at the core of this hymn and its fundamental argument that Israel shall overcome the "enemies" (אויבים).

As for lines 7b–18 they take the prophetic promise of military success and expand it to an eschatological sphere. Like the preceding lines here the testimony of the "seers of decrees" (חוזי תעודות) provides the foundation for the prophetic expectation of God's wars. By referring to the "seers" these lines do not focus on any particular speaker, but in a creative fashion they recall the prophecies and descriptions that allude to the passages of the prophets like Moses, Isaiah, and Ezekiel. In addition, there are a couple of turns that this section makes in comparison to the preceding hymn. For instance, Israel is not depicted with the language of military might. Instead we find a lowly Israel humbled and prostrated to the ground whose heart needs to be ignited. Thus, the references to the "poor" and those who are "prostrate in the dust" representation of the sectarians. These representations further connect to the previous columns, where the sectarians have been depicted as the "seers" and "hearers" of the mysteries of God. These metaphorical representations, in addition, tap into the aspects of the sectarians that makes them recipients of God's favor; that is, whereas in column 10 they are wise people, here in column 10 they are the humble people who wholly depend on God for their deliverance. The "enemies" (אויבים) on the other hand are mighty figures who possess a mythical dimension. The references to Pharaoh, Assyria, and Gog are markers that trigger memories from the Scriptures of how God dealt with these enemies. These allusions, therefore, are examples that substantiate the hope that God will deal with Belial and the nations in the same fashion as the enemies of the past were defeated. Thus, by triggering these allusions the scroll creates a set of associations that prove that Belial and the nations are as vulnerable to God's power as the major powers of the past were.

1QM 11 is a rich text with numerous intertextual markers. Our approach has been to divide this text into two parts for the sake of developing these markers. This direction, however, should not necessarily imply that these two parts are disjointed and cannot be read together. The link that joins these parts is the prophetic testimony. We observed in lines 6–7a that the oracle in Num 24:17–19 becomes the promise that Israel will overcome and possess its enemies. This prophecy is confirmed and taken to an eschatological direction when lines 7b–8 refer to the testimony of the seers. Thus, the imaginative development of these prophetic traditions becomes the conduit by which the scroll both predicts and prescribes faith in God's promises. Prophetic exegesis becomes the sword in the hands of the sectarians.

The other consistent theme that these parts share is the imaginative portrayal of the fight as a lopsided encounter between the underdog and a more powerful enemy. From David and Goliath to the poor and Gog, this column replays these images thus creating a web of meaning through the repetition of key words and images of the underdog overcoming its adversary, which only an informed reader/hearer can make. It is the power of these associations that ultimately makes the rhetorical effect of this column as it uplifts the faith of the combatants.

CHAPTER 5

PROPHETIC EXEGESIS IN 1QM 12

Preliminary Considerations

1QM 12 ANTICIPATES THE END OF THE WAR with a heavenly gathering that wraps up with a triumphant celebration to Zion. Like in the preceding columns here we have several indicators that point to a switch of themes that make it necessary to organize the content accordingly. The first piece in 1QM 12.1–5 consists of a heavenly vision where God chooses a holy people and establishes their names for eternity. The second piece in 1QM 12.7–18 is a celebratory march that ends, as the Scriptural counterparts, with a procession to Zion. Scholars have recognized the distinctive character of this column and proposed various approaches to organize its content.

Yigael Yadin holds that the initial lines of 1QM 12 continue with the theme of Israel's election that started in column 11.[1] 1QM 11.13–18 and 1QM 12.1–5 are part of the Serekh series, that emphasizes that Israel deserves God's help because they are the elect people. The descriptions of havoc against the wicked at the end of column 11 lead into 1QM 12.1–5 and the consecration of Israel. As for the rest of column 12, Yadin views these lines as the culmination of the Serekh series and the climax of the prayer for the appointed time of battle. He adds that in this final section the Chief Priest invokes God as the Mighty Hero, which leads them in the battle against the enemies. Yadin intuitively detects that column 12 alludes to passages in Isaiah and Maccabees, in both the descriptions of victory to Zion and the call for God to intervene in the battle. He also observes that lines 13–18 appear with slight changes in 1QM 19, which points to the repetition of the "prayer for the appointed time of battle" (תפלת

---

1 Yigael Yadin, *The Scroll of the War of the Sons of Light against the Sons of Darkness*, trans. Batya Rabim and Chaim Rabim (London: Oxford University Press, 1962), 214–216.

מועד המלחמה; 1QM 15.5) before the final pursuit of the Kittim.

Different from Yadin, Peter von der Osten-Sacken analyzes 1QM 12 as part of his investigation on the issue of the sectarians communion with the celestial beings.[2] Osten-Sacken observes that 1QM 12, like 1QM 7 before, becomes the context where the sectarians have a connection with the heavenly beings. He proposes that these descriptions have a priestly background that taps into Temple symbolism. Further, he draws a connection between this symbolism in 1QM and the Christian understanding of the Church as a temple. In his opinion, notwithstanding some differences, the War Scroll serves to solidify the Christian doctrine that angels are in the midst of the congregation. One last point that Osten-Sacken makes that bears major significance to our research is that the War Scroll, along with 1QH and 1QS, underscores that fellowship with angels is a privilege reserved for those who entered into the covenant of the community (cf. 1QS 4.22). As we shall see below, 1QM 12.1 explicitly states that fellowship with the angels comes to the elect which it labels as בחירי עם קודש ("chosen ones of the holy people").

For his part, Philip Davies splits 1QM 12 into different compositions because of the shift in themes throughout this column.[3] He places special attention to lines 1–5 and the description of the בחירי עם קודש, and observes that the term "chosen" (בחיר) appears elsewhere in the scrolls to denote both the people who will be saved in the end of time and the elite who will lead the nation. Davies believes that the use of "chosen" makes this phrase unnecessarily cumbersome, thus he posits that this is a later insertion that wanted to further narrow the scope of the "righteous party."[4]

As for lines 7–10 Davies notices that this is a metrical hymn that focuses on the presence of the קדושים ("holy ones") in the midst of the warriors. The curious aspect of this discussion is that Davies devotes little to no attention to the possible connections that this hymn has with Psalm 24 and the invocation of the מלך הכבוד ("king of glory") and the גבור המלחמה ("mighty one of war"). Finally, Davies observes that lines 10–15 consist of a war cry whose historical backdrop points to traditions like Num 10:35, where God is called upon to rise and defeat the enemies. In this final section Davies sees a

---

2 Peter von der Osten-Sacken, *Gott und Belial: Traditionsgeschichtliche Untersuchungen zum Dualismus in den Texten aus Qumran* (Gottingen: Vandenhoeck & Ruprecht, 1969), 230–232.

3 Philip R. Davies, *1QM, the War Scroll from Qumran: Its Structure and History* (Rome: Biblical Institute Press, 1977), 100–104.

4 Davies (ibid.) uses 1QM 14.2 and the reference to the עם קודשכה to suggest that in column 12 an editor narrows the scope by adding בחיר. Thus, it is not only a "holy people" but the "chosen of the holy people."

continuation with the spirit of columns 2–9, where Israel is to have dominion over all the nations. Despite the fragmentary nature of his analysis, Davies raises important points like the narrowing of the scope of who the chosen people are as well as the thematic links that this column has with the War of Divisions in 1QM 2–9, which we will cover below.

In a similar vein as Davies, Brian Schultz observes that column 12 has elements that relate to the other major parts of the scroll.[5] He proceeds from the standpoint of describing the intersecting points that this prayer has with the War of Divisions in particular the reference to "our commissioned" in line 8 and to Jerusalem in line 13. The mention of the בפקודינו ("commissioned") fits with the context 1QM 2, where the soldiers enlist to the army (1QM 2.7–8), while the reference to Jerusalem demonstrates a choice to express a more intimate connection with the city that will exist after the battle with the Kittim. Schultz also observes that lines 7–18 consist of a different composition, a prayer that he labels "And you, O God." This prayer is the only text that is repeated in 1QM 19 (and 4Q492) albeit with some variations. He goes on to explain that the presence of this prayer in columns 12 and 19 demonstrates a common structure between columns 10–14 and 15–19, where the prayers in 10–12.5 correspond to the instructions given in 14–16 and columns 12–14 parallel the depictions in 17–19. The merit of this approach is that it tries to bring together both of the major parts of the scroll together, and it looks for the redactional moves behind the addition of themes throughout these liturgies. We concur with Schultz that column 12 has textual snippets that relate thematically with both the War of Divisions and the War Against the Kittim. Furthermore, we hold to this opinion because the liturgies in 1QM 10–12 are the link between these two stages; they are the prophetic evidence of hope that the army can have in the promises of God.

The previous scholarly discussion consistently acknowledges that 1QM 12 deals with the consecration of a chosen people and the involvement of celestial beings in bringing about the final triumph. Although there is a diversity of approaches in the organization of this column, what becomes apparent is that lines 1–5 and 7–18 emphasize different themes. Our analysis below will, therefore, focus on both of these sections by paying close attention at some of the more salient intertextual points. In lines 1–5 we will devote our attention to the interpretation that the sectarians are the "chosen of the holy people." We will proceed with an exploration that will consider the influence that the prophecies of Daniel 11–12 have on these lines. On the other hand, in

---

5 Brian Schultz, *Conquering the World: The War Scroll (1QM) Reconsidered* (Leiden: Brill, 2009), 275–283.

lines 7–18 we will proceed with a different type of analysis. Whereas before we have focused on specific markers and their connection to other mainly sectarian scrolls, in this part we will compare and contrast this prayer with its counterpart in 4Q492 (cf. 1QM 19). This comparative exercise will allow us to draw some insights on how this prayer is used in 1QM. The last part of our intertextual analysis will focus on the themes of God as the King of Glory and the War Hero, and how 1QM combines them into one piece that envisions triumph and the restoration of Jerusalem.

a.   1QM 12.1–5: Israel as the Chosen People

i.   Text and Translation

1QM 12.1–5	1QM 12.1–5
1ו כיא רוב קדושים [א]לה בשמים וצבאות מלאכים בזבול קודשכה לה[ו]דות אמת[]כה ובחירי עם קודש	1 For there is a multitude of these holy ones in heaven, and the hosts of angels are in your holy abode to praise your name. The chosen of the holy people
2ו שמתה לכה בן ס[פר שמות כול צבאם אתכה במעון קודשכהומ] [י]ם בזבול כבודכה	2 you have established for yourself in the [book][6] of names of all the hosts with you in your holy dwelling and [ ], in the abode of your glory.
3ו וחסדי ברכו[תיכה] וברית שלומכה חרתה למו בחרט חיים למלוך [ ] בכול מועדי עולמים	3 The mercy of your blessings and a covenant of your peace you engraved for them with a stylus of life to reign for all appointed times of eternity,
4ו ולפקוד צן [י]ריכה לאלפיהם ולר־ בואותם יחד עם קדושיכה] [ ] מלאכיכה לרשות יד	4 and to appoint [ ] to a thousand and ten thousands together with your holy ones [ ] your angels to direct the hand
5ו במלחמה [ ] [ק]מי ארץ בריב משפ טיכה ועם בחירי שמים נוצ[חים]	5 in battle [ ] adversaries of the earth in the trial of your judgments and with the elect of heaven they shall prevail

---

6 There is a gap in the manuscript in line 2 after לכה and between the ב and the פר. The gap is significant enough to fit more than one word, but our translation only adds "book" (ספר). Another possible reconstruction is "number" (מספר); 1Q177 1–4.8 mentions the "number of the names" (מספר שמות) in its interpretation of Deut 7:15. 4Q365 26a–b.6 mentions the "number of the written names" (מספר כתב שמות) in reference to the census in Num 1.1–5. Our use of ספר is informed by the accounts in Daniel 12, where the משכלים are written in the book that contains the names of those who will be saved. Another important aspect is that this liturgy, as well as 1QM 10–11, are part of the "Book of the Rule of Its Time" (ספר סרך עתו) in 1QM 15.5.

Prophetic Exegesis in 1QM 12

ii. Content

The following is the content of 1QM 12.1–5

- 12.1–5
    1. Introduction of the "hosts of angels" (צבאות מלאכים)
    2. The Chosen of the Holy People added to the "book of the names of all the hosts" (ספר שמות כול צבאת)
    3. God's Covenant with the Chosen People
    4. Eternal Rule and Authority of the Chosen People

The first structural marker comes in line 1 with the conjunction כיא ("for"), which indicates that lines 1–5 follow the content from the end of column 11. However, because the bottom of the manuscript was not preserved, we cannot ascertain with certainty the relation of these lines with the prior column. Following כיא lines 1–2 introduce the צבאות מלכים ("hosts of angels") and the בחירי עם קודש. Once lines 1–2 bring up the main subjects, line 3 turns its attention to the benefits received by the chosen ones; they are not only written in the book of God's army but they have been endowed with blessings inherited from the covenant of peace. Further, they have been put in charge to reign for all the מועדי עולמים ("eternal times") and they will prevail along with the angels. Lines 1–5 proceed from the standpoint of something that was described in column 11. We can speculate that the lifting up of the "humble in spirit" and those "whose face is down to the dust" in 1QM 11.8–18 leads to this vision in heaven, where those same meek characters are now elevated to share in God's abode. Lines 3–5 further highlight that this chosen people are in charge for eternal times, because they have not only been added to the book of the warriors but also the covenant has been renewed in them. Thus, the concepts of being chosen and the eternal intimacy in heaven are the key markers that point to the Scriptural traditions which we will explore below.

iii. Sectarian Intertextuality

1QM 12.1–5 reflects on God's favor for Israel with the reference to בחירי עם קודש. These lines also describe that this chosen people are written in the book of all the hosts.[7] The focus of our inquiry at this junction is the concept of Israel being the chosen people and how the sectarians adopted this belief. Our argument is that this description points to the sectarians not only as the

---

7 The war text in 4Q491 Frg. 5–6.1 preserves this same line.

recipients of the renewed covenant, but as we will see further in lines 7–10a, as the ones who will bring about the blessing to the entire nation.[8] We will tap into the language of election elsewhere in the DSS and compares it with what this column has to say about the sectarians and their critical role in the latter times.

The Rule Books provide important descriptions of the elect and how they fit in God's plan. Often these books adopt the language of separation between the insiders and those outside of the community. In the Community Rule, for instance, the concept of being chosen points to the members of the Yahad. 1QS 4 provides one of the clearest descriptions of the distinction between those who are inside the group and those who are not. Lines 18–23 illustrate that God has allowed wickedness to rule, but that this state of affairs will soon come to an end for there will come a time of purification when the upright shall have insight into the knowledge of the Most High and the wisdom of angels. Lines 22–23 argue that God chose them for an eternal covenant and that they will have all the "glory of Adam." This reference to Adam appears in 1QHa 4.14–15, where the speaker thanks God for giving those who serve God "all the glory of Adam." 1QS 11.7–9 expand on these promises by concluding that those whom God chose shall receive an eternal possession; they are heirs with the holy ones and the sons of heaven. 1QS 4 and 11 evince the sectarian belief that they were the favored ones who would inherit an eternal communion with God and the angels because of their obedience to the rules of the Yahad.

The concept of election also points to the leaders of the Yahad. 1QS 9.12– 16 describe the duties of the משכיל ("Instructor") who is entrusted to teach and correct those within the Yahad. Lines 14–17 state that the Instructor is to discern who the true "Sons of Righteousness" are and to strengthen the chosen ones. The teacher is also charged with avoiding any encounter with individuals outside of the community, which line 16 represents as the "Men of the Pit." We can discern in these descriptions that בחיר represents a concept loaded with ideological beliefs used to set the boundaries between those who have been entrusted to the Instructor and those who are not; that is, between insiders and outsiders. This also appears in 1QS 11.16 where the speaker prays to God to be enlightened and included among the "chosen ones of man." We

---

8 This proposal fits with the chronology that columns 10–12 have established. In illustrating the advent of the war and future defeat of Belial columns 10–11 set the stage for the glorification of God and the restoration of Israel. The gathering of the chosen ones and their communion with angels in lines 1–5 lead to the consummation of this renewed relationship with God through a covenant of peace (ברית שלומכה, 1 QM 12.3). This new covenant leads into the victory for the chosen ones and final procession to Zion according in lines 7–18.

Prophetic Exegesis in 1QM 12

saw previously in lines 7–9a that the speaker had already described the Yahad as the heirs of an eternal possession along with the holy Angels. Further, the speaker here describes the Yahad as the "eternal plant" (מטעת עולם) (cf. 1QS 8.5), which is a metaphor that Isa 61:3 uses for the restored community of Israel. In essence, 1QS guides the readers to accept the duties and responsibilities of being part of this separate people, the Yahad. The use of the language of election demonstrates the conviction that the Yahad needs to maintain distance from unrighteousness if they are going to receive the eternal benefits of closeness to God. This same ideology permeates across other sectarian texts.

The Damascus Document shares this language of election and separation from the outsiders. CD 2 begins with the Instructor calling out "all the members of the covenant" to hear the ways of God. In these initial lines the teacher differentiates between those who repent and those who continue in disobedience. Likewise, in this statement the teacher sets the stage for a division between the insiders and the outsiders. In reference to the wicked, lines 7–9 relay that God did not choose them but waited until they were all gone to start something new. Lines 11–13 introduce that God had actually arranged everything so that there would be a people called by God's name; a people who would choose to do what God pleases. The themes of separation and foreknowledge are important in this column, as God predestined to reject the wicked because their deeds were established beforehand. There is a sense also in this column that God had pre-ordained things to be arranged in a particular way and had therefore set the stage for a remnant to be preserved. These descriptions correlate with what CD had already stated in column 1, where God not only differentiated between the wicked and the remnant but also raised the Teacher of Righteousness to steer this new people.

The Pesher Micah (1Q14 Frg. 8–10) shares this description when it interprets that the ministry of the Teacher of Righteousness is to teach the chosen ones; that is, the doers of Torah and the council of the Yahad who will be saved on the day of judgment. The Pesher Habakkuk in 1QpHab 5.4 also describes the chosen as those who have followed the commandments, and 1QpHab 9.12 and 10.13 describe the trials that the chosen ones experienced at the hands of the "dripper of the lie" (מטיף הכזב, 1QpHab 10:9). For its part 4Q171 Frg. 1–10 4.12–14 interprets Ps 37:34–36 with the restoration of the "chosen ones" and the punishment of the Man of Lies. As we can see the Damascus Document along with these Pesharim underscore not only that God has separated a people, as a remnant, but that in the same process God has left out other people. This separation of the chosen and the rejected, therefore, brings trials that will endure till the end of time. And like 1QS before, the Damascus Document also brings up that the leaders, priests, and teacher were chosen to serve this remnant.

Further, the Zadokite priests are labeled as "chosen ones" and responsible in these latter days to guide the flock. CD 3.19–4.3a discusses how God shall build a new house for Israel in fulfillment of the prophecy in Ezek 44:15. According to this prophecy the priests, Levites, and the sons of Zadok will serve in God's future Temple. CD interprets that the exiles from Judah are the priests along with the Levites, while the sons of Zadok are the "chosen ones" who will appear in the latter days. A similar perspective appears in 4Q174 Frg. 1–2i 21.19, where the Zadokite priests figure prominently in preserving the council of the Yahad to remain in the path of Torah. The Pesher Isaiah in 4Q164 1.3 interprets Isa 54:11–12 and the mention of "foundations made of sapphire and precious stones" to represent the priestly figures who founded the council of the Yahad and the chosen congregation. Lines 4–7 also mention "the twelve" and the heads of the tribes of Israel, which recall the reference in 1QS 8 of the twelve laymen of the council who will work along with the three priests. As for the Psalms Pesher it likewise mentions the chosen congregation in its interpretation of Ps 37:20. 4Q171 Frg 1–10 3.5–11 describe that this chosen people will be chiefs and princes who one day will receive their inheritance and enjoy their reward on the holy mountain, which is an allusion to Zion.

The Rule Books as well as the Pesharim use terms like בחר and בחיר to denote the remnant of Israel and the leaders in charge of steering the sectarians. Both terms carry the conviction that God has preserved this special group to carry on with the teachings of Torah and inherit God's blessings. This is not uncommon considering that during the historical period when the DSS where written, many groups vied for that special category of being "God's people." One key distinction, however, that we need to bear in mind is that while 1QS and CD describe their groups as the "chosen" ones, these groups are not necessarily the same sect. Likewise, the ways these Rule Books go about relaying their beliefs of being the elect is not identical. Although the language of being chosen is a common denominator, it is one that we still need to nuance.

In 1QM 12 the use of בחיר points to a special group within the holy people - Israel. This use correlates with 1QM 10.10, where the sectarians represent the favored people who are endowed with wisdom and the ability to see the holy angels. Taken together the descriptions in 1QM 10.10 and 12.1 are comparable with the images in 1QS 4.22–23, where God favors the upright with an

Prophetic Exegesis in 1QM 12

eternal covenant as well as closeness with the angels. This renewed covenant also appears in 1QM 12.3, but this time it is depicted as a "covenant of your peace." As for the Damascus Document it uses בחיר to denote both the people and the leaders. In 1QM 12 we will see these two aspects as well, since the army is not just the elect who share in the fellowship with God in heaven, but they are also the leaders who will spread judgment on the earth. They are the ones whom God will use to bless God's inheritance, that is, Israel.

Hence, the "chosen of the holy people" (בחירי עם קודש) represent the sectarians who have been favored with a covenant of peace and the sharing of God's eternal abode. As we proceed in this column, we will get a clearer perspective of their mission and how it impacts Israel. For now, our inquiry will focus on the sectarian belief that they lived among the angels.

iv. Scriptural Intertextuality

1QM 12.1–5 mention celestial beings including קדושים, מלאכים, and the בחירי שמים. The role of the angels in these lines is significant because they not only praise God but they partner with the sectarians to accomplish the victory. The image of the army sharing the same space with the angels is one that we touched upon when we discussed the camp of the soldiers in 1QM 7. The descriptions in column 12, however, are rather different for instead of focusing on an earthly setting they take place in heaven. Also, the inclusion of these lines following the defeats of Pharaoh, Assyria, and Gog in column 11, underscore that this gathering is a type of military celebration reminiscent of the Scriptural traditions. We can think of the Exodus from Egypt (Exodus 15), David's military triumphs, and the images of Ezekiel 38–48, where the defeat of Gog ushers an Eden type vision of the new Temple. Aside from this continuum from conflict to peace the one key aspect that jumps out from this vision is the preservation of the elect. Scriptural traditions like Enoch and Daniel prove to be influential.

Yadin devotes a section of his work to discuss the similarities between 1QM and Enoch including God's promise to protect the faithful.[9] He notes that there is a heavenly scene in 1 Enoch 43, where "the believers" on earth are counted among the hosts of angels. Also, 1 En. 89:70–77 relays the vision of the "sheep" that were recorded in a book that the angel used to intercede to God on their behalf. And 1 En. 104:1–4 has a promise to the faithful that they will be joyful as the angels since their names are written before the glory of God. Yadin uses these instances to argue Enoch has a direct influence on

---

9 Yadin, *The Scroll of the War*, 240–242.

1QM and its depiction that the "former earth-dwellers" collaborate with the angels in accomplishing God's will. Although Yadin's analysis is not exhaustive, it does highlight a common theme that the faithful will not be forgotten because their destiny is in God's hands. Specifically, the description in 1 Enoch 104 that the names of the faithful are "written" before the glory of God is an important one, because it coincides with the prophecies in Daniel 12 and with 1QM 12.

Our translation of 1QM 12.2 above describes that God established the chosen ones in the "book of the names of all their hosts" (ספר שמות כול צבאם), which denotes not only that the elect were preserved but that they were predestined to be established in the end. Because the gap in the manuscript is wide enough to fit more than one word, the reconstruction of this line has been open to different interpretations. Yadin reconstructs it as "a community and enumeration" (i.e. מספר) while J. van der Ploeg renders it "les vivants. Et le livre" (i.e. "the living, and the book"; ספר).[10] Also, the translation of Florentino García Martínez uses "book" rather than number.[11] Whether that line originally had "number" or "book," the context in column 12 depicts that the elect were indeed established among the troops, and that they were the ones preserved to this point. There is a sense of election and preservation linked to these lines that coincides with the accounts in Enoch. If our reconstruction of line 2 is correct, then what we have here is a clear marker ("book") that along with the angelic presence creates an allusion to Dan 12:1 and the eternal reward for "all who are found written in the book" (כל הנמצא כתוב בספר).

Daniel 11–12 describe the maneuvers of the king of the north and the persecution of many in Israel.[12] Dan 11:32–35 state that the "wise" (משכלים) will endure persecution, in order that they would be refined and purified until the end of the "appointed time" (מועד). The account wraps up with the fall of the king of the north and the rise of the archangel Michael. The key in Dan 12:1–5 is the reference to a book, which not only contains the turn of events of

---

10 Yadin reconstructs this line as מספר, that is "the number" (ibid., 314). J. van der Ploeg on the other hand renders this gap as ספר, that is *"livre."* See Johannes van der Ploeg, "La Règle de la Guerre: Traduction et Notes," *VT* 5 (1955): 386.

11 Florentino García Martínez, *The Dead Sea Scrolls Translated: The Qumran Texts in English* (Grand Rapids: Eerdmans, 1996), 105.

12 A.S. van der Woude, "Prophetic Prediction, Political Prognostication, and Firm Belief: Reflections on Daniel 11:40–12:3," in *The Quest for Context and Meaning: Studies in Biblical Intertextuality in Honor of James A. Sanders*, ed. Craig A. Evans and Shemaryahu Talmon (Leiden: Brill, 1997), 63–73. Daniel Harrington, "The Ideology of Rule in Daniel 7–12," *Society of Biblical Literature Seminar Papers* 38 (1999): 540–551. Benjamin Scolnic, "The Milesian Connection: Dan 11:23 and Antiochus IV's Rise to Power," *VT* 63 (2013): 89–98.

Prophetic Exegesis in 1QM 12

the latter days but more significantly it has the record of the people who will be delivered. Verses 2–3 depict in eschatological fashion that some will resurrect to either eternal life or contempt, while the משכלים will have a teaching ministry that will lead many to righteousness. This allusion to the prophecies in Daniel 12 represents a second passage where the War Scroll is heavily dependent on the visions and aspirations in the book of Daniel.

It is well documented the introduction to the War Scroll is heavily dependent on the chronology of Daniel 11–12.[13] The military encounters in lines 2–4 coincide with the maneuvers of the King of the North in Daniel 11. The depictions in lines 6–8 that Asshur will fall with no one coming to help (cf. Isa 31:8 and 1QM 11.11–12) and that the sons of light will shine in long life coincide with the end of the King of the North and the coming to life of the wise (משכלים). Lines 11–12 also indicate that the war will be a "time of distress" (עת צרה) and that after the back and forth between the armies, God along with the "holy ones" (קדושים) will intervene to eliminate the sons of darkness (1QM 1.16). This portrayal and the sequence that they follow are clear allusions to Daniel. Not only that but the mention of the holy ones coming to the aid of the sons of light provides an interesting parallel with 1QM 12.1–5, where the chosen ones of the heavens will fight side by side with the chosen ones of the holy people. Lastly, although Michael is not mentioned in 1QM 12, his name does appear in the shields of the soldiers (1QM 9.15–16) and more significantly in 1QM 17.5–9 where the chief priest prays for his help. The previous evidence underscores that the eschatological war, more specifically the War Against the Kittim in 1QM 1 and 15–19, was seen as the fulfillment of the visions in Daniel. 1QM 12, along with columns 1 and 15–19, evinces the influence from the prophecies of Daniel.

The heavenly vision in 1QM 12.1–5 demonstrates the hope for eternal fellowship with God that recalls passages in both Enoch and Daniel. Different from these traditions, however, 1QM proceeds from the standpoint of a partnership between the warriors and the heavenly beings. This partnership

---

13 Outside of 1QM the angel Michael is mentioned in 4Q285 1.1–4, which is another war scroll. Interestingly enough lines 3–4 mention Michael along Gabriel, Sariel, and Raphael. Plus, it adds a reference to the "chosen ones" (בחירי). Other manuscripts that mention Michael include 4Q529 which relays the visions of Michael. Also, manuscripts 4Q201 1iv.6 and 4Q202 1iii.7–13, 1iv.8 preserve the accounts of the book of Enoch where Michael appears. Lastly, a recent manuscript 4Q470 1.1–7 describes the word that the angel Michael delivers to King Zedekiah announcing the renewal of the covenant before the congregation. For additional information regarding Michael and the DSS, see: Erik Larson, Lawrence Schiffman, and John Strugnell, "4Q470 Preliminary Publication of a Fragment Mentioning Zedekiah," *RevQ* 16 (1994): 335–349. Rick van de Water, "Michael or Yhwh?: Toward Identifying Melchizedek in 11Q13," *Journal for the Study of the Pseudepigrapha* 16 (2006): 75–86. Joseph Angel, "The Liturgical-Eschatological Priest of the Self-Glorification Hymn," *RevQ* 24 (2010): 585–605.

demonstrates an interpretive development, where the sectarians no longer held to a patient waiting for the promises of God to take place, but they became direct actors in effecting change. 1QM 12.1–5 ultimately highlight that the sectarian army envisioned itself in the same light as the משכלים in Daniel. They are the ones "chosen" among the holy people to bring judgment, and as we will see in the next section, they will be the ones to serve God in the future restoration of Zion.

v. Prophetic Exegesis

The previous exploration has shown that the reference to a ספר in line 2 represents a direct allusion to Dan 12:1. The intriguing aspect of this allusion, however, is that the marker takes on a different direction. Whereas the verse in Daniel refers to the record of those who will be saved, 1QM uses the book for those who are enlisted in the armies of God. This difference is corroborated in the mission of the chosen ones. In Daniel the משכלים have a teaching ministry that leads many to righteousness, while the בחירי עם קודש lead the thousands in battle. A similar case happens in 1QM 1, where the narratives of Daniel 11–12 provide the foundational traces of the future battle between the forces of light and darkness, but the scroll still takes a slightly different direction.

1QM 1.1–7 predict the eschatological battle by alluding to the prophecies in Daniel 11–12.[14] After this initial chronology the scroll transitions in line 8 with a depiction of the last days, when the Sons of Righteousness (בני צדק) will shine to the ends of the earth. Further, lines 9–12 describe the battle between the forces of light and darkness, and they specifically mention that this will be a time of trial for all the people redeemed by God. Throughout these initial lines the narrative of Daniel provides the core of what the scroll anticipates. In lines 10–13, however, the scroll transitions; whereas the משכ־לים in Daniel are the persecuted people who receive deliverance from God

---

14 For a survey of different studies regarding the relationship of Daniel 11–12 with 1QM see: Jean Duhaime, *The War Texts: 1QM and Related Manuscripts* (New York: T&T Clark, 2004), 64–73. Other studies include: John Collins, "The Mythology of Holy War in Daniel and the Qumran War Scroll: A Point of Transition in Jewish Apocalyptic," *VT* 25 (1975): 596–612. G. K. Beale, *The Use of Daniel in Jewish Apocalyptic Literature and in the Revelation of St. John* (Lanham, MD: University Press of America, 1984), 60–66. David Flusser, "Apocalyptic Elements in the War Scroll" in *Judaism of the Second Temple Period*, trans. Azzan Yadin (Grand Rapids: Eerdmans, 2007), 1:140–158. Hanna Vanonen, "The Textual Connections between 1QM 1 and the Book of Daniel," in *Changes in Scripture Rewriting and Interpreting Authoritative Traditions in the Second Temple Period*, ed. Hanne von Weissenberg, Juha Pakkala, Marko Marttila (Berlin: De Gruyter, 2011), 223–246.

Prophetic Exegesis in 1QM 12

through the angel Michael, the Sons of Light in 1QM are a bellicose group that engages in their fight against the forces of darkness. Also, Daniel anticipates God's unilateral deliverance of the משכלים, which 1QM 1.13–17 describe as God breaking through the gridlock between the forces of light and darkness.

In essence, the prophecies of Daniel provide the periodization of history and more specifically they point directly at the sectarians as the ones who will receive the gift of life. 1QM 12 as well assumes that the sectarians will reap the blessings of God's predestined will. Moreover, the description of the sectarians as the "chosen from the holy people" and the recording of their names in the "book of the names of all their hosts", reinforce the belief that they were the favored ones for these latter days. This brings us to the sectarian belief of being the "chosen ones."

Our research demonstrates that the concept of being chosen appears in the Rule Books to denote both the remnant of Israel and the priestly figures that have the responsibility of steering the sectarians. 1QM 12.1–2 likewise uses this notion to show that there will be some who will be preserved, and that this same people have the duty of leading the thousands. These two aspects are highlighted in lines 3–4 where the chosen ones receive a covenant of peace that enables them "to reign for all appointed times of eternity" and empowers them to "appoint" and "direct the hand" in battle. Essentially, lines 1–5 envision the sectarians as the ones who will be preserved, and the responsible group that will lead the people back to God. This last point will become more apparent in the subsequent lines where the ascent to Zion takes place. We will see that just like the Scriptural traditions use the processions to Zion as a sign of consecration, 1QM 12 aspires that the triumph over darkness results in the sectarians leading the people back to their God.

b.   1QM 12.7–18: Final Restoration of Zion

i.   Text and Translation

1QM 12.7–18	1QM 12.7–18
7 ואתה אל נ[ ] בכבוד מלכותכה ועדת קדושיכה בתוכנו לעזר עולמי[ם]נו בוז למלכים לעג	7 You, O God, ... in the glory of your majesty, and the congregation of your holy ones is in our midst for eternal help [] contempt to the kings, derision
8 וקלס לגבורים כיא קדוש אדוני ומלך הכבוד אתנו עם קדושים גבו[רים] צבא מלאכים בפקודינו	8 and mockery to the powerful. For Holy is the Lord, and the King of Glory is with us, with the holy ones. The mighty of the host of angels are enlisted with us,

9 וגבור המלח[מה] בעדתנו וצבא רו־חיו עם צעדינו ופרשינו כ[עננים וכעבי טל לכסות ארץ	9 and the War Hero is with our congregation and the army of his spirits are with our steps. Our horsemen are like the clouds and the midst to cover the earth,
10a וכזרם רביבים להשקות משפט לכול צאצאיה	10a as a torrential rain that pours judgment on all that grows.
10b קומה גבור שבה שביכה איש כבוד ושול	10b Rise, O Hero! Take your captives, O Glorious One! Take
11 שללכה עושי חיל תן ידכה בעורף אויביכה ורגלכה על במותי חלל מחץ גוים צריכה וחרבכה	11 your spoil, Doer of Mighty Deeds! Place your hand on the neck of your enemies, and your foot on the back of the slain. Strike the nations, your adversaries, and let your sword
12 תואכל בשר אשמה מלא ארצכה כבוד ונחלתכה ברכה המון מקנה בחלקותכה כסף וזהב ואבני	12 consume guilty flesh! Fill your land with your glory and your inheritance with blessing; multitude of cattle in your fields, silver, gold, and precious
13 חפץ בהיכל[ו]תיכה ציון שמחי מאדה והופיעי ברנות ירושלים והגלנה כול ערי יהודה פתחי	13 stones in your palaces. Rejoice exceedingly, O Zion! Shine with jubilation, O Jerusalem! Rejoice all the cities of Judah. Open
שער[י]ך תמיד להביא אליך חיל גואים ומלכיהם ישרתוך והשתחוו לך כול מעניך ועפר	14 your gates continually, so the wealth of the nations can come in and their kings shall serve you and all your oppressors will bow to you, and the dust
15 [רגליך ילחכו בנו[ת עמי צרחנה בקול רנה עדינה עדי כבוד ורדינה ב[מ]ל[כות]	15 of your feet they will lick. Daughters of my people, shout with jubilant voice! Adorn yourselves with fine ornaments, and rule over the kingdom
16 [ ] י[שראל למלוך עולמים [ ]	16 ... Israel, to reign forever ...
17 ל[ ]הם גבורי המלחמה ירושלים [ ]	17 ... heroes of war Jerusalem ...
18 [ ]ם על השמים אדוני[ן]	18 ... above the heavens, the Lord ...

ii. Content

The following is the content of 1QM 12.7–10a

- 12.7–10-a
    1. Call to God and the Holy Ones
    2. The King of Glory in the midst of the army

Prophetic Exegesis in 1QM 12

- 12.10b–13a
  1. Call to God the War Hero
  2. Blessing of God's Inheritance
- 12.13b–18
  1. Celebration to Zion
  2. Israel's eternal reign

The content above shows a rhetorical strategy where a call precedes a deeper reflection about God's deeds. Lines 7–8a proclaim that God and the holy angels are to help the army. These images continue in lines 8b–10, by citing two key markers. The reference to the "King of Glory" (מלך הכבוד) and the "War Hero" (גבור המלחמה) allude to Psalm 24, and they hint at the celebratory images that come in lines 13b–18. Before we get to this celebration, there is another call this time to the War Hero in lines 10b–13a that recall passages where God defeats the enemies and fills the earth with blessing. The markers of the "enemy" and "God's sword" continue with the depictions in 1QM 11, where the "sword of no man" brings down the Kittim.[15] Another key to these lines is the addition of images of prosperity, like "cattle in the fields" and "precious stones" in God's abode. These depictions of richness evoke Scriptural traditions like Amos 9 and Ezekiel 40–48 where God brings prosperity and they confirm that the sectarian aspiration of turning chaos into prosperity follows the prophetic pattern in Scripture.

The mention of Zion at the end of this column introduces an interesting take about the sectarian aspirations, and it provides another example that suggests that Zion was part of the future visions and hopes for the sectarians.[16] The subsequent analysis will pick up some of the most salient intertextual

---

15 Notice that lines 8–10a depict the partnership between the army of God and the soldiers. This time different from 1QM 11, the army is depicted in a more intimidating light. The image of "horsemen" like clouds that cover the earth presents an interesting contrast. In Scripture the image of armies covering the earth like the clouds that bring rain recall enemy armies like in Ezek 38:9–16 and the army of Gog of Magog.

16 Along with 1QM 12 other manuscripts like 4QMMT (4Q394 2.1–19; 4.10–11; 4Q396 2.11–3.1), 11Q5 22, and 11Q19 attest to the hope within the DSS that Zion and the Temple in Jerusalem will one day experience past glories. For recent research on the place of Jerusalem in the sectarian library, see: John Kampen, "The Eschatological Temple(s) of 11QT," in *Pursuing the Text: Studies in Honor of Ben Zion Wacholder on the Occasion of His Seventieth Birthday*, ed. John C. Reeves and John Kampen (Sheffield: Sheffield Academic Press, 1994), 85–97. Daniel Falk, "Qumran Prayer Texts and the Temple," in *Sapiential, Liturgical and Poetical Texts from Qumran: Proceedings of the Third Meeting of the International Organization for Qumran Studies, Oslo, 1998*, ed. Daniel Falk, Florentino García Martínez (Leiden: Brill, 2000), 106–126. Hanne von Weissenberg, "The Centrality of the Temple in 4QMMT," in *The Dead Sea Scrolls: Texts and Context*, ed. Charlotte Hempel (Leiden: Brill, 2010), 293–305. Emile Puech, "Jérusalem dans les manuscrits de la Mer Morte," *RevQ* 25 (2012): 423–444.

examples and how these inform the prophetic exegesis of Scripture. Different from our previous chapters here we will compare 1QM 12.7–18 with its counterpart in 4Q492, and it will look at the differences between these texts to highlight the interpretive moves in 1QM. The Scriptural intertextuality will focus on the allusion to the "King of Glory" and adopt an eschatological reading of Psalm 24 that will inform our reading of lines 7–18.

iii. Sectarian Intertextuality

1QM 12.7–18 has a parallel version with some variants in 1QM 19 and 4Q492. Jean Duhaime devoted a section of his work in assessing 4Q492 and some of the intersecting points with 1QM 19.[17] He highlights two important aspects to consider when comparing these manuscripts. One is that 4Q492 has the same Herodian script as 1QM 19, which points to a dating around the first century BCE, and he concurs with Maurice Baillet who originally suggested that lines 1, 7, and 12 in 4Q492 were shorter than in 1QM 19. Thus, the shorter version of these lines would indicate perhaps that 4Q492 is an earlier text.[18] Our analysis will directly compare 1QM 12 and 4Q492, and when it is necessary we will refer to 1QM 19 for additional editorial insights. The aim of this analysis is to look closely at the differences between 1QM 12 and 4Q492 that may point at possible rhetorical strategies behind those edits.

1QM 19.1–14	Final Restoration of Zion 4Q492 1.1–13	1QM 12.7–18
1 [לן]בורים כיא קדוש אדירנו ומלך[הכבוד אתנו וצ]בא[	1 לגבורים כי[א קדוש אדירנו ומלך הכבוד אתנו וצבא רוחיו עם צעדינו ופרשינו כעננים](	7 ואתה אל נ[ן] בכבוד מלכותכה ועדת קדושיכה בתוכנו לעזר עולמי[ם]נו בוזלמלכים לעג
2 [ט]ל לכסות ארץ וכזרם רביבים להשקות משפט כ]ול[	2 לכסוֹת אָ[רץ וכזרם רביבים להשקות משפט לכול צאצאיהקומה גבור שבה שביכה איש[	8 וקלס לגבורים כיא קדוש אדוני ומלך הכבוד אתנו עם קדושים גבו]רים [צבא מלאכים בפקודינו

17 Duhaime, *The War Texts*, 20–21

18 Maurice Baillet, *Qumrân Grotte 4.III (4Q482–4Q520)* (Oxford: Clarendon, 1982), 47–49. Esther Eshel and Hanan Eshel, "Recensions of the War Scroll" in *The Dead Sea Scrolls Fifty Years After Their Discovery: Proceedings of the Jerusalem Congress, July 20–25, 1997*, ed. Lawrence H. Schiffman et al. (Jerusalem: Israel Exploration Society, 2000), 352–356.

3] וש[נ]ול שללכה עושי חיל תן ידכה בעורף אויביך ור]ג[ל]ך[ ]	3 כבו]ד ש(ש)ול]שללכה עושי חיל תן ידכה בעורף אויביך ורגלך (על במותי חלל מחץ גוים]	9 וגבור המלח[מה] בעדתנו וצבא רוחיו עם צעדינו ופרשינו כ[ענני]ם וכעבי טל לכסות ארץ
4 צריכ]ה וחרבך תואכל בשר מלא ארצכה כבוד ונחלתכה ברכה ה[מון]	4 צריכ)ה וחרבך תואכל ב]שר מ[ל]א]ארצכה כבוד ונחלתכה ברכה המ(ון מקנה בחלקותיך כסף]	10 וכזרם רביבים להש- קות משפט לכול צאצאיה קומה גבור שבה שביכה איש כבוד ושו
5 [[בֹהיכלותיך ציון שמחי מואדה והגלנה כול ערי יהו[ד]ה]	5 [וזה]ב בהיכלותיך ציון שמחי מאֹוד [] vacat [והגלנה כול ערי יהו(דה פתחי]	11 שללכה עושי חיל תן ידכה בעורף אויביכה ורגלכה על במותי חלל מחץ גוים צריכה וחרבכה
6]חיל גוים ומלכיהם ישרתוך והשתחוו לך [כו]ל[מעני]ך	6 שעריך תמיד להביא אל[יך] חיל גוים ומל- כיהם ישרתוך ו[השתחוו לך (כול מעני)ך (ועפר]	12 תואכל בשר אשמה מלא ארצכה כבוד ונח- לתכה ברכה המון מקנה בחלקותיכה כסף וזהב ואבני
7]בֹנֹות עֹמֹי הבענה- בקול רנה עדינה עדי כבוד ור[ד]ינה במלכות	7 רגליך ילחכו [] ב)נות עמי הבענה] ב[ק]ול רֹנֹה עדינה [עדי כבוד ור(ד) ינה במלכות ( ]	13 חפץ בהיכל[ו]ן תיכהצ ציון שמחי מאדה והופיעי בר- נות ירושלים והגלנה כול ערי יהודה פתחי
8 למחנ]יכה וישראל למלכות עֹולמים vacat	8 למחנ]יכה וישראל למ- לכות עולמים [] (ואחר יאספו המח(נה(ב)ל(י) להן ההוא למנוח עד הבוקר]	14 שער[י]ך תמיד להביא אליך חיל גואים ומלכיהם ישרתוך והשתחוו לך כול מעניך ועפר
9 המח]נֹה [ב]ל[נ]לה ההוא למנוח עד הבוקר ובבוקֹר יבואו עֹד מֹקֹום המערכה	9 [וב]בוקר יבואו עד מקום המערכה (אשֹר נפלו שם ג)בורי כתֹ[נֹי] ים והמוֹ[ן אשור וחיל כול הגוים]	15 [רגליך ילחכו בנו]ת עמי צרחנה בקול רנה עדינה עדי כבוד ורדינה ב[מ]ל[כות]
10 ג]בֹורי כתיים והמון אשור וחיל כול הגוים הנקהלים אם[ ] חללים	10 [הנקהלים אם (מ] תֹו) רֹוֹב חללֹין]סֹ(לֹאֹין מֹ[קב]רֹ אשר) נֹפלֹו שם בֹחֹרֹ[ב]אֹל[ן וננש שם כוהן הרו(אש]	16 [י]שראל למלוך עולמים vacat [ ]

11 [ ] נ]פלו שם בחרב אל ונגש שם כוהן הרו]אש [הו ואחיו [ ]	11 [ומ]שנהו ו(הכוהנים [והלוים [עם נשיא ה)מלח־ מה וכו]ל ראשי המערכות [ופקוד(יהם	17 [ל] [הם גבורי המלח־ מה ירושלים] [ ]
12 [מ]לחמה וכול ראשי המערכות ופקוד]הם[	12 [ ] יחד בעומדם ע]ל(ח)ללין כתי(ים וה)ללו שם [(א)ת אל (ישראל ו]ענו ואמרו	18 [[ם על השמים אדוני]]
13 ע]ל]ן ח]ללי כתי]ים וה]ללו שם [א]ת אל] [14 [[ל]]	13 [ ] לא]ל עליון [ן [ל [ ] ל [ל]]ל[[ ] [[ ]][[ל	

1QM 12.7–8a begins with a statement about God being in the midst of the
army for eternal help. Following a gap in line 7 there is a description of "contempt to the kings, derision and mockery to the powerful" (בוז למלכים לעג
וקלס לגבורים). The reference to the גבורים is the first word preserved in
both 4Q492 and 1QM 19. It is possible that the prayer originally began with
the content in 1QM 12.7–8a although we do not know for certain.

Lines 7–8a are significant because they transition from the heavenly
gathering to the celebration in Zion in the latter part of column 12. Yadin believes that 1QM 12.7–8a begin to explain "how" the King of Glory and the host
of angels fight along the combatants.[19] For his part, Philip Davies holds that
lines 8b–10a consist of a hymn that possesses a metric style, and that lines
7–8a were added to this hymn although he does not offer much of a discussion to explain this view.[20] From a rhetorical standpoint we can gather a strategy as lines 7–8a are the beginning of a call to God (אתה אל) that introduces
a song to the King of Glory. This same approach happens in line 10b where the
interjection "rise, O Hero" (קומה גבור) introduces a call that is followed by a
song to Zion in lines 13–18.

Following the invocation to the King of Glory lines 8b–9a describe the
partnership between the soldiers and the celestial armies. In these lines we
learn that the קדושים and the "mighty of the host of angels" (גבורים צבא
מלאכים) are enlisted in the army. The use of "enlisted" (פקד) is key because
it also appears in 1QM 2.4, 16 in reference to the commissioned men of the
army. 1QM 12.4 adds that the "chosen ones" will commission and direct the

---

19 Yadin, *The Scroll of the War*, 215.

20 Davies, *1QM, the War Scroll*, 102. Davies' observation is important because lines 8b–10a
are absent from 4Q492 and 1QM 19, and they show us the first editing instance.

Prophetic Exegesis in 1QM 12   217

thousands in the battle. Line 9 also describes that the War Hero is with the "congregation," which recalls passages in the War of Divisions (1QM 2, 3, and 5). Lines 8b–9a emphasize not only that the angels are with the army, but that God as the War Hero is fighting for them. These descriptions, however, are different in 4Q492 where we find a shorter description of the "host of his spirits" partnering with the army. The previous references that recall the War of Divisions are significant, because as Brian Schultz suggested they demonstrate the redactional activity of an editor who adapted the prayer in 4Q492 to a new context.[21] Although Schultz does not state what this new context is, we can gather from his discussion that this prayer, and thus the liturgies in 1QM 10–12, are a transition point from one stage of the war to the other as they are filled with intersecting points to the each of the stages of the war that seamlessly integrate these major parts of the scroll.

1QM 12.9b–10a finish this section with the horsemen spreading judgment. The horsemen in line 9 recall 1QM 6.8–14, where we have an extended account of their role in the War of Divisions. 4Q492 has the same description of the horsemen as "clouds that cover the earth" while 1Q19 skips the horsemen and talks about the "dew that covers the earth." Notwithstanding these differences the marker of horsemen covering the earth is significant because it comes on the heels of the eschatological lines in column 11. We recall that 1QM 11.16–18 depicts, albeit in fragmentary fashion, the attack on Gog whose army according to Ezek 38:9, 16 comes as a "cloud that covers the earth" (כענן לכסות הארץ).

The representation of the sectarians as horsemen that cover the earth represents a pun, where 1QM describes that God's army is mightier than the horsemen of Gog. As for the depiction of a "torrential rain that pours judgment" it recalls passages of judgment such as the deluge in Genesis and Elijah's prayer for rain, which the letter of Jas 5:7–17 uses to teach patience to his audience as they anticipate the coming of the Lord.[22] Lines 8b–10a essentially have the main contours of 4Q492 plus the addition in lines 8b–9a of the enlistment of the angels, which along with the reference to the horsemen recall passages in the War of Divisions. The appearance of themes linked with the War of Divisions continues with the trend in the liturgies in 1QM 10–11, where different markers recall the main parts of the scroll.

In line 10b there is an interjection that transitions the column into another direct address to God. Here we have a call for the גבור to rise and "take

---

21 Schultz, *Conquering the World*, 281–282.

22 Robert Eisenman, "Eschatological 'Rain' Imagery in the War Scroll from Qumran and in the Letter of James," *JNES* 49 (1990): 173–184. Eisenman sees several connections of the rain imagery in 1QM with the coming of the Son of Man and James allusion to Elijah's prayer for rain.

your captives" (שבה שביכה). The form of this interjection recalls passages in the book of Psalms, where the speaker calls on God for assistance. Examples of this type of call appear in Pss 3:8; 7:7; 9:20; 10:12; 17:13; 44:27; 74:22; 82:8; 132:8. And in Solomon's prayer in 2 Chr 6:41 the king uses this exact phrase to call on God to come and reside in the Temple. Likewise, in Num 10:35 Moses calls on God to rise and scatter the enemies as Israel follows the Ark of the Covenant. Although the call in line 10b is attested in Scripture, it has slight variations. For example, Psalms uses "rise, O Lord" (קומה יהוה) or "rise, O God" (קומה אלהים), rather than "rise, O Hero" (קומה גבור). Aside from 1QM 12 and 4Q492 the call "rise, O Hero" (קומה גבור) appears only in 11Q14 2.2, where it utters "rise, O Hero take the Philistines" (קומה גבור שבה פלשתים). The invocation to God the Hero has connections with liturgical pieces where God is called upon to take back or inhabit in God's abode. The use of this call and the fact that it alludes to Psalm 24 is significant, because God will take back Zion and everything that surrounds it.[23]

Following the call on the Hero to rise lines 11–12a prompt the "Doer of Mighty Deeds" (עושה חיל) with imperatives including: "take the spoil" (שול שללכה), "lay the hand" (תן ידכה) on the necks of his enemies, "strike" (מחץ) the nations, and "fill" the earth with his glory (מלא). Added to these commands are the targets of God's wrath: the "enemies" (אויבים), the "slain" (חלל), the "nations, your adversaries" (גוים צריכה) and the "guilty flesh" (בשר אשמה). The inclusion of the "enemies" and "oppressors" continue with the rhetorical strategy of columns 10–11, where these markers represent those forces that God needs to overcome on behalf of Israel. Plus, the pairing of an imperative and its target creates an overwhelming picture of violence; it gives the impression that lines 11–12a works as the capstone and the overthrow of the enemies that must precede the blessing of God's inheritance.

Line 12b is comprised of two requests: one is for God to fill the earth with glory and for God's inheritance to be blessed with all sorts of riches. A closer look at this line reveals that a subsequent editor tried to align these descriptions with 4Q492, as we see the insertion of כסף ("silver") between בחלקו־ תיכה ("in your fields") and זהב ("gold"). The aspiration for richness and blessings evokes several accounts in Scripture, where the defeat of the enemies ushers a period of bountiful riches on Israel. One important example of this theme comes from the Words of the Luminaries (4Q504).[24]

---

23 The other instance where גבור appears in 1QM is in reference to Goliath as a "mighty man of valor" (איש גבור חיל) who God handed over to David in defeat (1QM 11.1). This naturally works as a contrast and a pun that differentiates between Goliath as the would-be hero and God as the true war hero.

24 The Words of the Luminaries (4Q504) is a manuscript dated from the mid-second

Prophetic Exegesis in 1QM 12

4Q504 is a collection of non-sectarian liturgies that was preserved in the context of Qumran. The presence and use of these liturgies have been a question for scholars like Esther Chazon. In her study of 4Q504 Chazon problematizes the seeming contraction that a non-sectarian text was important in the context of Qumran.[25] She discerns that the Words of the Luminaries convey beliefs that align with the social identity of the sectarians. Of the principles that Chazon lists, two in particular are helpful in our study of 1QM 12 including: election and covenant.[26]

For instance, 4Q504 17.3–16 displays these two major concepts. In lines 3–7 the language of election figures prominently as God "chose" (בחר) Jerusalem as the place of worship. Likewise, the tribe of Judah was chosen as the one from where the Shepherd of God's people will come. And Israel was "loved more than all the peoples of the earth." In terms of the covenant, lines 7–9 describe that God made a covenant with David that he may sit on the throne eternally.

These two concepts bring us to 4Q504 17.9b–16 where the prayer transitions into a glorification of God before the nations of the world. This part of the prayer presents a similar aspiration as 1QM 12.12bff. where God's glory is lifted up and the nations will bring gifts of gold, silver, and every precious stone. The other significant aspect of these lines is that they envisage that Israel will be consecrated, and that Zion will be epicenter of this consecration. Interestingly, line 12 uses the phrase "there is neither adversary nor evil deed" (ואין שטן ופגע רע), which is a quotation of 1 Kgs 5:18 where Solomon announces to Hiram his desire to build the Temple. The citation of Kings implies that 4Q504 aspires for the reconstitution of the Temple in Jerusalem as the images of peace and prosperity introduced in lines 14–16 reveal. The notions of election and covenant in 4Q504 17 lead into the hope for a restoration of worship in Zion. This same strategy appears in 1QM 12, where the "elect of the holy people" who have a renewed covenant with God usher a time of blessing, prosperity, and worship of God in Zion.

This last point brings us back to 1QM 12.13 where the scroll interjects with a parallel exhortation to Zion to "rejoice exceedingly" (שמחי מאדה) and

---

century BCE. For a discussion about this non-sectarian collection of liturgies and their dates, see: Esther G. Chazon, "Is Divrei Ha-me'orot a Sectarian Prayer?" in *The Dead Sea Scrolls: Forty Years of Research*, ed. Devorah Dimant and Uriel Rappaport (Leiden: Brill, 1992), 3–17; Eileen M. Schuller, "Prayers and Psalms from the Pre-Maccabean Period," *DSD* 13 (2006): 306–18.

25 Esther G. Chazon, "Prayer and Identity in Varying Contexts: The Case of the Words of the Luminaries," *Journal for the Study of Judaism* 46 (2015): 484–511.

26 Ibid., 490–498. Aside from election and covenant, the other major societal values that Chazon points out include a reflection on historical recollections, the forgiveness of sin, and knowledge.

Jerusalem to "shine in jubilation" (והופיעי ברנות).[27] Line 14 continues with the command to "open your gates continually" so the wealth of the nations can come. The charge to open the gates in line 14 as well as the mention of the "King of Glory" in line 8 demonstrates the influence that traditions like Isaiah 60 and Psalm 24 have on this column, which we will discuss below. At this junction, however, it suffices to point out that this eschatological account foresees, via the language of Scripture, that God will retake the city and cause it to flow with the blessings from the nations. Moreover, these lines establish a turning point; in particular, lines 14–15a depict that the forces that once oppressed Israel will come to serve them. There are key markers within this line that not only allude to Scriptural accounts, but these same markers tie back to the descriptions that we have seen in 1QM 10–11.

The mention of the "nations" (גואים) recall the enemies in 1QM 10.1–8, specifically the "seven nations of vanity" (שבעת גוי הבל) under the rule of Belial and the "remnant of the nations" (שאר הגוים) that will see the glory of God in 1QM 11.9–15. Likewise the mention of the "kings" (מלכים) recalls figures like Pharaoh in 1QM 11.9, and the reference of those that "oppress you" (מעניך) recalls the adversaries in 1QM 10.7 and 12.11. And the enemies that will come to "lick the dust" (ועפר רגליך ילחכו) off the feet of Israel fulfills the prediction in 1QM 11.13, where God will submit the enemies into the hand of those who are "prostrate in the dust" (כורעי עפר). This sequence of events wraps up in lines 15–18 with the "daughters of my people" celebrating and Israel reigning forever.

The phrase "daughters of my people" (בנות עמי) appears only in this column and in the parallel versions in 1QM 19 and 4Q492.[28] The interesting aspect about this phrase is that despite the fact that it recalls Scriptural passages of celebration, the tone of war is still present. The encouragement to "shout" with a jubilant voice uses the verb צרח, which appears in 1QHa 11.33 when the "earth shouts" (ארץ תצרח) because of the disaster that God brings on Belial. In Scripture the verb צרח appears in passages like Isa 42:13 and Zeph 1:14 that describe contexts of war and judgment. Line 16 has a gap that precedes the mention of Israel. However, 1QM 19.8 and 4Q292 1.8 have the word "camp" (מחנה) which points back to the camps of the soldiers in the War of Divisions (1QM 7). The use of צרח and מחנה show traces of war amidst the celebration. The other significant question that the phrase "daughters of my people" brings is about the identity of God's people.

---

27 The call for Jerusalem to shine in jubilation is missing from both 4Q492 and 1QM 19.

28 In line 15 we see a change from the parallel version in 1QM 19 and 4Q492, where the הבענה is substituted for צרחנה. Also of note is that 1QM 19 and 4Q292 preserve the מחניכה before the mention of Israel.

Prophetic Exegesis in 1QM 12   221

In the DSS the phrase "my people" has many uses. It is used in reference
to Israel's ancestors in the re-written Scriptural accounts (4Q385 2.1) and the
Pesharim (4Q174 1–2i.21.2). "My people" can also be used for the faithful that
live in the current age. Pseudo-Ezekiel (4Q386 2.3) predicts the rise of a Son of
Belial who will come and try to oppress God's people. This prophecy follows
column 1, where we find Ezekiel's prophecy of the dry bones and the reconstitution of Israel. The Temple Scroll (11Q19) proceeds from the standpoint
of revisiting the different legal prescriptions from Torah in order to steer the
people of God. The idea of God's people is fundamental to this manuscript,
as it constantly makes reference to the precepts of law being established for
the people's sake. 11Q19 talks about the "assembly of the people" (עם קהל)
in 18.7 and 26.7–10 for whom atonement is to be made.[29] 11Q19 29 (cf. 59) lists
the offerings that the people shall bring to God in the "appointed times". Lines
9–10 conclude with the consecration of the people and the "creation" of the
Temple: "I will create my Temple to establish it for myself for all days according to the covenant I made with Jacob in Bethel."[30] This last description in the
Temple Scroll shares the ideology in 1QM 12, where the reconstitution of the
people of Israel is concomitant with the restoration of the sacred space.

Our analysis of 1QM 12.7–18 has shown continuity between this manuscript and 4Q492. Outside of lines 8b–9a, and their allusion to the War Hero
and the angels "enlisted" (פקודינו) along the sectarian army, column 12 does
not deviate from its Cave 4 counterpart. Because 1QM 12 is in better condition
than column 19 and 4Q492, we are in a much better position to discern the
editorial and rhetorical moves within this column, such as the puns against
the army of Gog and Goliath the Philistine, and how the calls to God, the King
of Glory, and the War Hero hope for a turn of events that envision a restoration of the people and their sacred space. Overall, we are able to see clearly
how column 12 integrates themes from the previous columns.

This is an important insight, because it corroborates that the liturgies
from 1QM 10–12 reflect on the stages in columns 2–9 and 15–19, while at the
same time interjecting markers that speak prophetically of what God will do

---

29 The representation of the people as an assembly (קהל) correlates with the Damascus
Document where the sectarians as a group are represented as a קהל (CD 7.17; 11.22; 12.6; 14.18).
Likewise, 1Q28a 1.25 describes that the קהל shall be consecrated when they gathered in fellowship. Notice also that lines 25–29 describe that the קהל shall gather to learn about cultic matters and for times of war. Interestingly, this text present similar restrictions on who can access
the קהל and the council of the Yahad as we see both in 1QM 2 and 7.

30 11Q19 48.7 proceeds from the standpoint of the assumptions in 1QM19 29, because in
this passage the people are urged to walk in the ways of God and abstain from abominable
things based on the fact that they are "holy people to God" (כי עם קדוש אתה ליהוה אלוהיכה)
and "sons of God" (בנים אתמה ליהוה אלוהיכמה).

at the end of time. Furthermore, the use of these markers points to the intertextual character of these liturgies and the dialogical links that they establish with other manuscripts in their surrounding context. As we turn our attention to the Scriptural traditions, we will keep an eye at how the allusions to Psalm 24 and Isaiah 60, proclaim the fulfillment of God's promises to Israel.

iv.   Scriptural Intertextuality

1QM 12.7–18 celebrates the victories of God with a procession to the holy city Jerusalem. In this part of our discussion we will pay close attention to a couple of lines in this hymn. In lines 8b–10a we have a reflection that describes how God and the holy angels help the army to become this formidable force that brings judgment upon the earth. Specifically, the invocation to the מלך הכ־ כוד and גבור המלחמה allude to Ps 24:7–10. In addition, in lines 13b–14 there is a command that the "gates open perpetually" so the wealth of the nations can come. This line is a clear allusion to Isa 60:11, where the prophet describes how the nations will one day come to serve Israel. As we look into how these two traditions are used in 1QM 12, we want to consider what this eschatological text reveals about the sectarian hope to bring restoration to Israel.

The reference to the מלך הכבוד follows a direct address to God in lines 7–8a. With the demonstrative particle כיא the column transitions into a prayer that calls on God to act on Zion's behalf. This transition provides a clue to us as readers that we are shifting from the original invocation and into the content of the prayer. Another important insight from this rhetorical strategy is that the invocation in lines 7–8a states in a matter of fact a religious belief that the sectarians hold to be true, and with the particle כיא the column begins to demonstrate how this belief will become a reality for Israel. The use of different titles for God represents one of the main strategies that stamp in the mind of the reader that Scripture is being fulfilled.

Outside of 1QM 12, 19, and 4Q492 the title מלך הכבוד appears nine times across the DSS including poetic and liturgical texts like the Hodayot (1QHa; 4QHe) the Songs of the Sabbath (4Q403; 11Q17), and other songs (4Q510–11). The interesting aspect about the use of this title is that it only appears in Psalm 24, where the text deals with a diversity of themes such as creation, the observance of Torah, and the final dawn of the divine warrior. Obviously, this last theme correlates with the descriptions in 1QM 12. The argument can be made, however, that the notions of Torah observance and the rededication of the sanctuary are also present in 1QM 12. Before we proceed, we will take a closer look at this Scriptural psalm.

Prophetic Exegesis in 1QM 12

Psalm 24 is comprised of ten verses including a statement about God's supremacy over creation (vv. 1b–2), a statement about Torah observance as a prerequisite for intimacy with God (vv. 3–6), and a liturgical procession for God's enthronement (vv. 7–10). The diversity of these topics and the seemingly disjointed sequence of events have called into question the integrity of this psalm. Scholars have come up with different proposals that attempt to find not just the historical background and form of this piece, but also a theory that would explain how these three pieces came together.[31] One particular approach that deserves special consideration adopts an eschatological interpretation of this psalm.

In his article "The Coherence of Psalm 24," Philip Sumpter explores the scholarly contributions to the analysis of Psalm 24.[32] In his view, this seemingly random text can be coherently organized by following its poetic form and content, which he categorizes in terms of time and space. Sumpter argues that in vv.1–2 the topic is not "the act of creation" but rather the divine ownership of the cosmos. Here he relies on the use of the verbs "to establish" (יסד, כון) in v. 2, to suggest that creation was already established as a house (or temple). Verses 1–2 establish that creation (as a macrocosm of the Temple) is God's possession to be shared and enjoyed by those who inhabit it. Sumpter adds that in these verses we see the convergence of the priestly and prophetic traditions, where the primal state of creation is made accessible via the cult (priestly) and where the redemption of the cosmos is envisioned in the future (prophetic).[33]

This leads into vv. 3–6, where the psalm narrows its focus from the universal to the particular; that is, from the earth to the mount of God and from those "who live on earth" to a specific people, Jacob.[34] Sumpter notes that these verses assume that the meaning of creation is intimacy with God, whether it is in its protological state (i.e. Genesis 2) or in its future eschatological sense (i.e. Isaiah 56–66). Likewise, there is a shift in the tone of the verbs; whereas vv. 1–2 have a firm conviction that God has "established" creation, vv.

---

31 For a variety of readings of Psalm 24, see: David Clines, "A World Established On Water (Psalm 24): Reader-Response, Deconstruction and Bespoke Interpretation," in *The New Literary Criticism and the Hebrew Bible*, ed. J. Cheryl Exum and David Clines (Sheffield: JSOT Press, 1993), 79–90. Nancy DeClaisse-Walford, "An Intertextual Reading of Psalms 22, 23, and 24," in *The Book of Psalms: Composition and Reception*, ed. Patrick D. Miller and Peter W. Flint (Leiden: Brill, 2005), 139–152. M. D. Goulder, "David and Yahweh in Psalms 23 and 24," *JSOT* 30 (2006): 463–473. Alastair Hunter, "'The Righteous Generation': The Use of Dôr in Psalms 14 and 24," in *Reflection and Refraction: Studies in Biblical Historiography in Honour of A. Graeme Auld*, ed. Robert Rezetko, Timothy Lim, and Brian Aucker (Leiden: Brill, 2006), 187–205.

32 Philip Sumpter, "The Coherence of Psalm 24," *JSOT* 39 (2014): 31–54.

33 Ibid., 45–48.

34 Ibid., 48–50.

3–6 start from the standpoint of who "may" enjoy this intimacy. Sumpter surprisingly does not devote more space to address the answers that the psalm gives in v. 4. This verse is of prime importance, because it underscores that Torah observance and not ethnic heritage guarantees the redemption of the faithful. Sumpter closes this section accurately recognizing that vv. 3–6 do not depict an actual consummation of creation, but the conditions for God to realize the plan of creation.

In vv. 7–10 the psalm transcends from the cosmic scope of creation to the gates of the city and from the bottom of the mountain to the top of the holy place.[35] These verses proclaim in a manner typical of eschatological and apocalyptic thought that God will suddenly intervene, to assert authority and redeem the people from their enemies. Although Sumpter acknowledges that there is no mention of the "enemies" within this psalm, he nevertheless recognizes that this ambiguity underscores that anyone who stands in the way of God's plan is the enemy. This means on the one hand that there may be enemies in the periphery of Israel, but also within that attempt to thwart God's purpose for the people (cf. Isaiah 28). In vv. 7–10 God accomplishes what vv. 1–2 depict; that is, God becomes a direct actor who by inhabiting the holy abode empowers the people to live according to the principles laid out in vv. 3–6.

Sumpter concludes that the seemingly disjointed structure and rhetoric of Psalm 24 is its actual strength.[36] The juxtaposition of God's sovereignty over creation and the intervention in human affairs is in line with the strategy employed by the prophets of mixing Pentateuchal narratives along with eschatological themes. The editor of Psalm 24, therefore, adopts this same method to argue for a theocentric worldview that will be normative for Israel

The previous discussion of Psalm 24 has provided aspects that we need to consider as we turn our attention to 1QM 12. We observed that Psalm 24, read from an eschatological standpoint, presents a trajectory both in time and space that narrows the scope from God's sovereignty over the foundations of creation to a narrower scope of re-claiming the house and therefore the people of God. In pursuing this direction the psalm evokes Scriptural traditions that make a similar argument. In particular, we can think of the eschatological traditions in Second Isaiah (40–66), Ezekiel 37–48, and Daniel 7–12, where the sequence of events correlates with Psalm 24. One key aspect, however, that we must develop further from Psalm 24 *vis-à-vis* 1QM 12, is the role that the ethical/religious notions in vv.3–6 play in setting the boundaries of fellowship with God. Different from vv. 1–2 that depict a universal access

---

35 Ibid., 50–52.
36 Ibid., 54.

Prophetic Exegesis in 1QM 12

to God via creation, v. 3 consigns God to a separate holy place (i.e. בהר יהוה and במקום קדשו). Similarly, the DSS assume such a distance between God and the people, and also between the sectarians, as the people of God, and the rest of Israel. We see this separatist move in two particular ways: one is in the belief that the sectarians, as a group, are God's sacred space and the interpretation that they are the generation that God has kept in these latter days. The ensuing examples illustrate these beliefs and how they relate to the vision in 1QM 12.

Psalm 24:3 asks the questions, "Who can ascend to the mount of the Lord? And who can rise in his holy place?" The sacred space in these questions appears in the markers of the mountain of the Lord (הר יהוה) and the holy place (מקום קדשו). The reference to ascending to the "mount of the Lord" is an allusion to the encounter at Sinai (Exod 19; cf. Exod 24:16, 34:4), where God commands to Moses to come up the mountain so that he can receive the instruction from God.

The book of Jubilees (4Q216) begins its re-interpretation of Scriptural traditions exactly with this encounter at Sinai.[37] Jub. 1:1–6 (4Q216 1.4–13) describes that God summoned Moses to the mountain, and revealed to him "the beginning" (הראשונים), "the end things that will come" (ואת אשר יבוא הגיד), and "the divisions of all of the days of Torah and the testimony" (מחלקות העתים לתורה ולתעודה). God also commands Moses to write these things in a book so that "their generations" may know about God's faithfulness. These lines in Jubilees reveal that history is now interpreted with an eschatological language that attempts to unite the past with the future. Also, the language of revelation and the reference to a generation underscore that the instruction that Moses received is not only applicable for what is to come but is something preserved for a group of people. There is a sense of revelation and secrecy, disclosure and concealment as the instruction is given to a few that can decode the times and regulations. The notion of a selected group given God's revelation appears in the Rule Books.

1QS 8 describes the prescriptions that give people access to the Yahad. In it we get a perspective of the sectarian ideology as the members of this community see themselves as the chosen people. In line 5 the Yahad is depicted as a sacred place "an eternal planting," which alludes to Jub. 26:16 and the promise to Abraham. Lines 8–9 add to this description by representing the community as a "holy place for Aaron and those who know the Covenant."

---

37 Another manuscripts that preserves this tradition is 4Q364 14.3, which is the text of Exod 24:12. For its part 4Q364 26.3–9 preserves the tradition in Deut 10:1–4, where Moses is summoned to the mountain and puts God's instruction into an ark of wood.

The Yahad represents a new people, the "blameless and true house in Israel" and the community of the holy (1QS 9.2).

For its part, the Damascus Document also assumes that the sectarians are a holy habitation. CD 3.12–19 discusses how God preserved a remnant of faithful people in these latter days. The key concept within this account is the interpretation that God preserved this people because the rest of Israel had gone astray in the proper observance of the Holy Sabbaths. Line 19 specifically describes this remnant as a "faithful house in Israel" who will inherit eternal life as predicted by the prophet Ezekiel (CD 3.20–21). In addition, 1Q28a 1.1–8 begins by describing the rule that all the congregation of Israel shall observe in the latter days (סרך לכול עדת ישראל באחרית הימים). This rule is to be written and instructed from the "Book of Meditation" (ספר ההגי), and it applies to all the "troops of the congregation" and "any native-born from Israel" (צבאות העדה לכול האזרח בישראל).

The examples from the Rule Books underscore that the sectarians believed that those who observe Torah in the latter days are the ones who can enjoy fellowship with God. The book of Jubilees and the other sectarian texts from the DSS confirm this interpretation, and they move forward by making proper observance of Torah a prerequisite for not only being part of God's home but also the determining factor for remaining in it.

The War Scroll follows this same conviction, as it describes the precepts that the warriors must abide by as they share the "camp" with the holy angels (cf. 1QM 7). In 1QM 12.1–5 we find the confirmation that the obedience to the word of God paid off and the faithful can enjoy fellowship with God in the highest. The allusions to Psalm 24 via the references to the מלך הכבוד and the גבור המלחמה confirm the sectarian belief, that not only is God among them to win the battle on their behalf, but more significantly that they are co-participants, as a holy people, of effecting this victory. This is clearly delineated with the images of the armies as a "cloud that covers the earth," which not only represent a pun on the armies of Gog of Magog (Ezekiel 38), but they further demonstrate that in partnering with God and the holy angels, the sectarian armies become mighty as them. They have come to share not just God's abode, but also the righteous and powerful qualities of God and the angels.

v.   Prophetic Exegesis

The previous discussion has explored some of the most salient intersecting points that 1QM 12.7–18 has with the passages of Scripture. Psalm 24 figures prominently because of the explicit reference to the מלך הכבוד and the

גבור המלחמה in lines 8–9a. Other passages like Ezekiel 38–39 are alluded to in line 9b–10 with the descriptions of the "horsemen." The call to Zion to rejoice and for Jerusalem to shine with jubilation in line 13 echo passages like Isa 40:9, where the prophet announces the news of restoration to the city, and Zech 8:3 (and 9:9) where God returns to inhabit in the holy mountain. The call for the "gates to be perpetually open" recalls the opening of the "eternal gates" for the King of Glory to enter (Ps 24:7–10), and it is a direct allusion of Isa 60:11 where the riches of the nations flow through the gates.

As we come to the end of the analysis not just of 1QM 12.7–18 but, above all, of columns 10–12, the questions that we must address are: How these references culminate this section of the scroll, and what do they reveal about the sectarians and their prophetic use of Scripture? 1QM 12.7–18 demonstrate the prophetic fulfillment of the promises given to Israel, where God takes back what is rightly God's in the same manner to Psalm 24. Whereas the Scriptural poem envisions the eschatological redemption of God's abode via a procession that elevates the "King of Glory," 1QM 12.7–18 foresee God breaking through in a cosmic fashion to overthrow the powerful and reclaim Zion as the holy city. This vision wraps up, in a manner similar to the cosmic conflicts in Scripture and elsewhere in the ancient Near East, with God taking back the holy city and sanctuary in order to live among the chosen people.[38]

Lines 7–10 begin this latter section with a statement that God and the "congregation of the holy ones" assists the army in a show of mockery and derision on the powerful. Not only does this word recall God's presence where God is called upon to provide a blow to Israel's enemies, but it also evokes 1QM 11 where the more powerful enemies are defeated and handed over to the lowly people. There is an interesting strategy in line 8 as it mentions the "mockery and contempt" for the powerful, which is then followed by a pun against the army of Gog of Magog in Ezekiel 38, for it is the army of God, comprised of men and angels, that will cover the earth with judgment. The humiliation of the enemies as well as the empowerment of Israel continue in the subsequent lines.

---

38 In the ancient Near East deities where celebrated following their defeat of the forces of chaos with a procession to the main city. For instance, in the Enuma Elish, Marduk is celebrated as the patron deity with a celebration to Babylon after order to the cosmos is restored. For a good translation of this Akkadian myth, see: Bill T. Arnold and Bryan E. Beyer, eds., *Readings from the Ancient Near East: Primary Sources for Old Testament Study* (Grand Rapids: Baker Academic, 2002), 31–50. The other significant aspect from the ancient Near East is that peace was often times a sign that the cosmos was restored. Thus, 1QM 12 in its joyful depictions of restoration envisions the restoration of the world. For a reading on the topic of peace in the ANE, see: John H. Walton, *Ancient Near Eastern Thought and the Old Testament: Introducing the Conceptual World of the Hebrew Bible* (Grand Rapids: Baker Academic, 2006), 196–199.

Line 10b preserves the references of God as גבור and the "Glorious One" (איש כבוד) and introduces a new title as it calls on the "Doer of Mighty Deeds" (עושי חיל) to intervene. Like the previous columns, lines 11–12a describe God's actions in submitting the forces that threaten the integrity of Israel. The use of key terms that have been continuously used like: "the enemies" (אויבים), "the slain" (מותי חלל), "the adversaries" (צרים) and the "sword that consumes guilty flesh" (חרבכה תואכל בשר אשמה) encapsulate the descriptions of columns 10–11 into these lines. In that process these terms transition into the images of fullness in line 12b, where the land is lavished with richness and God's inheritance (נחל) enjoys all sorts of blessing. The reference to "your inheritance" (נחלתכה) recalls several passages in Scripture where Israel is represented as God's possession (i.e. Exod 15:17; Pss 28:9, 68:10, 74:2, 106:5; Isa 63:7; Joel 2:17; Mic 7:14). The question at this junction is: What does 1QM mean when it uses "your inheritance?" Is it Israel as a nation? Or is this term referring to the sectarians as the "new Israel?"

The immediate context in 1QM 10.8b–18, 11.13–18, and 12.1–5 would suggest that the sectarians are in scope. If we look outside of 1QM, however, "your inheritance" appears in prayers like 1QHa 14 and a communal confession in 4Q393 that expand the scope.[39] In the DSS the word נחלה appears in descriptions of an "inheritance" that the righteous shall receive. 1QS 11.7 describes the "eternal inheritance" that the chosen ones from the Yahad shall receive along with the holy ones. The other example comes in 1QHa 14, where the speaker lays out a prayer that calls on God for deliverance.

1QHa 14 (cf. 4Q428 8; 4Q429 4i, ii) picks up a discussion that started in column 13 where the speaker reflects on the challenges of living justly. The first two lines of this column are fragmentary but line 3 describes that God gave a revelation that brought the speaker to share in the "holy council." This is significant because the rest of the column proceeds from the standpoint of believing in God's promise to this consecrated group. Lines 6–8 go on to describe the hope that God will raise a remnant; specifically, that God will "raise a few survivors from your people and a remnant from your inheritance" (תרים למצער מחיה בעמכה ושארית בנחלתכה, 1QHa 14.11). The parallelism in line 8 places two pairs of concepts; the "survivors from the living" (למצער מחיה) and the "remnant" (שארית) on the one hand, while on the other hand are "your people" (בעמכה) and "your inheritance" (נחלתכה). At *prima facie* this parallelism would suggest that only a few people would be preserved, but the fact that this small group of people would be exalted evinces that they

---

39 4Q364 26c-d.4, which is a reconstruction of Deut 9:27–29 where Moses recalls his intercession for Israel and reminds God that they are God's inheritance. 4Q365 6b.2 (Exod 15:17); 4Q418 81a.3 Lamentation 4Q501 1.2; wisdom teaching 4Q525 14ii.1.

Prophetic Exegesis in 1QM 12

have a special place as line 17 describes them as "princes in the eternal lot" (שריכה בגורל עולם).

Lines 11–14 add that this group will declare God's mighty works and that all the nations will witness God's truth and glory. Further line 18 states that they will be an "eternal plant" (מטעת עולם) that will provide shade to the entire world. And lines 26–35 finish with war depictions that have similarities with 1QM.[40] 1QHa 14 like 1QM 12 hopes for the future that is not reserved solely for the sectarians. Although there is a clear role that this "remnant" plays, the scope of the mission is to fill the earth with the knowledge and truth of God. A similar perspective appears in 4Q493, where the notions of Israel being God's possession and remnant appear.

4Q393 is a communal prayer that revisits God's covenant with Israel.[41] 4Q393 3.2–4 remind God of the promise to keep those who obey the commandments and to not abandon God's "inheritance" despite the fact that they have walked in their own stubbornness. Following this confession, line 5 introduces the turning point where the speaker asks for deliverance. And, like 1QM 12 and 1QHa 14 before, this prayer uses the language of war in lines 7–10 to envision an era where God will snatch the riches of the nations and give them to Israel. Further, 4Q393 illustrates a hope for God's inheritance to transition from their current situation into one that reaches back to the perfect moments with God in Eden. Although 4Q393 does not bear the marks of a sectarian composition like 1QM and the Hodayot, it does share the aspiration that God will use this remnant to lead the people back to God.

This brief discussion of both 1QHa 14 and 4Q393 confirms that the reference to "your inheritance" goes beyond a sectarian scope, but it actually points to God's people, Israel. The key to this term and its use in the vision of 1QM 12.12–13 is that it broadens the scope of the blessing outside of the confines of just the sectarians. Also, whereas the hymn in 1QM 10.8b–18 narrows the scope of the knowledge of God to those who have been endowed with wisdom (i.e. the sectarians), the liturgy in 1QM 12.7b–18 opens the blessing to all Israel. The sectarians as the remnant that God preserved are responsible to win the battle and effect a ministry of truth that will impact all of Israel and usher a time of blessing. This last point leads us into the triumphant procession to Zion in 1QM 12.13b–18.

---

40 In particular, the mention of God's sword brining judgment and the opening of the "eternal gates" (שערי עולם) so the army will cover the earth echo the images in 1QM 11–12.

41 John Emerton, "A Note on Two Words in 4Q393," *Journal of Jewish Studies* 47 (1996): 348–351. Daniel Falk, "Biblical Adaptation in 4Q392 Works of God and 4Q393 Communal Confession," in *The Provo International Conference on the Dead Sea Scrolls*, ed. Donald Parry and Eugene Ulrich (Leiden: Brill, 1999), 126–146.

The tripartite call to Zion, Jerusalem, and the cities of Judah underscores the completeness of the victory and its full impact on Israel. Among the DSS this unique call occurs only here in 1QM 12.13.[42] Elsewhere the references to Zion and Jerusalem appear in the interpretation of the prophecies of Isaiah about a future deliverance. 4Q161 2–6.25–27 interprets the prophecy of Isa 10:28–32 as the moment when God will fight Philistia. 4Q163 2.15–20 is a citation of Isa 30:19–20 where God promises revelation and guidance to the people in Jerusalem that have eaten the bread of affliction. A similar promise takes place in 4Q176 Frg. 8–11.1–2, where the manuscript cites the prophecy of deliverance in Isa 52:1–3.

For its part 4Q177 provides the closest parallel to 1QM 12. In Frg. 12–13 1.10, the manuscript echoes the conflicts that the sons of light will experience at the hand of Belial. Lines 9–11 counter this time of testing with God's sudden intervention that would end the affliction and the righteous will be able to enter the Holy City. Lastly, the command "open your gates continually" in line 14 alludes to Isa 60:11, where the gates will be open so the wealth of the nations may flow into the city. The key to this marker is that it evokes images of God overturning Israel's fortunes and submitting its oppressors to servitude (Isa 60:12–16). Specifically, the description in verse 14 correlate with line 13, where those who afflicted Israel shall bow down and lick the dust of their feet. And like Isa 60:14–22, 1QM 12 also finishes in lines 14–18 with the eternal rule of God and Israel.

In conclusion, 1QM 12.7–18 caps this set of liturgies that began in column 10 with an extraordinary vision of God's victory and celebration in Zion. The images of jubilation in the Holy City following the extermination of Israel's enemies evoke a pattern seen in other prophetic writings, where God submits the forces of chaos and restores order in the universe. The fascinating aspect about this section of the scroll is that it references different passages of Scripture and it uses them prophetically to delineate an eschatological hope for the future. The markers of the מלך הכבוד and the גבור מלחמה partnering with the army to cover the earth like a torrential rain show the conflation of Psalms 24 with Ezekiel 38–39, where the army of God not of Gog of Magog is the one that will prevail. Likewise, the markers of the Hero consuming the wicked with the sword and breaking through the gates so the wealth of the nations can come evokes the prophecies of Isaiah, where God turns the tables in Israel's favor. Perhaps one of the most interesting aspects of these lines is

---

42 In Scripture, Isa 40:9 demonstrates a similar tripartite scope as the prophecy urges Zion and Jerusalem to bless the cities of Judah. Zech 9:9 similarly describe a call to Zion and Jerusalem to celebrate the coming of the king. Verses 13–17 further illustrate the effect that God the king will have in bringing restoration to all the people.

the role that the army plays in bringing blessing to the nation, which underscores that the hopes of this liturgy is for Israel, as God's inheritance, to enjoy an intimacy and richness with God. The implication of this interpretation is that the army in 1QM 12 partners with God to bring the nation back; they are "the chosen ones" who are enlisted with the host of heaven, to exterminate the forces of evil and to bring forth a new era that fulfills the prophetic hopes in Scripture.

This last reflection brings us 11Q5 22 where the poem states that the future of Zion is something that the prophets foresaw. Line 13b–14 states "take the vision spoken of you, the dreams of prophets sought for you! Grow high, spread wide, O Zion!" (קחי חזון דובר עליך וחלמות נביאים תתבעך רומי ורחבי ציון).[43] The future of Zion as depicted in 1QM 12.7b–18 is one that is in line with the aspiration of the prophets for a return to the glory days when the people and their God lived in the city as a sacred space.

c. Summary

1QM 12 is the culmination of the liturgies that began in column 10. As such it illustrates with vivid language the end of the war and a procession to Zion in the manner of the victories of God in Scripture. Lines 1–5 consist of a vision of a heavenly gathering, the only one of this kind in the entire scroll, where the "chosen ones" are among the holy angels. The presence of the elect in the heavenly abode along with the armies of God shows the reversal of fortunes that has taken place from the beginning of column 10 and into column 12. In addition, these columns have shown a trajectory where the warriors in column 10 have been lifted up to share in God' abode in column 12. Also, the references to the "seers" and "hearers" in column 10 become fulfilled in column 12, where the "chosen ones" not only see the holy angels but partake of the parade. Furthermore, the appearance of the "chosen ones" in this gathering and their partnership with the holy angels in lines 7–9, demonstrate the reversal where the meek in column 11 are empowered to defeat the enemy. In essence, the descriptions in lines 1–9 in column 12, demonstrate that the sectarians

---

43 Ruth Henderson, "Structure and Allusion in the *Apostrophe to Zion* (11QPsa 22:1–15), *DSD* 20 (2013): 64–65. In her analysis of this line, Henderson sees that the reference to the "dreams of the prophets" is an allusion to Daniel 9:24 and the eschatological hope for an eternal order to be established in Jerusalem. Matthew Morgenstern, "The Apostrophe to Zion: A Philological and Structural Analysis," *DSD* 14 (2007): 178–198. Morgenstern interprets the use of לקח in the imperative קחי to be forceful. The poet, he adds, not only aspires for the future rebuilding of Jerusalem that is promised in the visions of the prophets, but also urges Jerusalem to actively demand its promised reward. This is perhaps what 1QM 12 envisions, the forceful retake via military prowess of what is God's and the promises given to Israel.

are in scope as the combatants, whose complete dependence on God, makes them not only share in the mysteries of God but also the victories. Likewise, there is also a sense within these lines that God has established these "chosen ones" to not just be a separate people, privileged in their familiarity and knowledge of God, but also are ultimately responsible for leading the armies of God. This last point indicates a possible connection to the book of Daniel and the role of the "wise" (משכלים).

The combination of these descriptions and the reference to a "book" in 1QM 12.2 presents a compelling case that this part of the scroll represents an interpretation of the prophecies of Dan 12:1–4, where the sectarians as the משכלים are the chosen ones who will be redeemed and lead the nation back to a place of intimacy with God. This is not the only time that 1QM taps into the prophecies of Daniel. As we saw before the introduction to the scroll in column 1 predicts the events of the end with the chronology of Daniel 11–12 as the overarching structure. Specifically, the reference to a "time of distress" (עת צרה) and the deliverance that will happen when God breaks the gridlock between the Sons of Light and the Sons of Darkness recorded in 1QM 1.12–16, allude to the prophecies of Daniel and hint early on at the deliverance that we see in full blown in 1QM 12.1–5. Also, the role that the angels play, in particular the archangel Michael during the War Against the Kittim in 1QM 17.6–7, demonstrates that the mysteries of Daniel are foundational to the prophetic interpretation in 1QM, in particular to column 12 and the redemption of Israel through the "chosen ones."

1QM 12.7–18 transition the vantage point from a gathering in heaven to the defeat of the enemy on earth. The prophetic interpretation of Scripture continues but this time rather than focusing on the aspirations of Daniel, the scroll taps into Psalm 24 and the cosmological order that God brings in taking back the city. The eschatological interpretation of Psalm 24 happens with the direct reference to the titles מלך הכבוד and the גבור המלחמה. Although the allusions reveal a direct dependence on this piece, lines 7–10a take on a different direction by alluding to the prophecy of Ezekiel 38–39. Whereas the מלך הכבוד comes to the city to proclaim authority over the city by commanding the doors to open, lines 7–10a demonstrate a partnership in which the horses of the army will cover the earth with power. This interpretive move evinces something that we have seen all along columns 10–12, which is that the sectarians hoped for God to lead them in battle. As such, this hope conflates faith and a bellicose activism that has interpreted the prophecies of Scripture to be taken rather than waited.

Lines 10b–18 wrap up with call on God as the Hero to take the captives

Prophetic Exegesis in 1QM 12   233

and bring prosperity that will flow to the city of God. The tripartite call to
Zion celebrates the prophetic aspirations of Isaiah and Zechariah, where the
city enjoys richness and authority over the enemies. The end of the war is the
restoration of everything that Israel, as God's inheritance, was promised in
Scripture. This vision of restoration culminates what the War Scroll began to
illustrate in 1QM 11.13–18, where the nations will see God's greatness and holiness (cf. 247–258). This last point brings up the implications that this vision
has for the sectarians.

From the outset 1QM set the stage for a war where God will intervene and
break the gridlock between the forces of light and darkness (1QM 1.8–17). If
we keep these descriptions in mind along with the images in columns 11–12,
we can see the sectarian ideology that aspires for the overthrow of God's enemies. The mention of Belial and the powerful enemies in 1QM 11.8–18, coincides with the mention of army of Belial and the companies of Edom, Moab,
Ammon, Assyria, and Philistia in 1QM 1. In addition, the use of the title מלך
הכבוד and its allusion to Psalm 24 in 1QM 12.8–9, underscore that God will
take the city and everything in it as we see in full display in 1QM 12.13–18 (cf.
1QM 19.5–8). These descriptions not only have an impact on the foreign enemies, but it could also have an impact on the locals who assist them. This
points back to 1QM 1, where the "violators of the covenant" (מרשיעי ברית)
are enlisted among the enemies.[44]

In essence, 1QM 11–12 show the fulfillment of the overthrow of the adversaries that the scroll introduces in column 1. The descriptions in these columns emphasize that the retake of Zion, as a microcosm of the earth, signi-
fies the restoration of God's kingdom over the earth. The implication of these
columns for our understanding of the sectarian ideology is that the sectarians
hoped for the consecration of Israel. Just like the book of Daniel foresees that
the משכילים will lead the people back to God, 1QM 12 anticipates that the sectarians, as the "chosen ones," will bring Israel back to God. The sectarian aspiration was therefore to bring a purification of the city and to see the oppressors (i.e. the foreign nations and/or the violators of the covenant) serving the
true people of Israel. The significance of this aspiration was very important
to 1QM in that it repeats the same account in column 19. Therefore, the hope
for the restoration of Zion is fundamental to the religious aspirations that can
only be constructed by a careful study of Scripture that combines prophecy
with liturgy and where God as king of Israel stands supreme.

---

44 The reference to the מרשיעי ברית appears in 1QM and in two apocryphal manuscripts
of Jeremiah: 4Q385 5a–b.8–9 and 4Q387 3.6. In all of these texts the reference are Israelites who
violated God's covenant.

Conclusion

THIS DISSERTATION HAS DEMONSTRATED that 1QM 10–12 interprets the passages of Scripture to embolden the combatants for the future eschatological skirmish. This interpretive approach, which we have labeled as prophetic exegesis, foretells what God will accomplish on the army's behalf as it revisits the past to substantiate these predictions. The citations and allusions spread across these columns work as signs, where the present and the future intersect with the past. The words of Scripture, therefore, become the precepts that have been established in ages past, and that the sectarians decode to discern how they will be used as the future events unfold. The ensuing summary will bring together the main points from each chapter and end with possible new avenues of inquiry on 1QM.

a.   Intertextuality in 1QM

Our reading of 1QM 10–12 used a methodology from the field of literary studies that critics have labeled as intertextuality. Since intertextuality has become this catchall term that often lacks specificity, it was necessary to limits its scope and explain how it can be useful when reading ancient texts like 1QM. Since the 1960s literary critics like Julia Kristeva and Roland Barthes used intertextuality to illustrate the ability that texts have in establishing connections with other works via particular words, expressions, or references. This quality of the text, however, was something that Mikhail Bakhtin had originally described as a dialogical exchange, where works not only reference other works but in doing so they establish connections with other works that are part of the greater whole. This *dialogism*, as Bakhtin labels it, is the result of the interactive quality of language, where any utterance is in constant negotiation with other utterances. The utterance that Bakhtin uses became the "text," first in the hands of Kristeva and then Barthes. Thus, the text in French post-structuralism becomes the locus of meaning where the combination of words, as signs and symbols, create a network of associations. Intertextuality is therefore the study of these associations and dialogical exchange, where the text (as utterance) becomes the intersecting point with other texts (utterances).

But whereas Kristeva and Barthes saw intertextuality as this anonymous exchange, critics like Susan Stanford-Friedman and Nancy K. Miller asserted the authorial voice especially of the female writer to craft her own text. This assertion is an important contribution, because it gives a voice to those authors who have often experienced the silencing of their authorial voice and agency. In addition, it further highlights that the role of the author, especially of those who write from the periphery of the centers of power, is critical to assess not just a particular rhetorical agenda but also how the author introduces her/his own agency into the text.

In a similar fashion, the reading of ancient texts, especially those sectarian works like 1QM, must consider the points where text and author(s) meet and what these connections reveal about the ideological framework that shape the author(s) religious views. Thus, the intertextual exchange that we see in 1QM 10–12 proceeds from the agency of a group of people, whose faith and aspirations look back at the world of Scripture to envision a new age. Also, in presenting their religious views these sectarians went to the level of the "word," to argue that this sign of the past and promise for the future will impact their destiny as a group(s) and of Israel as a people. Thus, to be able to decipher how the sectarians in 1QM tried to push this rhetorical agenda we adopted a two-pronged approach that looked at the sectarians and Scriptural traditions.

The former started from the standpoint that 1QM is a sectarian text like other manuscripts including the Rule Books, the Pesharim, and the Hodayot. Like these other texts 1QM adopts the sacred traditions to demonstrate that the sectarians are the direct recipients of the promises and revelations that God gave to Moses and the Prophets. This is the same direction that we encounter in 1QS 8, as it describes the prophetic foundation of the Yahad, and how CD 1 depicts the preservation of a remnant during the latter days. By asking questions of these texts, we opened a dialogue to observe both the points of convergence and difference that 1QM has with these texts. This dialogue further demonstrated a consistent teaching foundation where the sectarians relied heavily on the words of Scripture.

This brings up the Scriptural trajectory that 1QM takes when adopting a particular tradition. Here we demonstrated that like any other work, 1QM

Conclusion   237

represents one example of how certain traditions evolved. For instance, 1QM 11.6–7 adopts the oracle in Num 24:17–19 as a promise of the military might and victories that Israel, as the sectarian army, will experience. This same prophetic tradition slightly edited appears in the Damascus Document (CD 7.18-21) where the oracle in Numbers predicts the coming of Interpreter of Torah and the Leader of the Congregation. These two passages are but one example among many of how one passage, as text and utterance, changes in its application once it comes in contact with other texts. This diversity of interpretations also suggests that the Scriptural word can have many applications, and that each of these directions depends on the context where the passage appears and the author(s) rhetorical goal.

The combination of sectarian and Scriptural focus offered a more comprehensive view of intertextuality. For it went beyond the mere acknowledgment that the sectarian texts allude to Scripture, but it asked further questions as to how a particular tradition (or *traditum* in the words of Michael Fishbane) evolved into a particular strand. And in this process, it allowed us as readers to view 1QM in a more complex way, where each intertextual exchange is a connection that opens new pathways of inquiry and creates a web of meaning and signification.

In essence, our approach to intertextuality continues with some of the efforts by scholars like George Brooke and Julie Hughes who adopt intertextuality and the study of allusions in their study of the DSS. Our discussion of the feminist intertextuality offers a new insight in that it not only considers intertextuality as the combination of two or more texts as they relate to one another, but in doing so it asks questions of ideology and authorial agency. This is especially important when considering sectarian texts like 1QM because Scripture is adopted to fuel a particular ideology that envisions a future that fits this sectarian hope. In addition, our use of intertextuality offers a new way of thinking about this method, as it underscores that texts do not relate to other works in a vacuum, but they are part of a bigger conversation. Therefore, the DSS with their ability not just to speak to the passages of Scripture but to other sectarian and non-sectarian texts offer a well of opportunities where intertextuality can be a helpful analytical method.

b.   Prophetic Exegesis

The concept of Prophetic Exegesis explains what 1QM does with the passages of Scripture. When 1QM alludes and cites these traditions it interprets these moments as predictions of the future and as tokens of faith that prepare

238   INTERTEXTUALITY AND PROPHETIC EXEGESIS IN THE WAR SCROLL OF QUMRAN

the soldiers for battle. This interpretive approach, however, has its roots in Scripture itself, and also in post-exilic works that carefully interact with the sacred texts as they wrestle with their historical vicissitudes. Michael Fishbane explains this dynamic via the concepts of *traditum* and *traditio,* where a kernel of instruction and/or revelation from Scripture (*traditum*) is revisited by subsequent traditions that seek to not only understand its meaning but ultimately use it for their communities (*traditio*). Daniel 9 is a classic example of these two concepts interacting with one another, as Daniel seeks to understand how Jeremiah's 70-year prophecy (*traditum*) will unfold. Towards the end of this chapter Daniel receives the revelation about how these 70 years, as weeks, will lead to the restoration of Israel. Thus, the prayer of Daniel and the ensuing angelic revelation becomes a *traditio* that ensues from the original engagement with the Scriptural tradition and that spurs other traditions as well such as those that happen in 1 Enoch. Daniel 9 is illustrative also of the fact that in analyzing prophecy some of these post-exilic texts evinced the belief that revelation was never static, but that it was constantly assessed from different vantage points.

The DSS adopt a similar direction as Daniel 9. For instance, the Thematic Pesharim and the Rule Texts underscore that prophetic exegesis was the interpretive direction by which the sectarians viewed the past and were inspired for the future. These sectarian writings demonstrate that textual snippets were used not just as "proof-texts", but as prophetic words and revelation that both foresaw the future and shaped the faith of the sectarians. This is a two-way encounter where the sectarian writing converses with the Scriptural words and introduces new interpretations. And it is also a way that Scripture was foundational to the sectarians. Essentially, prophetic exegesis as we see it in Daniel 9 and in the sectarian texts is the process by which the words from the Scriptures become signs that point to the fulfillment of prophetic reality and tokens that establish the faith of those who study these words. As a result of this interpretive approach, as it is demonstrated in 1QM 10–12, any word from the sacred traditions becomes a prophetic word as both predictive as well as prescriptive.

c.   1QM 10–12 and their Role in the War Scroll

The War Scroll contains two stages in the War of Divisions (1QM 2–9) and the War Against the Kittim (1QM 15–19). Between these two stages, columns 10–14 present an interpretive crux because they are a different type of composition from the other columns in the scroll. Specifically, 1QM 10–12, with their

Conclusion 239

allusions and citations of the Scriptures, present additional questions regarding the interpretation of Scripture and what this approach reveals about the sectarian ideology. Although we have attempted to deal with most of the questions relating to these columns, one final issue that must be addressed pertains to how these texts relate to the overall scope of 1QM.

We believe that the explicit reference to the sacred traditions within 1QM 10–12 underscores that these columns are the prophetic foundation as the war transitions from one stage to the other. Just as the prophecies of Daniel 11–12 set the chronology and establish the faith of the בני אור ("sons of light") in 1QM 1, the collage of prophetic texts in columns 10–12 becomes the evidence from Scripture that God has been with Israel. This in turn will help the sectarians as they move forward in their battle against the Kittim. Also, whereas the precepts from Torah played a major role in the formation and preservation of the army in the War of Divisions (e.g. 1QM 2, 7), in column 10 the scroll transitions into a different stage.

Once the army is formed the priestly prayer in 1QM 10.1–8a caps the War of Divisions with three explicit citations from Deuteronomy and Numbers. These texts not only wrap up the first stage of the war, but in using the words of Moses, as prophetic teaching, they demonstrate a change of scope and interpretive approach where Scripture will become the conduit by which the truths about God and the future plans for Israel are illustrated. This last point becomes apparent in 1QM 10.8b-18, where the hymn asserts that God has chosen the sectarians and has disclosed to them the plans, the seasons, and the mysteries of creation. The election of Israel continues in column 11, where the allusions to the past victories demonstrate that God has indeed kept the promise to protect and deliver them from their enemies. The oracle of Num 24:17–19 (1QM 11. 6-7) and the prophecy of Isa 31:8 (1QM 11.11–12a) serve not only as evidence that God kept the promises, but they also prove that God will act on behalf of the sectarians. The final vision in column 12 wraps up this image of the future success that will come to the sectarian army with a procession to Zion. Thus, from columns 10–12 we have a trace of election and promise, prophecy and vision that underscore that the sectarians will, via God's strength and power, succeed in the battle against the Kittim.

1QM 10–12 are the religious evidence that the sectarians draw from the passages of Scripture to believe that the looming battle against the Kittim is in God's hands. These columns are fundamental to demonstrate the transition from one stage of the war to the next. And they provide the first indication that the scroll goes from the prescriptive use of Scripture in the formation of the army, to the hortatory interpretation of Scripture via prayer, hymns, and prophecy. This style will continue in the subsequent columns, especially in the War Against the Kittim where the High Priest continually exhorts the combatants.

d. Next Steps in the Study of 1QM

The study of 1QM 10–12 has demonstrated the interpretive approach that the sectarians used when they read the current events in light of the predictions and prescriptions from Scripture. From the initial priestly prayer and call to action in column 10 to the procession to Zion in column 12, these passages rely heavily on the sacred traditions to establish the faith of the combatants and envision a future in Zion. Although scholars since Jean Carmignac have already observed the allusive character of these columns, most of the discussion has remained in ascertaining the extent to which 1QM uses the Scriptural passages and what these uses reveal about possible hermeneutical directions taken by the author(s) of the scroll.

We have attempted to go beyond the mere identification of the citations and allusions to Scripture within these columns and argue that in bringing these traditions, 1QM 10–12 establish a dialogue where we witness a sectarian interpretation via prophetic exegesis. In particular, these three columns have forced us to go at the level of the word to fully grasp how key expressions, as markers loaded with religious significance, become the intersecting points between this manuscript and other texts. Thus, the word in the War Scroll, as an utterance and confession of faith, became the center where our inquiry focused. It is at the intersection of the axes of sectarian and Scriptural traditions where we can observe not only a possible influence but how these columns both align and diverge with other sectarian texts and Scripture. The other significance of this study is that it has gone beyond the labels of "pesher" or "midrash" to describe and encapsulate the type of exegesis evinced in these columns. In adopting "prophetic exegesis" we have placed an emphasis on the dual quality of prophecy to both exhort and predict as well as to teach and align the people to a set of core cultic and ethical values. Likewise, prophetic exegesis has allowed us to use a methodological approach that could encompass other words, beyond פשר and דרש, that are also significant in ascertaining how the sectarians interacted with Scripture as instruction, wisdom, prophecy, and ultimately a celebration of God and Israel.

This last point brings us to possible new avenues of inquiry that go beyond 1QM 10–12 but into the War Scroll and other war texts among the DSS. Since its discovery in 1948 scholars like Jean Carmignac and Yigael Yadin have

Conclusion   241

worked to reconstruct and translate this manuscript. These early efforts were followed by other contributions in the form of commentaries and noted translations, where authors like Bastian Jongeling and J. van der Ploeg analyzed the scroll and commented on its structure line by line. For his part Philip Davies and more recently Brian Schultz sought to find the compositional layers in 1QM to propose a possible redactional history. In the case of Schultz, he not only pursued a redactional history of 1QM, but he also made the case to read it in its final form. Todd A. Scacewater picked up this proposal and advocated for a unified reading of 1QM in its extant form. We use this brief chronology to argue that we are at the point where we can produce a work that reads 1QM in its final form and clearly demonstrates how the seemingly disjointed parts of this scroll come together. This effort can now be aided by reading other war texts in Cave 4 and Cave 11. The manuscripts 4Q285 and 4Q491–495 not only attest to a holy war ideology among the sectarians, but they also evince their own use and interpretation of prophecy. They like 1QM see in the words of Scripture the signs of the future and the prescriptions that should steer the combatants not only as they wait for a final battle but in how they should align with the cultic precepts adopted by the sectarians. The same can be said of 11Q14 who like its counterparts envisions via the prophecies of Scripture a turn of events and an age where God is glorified, and Israel is restored.

Lastly, the studies of the different manuscripts can be put together into a piece that explores the role that the prophecies and teachings of the sacred traditions played in eliciting a holy war ideology among these sectarians. This in turn can inform how millenarian and other sectarian groups also adopted fundamental teachings to espouse, not just a war posture, but a worldview that sees any difference and deviation from these teachings as threats that need to be eradicated with violence or isolation. The opportunities for study of the War Scroll are many, especially when it comes to how this manuscript, like the other extant copies in the DSS, handle the core teachings of Scripture to establish and expand an ideological view of the future in light of the past.

Bibliography

Allen, Graham. *Intertextuality*. New York: Routledge, 2011.

Allegro, John M. and Arnold Anderson. *Qumrân Cave 4.I (4Q158–4Q186). Discoveries in the Judean Desert 5*. Oxford: Clarendon Press, 1968.

Alter, Robert. *The Art of Biblical Poetry*. Edinburgh: T&T Clark, 1990.

Amit, Yairah. "The Role of Prophecy and Prophets in the Chronicler's World." Pages 80–101 in *Prophets, Prophecy, and Prophetic Texts in Second Temple Judaism*. Edited by Michael H. Floyd and Robert D. Haak. New York: T&T Clark, 2006.

Angel, Joseph. "The Liturgical-Eschatological Priest of the Self-Glorification Hymn." *Revue de Qumrân* 24 (2010): 585–605.

Arnold, Bill T. and Bryan E. Beyer, eds., *Readings from the Ancient Near East: Primary Sources for Old Testament Study*. Grand Rapids: Baker Academic, 2002.

Aune, David E. *Prophecy in Early Christianity and the Ancient Mediterranean World*. Grand Rapids: Eerdmans, 1983.

_____. "Charismatic Exegesis in Early Judaism and Early Christianity." Pages 126–150 in *The Pseudepigrapha and Early Biblical Interpretation*. Edited by J.H. Charlesworth and C.A. Evans. Sheffield: JSOT Press, 1993.

Baillet, Maurice. *Qumrân Grotte 4.III (4Q482-4Q520). Discoveries in the Judean Desert 7*. Oxford: Clarendon Press, 1982.

Bakhtin, Mikhail. *The Dialogic Imagination: Four Essays*. Edited by Michael Holquist. Translated by Caryl Emerson and Michael Holquist. Austin: University of Texas Press, 1981.

Barthes, Roland. *Image, Music, Text*. Translated by Stephen Heath. London: Fontana, 1977.

Batsch, Christophe. "Priests in Warfare in Second Temple Judaism: 1QM, or the Anti-Phinehas." Pages 165–178 in *Qumran Cave 1 Revisited Texts from Cave 1 Sixty Years After Their Discovery: Proceedings of the Sixth Meeting of the IOQS in Ljubljana*. Edited by Daniel K. Falk, Sarianna Metso, Donald W. Parry and Eibert J.C Tigchelaar. Leiden: Brill, 2010.

Baumgarten, Albert I. "The Name of the Pharisees." *Journal of Biblical Literature* 102 (1983): 411–428.

Baumgarten, Joseph M. "The Calendars of the Book of Jubilees and the Temple Scroll," *Vetus Testamentum* 37 (1987): 71–78.

Beale, Gregory K. *The Use of Daniel in Jewish Apocalyptic Literature and in the Revelation of St. John*. Lanham: University Press of America, 1984.

Beentjes, Pancratius. "War Narratives in the Book of Chronicles: A New Proposal in Respect of their Function." *Hervormde Teologiese Studies* 59 (2003): 587–596.

Ben-Dov, Jonathan. "The Elohistic Psalter and the Writing of Divine Names at Qumran." Pages 79–104 in *The Dead Sea Scrolls and Contemporary Culture: Proceedings of the International Conference Held at the Israel Museum, Jerusalem (July 6-8, 2008)*. Edited by Adolfo D. Roitman, Lawrence H. Schiffman and Shani Tzoref. Leiden: Brill, 2011.

Ben-Porat, Ziva. "The Poetics of Literary Allusion," *PTL: A Journal for Descriptive Poetics and Theory of Literature* 1 (1976): 105–128.

Bergsma, John S. "Qumran Self-identity: 'Israel' or 'Judah'?." *Dead Sea Discoveries* 15 (2008): 172–189.

Bernstein, Moshe. "Scriptures: Quotation and Use." Pages 839–842 in *Encyclopedia of the Dead Sea Scrolls*. Edited by Lawrence H. Schiffman and James C. VanderKam. Oxford: Oxford University Press, 2000.

Berrin (Tzoref), Shani. "Qumran Pesharim." Pages 134–157 in *Biblical Interpretation at Qumran*. Edited by Matthias Henze. Grand Rapids: Eerdmans, 2005.

Beyerle, Stefan. "'A Star Shall Come Out of Jacob': A Critical Evaluation of the Balaam Oracle in the Context of Jewish Revolts in Roman Times." Pages 163–188 in *The Prestige of the Pagan Prophet Balaam in Judaism, Early Christianity and Islam*. Edited by George H. van Kooten and J.T.A.G.M. van Ruiten. Leiden: Brill, 2008.

Blenkinsopp, Joseph. *Prophecy and Canon*. Notre Dame: University of Notre Dame Press, 1977.

Boyarin, Daniel. *Intertextuality and the Reading of Midrash*. Bloomington: Indiana University Press, 1994.

Brenner, Martin. *The Song of the Sea: Exodus 15:1–21*. Berlin: De Gruyter, 1991.

Brooke, George J. "Qumran Pesher: Towards the Redefinition of a Genre," *Revue de Qumrân* 10 (1981): 483–503.

———. *Exegesis at Qumran: 4QFlorelegium in The Jewish Context. Journal for the Study of the Old Testament Supplement Series* 29. Edited by David J. A. Clines and Philip R. Davies. Sheffield: JSOT Press, 1985.

———. "The Explicit Presentation of Scripture in 4QMMT." Pages 67–88 in *Legal Texts and Legal Issues: Proceedings of the Second Meeting of the International Organization for Qumran Studies*. Edited by Moshe Bernstein, Florentino García Martínez, and John Kampen. Leiden: Brill, 1997.

———. "Thematic Commentaries on Prophetic Scriptures." Pages 134–157 in *Biblical Interpretation at Qumran*. Edited by Matthias Henze. Grand Rapids: Eerdmans, 2005.

_____. "Prophecy and Prophets in the Dead Sea Scrolls: Looking Backwards and For-wards." Pages 151–165 in *Prophets, Prophecy, and Prophetic Texts in Second Temple Judaism*. Edited by Michael H. Floyd and Robert D. Haak. New York: T&T Clark, 2006.

_____. *Reading the Dead Sea Scrolls: Essays in Method*. Atlanta: Society of Biblical Literature, 2013.

Brownlee, William H. *The Midrash Pesher Habakkuk*. Atlanta: Scholars Press, 1979.

Campbell, Jonathan G. *The Use of Scripture in the Damascus Document 1-8, 19–20*. New York: De Gruyter, 1995.

Carmignac, Jean. "Les citations de l'Ancien Testament dans la Guerre des Fils de lu-mière contre les Fils de Ténèbres." *Revue Biblique* 63 (1956): 234–260.

_____. *La Règle de la Guerre Des Fils de Lumière Contre les Fils de T*énèbres. Paris: Letouzey et Ané, 1958.

_____. "Le document de Qumrân sur Melkisédeq," *Revue de Qumrân* 7 (1969–71): 342–378.

Chazon, Esther G. "Is Divrei Ha-me'orot a Sectarian Prayer?" Pages 3–17 in *The Dead Sea Scrolls: Forty Years of Research*. Edited by Uriel Rappaport and Devorah Dimant. Leiden: Brill, 1992.

_____. "Liturgical Communion with the Angels at Qumran." Pages 95–105 in *Sapiential, Liturgical and Poetical Texts from Qumran*. Edited by Daniel K. Falk, Florentino García Martínez, and Eileen Schuller. Leiden: Brill, 2000.

_____. "Lowly to Lofty: The Hodayot's use of Liturgical Traditions to Shape Sectarian Identity and Religious Experience." *Revue de Qumrân* 26 (2013): 3–19.

_____. "Prayer and Identity in Varying Contexts: The Case of the Words of the Luminaries." *Journal for the Study of Judaism* 46 (2015): 484–511.

Clines, David. "A World Established On Water (Psalm 24): Reader-Response, Deconstruction and Bespoke Interpretation." Pages 79–90 in *The New Literary Criticism and the Hebrew Bible*. Edited by J. Cheryl Exum and David J. A. Clines. Sheffield: JSOT Press, 1993.

Collins, John J. "The Mythology of Holy War in Daniel and the Qumran War Scroll: A Point of Transition in Jewish Apocalyptic." *Vetus Testamentum* 25 (1975): 596–612.

_____. *Apocalypticism in the Dead Sea Scrolls*. London: Routledge, 1997.

_____. "Powers in Heaven: God, Gods, and Angels in the Dead Sea Scrolls." Pages 9–28 in *Religion in the Dead Sea Scrolls*. Edited by John J. Collins and Robert A. Kugler. Grand Rapids: Eerdmans, 2000.

_____. *Beyond the Qumran Community*. Grand Rapids: Eerdmans, 2010.

Cook, Edward. "What did the Jews of Qumran Know about God and How Did They Know It?: Revelation and God in the Dead Sea Scrolls." Pages 3–22 in *Judaism in Late Antiquity: A Systemic Reading of the Dead Sea Scrolls*. Edited by Alan J. Avery-Peck, Jacob Neusner, and Bruce D. Chilton. Leiden: Brill, 2001.

Cook, Stephen L. *The Apocalyptic Literature*. Nashville: Abingdon Press, 2003.

_____. *On the Question of the "Cessation of Prophecy" in Ancient Judaism*. Texte und Studien zum antiken Judentum 145. Tübingen: Mohr Siebeck, 2011.

Cross, Frank Moore. "The Priestly Tabernacle in the Light of Recent Research." Pages 169–178 in *Temples and High Places in Biblical Times*. Edited by Avraham Biran. Jerusalem: Hebrew Union College-Jewish Institute of Religion, 1981.

Crouch, Carly. "Made in the Image of God: The Creation of אדם, the Commissioning of the King and the Chaoskampf of Yhwh." *JANER* 16 (2016): 1–21.

Cudworth, Troy. *War in Chronicles: Temple Faithfulness and Israel's Place in the Land*. London: Bloomsbury T&T Clark, 2016.

Culler, Jonathan. *The Pursuit of Signs: Semiotics, Literature, Deconstruction*. Ithaca: Cornell University Press, 1981.

Davis, Ellen. "'And Pharaoh Will Change His Mind...' (Ezekiel 32:31): Dismantling Mythical Discourse." Pages 224–239 in *Theological Exegesis: Essays in Honor of Brevard S. Childs*. Edited by Christopher R. Seitz and Kathryn Greene-Mc-Creight. Grand Rapids: Eerdmans, 1999.

Davies, Philip R. *1QM, the War Scroll from Qumran: Its Structure and History*. Rome: Biblical Institute Press, 1977.

———. "'Old' and 'New' Israel in the Bible and the Qumran Scrolls: Identity and Difference." Pages 33–42 in *Defining Identities: We, You, and the Other in the Dead Sea Scrolls*. Edited by Florentino Garcia Martinez and Mladen Popović. Leiden: Brill, 2008.

DeClaisse-Walford, Nancy. "An Intertextual Reading of Psalms 22, 23, and 24." Pages 139–152 in *The Book of Psalms: Composition and Reception*. Edited by Peter W. Flint, Patrick D. Miller, Aaron Brunell, and Ryan Roberts. Leiden: Brill, 2005.

Dillard, Raymond. "The Literary Structure of the Chronicler's Solomon Narrative." *Journal for the Study of the Old Testament* 30 (1984): 85–93.

Dimant, Devorah. "The Hebrew Bible in the Dead Sea Scrolls: Torah Quotations in the Damascus Covenant." Pages 113–122 in *'Sha'arei Talmon': Studies in the Bible, Qumran, and the Ancient Near East presented to Shemaryahu Talmon*. Edited Michael Fishbane, Emanuel Tov, and Weston W. Fields. Winona Lake: Eisenbrauns, 1992.

———. "Men as Angels: The Self-Image of the Qumran Community." Pages 93–103 in *Religion and Politics in the Ancient Near East*. Edited by Adele Berlin. Bethesda: University of Maryland Press, 1995.

———. "The Blessing of Judah in 4Q252." Pages 250–260 in *Studies in the Hebrew Bible, Qumran, and the Septuagint Presented to Eugene Ulrich*. Edited by James C. VanderKam, Peter W. Flint and Emanuel Tov. Boston: Brill, 2006.

———. "Sectarian and Non-Sectarian Texts from Qumran: The Pertinence and Usage of a Taxonomy." *Revue de Qumrân* 24 (2009): 7–18.

———. *History, Ideology and Bible Interpretation in the Dead Sea Scrolls. Forschungen zum Alten Testament* 90. Tübingen: Mohr Siebeck, 2014.

Duhaime, Jean. "La Règle de la Guerre de Qumrân et l'apocalyptique." *Science et Esprit* 36 (1984): 67–88.

———. *The War Texts: 1QM and Related Manuscripts*. London: T&T Clark, 2004.

Dupont-Sommer, André. "'Règlement de la guerre des fils de lumière': traduction et notes." *Revue de l'histoire des religions* 148 (1955): 141–180.

Eisenman, Robert. "Eschatological "Rain" Imagery in the War Scroll from Qumran and in the Letter of James." *Journal of Near Eastern Studies* 49 (1990): 173–184.

Ellis, Edward. *Prophecy and Hermeneutic in Early Christianity.* Grand Rapids: Eerdmans, 1978.

Emerton, John. "A Note on Two Words in 4Q393." *Journal of Jewish Studies* 47 (1996): 348–351.

Endres, John. "Theology of Worship in Chronicles." Pages 165–188 in *The Chronicler as Theologian: Essays in Honor of Ralph W. Klein.* Edited by M. Patrick Graham, Steven L. McKenzie and Gary N. Knoppers. New York: T&T Clark, 2003.

Fishbane, Michael. *Biblical Interpretation in Ancient Israel.* New York: Oxford University Press, 1985.

Eshel, Esther and Hanan Eshel. "Recensions of the War Scroll." Pages 352–356 in *The Dead Sea Scrolls Fifty Years After Their Discovery: Proceedings of the Jerusalem Congress, July 20-25, 1997.* Edited by Lawrence H. Schiffman, Emanuel Tov, James C. VanderKam, and Galen Marquis. Jerusalem: Israel Exploration Society, 2000.

Eshel, Hanan. "The Kittim in the War Scroll and in the Pesharim." Pages 29–44 in *Historical Perspectives: From the Hasmoneans to Bar Kokhba in Light of the Dead Sea Scrolls.* Edited by D. Goldblatt, A. Pinnick, and D.R. Schwartz. Leiden: Brill, 2001.

Evans, Craig A. *Opposition to the Temple: Jesus and the Dead Sea Scrolls.* New York: Doubleday, 1992.

_____. "David in the Dead Sea Scrolls." Pages 183–197 in *The Scrolls and the Scriptures: Qumran Fifty Years After.* Edited by Stanley E. Porter and Craig A. Evans. Sheffield: Sheffield Academic Press, 1997.

Fabry, Heinz-Josef. "Priests at Qumran: A Reassessment." Pages 243–262 in *The Dead Sea Scrolls: Texts and Context.* Edited by Charlotte Hempel. Leiden: Brill, 2010.

Falk, Daniel. *Daily, Sabbath and Festival Prayers in the Dead Sea Scrolls.* Leiden: Brill, 1998.

Falk, Daniel. "Biblical Adaptation in 4Q392 Works of God and 4Q393 Communal Confession." Pages in 126–146 in *The Provo International Conference on the Dead Sea Scrolls.* Edited by Donald Parry and Eugene Ulrich. Leiden: Brill, 1999.

_____. "Qumran Prayer Texts and the Temple." Pages 106–126 *Sapiential, Liturgical and Poetical Texts from Qumran: Proceedings of the Third Meeting of the International Organization for Qumran Studies, Oslo, 1998.* Edited by Daniel K. Falk, Florentino García Martínez and Eileen Schuller. Leiden: Brill, 2000.

Fitzmyer, Joseph A. *Essays on the Semitic Background of the New Testament.* London: Geoffrey Chapman, 1971.

Flint, Peter W. "The Daniel Tradition at Qumran." Pages 359–397 in *The Book of Daniel: Composition and Reception.* Edited by John Collins and Peter Flint. Leiden: Brill, 2001.

_____. "The Prophet David at Qumran." Pages 158–167 in *Biblical Interpretation at Qumran.* Edited by Matthias Henze. Grand Rapids: Eerdmans, 2005.

Flusser, David. *Qumran and Apocalypticism*. Translated by Azzan Yadin. Grand Rapids: Eerdmans, 2007.

Fischer, Georg. "Das Schilfmeerlied Exodus 15 in Seinem Kontext" *Biblica*, 77 (1996): 32–47.

Flint, Peter. "The Prophet David at Qumran." Pages 158–167 in *Biblical Interpretation at Qumran*. Edited by Matthias Henze. Grand Rapids: Eerdmans, 2005.

García Martínez, Florentino. *Qumran and Apocalyptic. Studies on the Texts of the Desert of Judah* 9. Leiden: Brill, 1992.

_____. *The Dead Sea Scrolls Translated: The Qumran Texts in English*. Grand Rapids: Eerdmans, 1996.

_____. "Balaam in the Dead Sea Scrolls. Pages 163–188 in *The Prestige of the Pagan Prophet Balaam in Judaism, Early Christianity and Islam*. Edited by George H. van Kooten and J.T.A.G.M. van Ruiten. Leiden: Brill, 2008.

––– and A.S. van der Woude. "A 'Groningen' Hypothesis of Qumran Origins and Early History." *Revue de Qumrân* 14 (1990): 521–541.

–––, Eibert J.C. Tigchelaar, and Adam S. van der Woude. *Qumran Cave 11.II: (11Q2–18, 11Q20–31)*. Discoveries in the Judean Desert 23. Oxford: Clarendon Press, 1998.

Gmirkin, Russell. "Historical Allusions in the War Scroll." *Dead Sea Discoveries* 5 (1998): 172–214.

Goodman, Martin Goodman. "The Qumran Sectarians and the Temple in Jerusalem." Pages 263–273 in *Dead Sea Scrolls: Texts and Context*. Edited by Charlotte Hempel. Leiden: Brill, 2010.

Gottstein, Moshe. "Bible Quotations in the Sectarian Dead Sea Scrolls," *Vetus Testamentum* 3 (1953): 80–92.

Goulder, M.D. "David and Yahweh in Psalms 23 and 24." *Journal for the Study of the Old Testament* 30 (2006): 463–473.

Green, Dennis. "Divine Names: Rabbinic and Qumran Scribal Techniques." Pages 497–511 in *The Dead Sea Scrolls Fifty Years After Their Discovery*. Edited by Lawrence H. Schiffman, Emanuel Tov, James C. VanderKam, and Galen Marquis. Jerusalem: Israel Exploration Society, 2000.

Grossman, Maxine L. *Reading for History in the Damascus Document: A Methodological Method*. Leiden: Brill, 2002.

Harkins, Angela. "Elements of the Fallen Angels Traditions in the Qumran Hodayot." Pages 8–24 in *The Fallen Angels Traditions: Second Temple Developments and Reception History*. Edited by Angela Kim Harkins, Kelley Coblentz Bautch, and John C. Endres. Washington: Catholic Biblical Association of America, 2014.

Harrington, Daniel. "The Ideology of Rule in Daniel 7–12." *Society of Biblical Literature Seminar Papers* 38 (1999): 540–551.

Hempel, Charlotte. *The Laws of the Damascus Document: Sources, Tradition and Redaction*. Leiden: Brill, 1998.

_____. *The Damascus Texts*. Sheffield, England: Sheffield Academic Press, 2000.

_____. "Do the Scrolls Suggest Rivalry Between the Sons of Aaron and the Sons of Zadok and If So Was It Mutual?" *Revue de Qumrân* 24 (2009): 135–153.

_____. *The Qumran Rule Texts in Context.* Texte und Studien zum antiken Judentum 154. Tübingen: Mohr Siebeck, 2013.

Henderson, Ruth. "Structure and Allusion in the *Apostrophe to Zion* (11QPs^a 22:1–15)." *Dead Sea Discoveries* 20 (2013): 64–65.

Hughes, Julie A. *Scriptural Allusions and Exegesis in the Hodayot.* Studies on the Texts of the Desert of Judah 59. Leiden: Brill, 2006.

Hunter, Alastair. "'The Righteous Generation': The Use of Dôr in Psalms 14 and 24." Pages 187–205 in *Reflection and Refraction: Studies in Biblical Historiography in Honour of A. Graeme Auld.* Edited by Robert Rezetko, Timothy Lim, and Brian Aucker. Leiden: Brill, 2006.

Jakobson, Román. "Two Aspects of Language and Two Types of Aphasic Disturbances." Pages 95–114 in *Fundamentals of Language.* The Hague: Mouton, 1956.

Jarick, John. "The Bible's 'Festival Scrolls' Among the Dead Sea Scrolls." Pages 170–182 in *The Scrolls and the Scriptures: Qumran Fifty Years After.* Edited by Stanley Porter and Craig Evans. Sheffield: Sheffield University Press, 1997.

Jassen, Alex P. *Mediating the Divine: Prophecy and Revelation in the Dead Sea Scrolls and Second Temple Judaism.* Studies on the Texts of the Desert of Judah 68. Leiden: Brill, 2007.

_____. "Re-Reading 4QPesher Isaiah A (4Q161). Forty Years After DJD V." Pages 57–90 in *The Mermaid and the Partridge: Essays from the Copenhagen Conference on Revising Texts from Cave Four.* Edited by George Brooke and Jesper Høgenhaven. Leiden: Brill, 2011.

Jokiranta, Jutta. "'Sectarianism' of the Qumran 'Sect': Sociological Notes." *Revue de Qumrân* 20 (2001): 223–239.

Jongeling, Bastiaan. *Le rouleau de la guerre des manuscrits de Qumrân.* Assen: Van Gorcum, 1962.

Kampen, John. "The Eschatological Temple(s) of 11QT." Pages 85–97 in *Pursuing the Text: Studies in Honor of Ben Zion Wacholder.* Edited by John Kampen and John Reeves. Sheffield: Sheffield Academic Press, 1994.

Kapfer, Hilary Evans. "The Relationship between the Damascus Document and the Community Rule: Attitudes Toward the Temple as a Test Case," *Dead Sea Discoveries* 14 (2007): 152–177.

Katzin, David. "The Time of Testing': The Use of Hebrew Scriptures in 4Q171's Pesher of Psalm 37." *Hebrew Studies* 45 (2004): 121–162.

_____. "The Use of Scripture in 4Q175." *Dead Sea Discoveries* 20 (2013): 200–236.

_____. "A Paradigm for Identifying the Use of Scriptural Allusion in Lemma-Based Exegesis within the Qumran Library using 4QpPsa (4Q171) As an Example." *Hebrew Union College Annual* 87 (2016): 61–92.

Klein, Anja. "Hymn and History in Ex 15: Observations on the Relationship Between Temple Theology and Exodus Narrative in the Song of the Sea." *Zeitschrift für die alttestamentliche Wissenschaft* 124 (2012): 516–527.

Knibb, Michael A. *The Qumran Community.* Cambridge: Cambridge University Press, 1987.

Knoppers, Gary. "Jerusalem at War in Chronicles." Pages 57–76 in *Zion, City of Our God.* Edited by Richard S. Hess and Gordon J. Wenham. Grand Rapids: Eerdmans, 1999.

———. "Battling Against Yahweh': Israel's War Against Judah in 2 Chr 13:2–20." *Revue Biblique* 100 (1993): 511–532.

Klein, Ralph. "Psalms in Chronicles." *Currents in Theology and Mission* 32 (2005): 264–275.

Knut Heim, "The (God-)Forsaken King of Psalm 89: A Historical and Intertextual Enquiry." Pages 296–322 in *King and Messiah in Israel and the Ancient Near East: Proceedings of the Oxford Old Testament Seminar.* Edited by John Day. Sheffield: Sheffield University Press, 1998.

Kooij, Arie van der. "Authoritative Scriptures and Scribal Culture." Pages 55–71 in *Authoritative Scriptures in Ancient Judaism.* Edited by Mladen Popovic. Boston: Brill, 2010.

Krieg, Matthias. "Mo'ed Naqam - ein Kulturdrama aus Qumran: Beobachtungen an der Kriegsrolle," *Theologische Zeitschrift* 41 (1985): 3–30.

Kristeva, Julia. *Desire in Language: A Semiotic Approach to Literature and Art.* Edited by Leon S. Roudiez. New York: Columbia University Press, 1980.

Kugel, James L. *The Bible As It Was.* Cambridge: Belknap Press of Harvard University Press, 1997.

———. "The Beginnings of Biblical Interpretation." In *A Companion to Biblical Interpretation in Early Judaism.* Edited by Matthias Henze, 3-26. Grand Rapids: Eerdmans, 2012.

Larsen, David. "Angels Among Us: the use of Old Testament Passages as Inspiration for Temple Themes in the Dead Sea." *Studies in the Bible and Antiquity* 5 (2013): 91–110.

Larson, Erik, Lawrence Schiffman, and John Strugnell, "4Q470 Preliminary Publication of a Fragment Mentioning Zedekiah." *Revue de Qumrân* 16 (1994): 335–349.

Lim, Timothy H. "Midrash Pesher in the Pauline Letters." Pages 280–292 in *The Scrolls and the Scriptures: Qumran Fifty Years After.* Edited by Stanley Porter and Craig Evans. Sheffield: Sheffield Academic Press, 1997.

———. "Kittim." Pages 496–471 in *Encyclopedia of the Dead Sea Scrolls.* Edited by Lawrence Schiffman and James VanderKam. Oxford: Oxford University Press, 2000.

———. *Pesharim.* Sheffield: Sheffield Academic Press, 2002.

———. "All These He Composed through Prophecy." Pages 61–73 in *Prophecy after the Prophets? The Contribution of the Dead Sea Scrolls to the Understanding of Biblical and Extra-Biblical Prophecy.* Edited by Kristin de Troyer and Armin Lange. Leuven: Peeters, 2009.

Lust, J. L. "Quotation Formulae and Canon in Qumran." Pages 79–93 in *Canonization and Decanonization: Papers Presented to the International Conference of the Leiden Institute for the Study of Religions (LISOR), Held at Leiden 9-10 January 1997.* Edited by A. Van der Kooij and K. Van der Toorn. Leiden: Brill, 1998.

Machacek, Gregory. "Allusion." *Publications of the Modern Language Association of America* 122 (2007): 522–536.

Manzi, Franco. *Melchisedek e t'angelotogia nell'epistola agli Ebrei e a Qumran*. Rome: Pontifical Biblical Institute, 1997.

Marzouk, Safwat. *Egypt as a Monster in the Book of Ezekiel*. Vol. 76 of *Forschungen zum Alten Testament*. Tübingen: Mohr Siebeck, 2015.

Menken, Maarten. "Genesis in John's Gospel and 1 John." Pages 83–98 in *Genesis in the New Testament*. Edited by Maarten Menken and Steve Moyise. New York: T&T Clark, 2012.

Metso, Sarianna. "The Use of Old Testament Quotations in the Qumran Community Rule." Pages 217–231 in *Qumran Between the Old and New Testaments*. Edited by Frederick H. Cryer and Thomas L. Thompson. Sheffield: Sheffield Academic Press, 1998.

Metzger, Bruce. "The Formulas Introducing Quotations of Scripture in the NT and the Mishnah," *Journal of Biblical Literature* 70 (1951): 297–307.

Miller, Nancy K. "Changing the Subject: Authorship, Writing, and the Reader." Pages 102–120. *Feminist Studies - Critical Studies*. Edited by Teresa de Lauretis. Bloomington: Indiana University Press, 1986.

_____. "Arachnologies: The Woman, the Text, and the Critic." Pages 77–101 in *The Poetics of Gender*. Edited by Nancy K. Miller. New York: Columbia University Press, 1986.

Morawski, Stefan. "The Basic Functions of Quotation." Pages 690–705 in *Sign, Language, Culture*. Edited by A.J. Greimas et al. The Hague: Mouton, 1970.

Morgenstern, Matthew. "The Apostrophe to Zion: A Philological and Structural Analysis." *Dead Sea Discoveries* 14 (2007): 178–198.

Newsom, Carol. "Apocalyptic Subjects: Social Construction of the Self in the Qumran Hodayot." *Journal for the Study of the Pseudepigrapha* 12 (2001): 3–35.

Nissim Amzallag, Gérard. "The Subversive Dimension of the Story of Jehoshaphat's War Against the Nations (2 Chron 20:1–30)." *Biblical Interpretation* 24 (2016): 178–202.

Nissinen, Martti. "Pesharim as Divination. Qumran Exegesis, Omen Interpretation and Literary Prophecy." Pages 43–60 in *Prophecy after the Prophets? The Contribution of the Dead Sea Scrolls to the Understanding of Biblical and Extra-Biblical Prophecy*. Edited by Kristin de Troyer and Armin Lange. Leuven: Peeters, 2009.

Nitzan, Bilhan. *Qumran Prayer and Religious Poetry*. Studies on the Texts of the Desert of Judah 12. Leiden: Brill, 1994.

North, Robert. "'Kittim' War or 'Sectaries' Liturgy?" *Biblica* 39 (1958): 84–93.

Olyan, Saul. "The Exegetical Dimensions of Restrictions on the Blind and the Lame in Texts from Qumran." *Dead Sea Discoveries* 8 (2001): 46–50.

O'Neill, John. "'Who is Comparable to Me in My Glory?': 4Q491 Fragment 11 (4Q491C) and the New Testament." *Novum Testamentum* 42 (2000): 24–38.

Osten-Sacken, Peter von der. *Gott und Belial: Traditionsgeschichtliche Untersuchungen zum Dualismus in den Texten aus Qumran*. Gottingen: Vandenhoeck & Ruprecht, 1969.

Pagels, Elaine. "Exegesis of Genesis 1 in the Gospels of Thomas and John." *Journal of Biblical Literature* 118 (1999): 477–496.

Pardee, Dennis. *Ugaritic and Hebrew Poetic Parallelism: A Trial Cut ('nt and Proverbs 2)*. Leiden: Brill, 1988.

Patte, Daniel. *Early Jewish Hermeneutics in Palestine*. Missoula: Scholars Press, 1971.

Paul, Shalom. *Amos*. Minneapolis: Fortress Press, 1991.

Penner, Jeremy "Mapping Fixed Prayers from the Dead Sea Scrolls onto Second Temple Period Judaism." *Dead Sea Discoveries* 21 (2014): 39–63.

Perdue, Leo. "Sages, Scribes, and Seers in Israel and the ancient Near East: An Introduction." Pages 1–34 in *Scribes, Sages, and Seers: The Sage in the Eastern Mediterranean World*. Edited by Leo Perdue. Göttingen: Vandenhoeck & Ruprecht, 2008.

Perri, Carmela. "On Alluding." *Poetics* 7 (1978): 289–307.

Ploeg, J. van der. "La Règle de la Guerre: traduction et notes." *Vetus Testamentum* 5 (1955): 373–420.

Puech, Émile. "4Q252: 'Commentaire de la Genèse A' ou 'Bénédictions Patriarcles'?" *Revue de Qumrân* 26 (2013): 227–251.

_____. "Les Manuscrits de Qumrân Inspirés du livre de Josué: 4Q378, 4Q379, 4Q175, 4Q522, 5Q9 et Mas1039-211." *Revue de Qumrân* 28 (2016): 45–116.

_____. "Jerusalem dans les manuscrits de la Mer Morte." *Revue de Qumrân* 25 (2012): 423–444.

Regev, Eyal. "Abominated Temple and a Holy Community: The Formation of the Notions of Purity and Impurity in Qumran." *Dead Sea Discoveries* 10 (2003): 243–278.

_____. "Comparing Sectarian Practice and Organization: The Qumran Sects in Light of the Regulations of the Shakers, Hutterites, Mennonites and Amish." *Numen* 51 (2004): 146–181.

Rowland, Christopher. *The Open Heaven*. New York: Crossroads, 1982.

Russell, Brian. *The Song of the Sea: The Date of Composition and Influence of Exodus 15:1–21*. New York: Peter Lang, 2007.

Saukkonen, Juhana Markus. "Selection, Election, and Rejection: Interpretation of Genesis in 4Q252." Pages 63–81 in *Northern Lights on the Dead Sea Scrolls: Proceedings of the Nordic Qumran Network 2003–2006*. Edited by Anders Klostergaard Petersen et al. Leiden: Brill, 2009.

Saussure, Ferdinand de. *Course in General Linguistics*. Chicago: Open Court, 1972.

Scacewater, Todd A. "The Literary Unity of 1QM and its Three-Stage War." *Revue de Qumrân* 27 (2015): 225–248.

Schaper, Joachim. "The Death of the Prophet: The Transition from the Spoken to the Written Word of God in the Book of Ezekiel." Pages 63–79 in *Prophets, Prophecy and Prophetic Texts in Second Temple Judaism*. Edited by Michael H. Floyd and Robert D. Haak. New York: T&T Clark, 2006.

Schiffman, Lawrence H. "The Sacrificial System of the Temple Scroll and the Book of Jubilees." *Society of Biblical Literature Seminar Papers* 24 (1985): 217–233.

_____. "Origin and Early History of the Qumran Sect." *The Biblical Archaeologist* 58 (1995): 37–48.

_____. "The Pharisees and Their Legal Traditions According to the Dead Sea Scrolls." *Dead Sea Discoveries*, 8 (2001): 262–277.

_____. "The Dead Sea Scrolls and the History of the Jewish Book," *Association for Jewish Studies Review* 34 (2010): 359–365.

Schniedewind, William. *The Word of God in Transition: From Prophet to Exegete in the Second Temple Period.* Sheffield: JSOT Press, 1995.

Schuller, Eileen M. "Worship, Temple, and Prayer in the Dead Sea Scrolls." Pages 125–143 in *Judaism in Late Antiquity: A Systemic Reading of the Dead Sea Scrolls.* Edited by Alan J. Avery-Peck, Jacob Neusner, and Bruce Chilton. Leiden: Brill, 2001.

_____. "Prayers and Psalms from the Pre-Maccabean Period." *Dead Sea Discoveries* 13 (2006): 306–318.

Schultz, Brian. *Conquering the World: The War Scroll (1QM) Reconsidered.* Studies on the Texts of the Desert of Judah 76. Leiden: Brill, 2009.

Scolnic, Benjamin. "The Milesian Connection: Dan 11:23 and Antiochus IV's Rise to Power." *Vetus Testamentum* 63 (2013): 89–98.

Shemesh, Aharon. "The Holy Angels are in Their Council: The Exclusion of Deformed Persons from Holy Places in Qumranic and Rabbinic Literature." *Dead Sea Discoveries* 4 (1997): 179–206.

_____. *Halakhah in the Making: The Development of Jewish Law from Qumran to the Rabbis.* Berkeley: University of California Press, 2009.

_____. "Biblical Exegesis and Interpretations from Qumran to the Rabbis." Pages 467–489 in *A Companion to Biblical Interpretation in Early Judaism.* Edited by Matthias Henze. Grand Rapids: Eerdmans, 2012.

Smith, Mark. "The Poetics of Exodus 15 and Its Position in the Book." Pages 23–34 in *Imagery and Imagination in Biblical Literature: Essays in Honor of Aloysius Fitzgerald.* Edited by Lawrence Boadt and Mark Smith. Washington: Catholic Biblical Association of America, 2001.

Sokolowski, Robert. "Quotation." *The Review of Metaphysics* 37 (1984): 699–723.

Showalter, Elaine. "Piecing and Writing." Pages 222–247 in *The Poetics of Gender.* Edited by Nancy K. Miller. New York: Columbia University Press, 1986.

Stanford Friedman, Susan. "Weavings: Intertextuality and the (Re)Birth of the Author." Pages 146–180 in *Influence and Intertextuality in Literary History.* Edited by Jay Clayton and Eric Rothstein. Madison: University of Wisconsin Press, 1991.

Stegemann, Harmut. *Die Entstehung der Qumrangemeinde.* Bonn: Univ zu Bonn, 1971.

Stern, Sacha. "The 'Sectarian' Calendar of Qumran." Pages 39–62 in *Sects and Sectarianism in Jewish History.* Edited by Sacha Stern. Leiden: Brill, 2011.

Strong, John. "Egypt's Shameful Death and the House of Israel's Exodus from Sheol (Ezekiel 32.17–32 and 37.1–14)." *Journal for the Study of the Old Testament* 34 (2010): 475–504.

Sukenik, Eleazar L. *The Dead Sea Scrolls of the Hebrew University.* Jerusalem: Magness Press, 1955.

Sumpter, Philip. "The Coherence of Psalm 24." *Journal for Study of the Old Testament* 39 (2014): 31–54.

Sweeney, Marvin. "Parenetic Intent in Isaiah 31." Pages 99–106 in *Proceedings of the Eleventh World Congress of Jewish Studies*. Edited by David Assaf. Jerusalem: World Union of Jewish Studies, 1994.

Throntveit, Mark. "The Idealization of Solomon as the Glorification of God in the Chronicler's Royal Speeches and Royal Prayers." Pages 411–427 in *The Age of Solomon: Scholarship at the Turn of the Millennium*. Edited by Lowell K. Handy. Leiden: Brill, 1997.

Tigchelaar, Eibert. "Balaam and Enoch." Pages 87–99 in *The Prestige of the Pagan Prophet Balaam in Judaism, Early Christianity and Islam*. Edited by George H. van Kooten and J.T.A.G.M. van Ruiten. Leiden: Brill, 2008.

Tiňo, Jozef. *King and Temple in Chronicles: A Contextual Approach to Their Relations*. Forschungen zur Religion und Literatur des Alten und Neuen Testaments 234. Göttingen: Vandenhoeck & Ruprecht, 2010.

Tzoref, Shani. "Covenantal Election in 4Q252 and Jubilees' Heavenly Tablets." *Dead Sea Discoveries* 18 (2011): 74–89.

VanderKam, James C. *The Dead Sea Scrolls Today*. Grand Rapids: Eerdmans, 1994.

_____. *Calendars in the Dead Sea Scrolls*. London: Routledge, 1998.

_____. "The Pre-history of the Qumran Community with a Reassessment of CD 1:5-11." Pages 59–76 in *Dead Sea Scrolls and Contemporary Culture*. Edited by Adolfo Roitman, Lawrence Schiffman, and Shani Tzoref. Leiden: Brill, 2011.

_____. *The Dead Sea Scrolls and the Bible*. Grand Rapids: Eerdmans, 2012.

_____. "Those Who Look for Smooth Things, Pharisees, and Oral Law." Pages 465–477 in *Emanuel: Studies in Hebrew Bible, Septuagint, and Dead Sea Scrolls in Honor of Emanuel Tov*. Edited by Shalom Paul et al. Leiden: Brill, 2003.

Vanonen, Hanna. "The Textual Connections Between 1QM 1 and the Book of Daniel." Pages 223–246 in *Changes in Scripture: Rewriting and Interpreting Authoritative Traditions in the Second Temple Period*. Edited by Hanne von Weissenberg, Juha Pakkala and Marko Marttila. Berlin: De Gruyter, 2011.

Walton, John H. *Ancient Near Eastern Thought and the Old Testament: Introducing the Conceptual World of the Hebrew Bible*. Grand Rapids: Baker Academic, 2006.

Wassen, Cecilia. "Visions of the Temple: Conflicting Images of the Eschaton." *Svensk exegetisk årsbok* 76 (2011): 41–59.

Water, Rick Van de. "Michael or Yhwh? Toward Identifying Melchizedek in 11Q13." *Journal for the Study of the Pseudepigrapha* 16 (2006): 75–86.

Weissenberg, Hanne von. "The Centrality of the Temple in 4QMMT." Pages 293–305 in *Dead Sea Scrolls: Texts and Context*. Edited by Charlotte Hempel. Leiden: Brill, 2010.

Wenthe, Dean O. "The Use of the Hebrew Scriptures in 1QM." *Dead Sea Discoveries* 5 (1998): 290–319.

Willits, Joel. "The Remnant of Israel in 4QpIsaiah (4Q161) and the Dead Sea Scrolls." *Journal of Jewish Studies* 57 (2006): 11–25.

Bibliography

Williamson Jr., Robert. "Pesher: A Cognitive Model of the Genre." *Dead Sea Discoveries* 17 (2010): 307–331.

Woude, A. S. van der. "Prophetic Prediction, Political Prognostication, and Firm Belief: Reflections on Daniel 11:40–12:3." Pages 63–73 in *The Quest for Context and Meaning: Studies in Biblical Intertextuality in Honor of James A. Sanders*. Edited by Craig A. Evans and Shemaryahu Talmon. Leiden: Brill, 1997.

Yadin, Yigael. *The Scroll of the War of the Sons of Light against the Sons of Darkness*. Translated by Batya Rabin and Chaim Rabim. London: Oxford University Press, 1962.

Zanella, Francesco. "Sectarian and Non-Sectarian Texts: A Possible Semantic Approach." *Revue de Qumrân* 24 (2009): 19–34.

Zakovitch, Yair. "Inner-biblical Interpretation." Pages 27–63 in *A Companion to Biblical Interpretation in Early Judaism*. Edited by Matthias Henze. Grand Rapids: Eerdmans, 2012.

Zelig Aster, Shawn. "Isaiah 31 as a Response to Rebellions Against Assyria in Philistia." *Journal of Biblical Literature* 136 (2017): 347–361.

INDEX

Genesis

1	36n50
1:1	36, 144
1–11	147
2	223
2:22	144
10:4	32
11:9	144
17:12	73
17:27	73
49	160
49:10	160n6, 161
49:10 MT	160n6

Exodus

2:24	122
6:5	122
9:35	119
12:43	73
14	62, 176
14:3	116
14:13–14	176
14:19	117
15	18, 127, 136, 136n53, 139-140, 139n64, 143, 145, 171, 189, 207
15:1	143, 171
15:1–21	136n52
15:6–9	113
15:11	137, 143
15:13	137, 139, 143
15:17	228, 228n39
15:17–18	70n3, 72
15:19–21	189
19	225
23:7	52, 104
24:12	225n37

24:16	225
25:9	144
31:3	165
34:4	225
34:22	144

Leviticus

18:5	132
18:13	106
22:25	73
23:2	144
23:2–4	144
23:37	144
25:9	78n25
25:13	77, 79
26:46	119

Numbers

1	119, 202n6
1.1–5	202n6
2:3	162
4:37–49	119
7:9	111
10:1–10	120
10:8	121
10:9	3, 102n7, 103-104, 110, 118-123
10:14	162
10:35	200, 218
22:31	142, 183
24	169
24:8	120
24:15–17	167
24:17–19	3, 16, 150-152, 153n5, 154-155, 159, 166-167, 170, 176, 179, 181, 183, 197, 237, 239
24:24	32

31:6	120			

Deuteronomy

1:30–33	117
3:24	127
4:16–18	144
5:1	115
5:28–29	167
6:4	115
7	119
7:1	112
7:15	202n6
7:21–22	3, 101n2, 102n7, 110-112, 123
9:1	115
9:27–29	228n39
10:1–4	225n37
15:2	77, 79
17	157
18:18–19	167
20	118-119
20:2–4	114
20:2–5	3, 102n5,7, 107, 110-111, 114, 123
20:3	115-116
20:4	117
20:8	118-119
23	106, 110, 121
23:3–4	73
23:8	73
23:10–15	103n8, 107
23:13	106
23:15	110-111
24:17	73
31:6	116
31:6–8	117
32	113
32:27	120
32:30	195
33:8–11	168
33:29	117, 122

Joshua

3:4	106
10:12–14	60

Judges

3:10	174
5:4	94
7:3	118
10:1	117
13:5	117
14:6	174
14:19	174
15:14	174

1 Samuel

16:18	157
17	18, 152, 155, 179
17:46–47	154-155
17:47	117
23:26	116

2 Samuel

7	72, 161
7:8–17	159
7:10	72
7:10–11	70n2, 72
7:11	70n7, 73
7:12–14	74
7:13–14	70n11
22:4	117

1 Kings

2:4	161
5:18	219
8:25	161
8:33	113
8:46	113
17:2–8 LXX	89

2 Kings

1:8	89
7:15	116
16:6	112
22:19	116

1 Chronicles

1:7	32
5	172
10	173
11–16	173
15–16	121n32
16:25	112
17–29	173

2 Chronicles

1–9	173
5–7	121n32
6	172
6:16	161
6:24	113, 172
6:36	113
6:41	218
10–12	173
12:1–8	62
13	173
13:2–20	172
13:12–15	121
14	173
14–16	173

Index   259

17–20	173
20	62, 100, 121n32, 152, 173, 175, 177, 179
20:1	174
20:1–30	172
20:15	172
20:17	117
20:20–28	121
20:24	156
21–22	173
23–24	173
25	173
26	173
27	173
28	173
29–32	173
33	173
34–35	173
36	173

Ezra

3:10	121
7:6	63
7:24	161

Nehemiah

1:5	111
4:8	112
8:1–8	56
9:27	120
9:32	112
12:35	121
12:41	121

Job

9:4	112
12	94
36	141-142
36:6	141
36:8–12	142
36:22	142
36:26–33	142
36:29	142
37:15–20	142
37:21	142
37:23	142

Psalms

1	72, 76
1:1	71n14, 75
2	72
2:1–2	71n19, 76
3:8	218
7:7	218
7:8–9	77, 80

9:20	218
10:12	218
14	223n31
17:13	218
18	45
18:4	44
22	223n31
23	223n31
24	16, 19, 200, 213-214, 218, 220, 222-224, 223n31-32, 226-227, 230, 232-233
24:3	225
24:7–10	222, 227
25:5	94
28:9	228
34:16	145
35	140
37	185
37:11	185
37:20	206
37:21–22	186
37:34–36	205
44:27	218
50:17	142
68:10	228
71:19	140
74:2	228
74:22	218
82:1	77, 80
82:2	77, 80
82:8	218
83:7–9	39
89	141n65
89:9	140
92:6	127
99:3	112
106:5	228
107:40	94
113:5–6	127
118:22	88
132:8	218
136	189

Proverbs

4:18	39
15:33	142

Isaiah

2:22	52, 104
4:2	74
7:4	116
7:17	169
8:11	71n16, 76
10:28–32	230
10:33–34	162n3, 164

10–11	164		38–39	150, 188, 190, 193-194, 196, 227, 230, 232
11	164		38–48	14, 19, 207
11:1–5	163-164		39:18	193
11:2	174		39:27	193
11:3	166		40–48	213
13:4	39		43:10	142
23:15–18	122			
28:16	84n7, 87			
30:19–20	230		**Daniel**	
31	191, 193		1	209
31:8	3, 13, 41, 151, 156, 182-183, 191-192, 195, 209, 239		4:14	161
			4:22	161
40:3	52, 85n14, 88-90, 104, 119n30		4:29	161
			5:21	161
40:9	227, 230n42		5:29	161
40:28	144		7	10
42:13	220		7:13	178
42:16	94		7–12	208n12, 224
45:22	117		9	96, 238
48:17	94		9:4	112
52:1–3	230		9:23–27	93
52:7	76, 78, 78n23, 81-82		9:24	231n43
54:11–12	206		9:25	76, 78, 81
56–66	223		10:6	39
60	220, 222		11	39-40, 209
60:1	230		11:11	39
60:11	222, 227, 230		11:23	208n12
60:12–16	230		11:30	32
60:14–22	230		11:32	39, 71n19
61	80, 87		11:32–34	41
61:1	79		11:32–35	208
61:2	78n20, 81		11:40–12:3	208n12
61:2–3	76		11:42	39
61:3	87, 205		11:44	39, 41
63:7	228		11:45	39
			11–12	2-3, 7, 11, 19, 35, 41, 61n1, 76, 201, 208-210, 210n14, 232, 239
Jeremiah				
23:5	74		12	11, 16, 41, 94, 202n6, 208-209
25:31	92			
29	61n1		12:1	40, 208, 210
33:15	74		12:1–3	41
33:17	161		12:1–4	61n1, 232
36	61n1		12:1–5	208
36:3	61n1		12:10	71n19, 76
49:19	137			
50:44	137		**Hosea**	
51:46	116		4:6	94
Ezekiel			**Joel**	
29–32	189		2:2	40
32	190		2:11	112
32.17–32	190		2:17	228
32:31	189		3:4	112
37–48	224		3:18	94
38	226-227			

Index

Amos

5:26	169
5:26–27	169-170
7:16	94
9	14, 19, 162, 213
9:1–15	94
9:11	70n12, 74, 169
9:13	94

Micah

2:11	94
7	141
7:14	228

Habakkuk

2:17	186-187
3:19	94

Zephaniah

1:14	220

Zechariah

3:8	74
5:1–4	61n1
6:12	74
8:3	227
9:9	230n42
10:4	88
13:2–3	65
14:13	41

Malachi

3:1	89
3:23	112

Sirach

1:11–13	39
46:4	60
50:1–16	121

2 Esdras

19:32	112

1 Maccabees

1:1	32
2:7	113
3:22	116
3:46–56	118
3:46–60	121
3:54	121n33
3–4	176
4	100
4:8	116
4:9	100, 149, 177, 189
4:18	113
4:30	100, 149, 177
4:36–43	121
4:40	121n33
5:31–33	121n33
6:33	121n33
6:41	39
7:41	100, 149
7:45	121n33
9:12	121n33
9:27	65
9:46	113
12	113
12:15	113
15:33	113
16:8	121n33

2 Maccabees

12:15	100
15	177
15:8–9	177
15:11	177

3 Maccabees

2:1–20	149
2:6–7	189
6:4–5	189

Matthew

3:1–3	89
3:2	89
3:4	89

Mark

1:1–3	89
1:2–4	89
1:6	89

Luke

3:1–4	89
3:2	89
3:2–6	89

John

1:1	36
1:21–23	89
1:23	89

Acts

1:15–26	86
2:25–31	159
15:15–16	74

James

5:7–17	217

1 Peter

1:10	177

1 Enoch

1–36	144
10	87
10.16	87
17–18	45
43	207
82	134
82.7	134
89:70–77	207
93:5	87
93:10	87
104	208
104:1–4	207

Jubilees

1:1–6	225
2	134
2.7–12	134
4	87, 134
4.17–18	134
16:26	84n5
21	87
21.24	87
23:19	132n49
26:16	225
31:12–19	161

1QpHab 1QPesher to Habakkuk

2	32n38, 63-64, 95
2.1	95
2.7–10	64
2.8–9	63
2.12–16	32n38
2:9	156
3.4–15	32n38
4.5–10	32n38
5	205
5.1	95
5.4	205
6.1–10	32n38
9	205
9.7	32n38
9.12	205
10:9	205
12	92, 186
12.9	92

1Q16 (1QpPs) 1QPesher to Psalms

9–10	32n38
9–10.1–4	32n38

1Q20

20	161
20.13	161
22	79
22.4–25	79

1Q22

4	139n61
4.1	139n61

1QS (1QS) 1QRule of the Community

1	45, 85n16, 86, 92, 108n16, 119n30, 131, 133, 156
1.1	108n16
1.1–3	85n16
1.3	119n30, 156
1.8	86
1.9	131
1.13–18	133
1.15	92
1.16–2.12	45
3	73, 107, 109, 129, 133
3.10	133
3.13	107, 129
3.14	109
3.24	73
3.25–26	73
4	39, 93, 109, 134, 200, 204, 206
4.7	39
4.13–15	109
4.14	93
4.22	200
4.22–23	206
5	104, 122, 131n46
5.9	131n46
5.13	93
5.13b–16a	104
5.21	122
6	75, 83, 88
6.7–8	83
6.24	75, 88
7	107
8	64, 68, 75, 84, 86-87, 90, 91n11, 93, 119n30, 131, 205-206, 236
8.1	86, 131, 131n46
8.1–16	84
8.4	87
8.5	93, 205
8.6–7	87
8.13–15	68
8.15	64, 75, 88, 119n30
8.15–16	86, 131n46
8.26	75, 88
8–9	64

9	74, 86, 90, 107, 128, 131, 168, 226
9.2	226
9.3	86
9.3–6	87
9.6	86
9.7	122
9.11	74, 90, 168
9.12–14	128
9.12–16	204
9.13	107, 131n46
9.13–14	131
10	95, 133
10.1–8	133
10.25	95
11	87, 131n47, 204, 228
11.7	228
11.7–9	204
11.8	87
11.16	204
11.19	131n47
15–16	131
19	131n46

1Q28a (1QSa) 1QRule of the Congregation

1	83, 107, 122, 221n29, 226
1.1–7	107
1.1–8	226
1.7	83
1.23–24	122
1.25	221n29
2.13	122

1Q28b (1QSb) 1QRule of Benedictions

1	93, 129
1.1	129
1.7	93
3	92
3.2	92
3.22	129
5.20	129

1QM (1QM) 1QWar Scroll

1	2n6, 5, 7, 11-12, 32, 32n38, 35, 38-39, 41-42, 50, 61n1, 93, 108, 137-138, 138n57, 151, 174, 191, 209-211, 210n14, 232-233, 239
1.1	174
1.1–2	39, 112
1.1–7	210
1.2	32n38, 50, 191
1.5	35
1.6	93
1.8	39
1.8–17	233
1.9	39, 138n57
1.9–11	138
1.10	108
1.10–11	138n57
1.11	39
1.12–16	232
1.13–17	211
1.16	209
1–2	6
2	2, 9, 33, 119, 137n54, 201, 216-217, 221n29, 239
2.3	137n54
2.4	216
2.4–7	133
2.7–8	201
2.9b–16	2
2.10–14	9
2–9	3, 35, 58, 58n10, 99-100, 103-104, 122n35, 174, 201, 238
2–14	5
3	175, 217
3.2	175
3.8	175
3–9	6
3–14	6
4	69, 76
4.2	93
5	165, 217
5.6–14	165
6	217
6.6	138n57
6.8–14	217
6.12–13	107
7	15, 17, 103-106, 103n8, 121, 128-129, 200, 207, 220, 221n29, 226, 239
7.1–3	105
7.4–6a	106
7.5	106
7.6	129
7.7	106
7.9–18	121
7.10–12	103
7.11	165
7.12–13	128
7.12–18	15
7.13	104
7–9	123
8	126
9	100, 103-104, 110, 123, 175, 209
9.10	103-104, 110, 123
9.15–16	209

9.17	123, 175
10	3, 10, 13, 15-16, 18, 50-51, 99, 101, 102n7, 103-105, 107, 109-114, 110n19, 115n23, 116, 118-120, 122-125, 127-129, 131, 134-137, 139-143, 145, 145n70, 147, 149, 151, 154-155, 157, 166-167, 173, 175, 180, 194-195, 206, 220, 228-229, 239
10.1	103, 105, 110-113, 110n19
10.1–2	50, 180
10.1–2a	110, 112
10.1–6	173
10.1–8	10, 220
10.1–8a	13, 15-16, 101, 102n7, 103-105, 110, 120, 122-123, 136, 151, 155, 239
10.2	103, 107-109
10.2b–5a	114
10.2–5	50
10.3	116
10.5b–8a	118
10.5b–8b	118
10.5–6	104, 119, 195
10.6	119
10.6–8	50
10.7	104, 220
10.7–8a	120
10.8	135
10.8a	139
10.8b	137, 139, 151, 154
10.8bâ€"16	145n70
10.8bâ€"18	239
10.8b–9a	127
10.8b–18	15, 109, 112, 125, 127-128, 135, 141-143, 145, 154, 157, 167, 228-229
10.8–9	143
10.9	137
10.9b–12a	127
10.9–12	137
10.10	128-129, 206
10.10–11	131
10.11	129
10.12–14	140
10.15	134
10.16	142
10.16b	127
10.17	154
10–11	8, 12, 16, 105, 154, 175, 202n6, 217, 220
10–12	3-4, 7, 12-13, 15, 17, 21, 30, 33, 38, 46, 52-53, 56, 99, 201, 217, 221, 235-236, 238-240

10–14	3, 5-6, 10
11	3, 10, 13-16, 18, 41, 50-51, 108, 116-118, 125, 143n67, 149-152, 153n5, 154-156, 159, 164, 166-167, 169-170, 172, 174, 176-179, 181-183, 185-193, 196-197, 199, 203, 209, 213, 217, 218n23, 220, 227, 233, 237, 239
11.1	155-156, 218n23
11.1–5a	155
11.1–7	149
11.1–7a	13, 15-16, 18, 152, 153n5, 154-155, 159, 170, 174, 176, 178-179, 181
11.1–7b	154
11.1–12	149, 151
11.2	156, 159
11.5–7	51
11.6	108
11.6b–8	166
11.6–7	154, 237
11.7b–8	14
11.7b–9a	183
11.7b–12	150
11.7b–17	182
11.7b–18	15-16, 164, 182-185, 187-188, 194
11.8–9	143n67
11.8–18	203, 233
11.9	187, 220
11.9–10	189-190
11.9–15	220
11.10	192
11.11–12	41, 50-51, 150, 156, 191, 209
11.11–12a	239
11.13	151, 220
11.13–12.5	10, 151
11.13–12.15	149
11.13–18	193, 199, 228, 233
11.14–18	186, 196
11.16	192
11.16–18	217
11–12	229n40, 233
12	2, 7, 13, 15-16, 19, 38, 45, 56, 79, 129, 133, 137, 149, 151, 156, 186, 196, 199-203, 207-211, 212n18, 213-214, 216-219, 221-222, 224-227, 227n38, 229-233, 231n43
12.1	129, 200
12.1	129, 200
12.1–2	211
12.1–4	45

Index

12.1–5	15, 19, 199, 202-203, 207, 209-210, 226, 228, 232
12.2	208, 232
12.3	133, 207
12.4	216
12.7b–18	229, 231
12.7–8a	216
12.7–10a	212n18
12.7–18	15-16, 19, 199, 211, 214, 221-222, 226-227, 230, 232
12.8–9	233
12.9b–10a	217
12.10	79
12.11	156
12.12b	219
12.12–13	229
12.13	219, 230
12.13b–18	229
12.13–18	186, 233
13	12, 93, 108, 127, 133, 141, 185
13.1	12
13.1–2	138n57
13.8	93, 133, 141
13.10	108
13.13	127
13.14	108
13.14–18	185
13–14	12, 99
13–14.1	99
14	12, 99, 107-108, 139n63, 141, 150, 193, 200n4
14.1–4	138
14.2	200n4
14.3–4	139n63
14.4b–8	150
14.4b–8a	193
14.5–9	93
14.6	107
14.6–9	141
14.9	108
14.15–16	138n57
15	2-3, 5, 7, 16, 50, 99-101, 115, 115n23, 151, 191, 200, 202n6
15.4	115
15.4–5	99-101, 191
15.4–6	7, 16
15.4–16.1	2
15.5	3, 5, 16, 83, 151, 200, 202n6
15.8–9	50
15.10–11	151
15.14	138n57
15–16	99
15–19	2-3, 5-6, 16, 99-100, 104, 120n31, 151, 209, 238
16	2, 16, 216

16.1	2
16.13–17	16
16.13–17.9	2
16.15	108
16–17	99
17	82, 138n58, 209, 232
17.5–8	138n58
17.5–9	209
17.6–7	232
17.7	82, 138n57
18	16, 138
18.3–6	138
18.5b–14	16
18.5–14	2
18.6	138n57
19	7, 16, 19, 56, 81, 137, 191, 196, 199, 201-202, 214, 216, 216n20, 220, 220n27-28, 222, 233
19.1–11	81
19.1–14	214
19.5–8	233
19.8	220
19.9–13	196
19.10	191
42	175
49	185

1QM19

29	221n30

1QHa

1	109n18, 143n67
1.1–4	109n18
2.7	109n18
3	138n58
4	131, 204
4.7–12	131
4.12	119n30
4.14–15	204
5	106n15, 131n47
5.2	109n18
5.8	131n47
5.21	106n15
9	127, 131
9.1–9a	127
9.1–37	127
9.13b–20	127
9.21	127
11	44-45, 138n60, 187, 220
11.20–37	44-45
11.22	138n60
11.25–26	187
11.33	220
12	81, 92

12.12	92
12.13–17	81
13	87, 187
13.16–18	187
13.21	87
14	93, 131, 228-229
14.4	131
14.8	93
14.11	228
14.32	93
15	127, 137, 138n60
15.10–14	128
15.28	127, 137
15.29	138n60
16	87
16.6	87
18	138
18.10	138
19	45, 87
19.13–17	45
19.22a	87
19.25	87
20	129n43
20.4	129n43
20.11	129n43
21	131
21.4–5	131
23	87
23.4	131
23.14	87
24	139
24.10	139
27.3	139

1Q37
1	76
1.3	76

4Q88
9	87
9.14	87

4Q158
1–2	111n21
1–2.6	111n21

4Q160
1	111n21
1.4	111n21

4Q161
2–6	230
2–6.25–27	230
8–10	159
8–10.15–29	159

4Q163
2.15–20	230
19	87
19.1	87

4Q164
1	206
1.3	206

4Q165
6	76, 87
6.1	76
6.5	87

4Q169
3–4	32n38

4Q171
1	95
1.26	95
2	87
2.9	87
11	76
11.2	76

4Q174 (4QFlor) 4QFlorilegium
1	67
1.1–13	67
1–2	159, 221
1–3	50
2	50

4Q175 (4QTest) 4QTestimonia
1	167
1.9–13	167

4Q177
1	73, 87
1.9	87
1–4	111n21
1–4.10	111n21
12–13	155

4Q179
1	165

4Q183
1	165

4Q201
1	209n13

4Q202
1	209n13

Index

4Q216	
1	225
1.4–13	225
2	92
2.8	92
6.2–8	134
6.8	92

4Q219	
2	87
2.30	87
2.33	87

4Q221	
1	87
1.8	87

4Q247	
4	32n38
4Q247	
6	32n38

4Q249	
1	75
1.1	75

4Q249a	
1	108
1.5	108

4Q251	
4–7	156
17	106, 106n15
17.4–6	106, 106n15

4Q252	
5	160
5.1–7	160
6	159
6.2	159

4Q256	
9	75
9.1	75

4Q258	
1	75
1.1	75
6	75
6.7	75
7	75
7.1	75

4Q259	
1	107

1.12	107
3	75, 82
3.6	75
3.10	82

4Q261	
5	107

4Q265	
7	83, 106n13
7.5	106n13
7.6	83

4Q266	
1	165
2	92-93, 129-130
2.11–12	93
3	167
5	75
8	129
10	107

4Q268	
1	92-93, 129-130
1.5–8	129-130
1.9	92
1.14	93

4Q269	
16	75
16.19	75

4Q270	
2	92
7	75, 107, 165

4Q285	
1	209n13
1.1–4	209n13
3	32n38
3.4	32n38
4.5	32n38
7	159, 162n3, 164
7.2	164
7.3–4	162n3
7.3–5	159
7.6	32n38

4Q286	
2	134

4Q287	
2	165

4Q289			**4Q396**	
1	129		2	213
			2.11–3.1	213
4Q292			4	122
1	220		4.8	122
1.8	220			
			4Q397	
4Q332			2	122
3	32n38		2.14	122
3.2	32n38		4	158
			4.10–15	158
4Q364			4.11	109n18
14	225n37			
14.3	225n37		**4Q398**	
26	225n37, 228n39		14–17	109n18, 158
26.3–9	225n37			
			4Q402	
4Q365			2	165
6	189, 228n39		2.3	165
10	165			
10.4	165		**4Q403**	
26	202n6		1	165
4Q378			**4Q405**	
22	156		14–15	165
26	110n19		16	165
26.2	110n19		16.4	165
			19	165
4Q379				
19	156		**4Q416**	
19.2	156		1	134
			1.12–14	134
4Q385			2	95
2	221		2.6	95
2.1	221			
5	233n44		**4Q417**	
			1	129n43
4Q385a				
18	79		**4Q418**	
18.3	79		2	134
			81	129n43, 165, 228n39
4Q386				
2	221		**4Q421**	
2.3	221		1	129n43
4Q393			**4Q423**	
3	229		8	165
3.2–4	229		8.1	165
4Q394			**4Q427**	
2	213		1	87
2.1–19	213		1.3–4	87
			7	137, 139
			10	131

Index

10.1–5	131

4Q428

4	228
8	228
9	137
9.3	137
10	128n42
10.7	128n42

4Q429

4	228

4Q431

1	137
1.4	137

4Q434

1	87
1.2	87
1.3	87

4Q440

3	131n47

4Q456

8	156
8.3	156

4Q457b

2	155
2.2	155

4Q462

1	165
1.5	165

4Q463

1	131n47
1.4	131n47

4Q470

1	209n13
1.1–7	209n13

4Q479

1	155
1.4–5	155

4Q491

1–3	106
1–3.7	106
8–10	138n57, 139n63
10	32n38
11	108, 115, 138n58, 185

4Q492

1	32n38, 139n63, 156, 196, 214
1.1–13	214
1.9–10	156
1.9–12	32n38
1.9–13	196
1.10	156
1.12	139n63

4Q495

1	128
1.2	128
2	108
2.1	108

4Q496

3	32n38
3.6	32n38

4Q501

1.2	228n39

4Q504

3	156
3.12	156
17	159, 219
17.3–16	161, 219
17.7	159
17.9b–16	219

4Q512

36–38	106n15
36–38.17	106n15
69	165
69.2	165

4Q522

22–26	155

4Q523

1–2	165
1–2.5	165

4Q525

14	228n39

4Q542

1	161

4Q544

1	161
1.12	161
2.16	161

CD Damascus Document

1	90, 91n11, 92-95, 109, 132, 236
1.1	92
1.1–11	90, 91n11
1.4	93
1.4b–8a	93
1.8–11	94
1.12	109
1.16	95
1:5–11	93
2	92-93, 95, 109, 130, 205
2.1	95
2.2	92, 130
2.6	93
2.8	109
2.14	92
3	92, 132, 206, 226
3.12–19	226
3.14	92
3.14–15	132
3.19–4.3a	206
3.20–21	226
4	18, 157
4.14–21	157
5	18, 81, 91n11, 95, 106, 119n30, 157
5.1–2	157
5.1–6	157
5.10	106
5.20	91n11, 95
5.20–6.3	81
5.21	119n30
6	87, 132n50, 165
6.5	87
6.15	165
6.18	132n50
6:5	80
7	50, 68, 159, 167-169, 221n29, 237
7.1	165
7.10–12	50
7.14–19	68
7.14–21	168
7.16	159
7.17	221n29
7.19	167
7.1821	237
7:13–18	67
8	75
8.8	165
8.16	75
10	83
10.6	83
11	106n13, 156

11.5–6	106n13
11.12	156
11.22	221n29
12	129
12.4	92
12.6	221n29
12.21–23	129
13	115
13.5	115
14	130
14.18	221n29
15	107, 129
15.14	107
15.17	129
16	83, 108n16
16.3–4	83
16.4	108n16
19	109
19.1–4	109
19.7–9	50
19.11–12	50
19.15–16	50
19.20	165
19.29	75
20	75, 107, 109, 128
20.4	107, 128
20.6	75
20.15–17	50
20.22	109
20.25	95

11Q5

4	155
11	111n21, 213
19	111n21
19.9	111n21
22	213, 231
22:1–15	231n43
27	157
28	155
37–38	18

11Q6

4–5	111n21

11Q11

5	157-158
5.4	157
5.5–14	158

11Q13 (11QMelch) 11QMelchizedek

2	63, 76, 87
2.1–25	76
2.4	87
2.18	63, 76

Index

11Q14

1	162n3, 164
2	218
2.2	218

11Q17 (11QShirShabb) 11QSongs of the Sabbath Sacrifice

4	165
4.10	165
6.6	165
7.13	165
9.7	165

11Q19

29	221
35	93
35.7	93
46.10	93
48	221n30
48.7	221n30
51	81
51.1–5	81
54.8–18	81